BYE BYE BABYLON

BEIRUT 1975-79

بيروت

LAMIA ZIADÉ

BYE BYE BABYLON

BEIRUT 1975-79

Interlink Graphic

An imprint of Interlink Publishing Group, Inc.
www.interlinkbooks.com

First American edition published in 2012 by

INTERLINK GRAPHIC
An imprint of Interlink Publishing Group, Inc.
46 Crosby Street, Northampton, Massachusetts 01060
www.interlinkbooks.com

Library of Congress Cataloging-in-Publication Data

Ziadé, Lamia.
    Bye Bye Babylon: Beirut 1975–1979 / by Lamia Ziadé. – 1st American ed.
       p. cm.
    "Translation copyright Olivia Snaije"—ECIP data
    ISBN 978-1-56656-877-7 (pbk.)
    1. Beirut (Lebanon)—History. 2. Lebanon—History—Civil War,
1975-1990—Personal narratives. 3. Ziadé, Lamia. I. Kiang-Snaije, Olivia.
    II. Title.
    DS89.B4Z53 2012
    956.9204'4092—dc23
    [B]
                          2011032505

Printed and bound in India

To request our complete 48-page full-color catalog, please call us toll
free at 1-800-238-LINK, visit our website at www.interlinkbooks.com,
or send us an e-mail: info@interlinkbooks.com

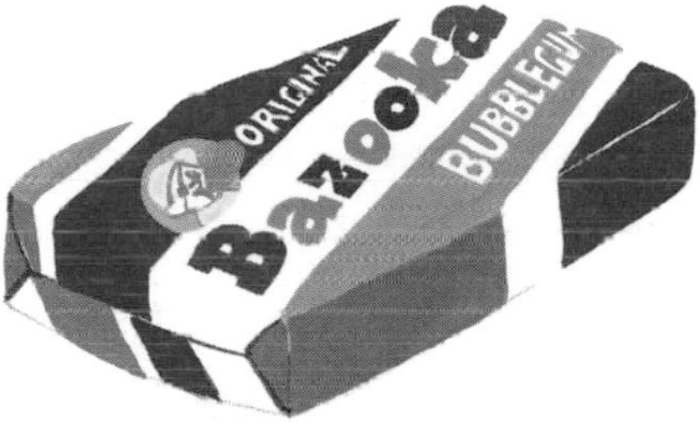
ORIGINAL
Bazooka
BUBBLEGUM

In 1975 I was seven years old and loved the Bazookas my mother bought for Walid and me at Spinney's in the Ramlet al-Baida neighbourhood.

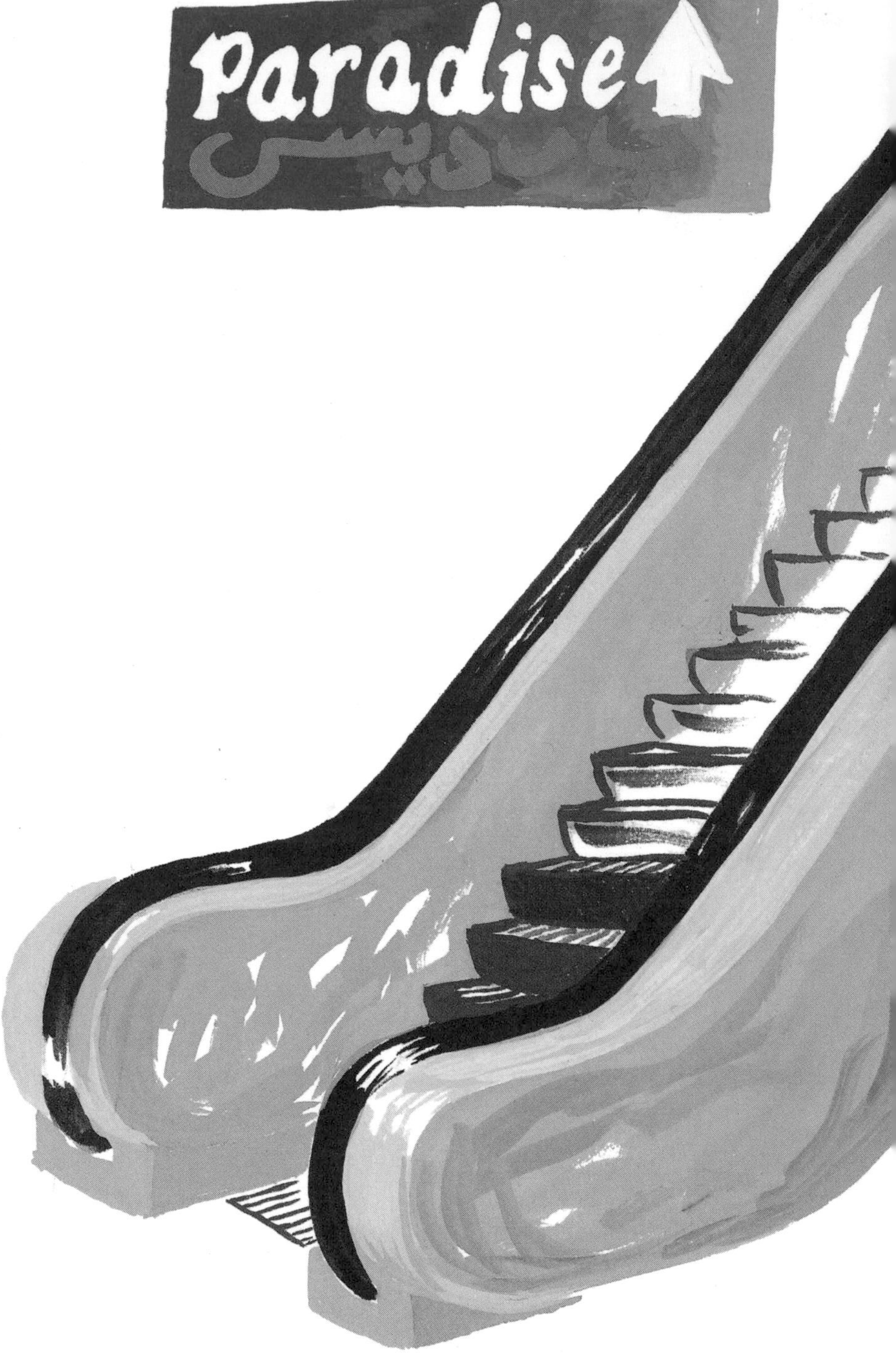
Paradise

Spinney's, an ultramodern supermarket, had opened in Beirut several years earlier. It is a monument to the best of what the Western world can offer with many firsts for Lebanon: trolleys, escalators (or maybe the first were in the Byblos department store, I'm not sure). It's a real paradise that is about to go up in smoke like everything else.

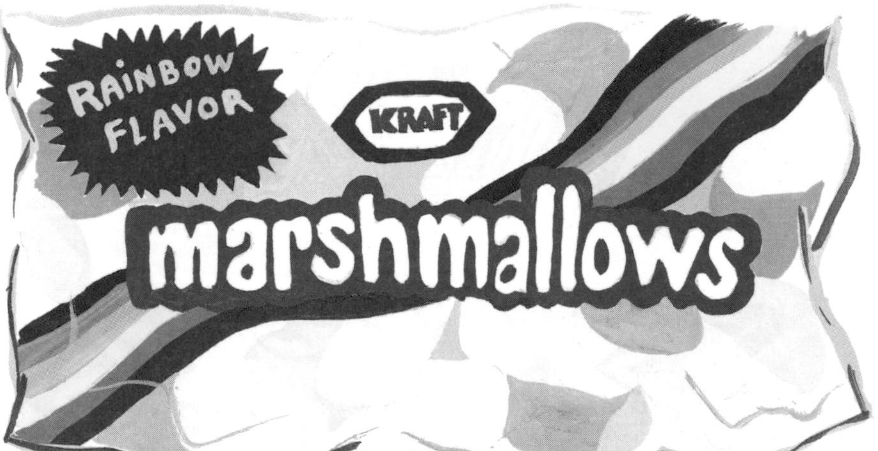
RAINBOW FLAVOR
KRAFT
marshmallows

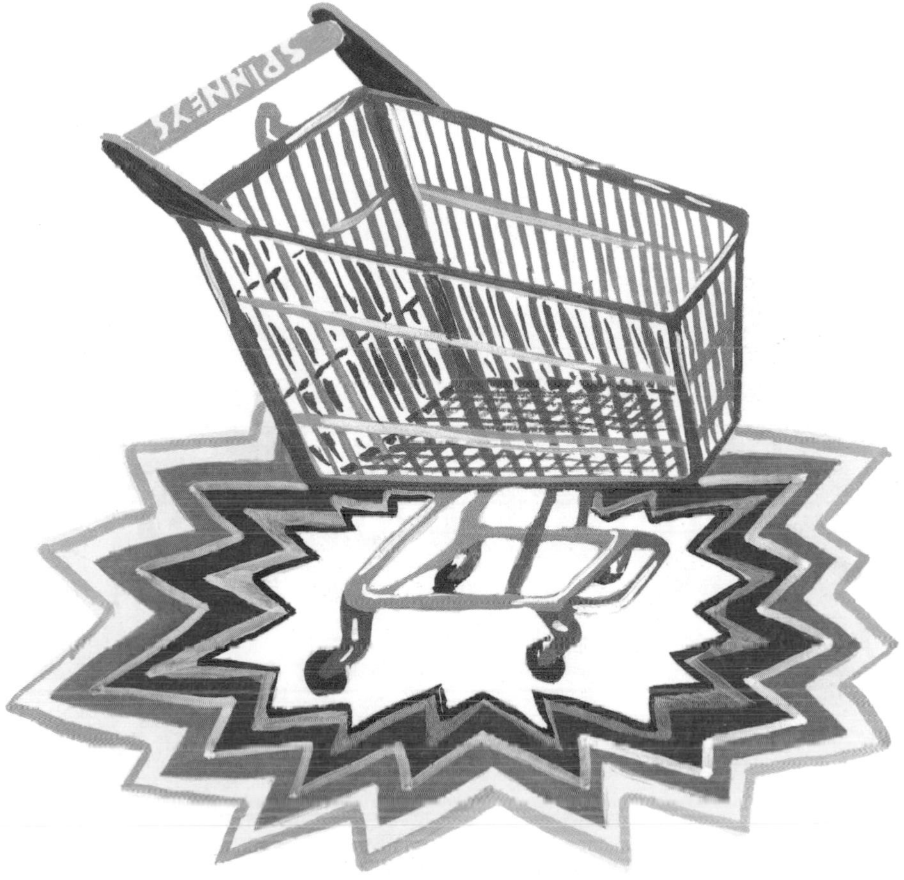
SPINNEYS

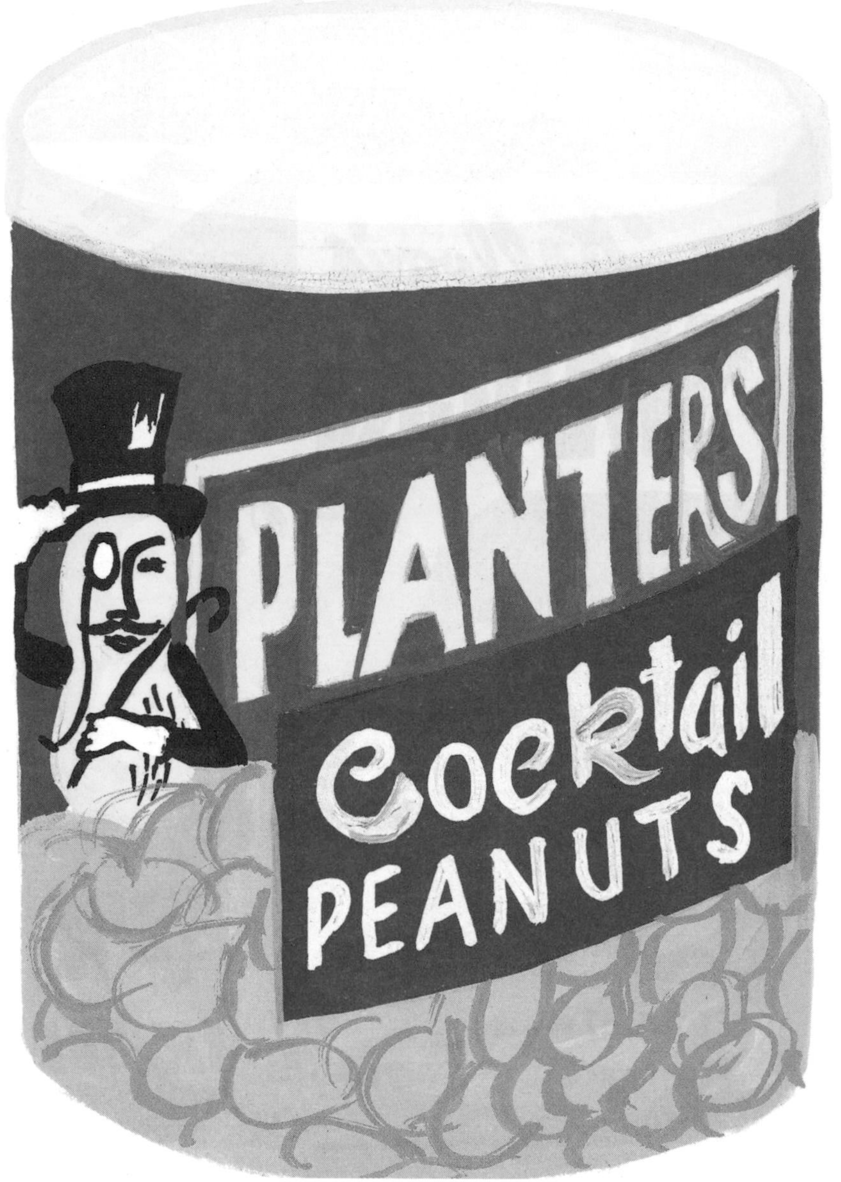
PLANTERS
Cocktail
PEANUTS

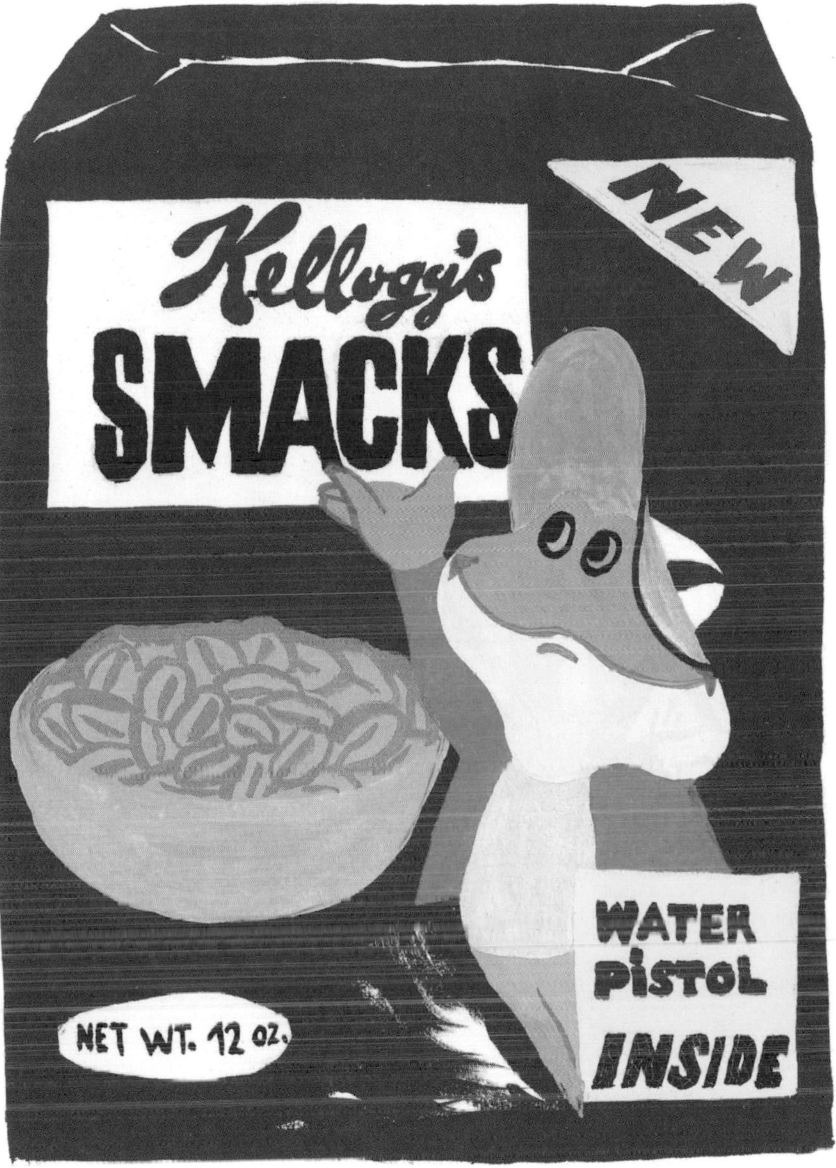
Kellogg's
SMACKS
NEW
WATER
PISTOL
INSIDE
NET WT. 12 OZ.

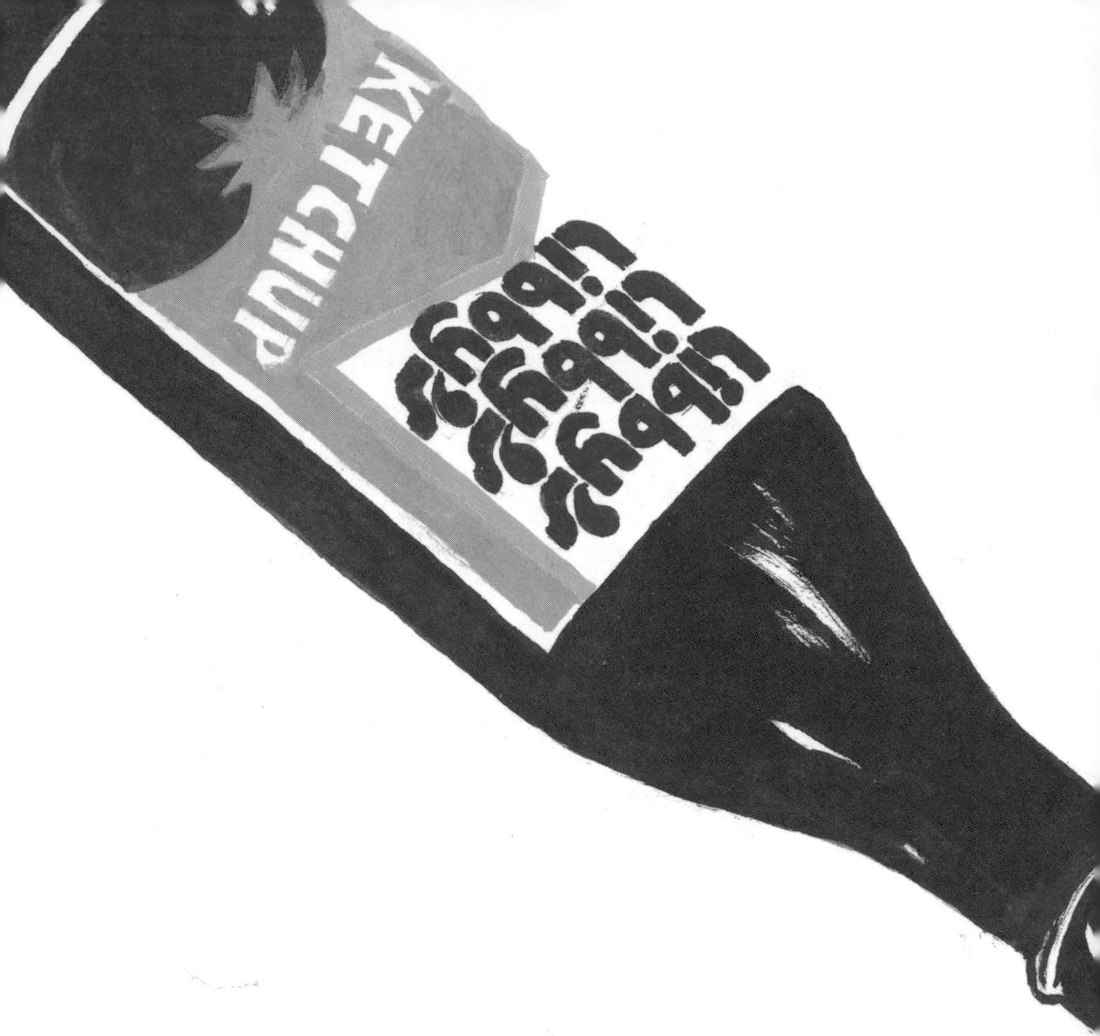
KETCHUP

To our delight, the supermarket shelves and our trolleys overflow with the same wondrous items one can find in New York or London. At the same time, the militias are stockpiling their arsenals with weapons and munitions of all kinds, of all calibres, and from a variety of sources. Lebanon is a veritable powder keg just waiting for a spark to ignite it.

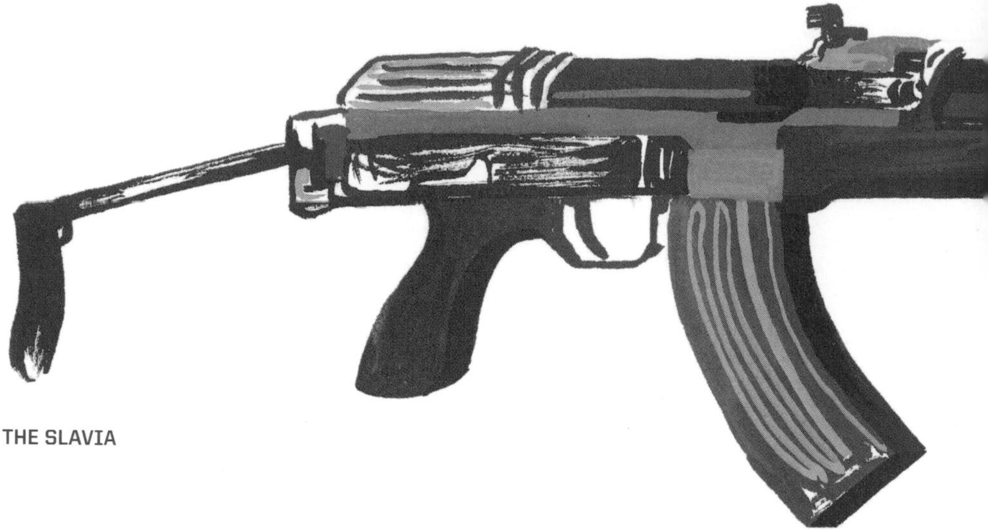

THE SLAVIA

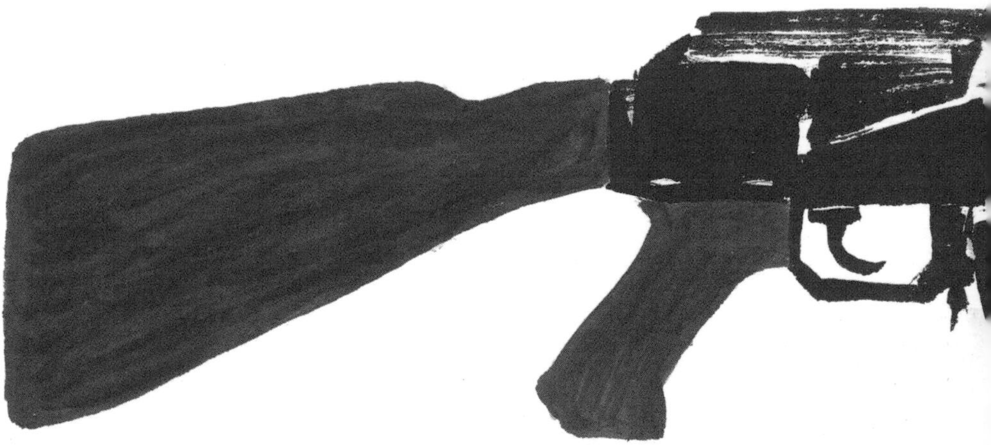

THE KALASHNIKOV AK 47

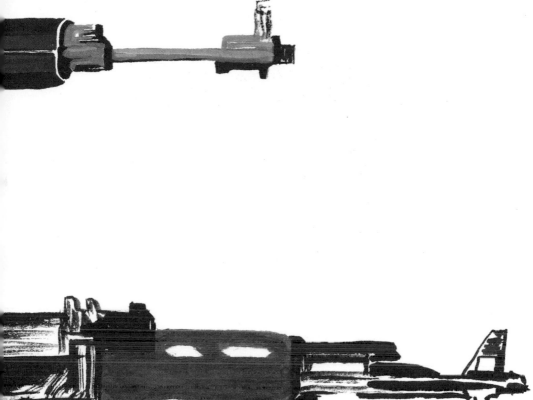

The **AK 47** is everyone's plaything, nicknamed *kalash* or *klashing* or *kleshen*. The **Slavia** is a derivative of the kalash, and during the first few months only the Palestinians have them. After that the Kataeb militiamen take them from the dead they rob.

THE MAKAROV

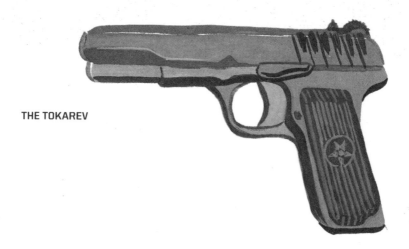

THE TOKAREV

The Belgian **FN Herstal** is nicknamed *arbaatash* (fourteen in Arabic) because it shoots fourteen rounds. The **Colt 45** is American, of course, and shoots 11.43 mm calibres. The **Makarov** and the **Tokarev** (pronounced *Tobariv*) are Russian. The **Walther** is called *tmeniyeh mhayar* (approximately eight) because it shoots 7.65 mm bullets.

THE G3

THE FAL

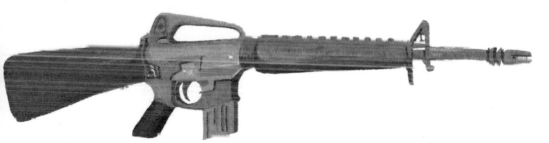

THE M16

The **FAL** is Belgian, the **M16** is American, the **G3** (*gé-tri* in Arabic) is German. The Christian militias primarily use these weapons. The **Dragunov** (for the Lebanese *Drakanof*) is a Russian sniper rifle. It will be used a great deal during the Battle of the Hotels. The **MAG** is an imitation of the **M60** and is a belt-fed machine gun. All these weapons shoot 7.62 mm bullets except the M16, which shoots 5.56 mm bullets.

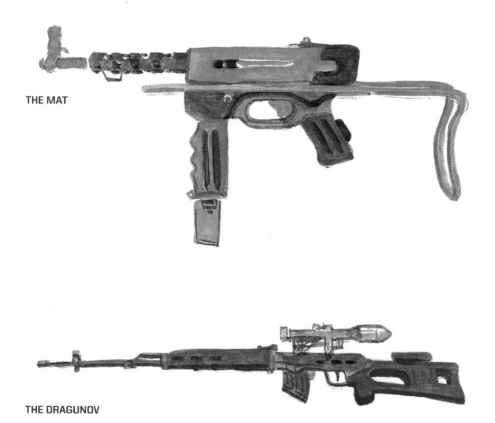

THE MAT

THE DRAGUNOV

Some machine pistols: the **Uzi** is made in Israel, and only the Lebanese Forces (Christian) have them. They also have the American **Ingram**. The **MAT** is French and is used by all sides. These machine pistols shoot 9 mm bullets.

All factions use the Soviet-made heavy machine gun **DShK** (Degtyarov-Shpagin). When mounted on a jeep it plays a starring role during the war; it is the famous dushka (*doshka* for the Lebanese). This anti-aircraft cannon will be used against people, cars and small trucks. The **RPG** rocket-propelled grenade launchers (pronounced RBG, the letter P doesn't exist in Arabic) are Soviet-made. The **RPG-7** is the newer, more sophisticated version of the **RPG-2**. Conceived as an anti-tank weapon, it too is put into practice against people. The **LAW** is originally American and is used only once – the launcher is then thrown away. It will do wonders against cars.

RPG-7

RPG-2

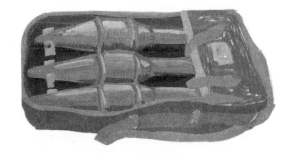

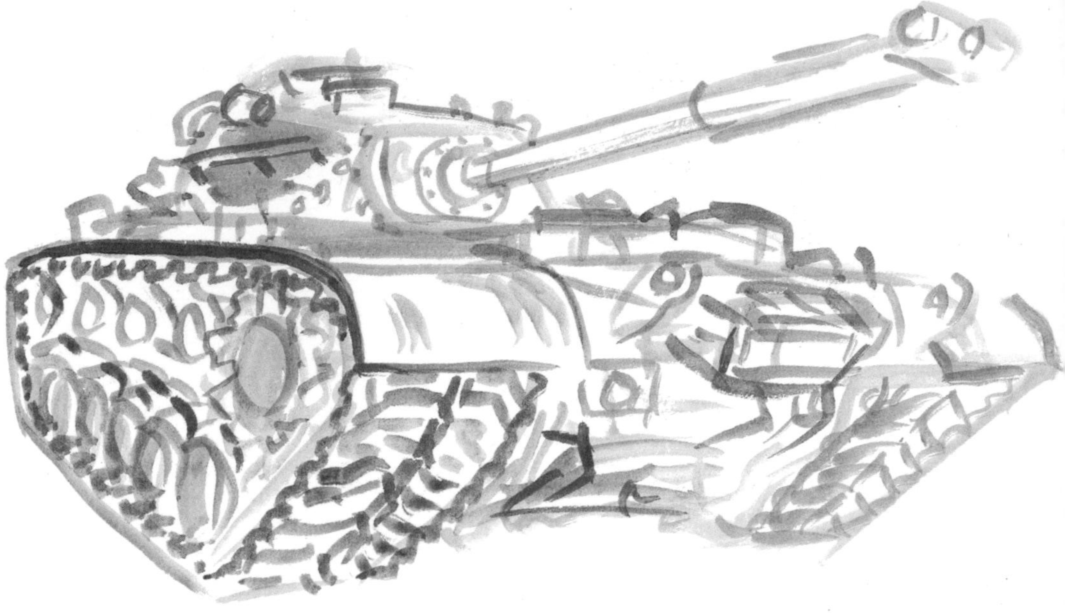

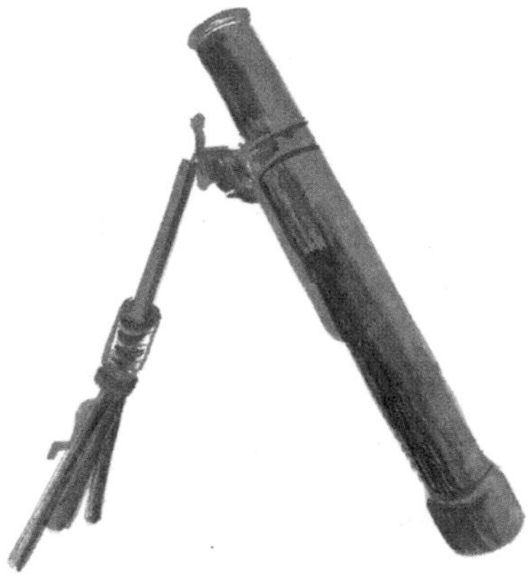

All factions use recoilless rifles and 60, 80 and 120 mm mortars. On the progressive Palestinian side Soviet-type 82 and 107 mm recoilless guns are used as well as 140 mm **Katyusha** rocket launchers that have a range of 9 km.

The Fatah party has a supply of **Grad missiles** that are like super-Katyushas and have a range of 15 km. **BM-21**s, or *rejmé*, are what the Germans called 'Stalin's organs' during World War Two. They will be used to destroy buildings and neighbourhoods. They are capable of tremendous firepower, but only relative target precision.

The **T54**, in a variety of models, is the only tank in Lebanon at the beginning of the conflict. It will be used by various factions over the years and as the situation evolves. At the outset, the T54s belong to the army. The Kataeb party will steal them and in turn will have them stolen by the Mourabitoun party. The Amal Movement will claim them after crushing the Mourabitoun, and so on . . .

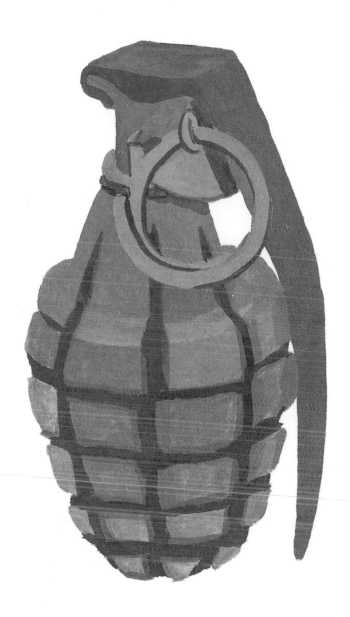

All factions use Russian grenades, or hand grenades. They are called *remmaneh* in Arabic, which means pomegranate.

There is a vast choice of artillery for militias and civilians alike. Both factions have two things in common: a suicidal appetite for violence, and a fascination with destruction. They are restlessly waiting for an opportunity to try out their weapons.

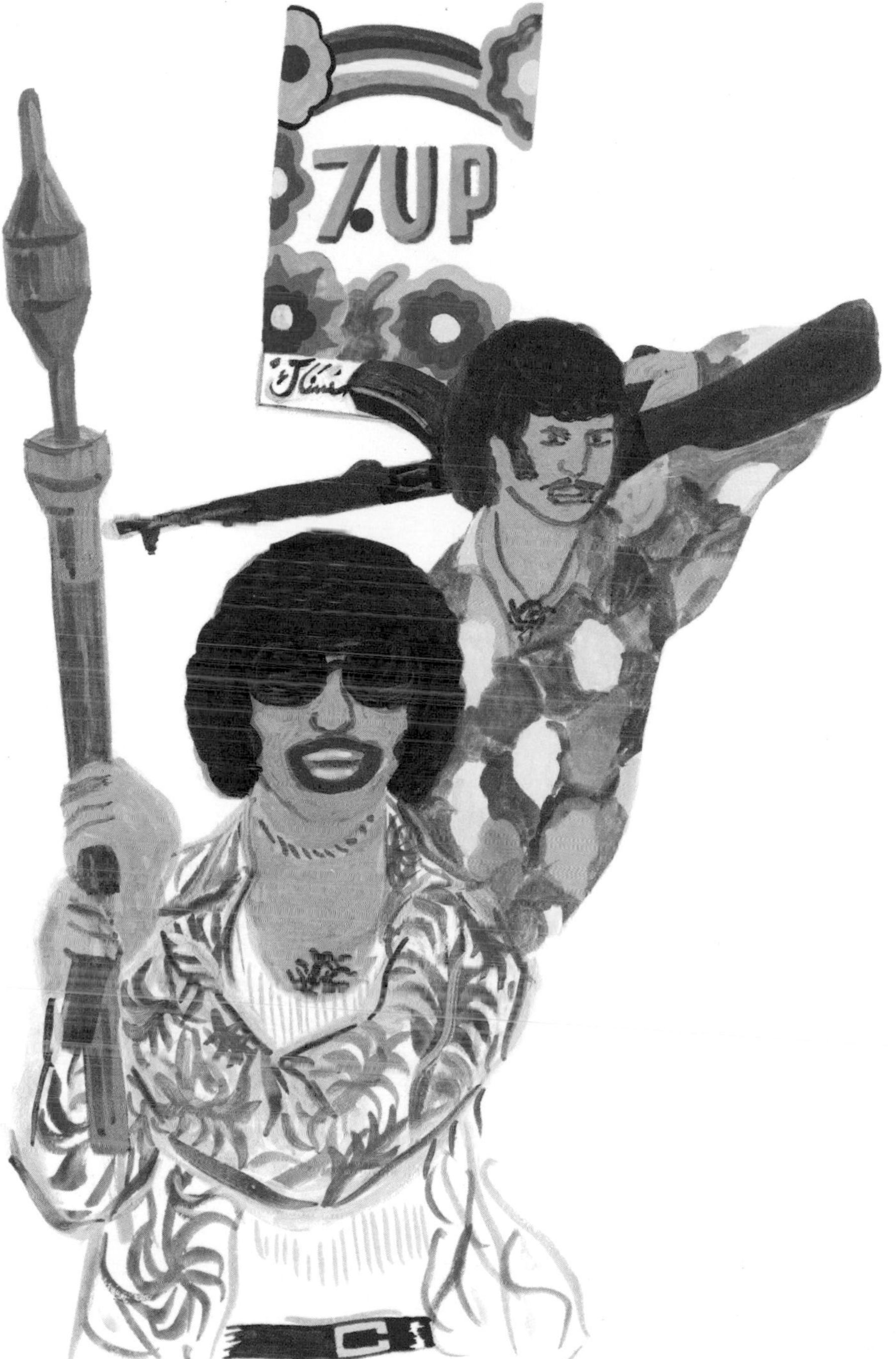
7UP

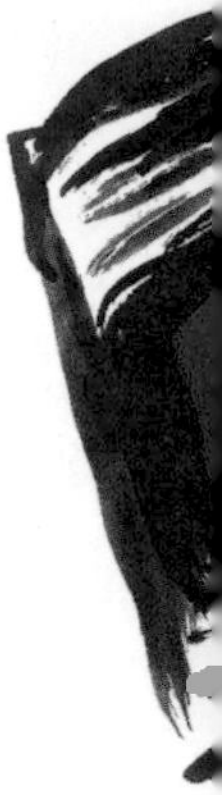

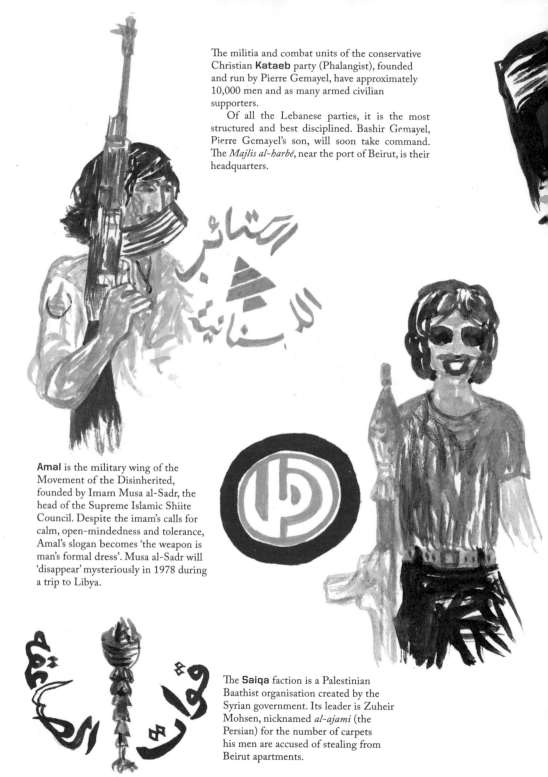

The militia and combat units of the conservative Christian **Kataeb** party (Phalangist), founded and run by Pierre Gemayel, have approximately 10,000 men and as many armed civilian supporters.

Of all the Lebanese parties, it is the most structured and best disciplined. Bashir Gemayel, Pierre Gemayel's son, will soon take command. The *Majlis al-harbé*, near the port of Beirut, is their headquarters.

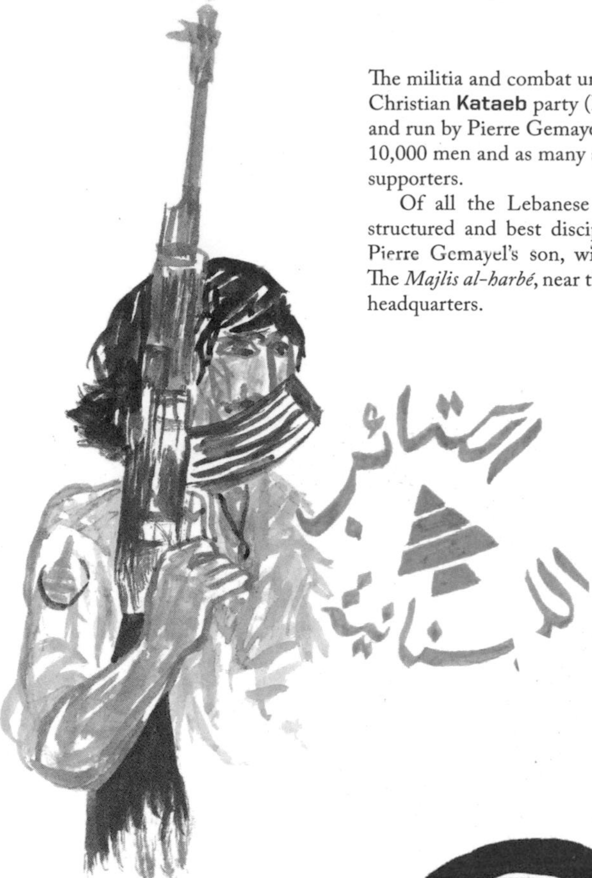

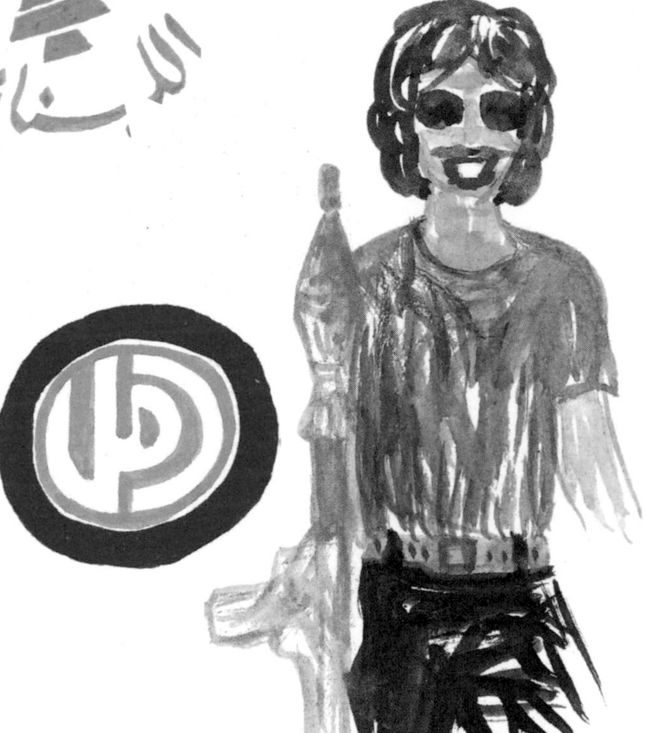

Amal is the military wing of the Movement of the Disinherited, founded by Imam Musa al-Sadr, the head of the Supreme Islamic Shiite Council. Despite the imam's calls for calm, open-mindedness and tolerance, Amal's slogan becomes 'the weapon is man's formal dress'. Musa al-Sadr will 'disappear' mysteriously in 1978 during a trip to Libya.

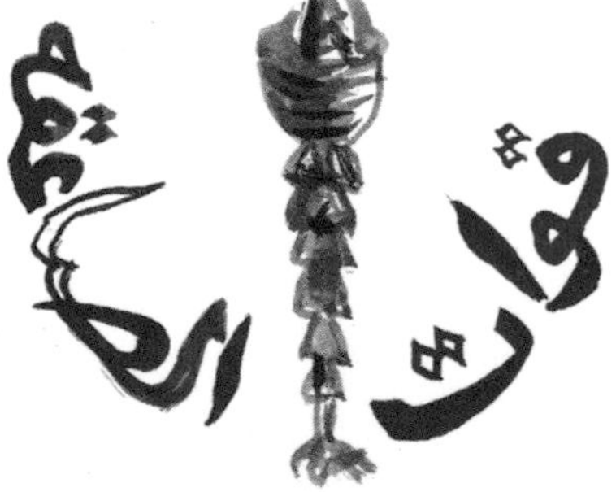

The **Saiqa** faction is a Palestinian Baathist organisation created by the Syrian government. Its leader is Zuheir Mohsen, nicknamed *al-ajami* (the Persian) for the number of carpets his men are accused of stealing from Beirut apartments.

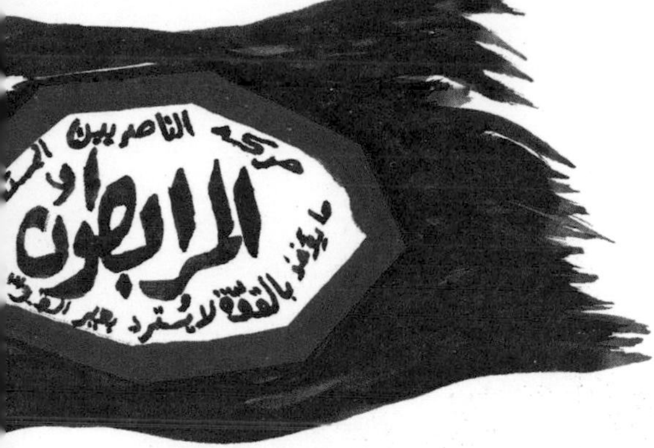

The **Mourabitoun** (Movement of Independent Nasserists), founded by Ibrahim Kulaylat, is a paramilitary 'progressive' organisation. The 3,000 or so fighters are trained by Fatah.

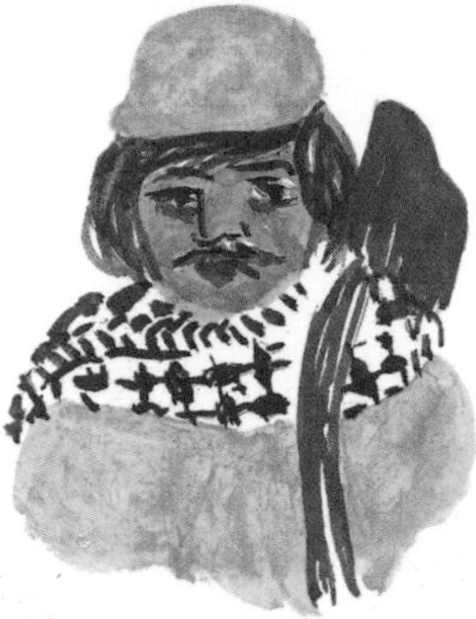

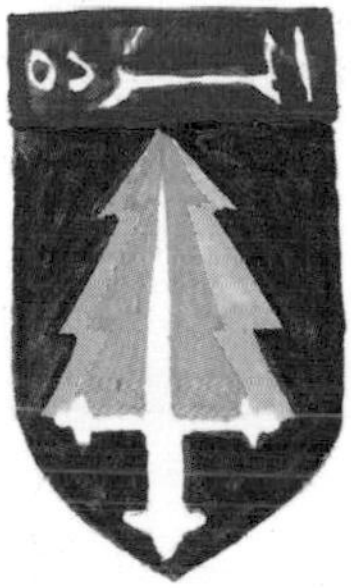

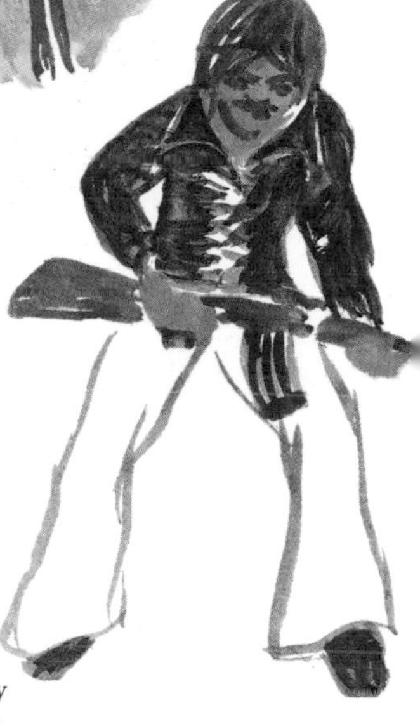

The **Marada** are Christian followers of President Suleiman Frangieh. The 900-odd fighters are based mainly in the region of Zgharta and Ehden in northern Lebanon.

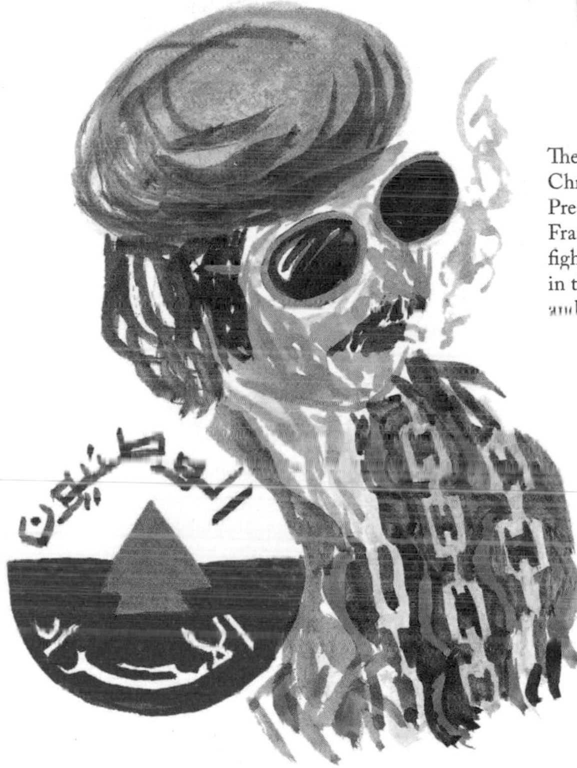

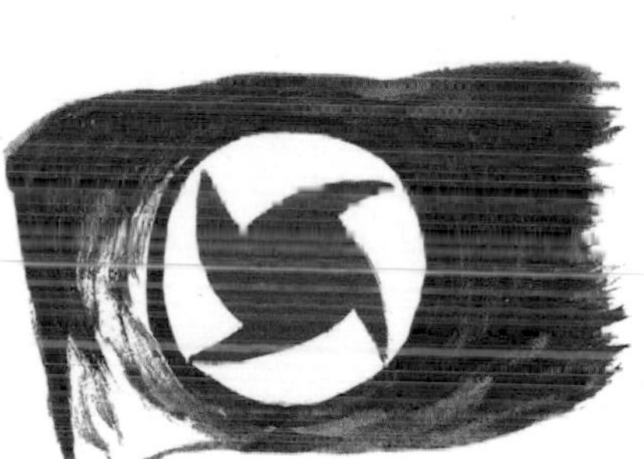

The **NLP** (National Liberal Party), established by the conservative Christian politician Camille Chamoun, has its own armed militia, *al-Noumour* (or the Tigers), which is 3,000-men strong.

The **SSNP** (Syrian Social Nationalist Party) is run by Dr Abdallah Saadeh. After veering from the extreme right to the extreme left, the party advocates uniting Greater Syria, social nationalism and the fight against Zionism. The militia includes about 2,500 men and other armed supporters.

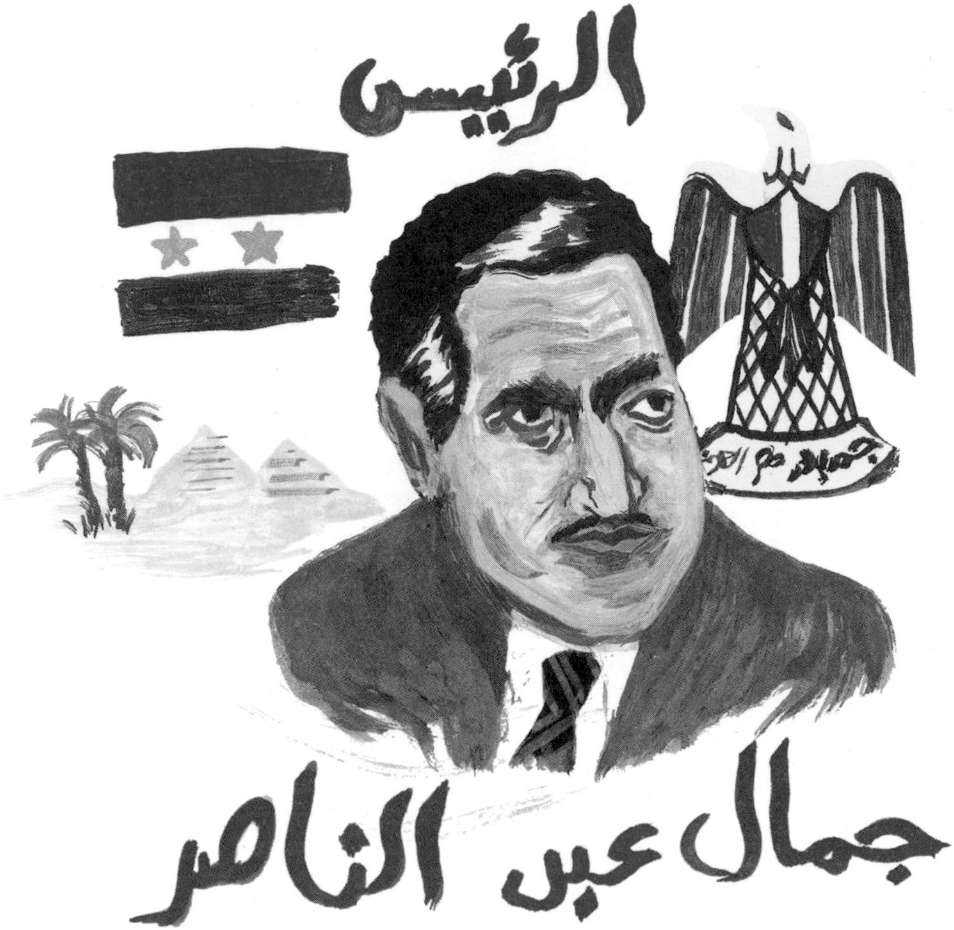
الرئيس
جمال عبن الناصر

Besides the Mourabitoun, several other movements take inspiration from Nasser, even though he had died several years earlier.

The Popular Nasserite Forces, founded by Maarouf Saad who was killed three months before the beginning of the war (2,000 men).

Arab Socialist Union, Nasserite ideology.

The Union of Working Peoples Forces, Nasserite ideology.

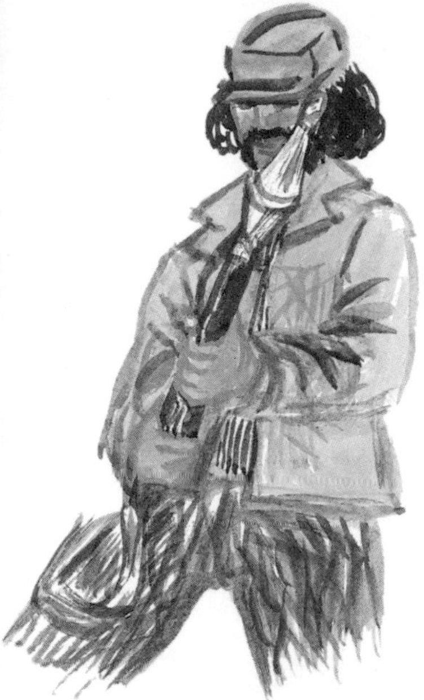

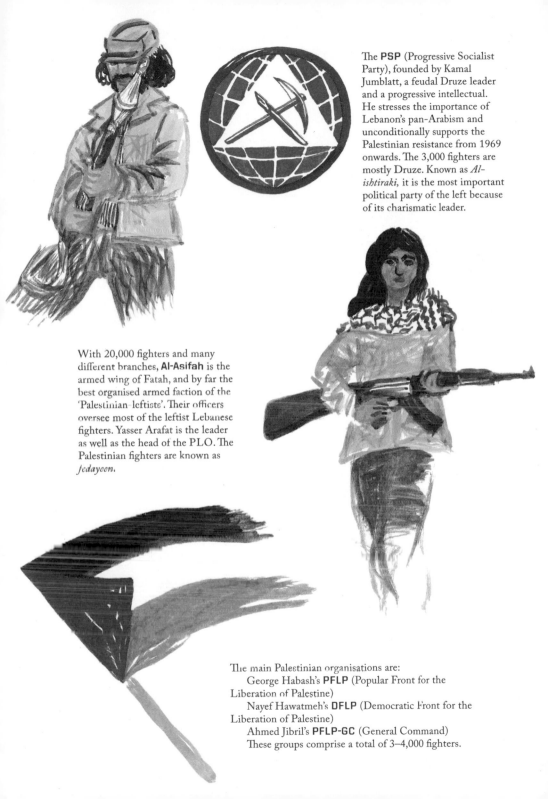

The **PSP** (Progressive Socialist Party), founded by Kamal Jumblatt, a feudal Druze leader and a progressive intellectual. He stresses the importance of Lebanon's pan-Arabism and unconditionally supports the Palestinian resistance from 1969 onwards. The 3,000 fighters are mostly Druze. Known as *Al-ishtiraki,* it is the most important political party of the left because of its charismatic leader.

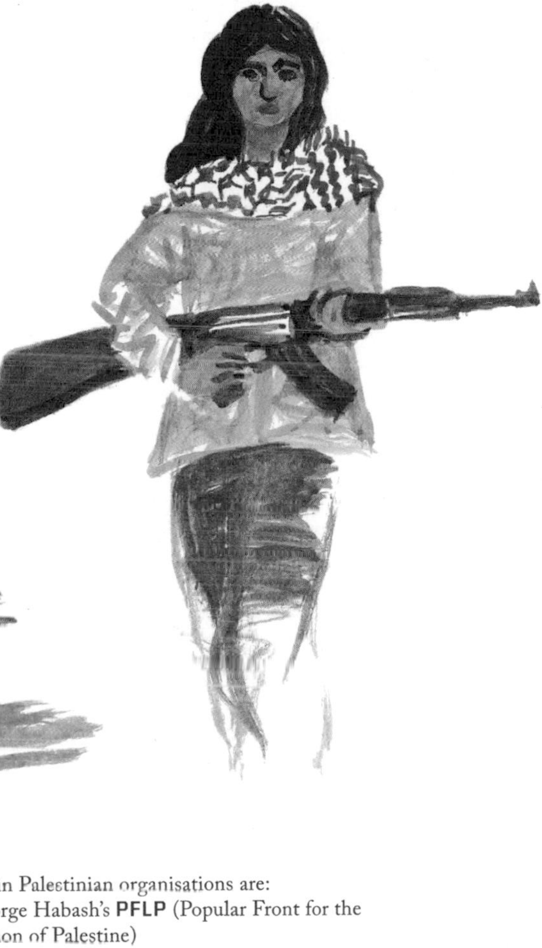

With 20,000 fighters and many different branches, **Al-Asifah** is the armed wing of Fatah, and by far the best organised armed faction of the 'Palestinian leftists'. Their officers oversee most of the leftist Lebanese fighters. Yasser Arafat is the leader as well as the head of the PLO. The Palestinian fighters are known as *Jedayoon.*

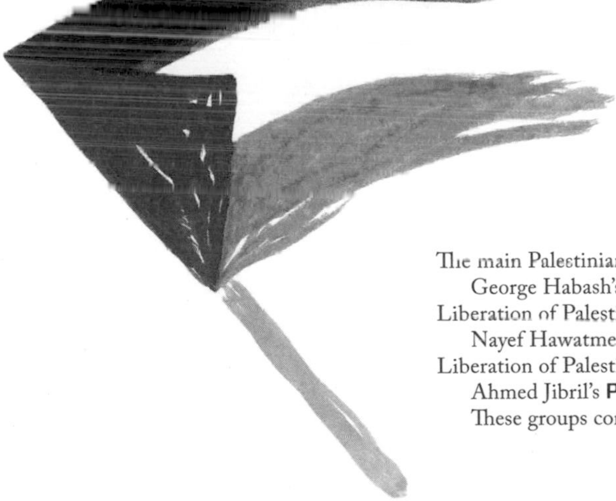

The main Palestinian organisations are:
George Habash's **PFLP** (Popular Front for the Liberation of Palestine)
Nayef Hawatmeh's **DFLP** (Democratic Front for the Liberation of Palestine)
Ahmed Jibril's **PFLP-GC** (General Command)
These groups comprise a total of 3–4,000 fighters.

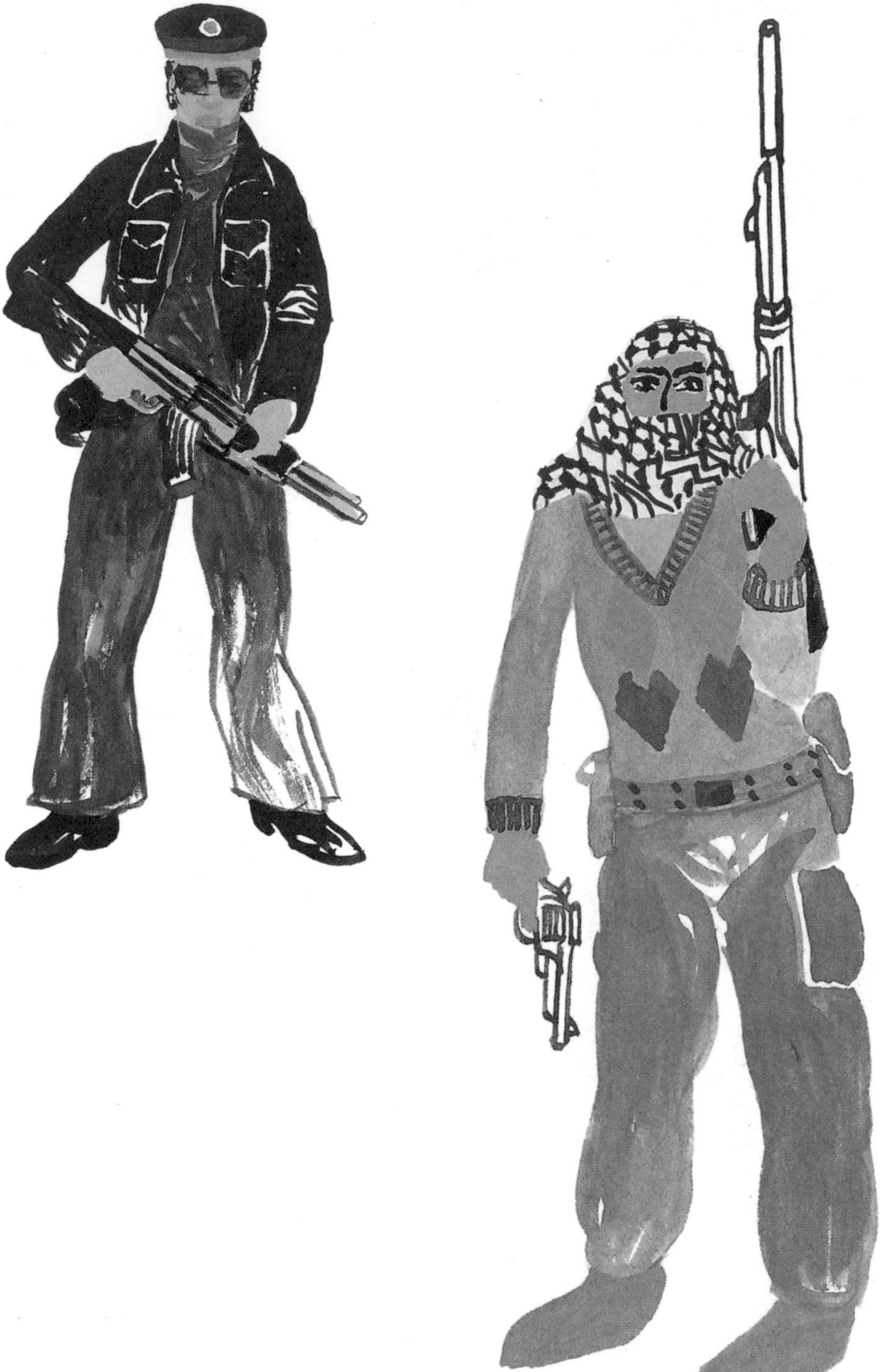

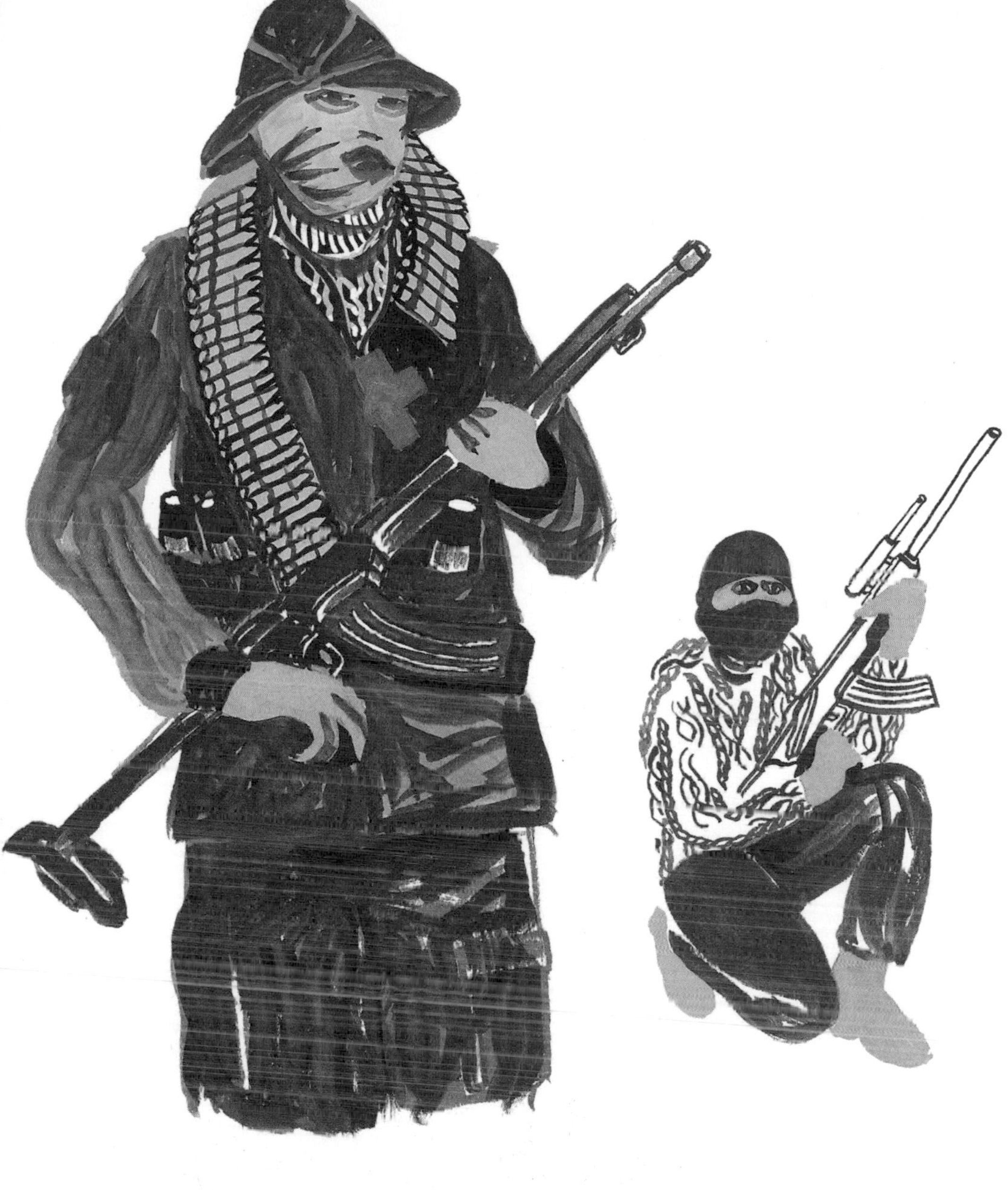

But we still want to think that our country is the Switzerland, the Paris, the Las Vegas, the Monaco and the Acapulco of the Middle East all in one, and what's more, we want to enjoy it. From the café terraces of Raouché or Ain Mreisseh, where we sometimes go for a banana split, we can't see the Shiite ghettoes or the Palestinian camps. And when we wear sunglasses we can't spot all the dirt either.

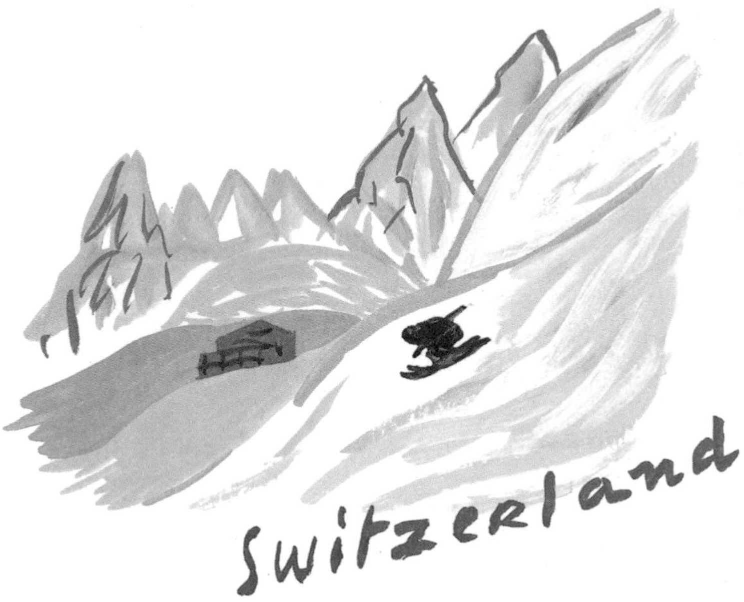
Switzerland

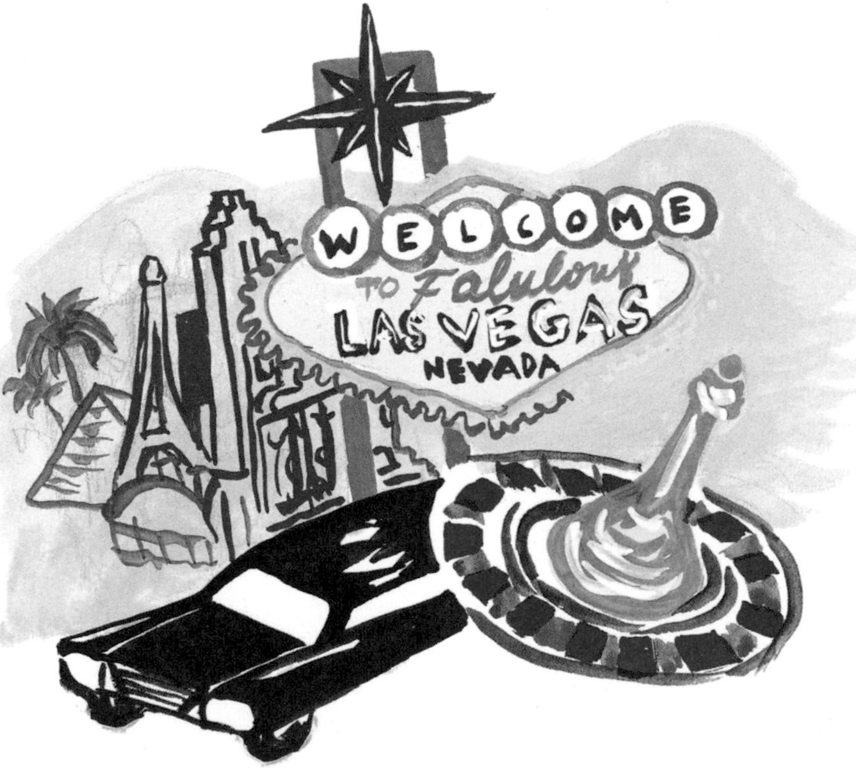
WELCOME
TO Fabulous
LAS VEGAS
NEVADA

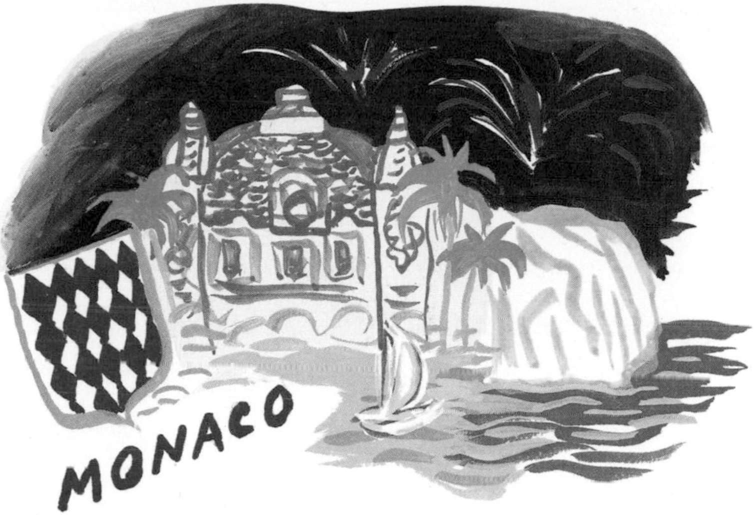
MONACO

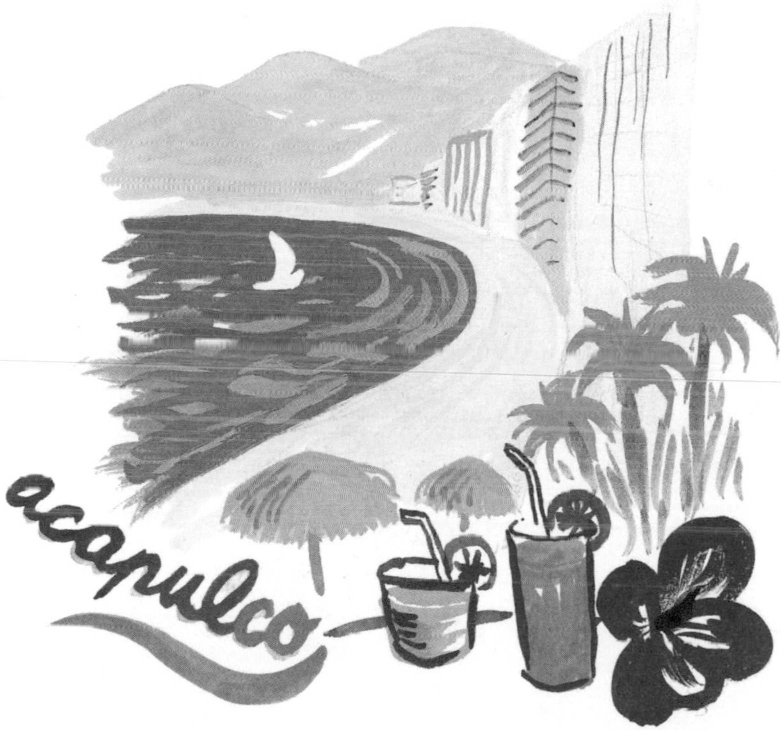
acapulco

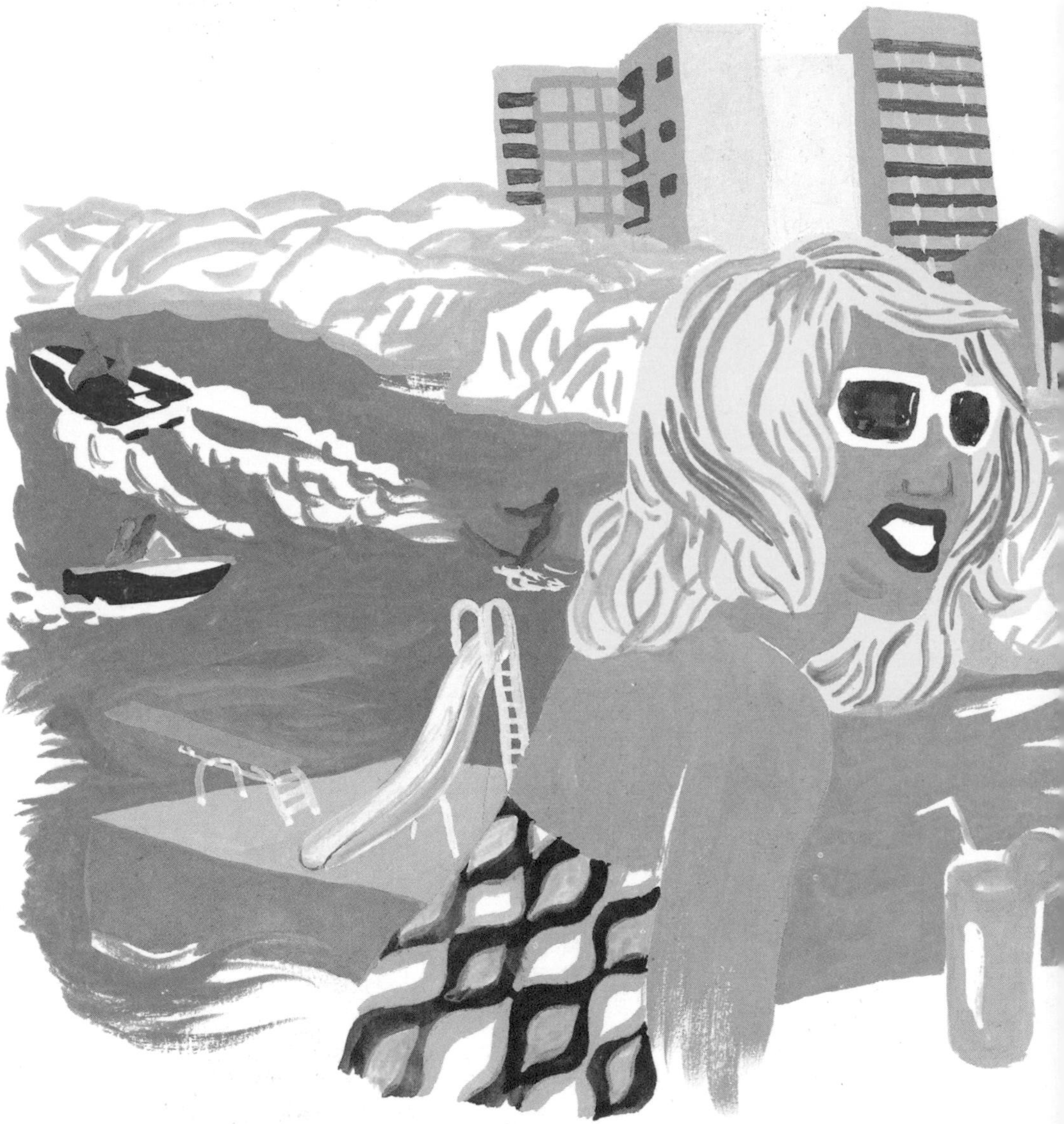

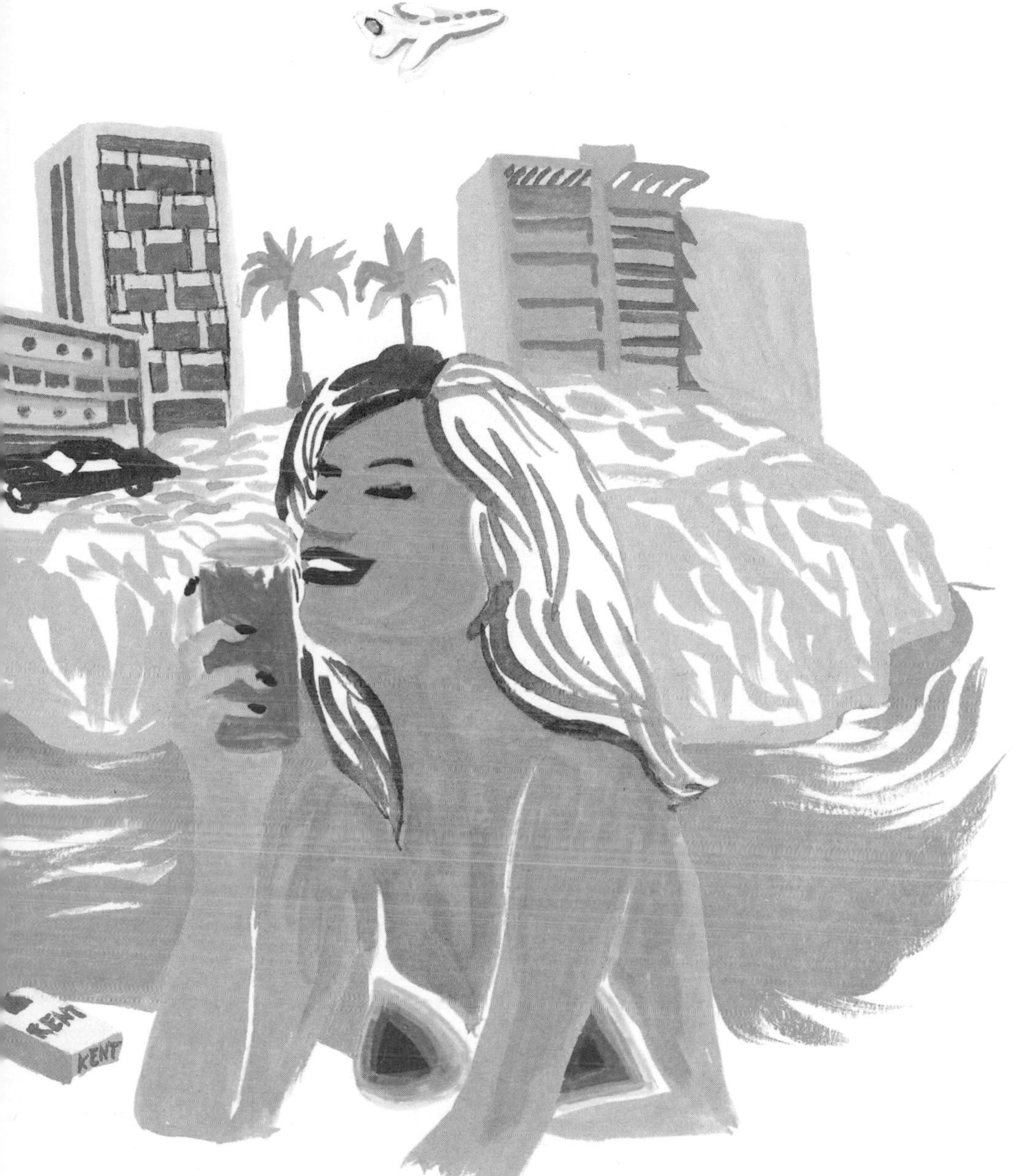
KENT
KENT

The spark ignites on 13 April, 1975. The shiny Western varnish, which the Lebanese are so proud of, is finally cracking.

That Sunday, Sheikh Pierre Gemayel, head of the Kataeb party, is attending a *tedchine*, the consecration of a church, in Ain el-Remmaneh, with his men. A bus filled with Palestinians from the Tal al-Zaatar refugee camp goes by. It's a fatal clash.

It's a Sunday, and my parents, my grandmother, my brother Walid and I have gone to have lunch in a restaurant in Chemlane, in the Aley region. On our way back we are met with visions of chaos as we near the neighbourhood of Ain el-Remmaneh: burnt tyres, armed men, blocked roads, the crackling of machine guns, panic, cries, flames and fumes. That Sunday lunch in the country marks in time the last moment of innocence.

The swings in the restaurant garden where we play while the adults are drinking their coffee, my Vichy-red gingham dress, my mother's shirt with pink and green zinnias on it, the *Petzi* comic book that Walid won't lend me, the story Teta* tells us during dessert about her cousin from Egypt who lost everything to gambling – these memories will be imprinted forever in my mind by what becomes a symbolic date – 13 April. It is like a rebirth; there is the before and after of that Sunday lunch which separates two distinct lives.

The clash that takes place in Ain el-Remmaneh between the Kataeb and the Palestinians unleashes a paroxysm of battles, massacres, kidnappings, destruction, pillage, assassinations and attacks . . .

And we're off, into the euphoria of the war.

* Grandmother

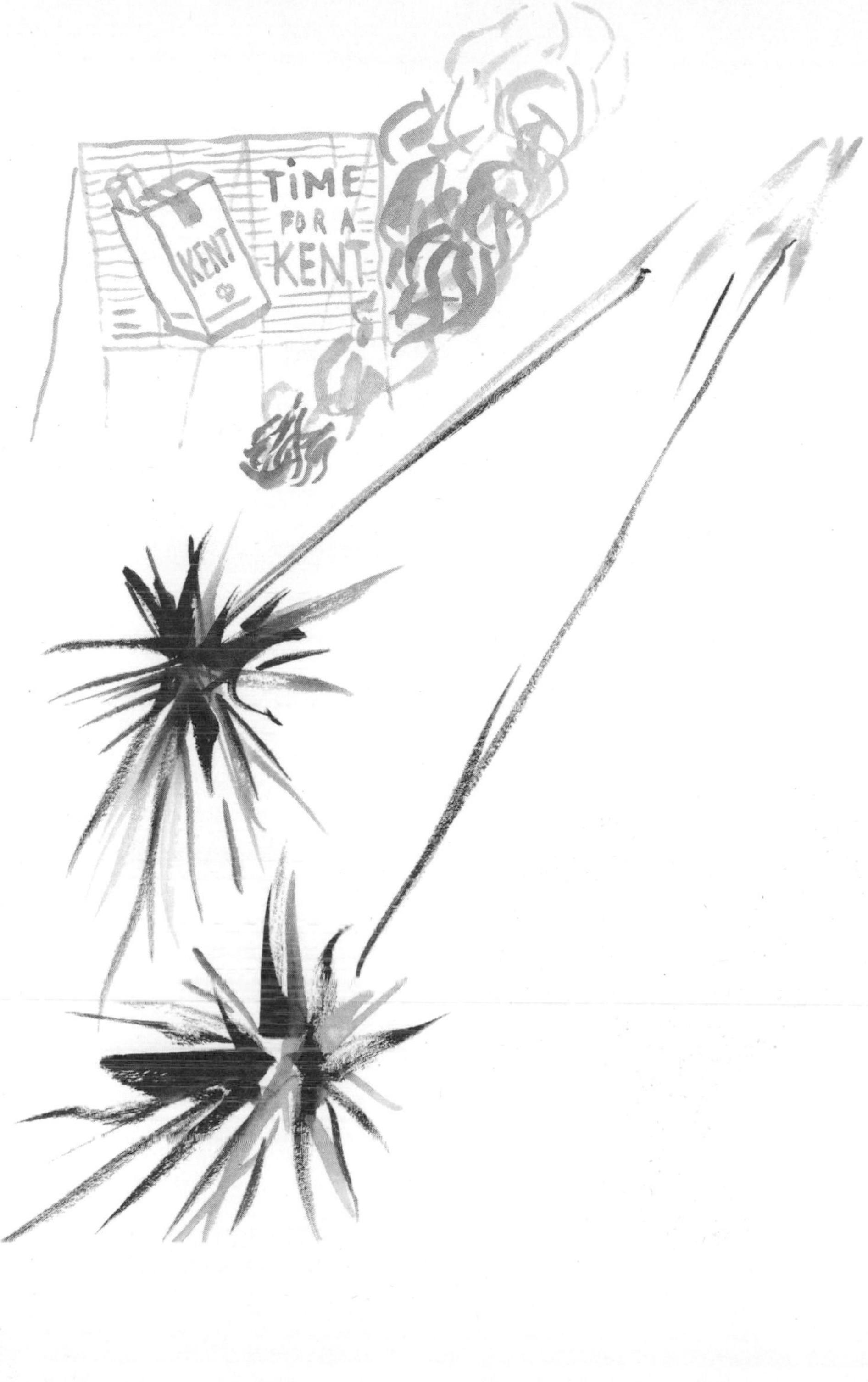
KENT
TIME FOR A KENT

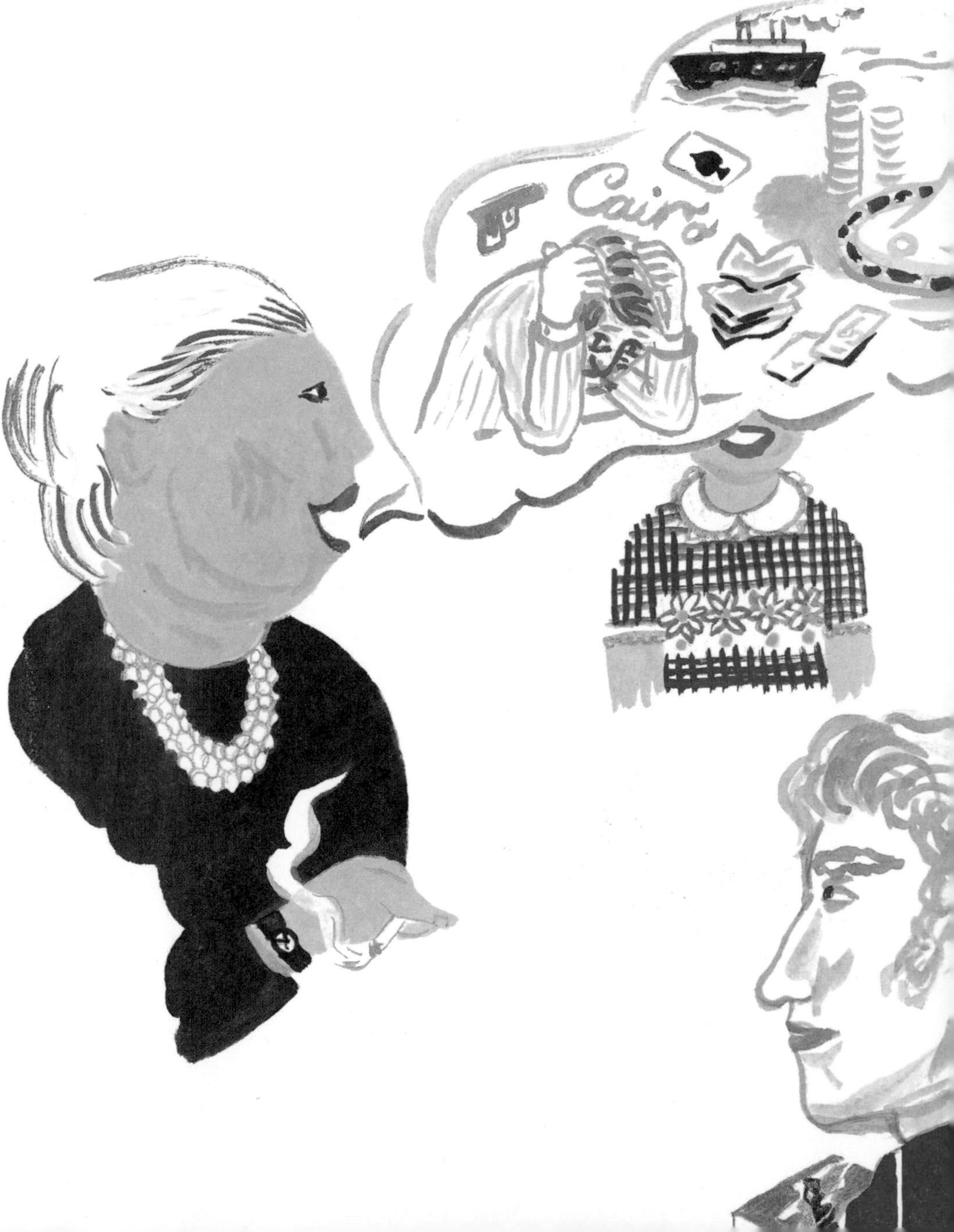
Cairo

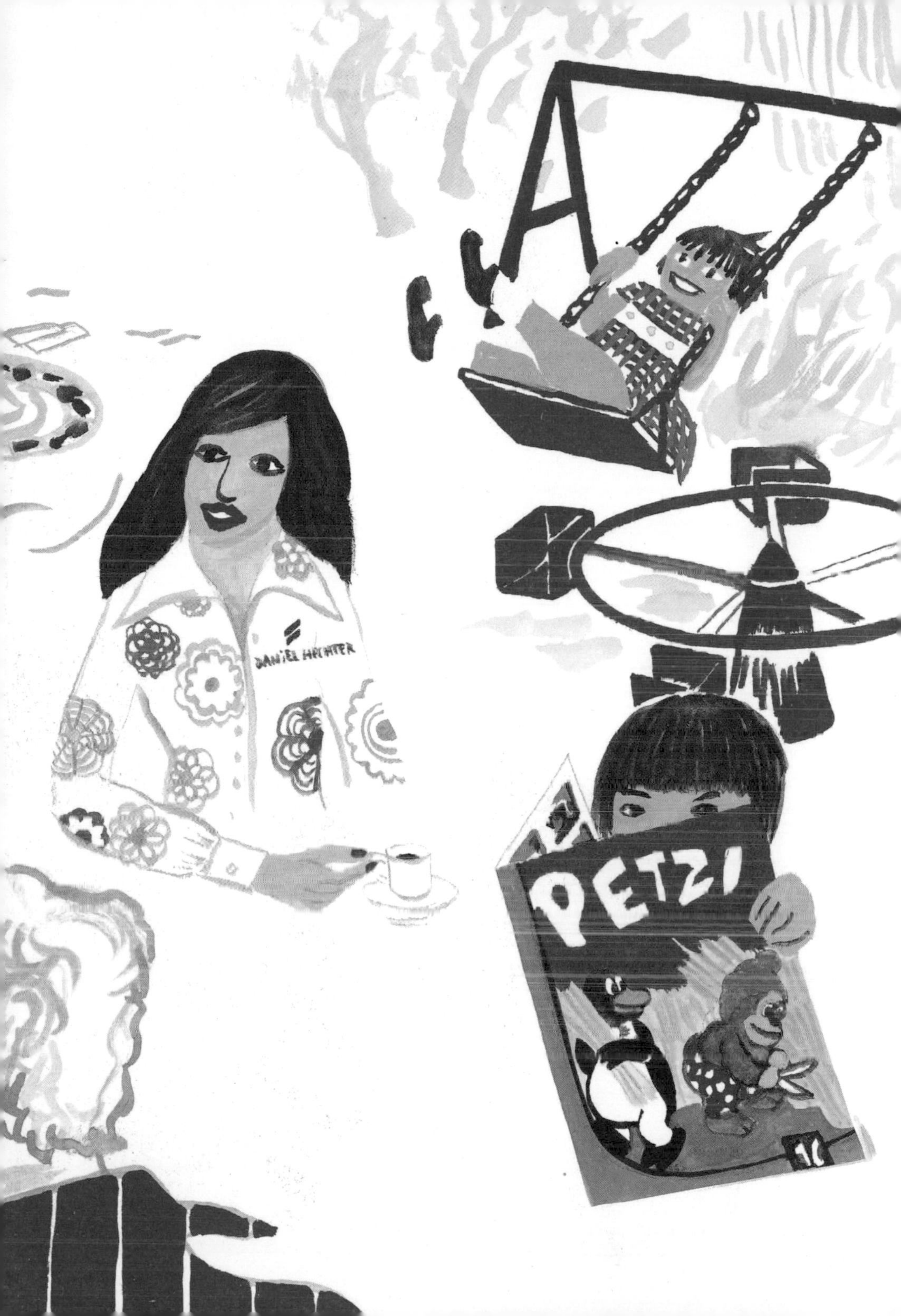
DANIEL HECHTER
PETZI

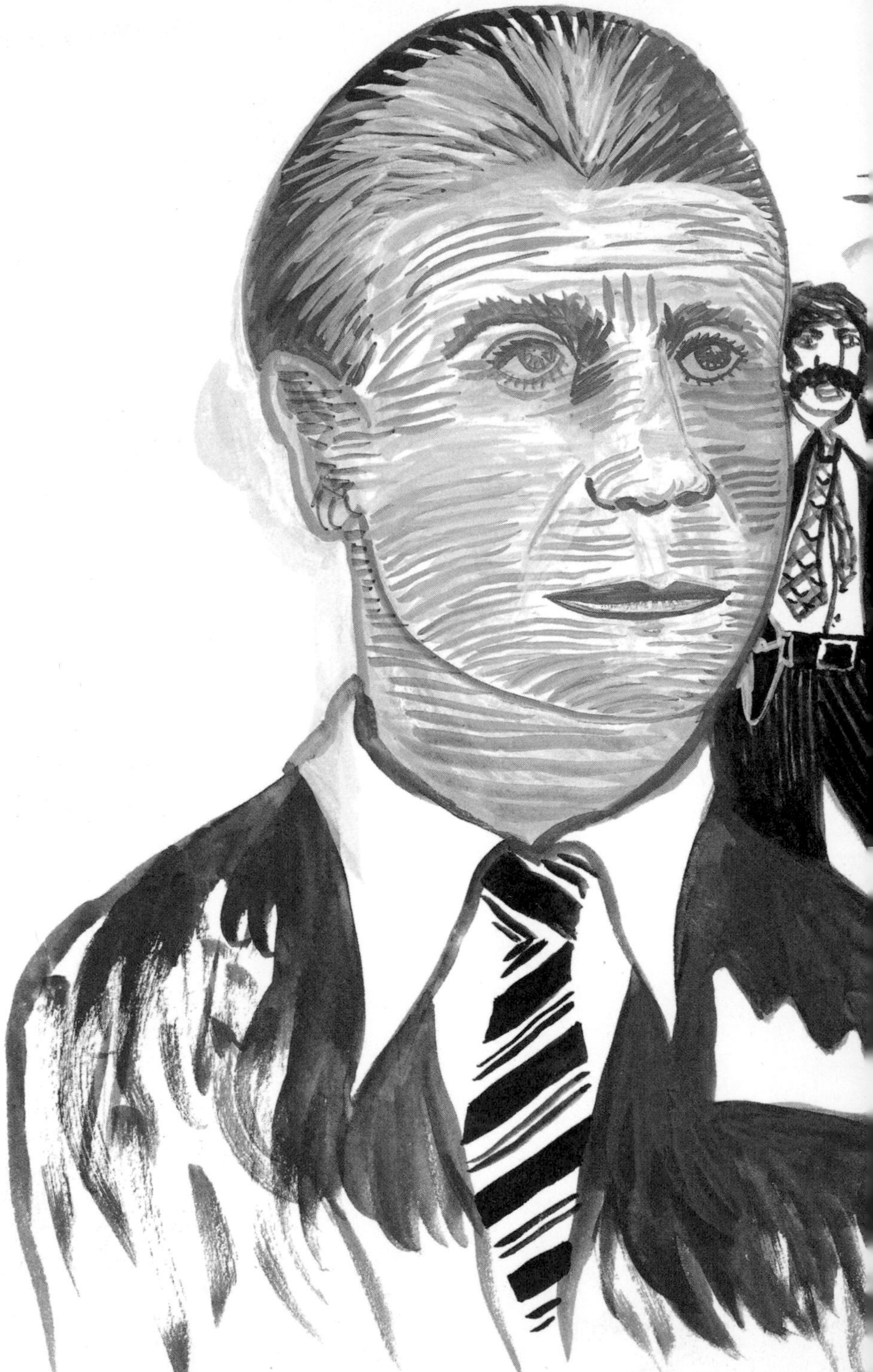

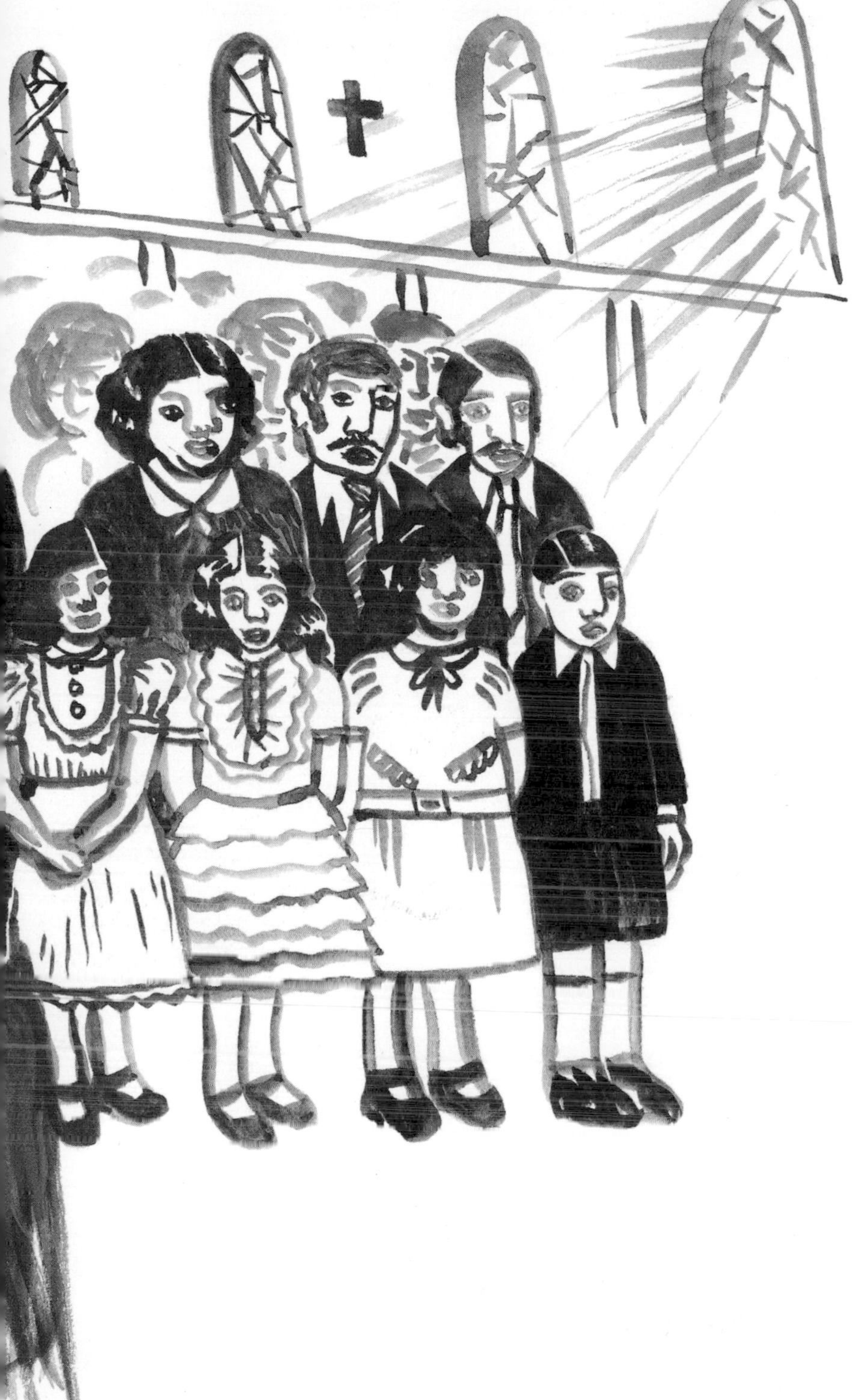

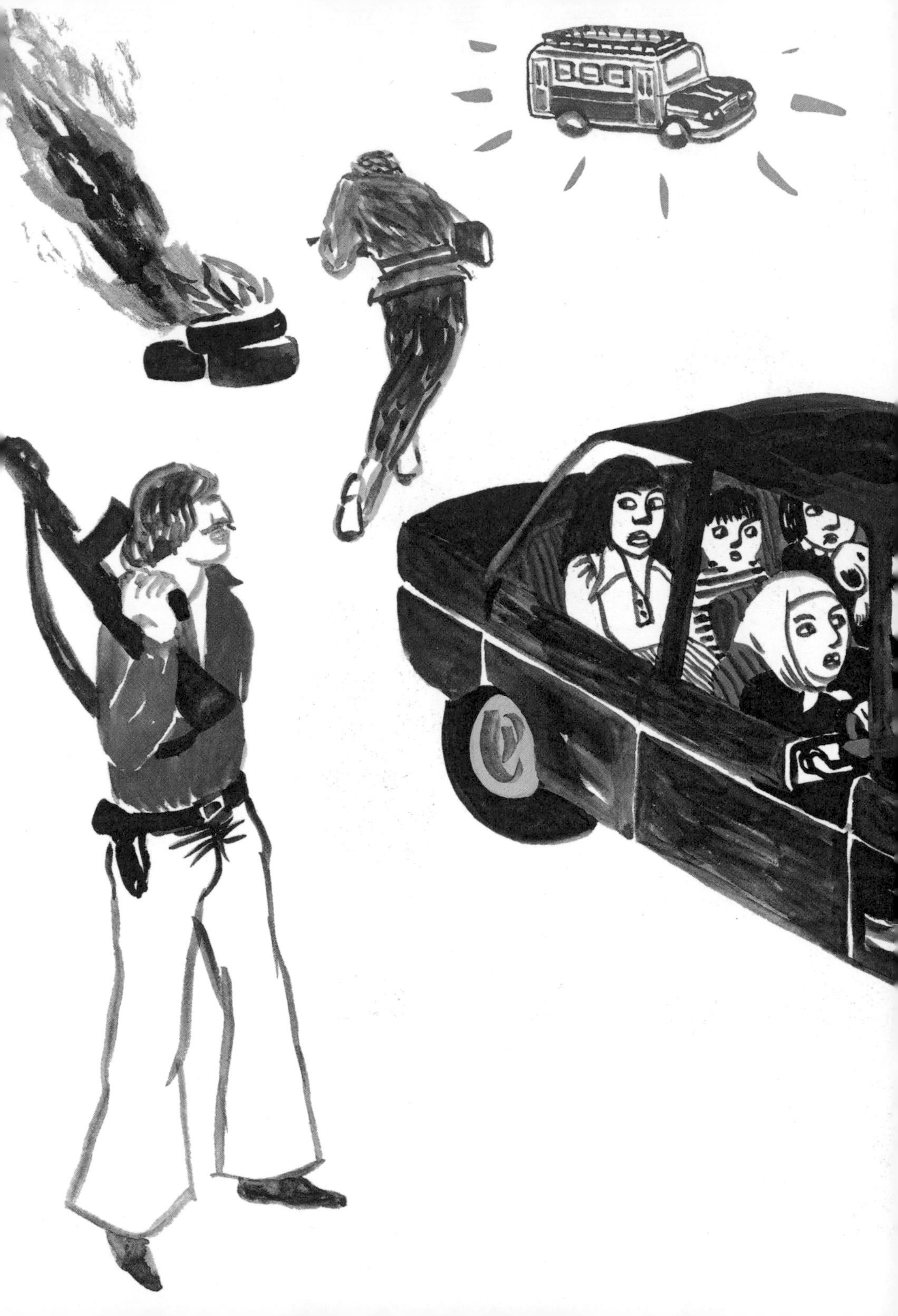

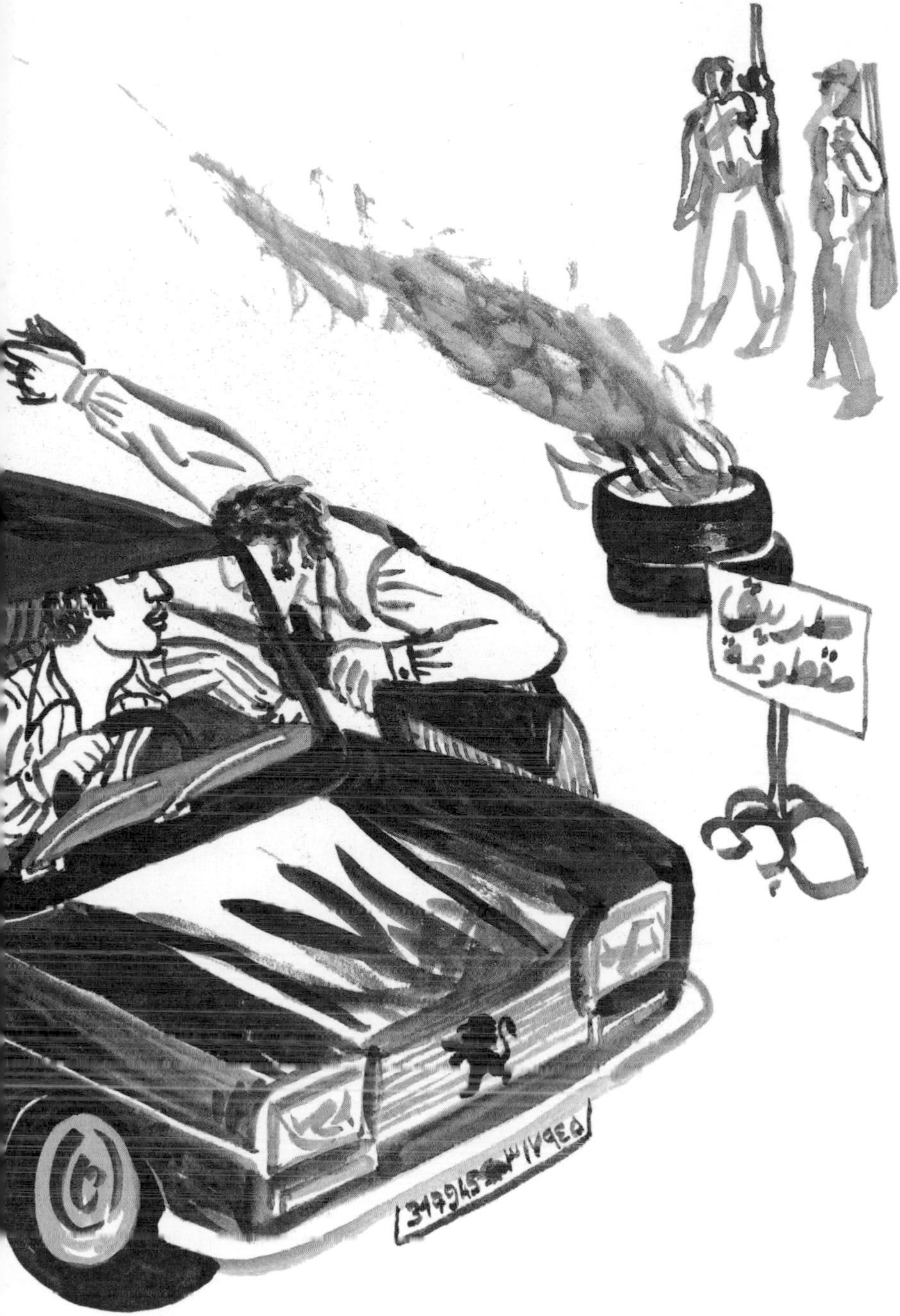
طريق
مقطوعة

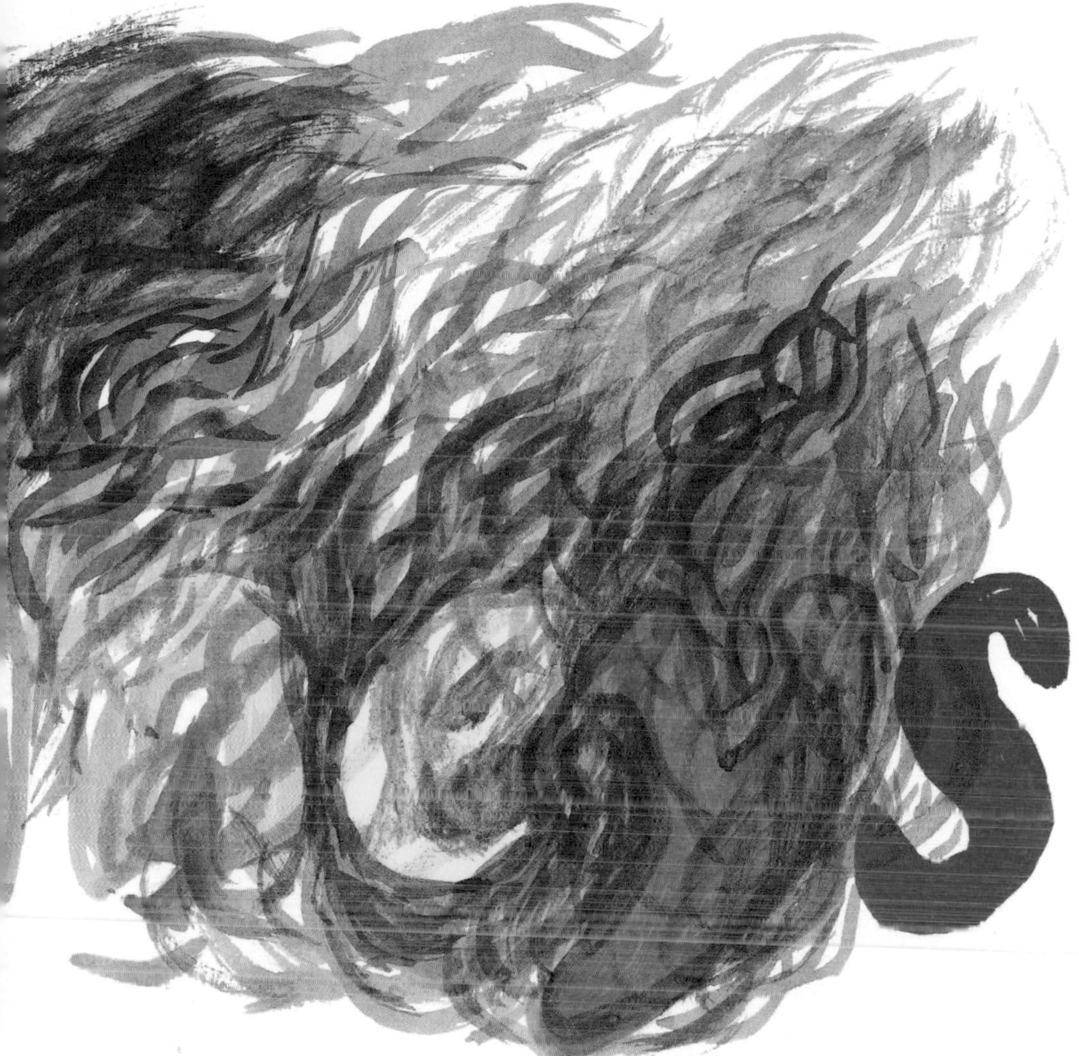

Far worse than the destruction of these temples to the Western way of life, the war does away with Beirut's soul from the outset. The Beirut souks, symbols of the co-existence, tolerance and openness of the Levant, will be pillaged, burned, destroyed and eliminated within a few weeks. Fighters from different militias, as if crazed, show no restraint.

After the clashes during the spring of 1975, known as the first three 'rounds' of the Lebanese 'crisis', and after a summer truce during which everyone rushes to the beach, the violence returns with a vengeance.

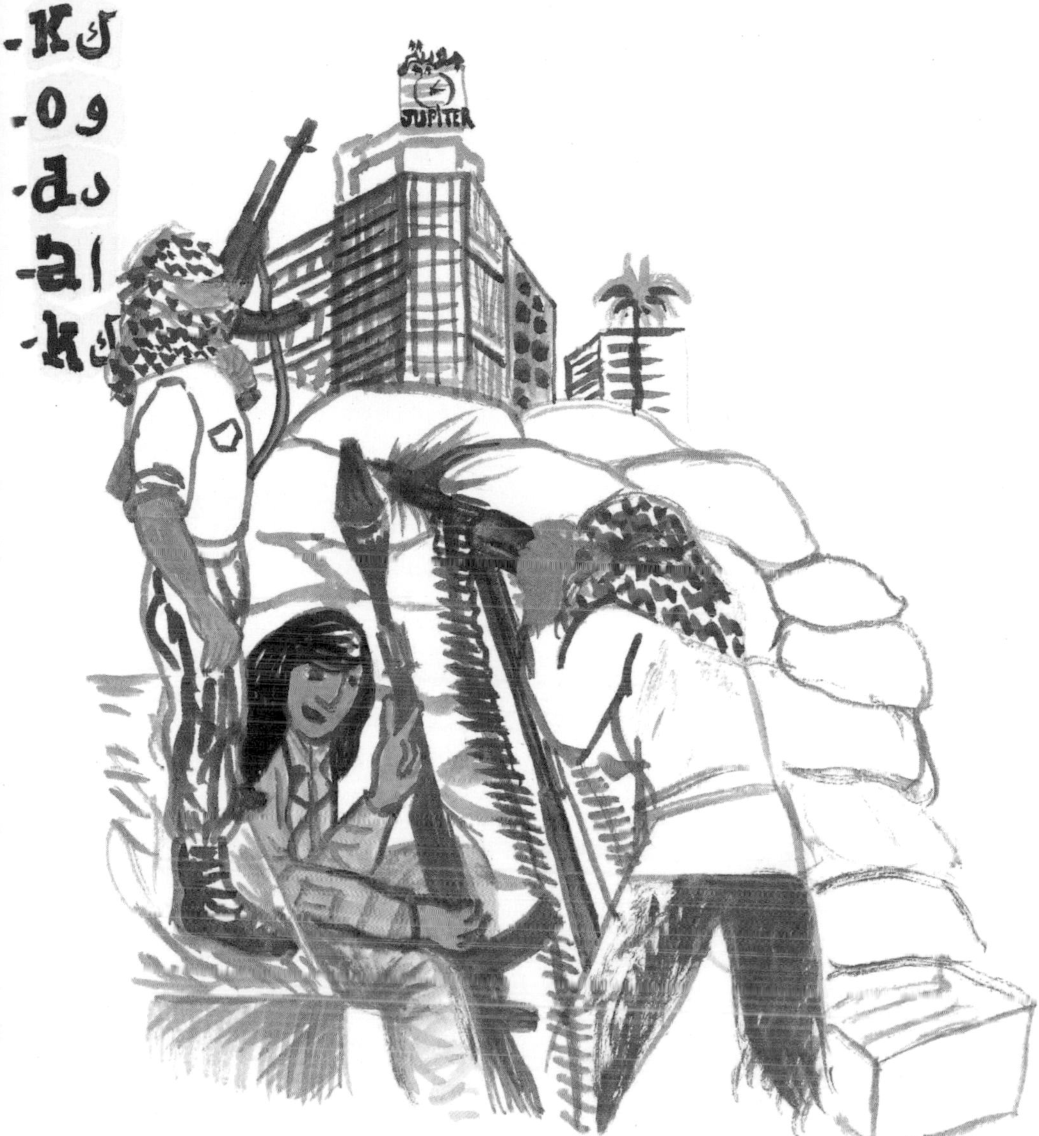
-K ك
-O و
-d د
-a ا
-k ك
JUPITER

Beirut gives a last gasp in that autumn of 1975, surrendering to Phalangist, Palestinian and other militias who are thirsting for violence, but still able to take occasional breaks during the ceasefire in order to plunder in peace. These ideological and bloody battles are cheerfully interchanged with profitable truces.

Enemy militias fighting on the same street agree to stop the battle to fill their bags with whatever happens to be in the vicinity of their respective positions. Once the shops have been emptied, they resume combat, picking up where they left off.

Before being completely torched, the souks are cleared of merchandise, some by shop owners trying to save what little they can, but mostly by looters. Metal shutters are blown up; façades are gutted and windows shattered, the shops are transformed into gaping holes. Part of the day's booty is hastily sold on the pavements of Hamra. Gold Cartier lighters can be found for two dollars! The militias collect whatever is useful for their families (Brandt, Philips, Moulinex) and whatever can be used for embellishment (feather boas, Hawaiian shirts, carnival masks) becomes combat wear.

The Phalangists wear balaclavas or masks during battle, to preserve the anonymity of some of their members, the civilians who work in leftist neighbourhoods, so that they can avoid recognition and reprisals during a truce. On the Palestinian side the *keffiyeh* wrapped around the face serves the same purpose. At the end of the month, when the war is well established, these precautions will no longer be necessary.

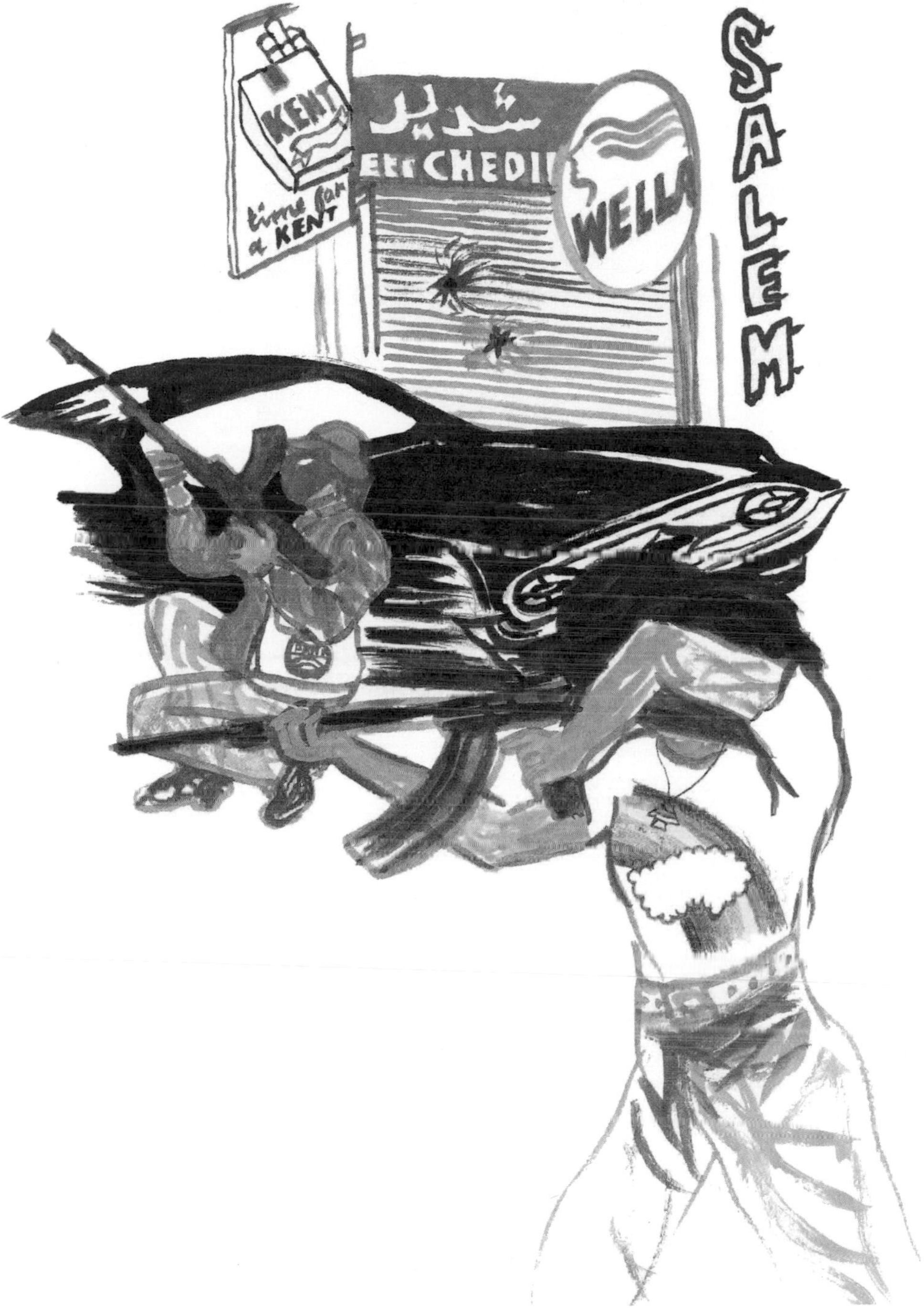
KENT
time for a KENT
شدير
WELLA
SALEM

Cartier

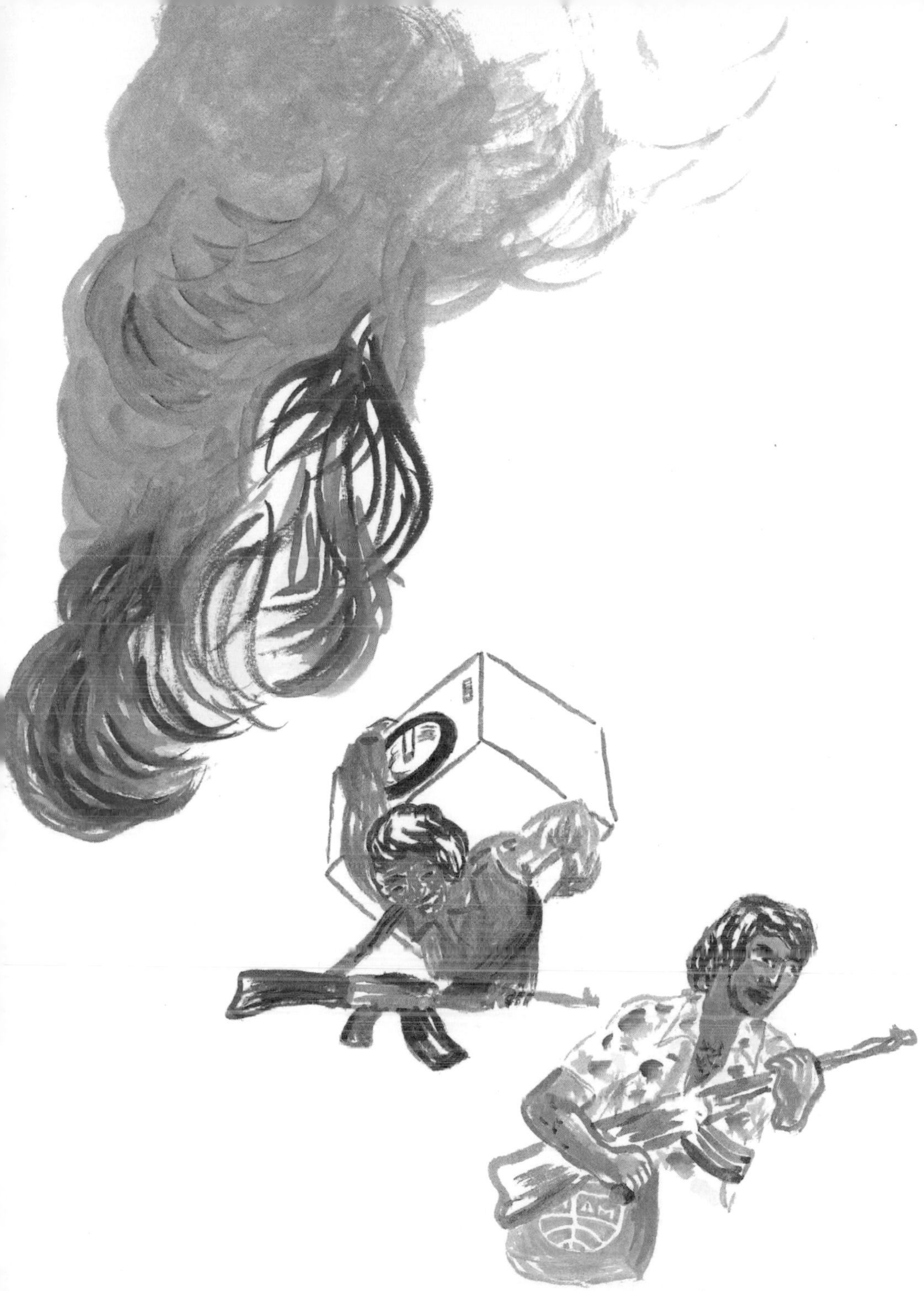

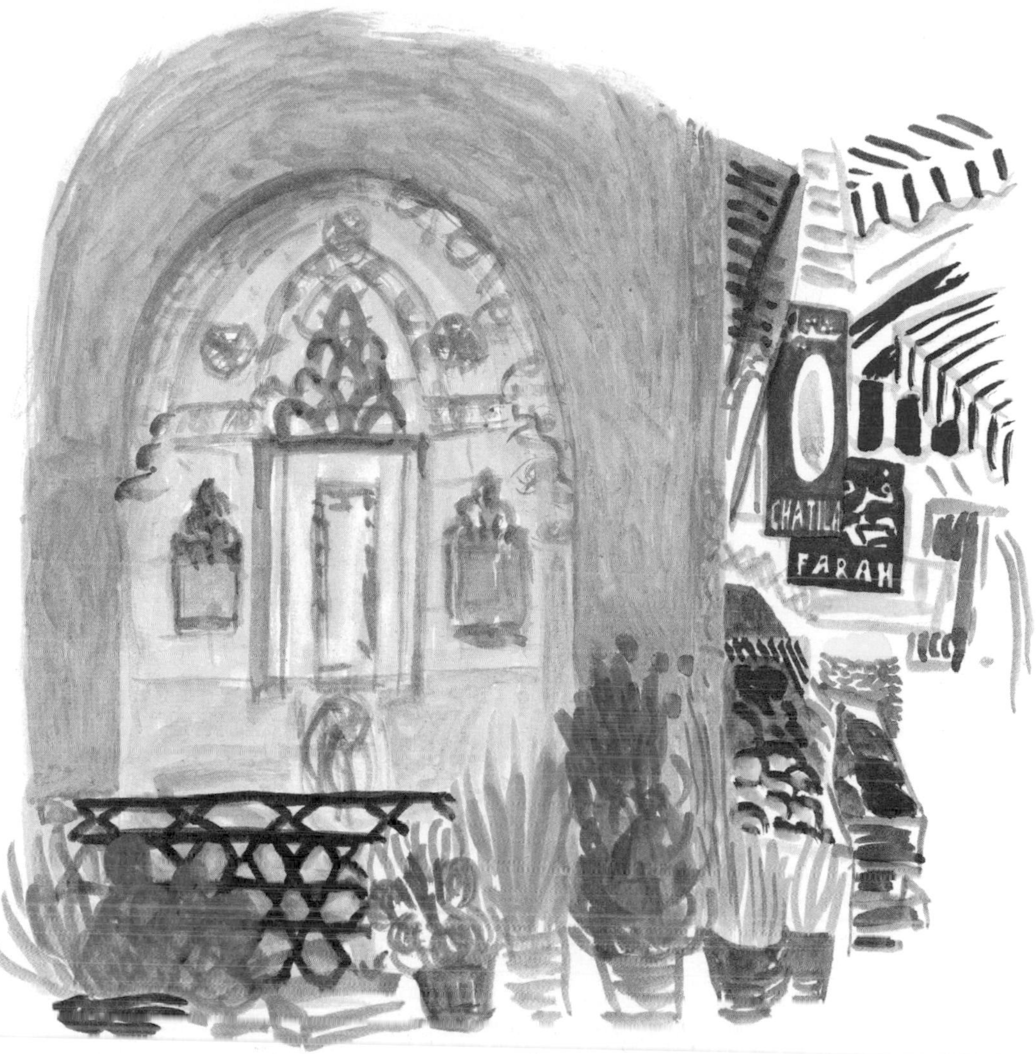
CHATILA
FARAH

The Ottoman fountain at the entrance of the Souk al-Franj in Bab Idriss

My grandfather Antoun's shop, *Ziadé Nouveautés*, is in the Souk al-Tawileh. He sells fabrics for evening gowns and bridal dresses. Silks from Lyon, *broderies anglaises,* Calais lace, organdies, organzas, crêpes, mousselines and taffetas. There's everything you might need to dazzle at the Palm Beach bar or the Vendôme, at the Paon Rouge or the Stéréo-Club, all these places that I dream of and that I'll never know.

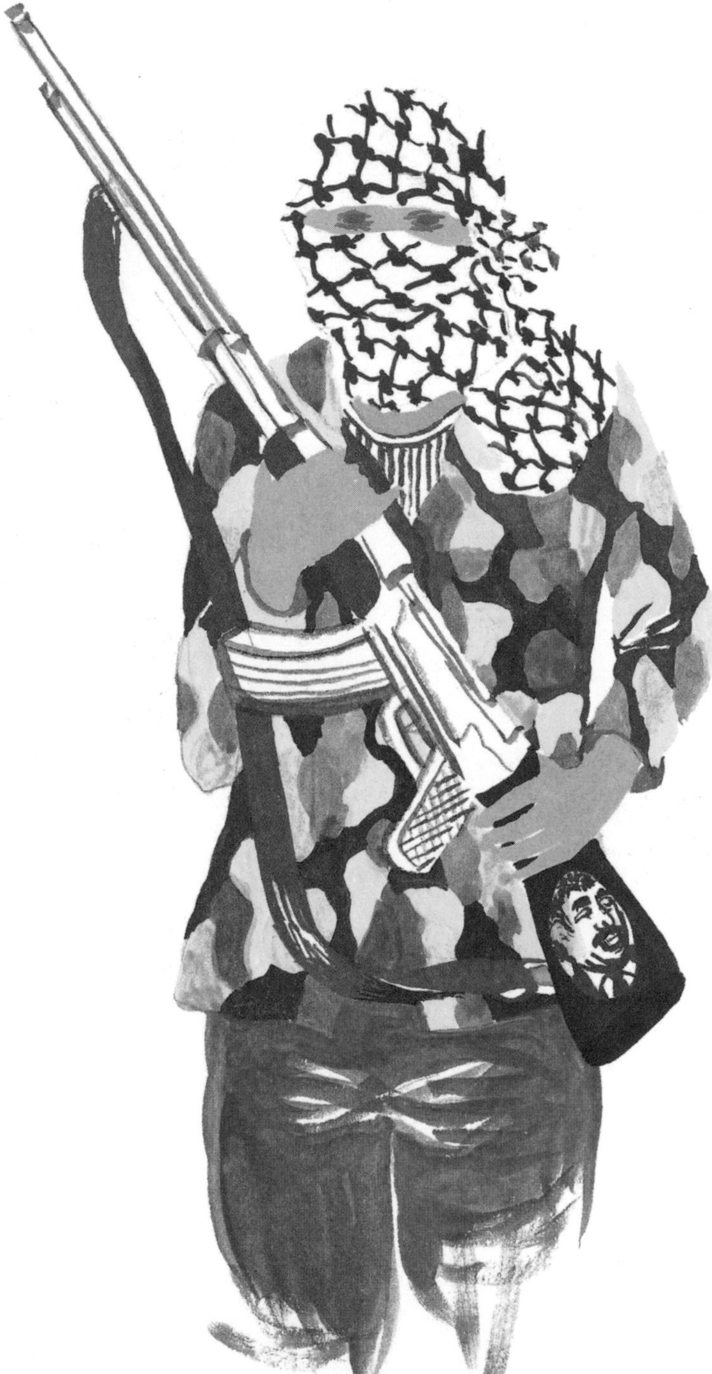

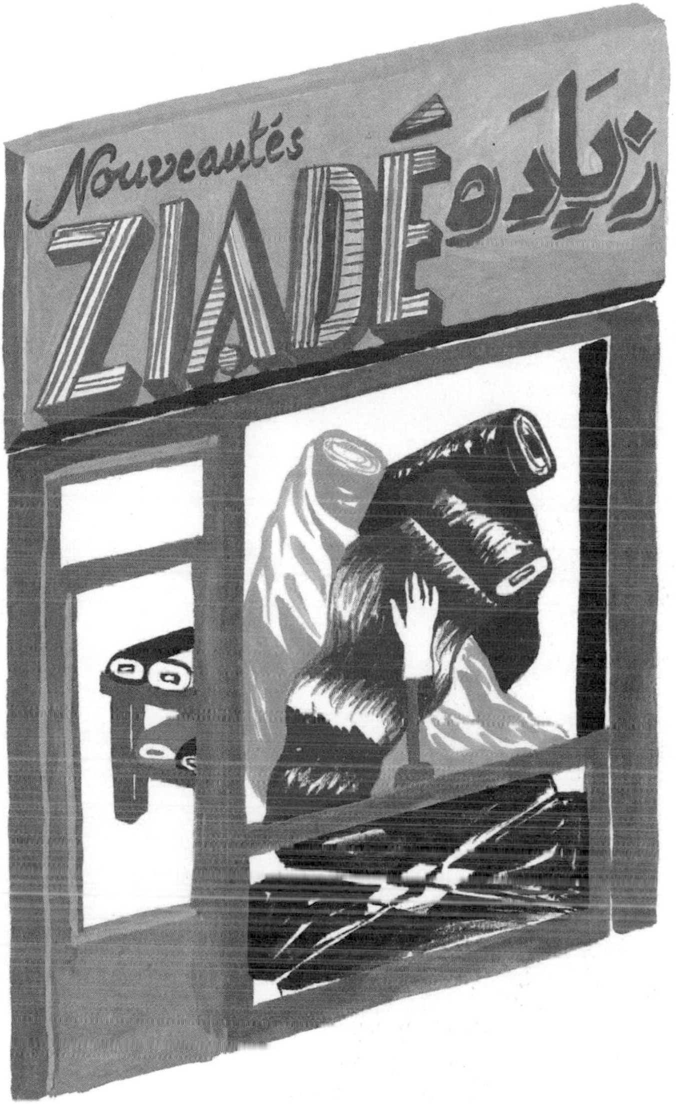
Nouveautés
ZIADE

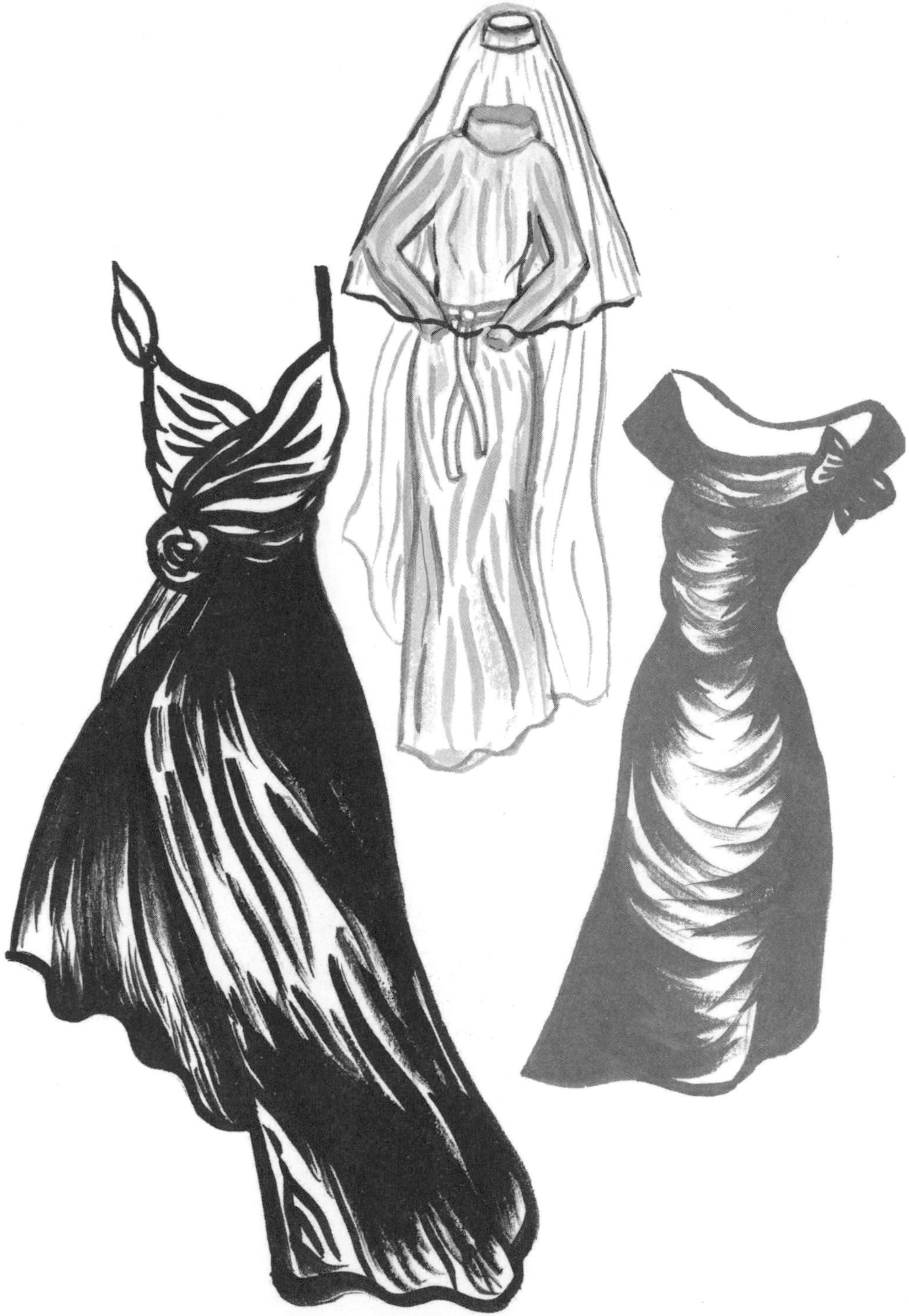

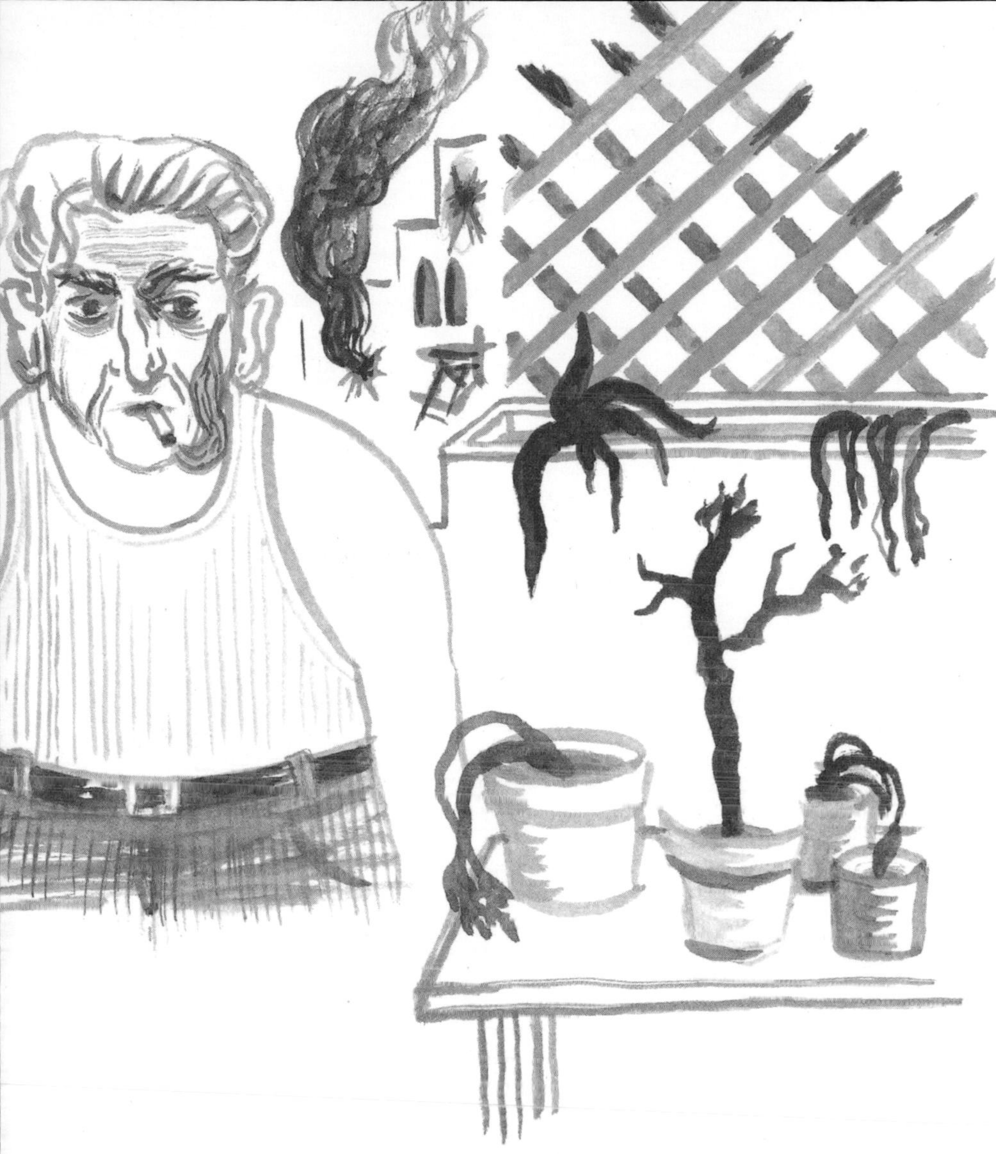

Jiddo* Antoun, a man who likes flowers, silk ties and a game of pinochle, has lost everything. The elegant ladies will no longer enter his shop saying 'Good morning, Monsieur Ziade', or 'My dear Antoine, *biffak habibi*!'

He will resign himself to spending the rest of his life watering and taking care of his flowers; jasmine, hibiscus, gardenias and begonias on the huge lush veranda of the apartment on rue Wadi Abu Jamil. But in a few weeks' time there will be no more water, and in a few months' time there will be no more plants on the terrace.

* Grandfather

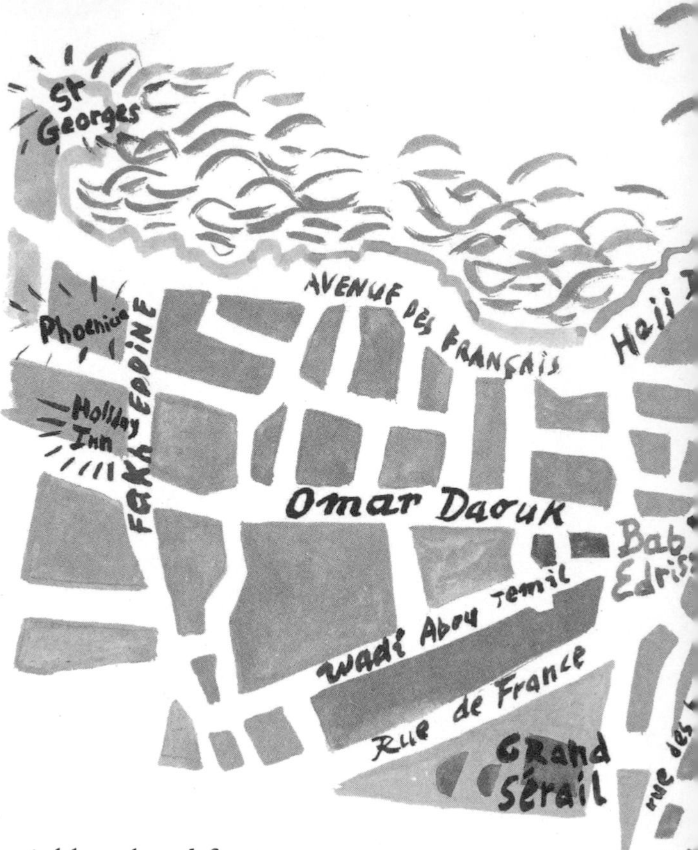
St Georges
Phoenicia
Holiday Inn
FAKh EDDINE
AVENUE DES FRANÇAIS
Omar Daouk
Bab Edriss
wadi Abou Jemil
Rue de France
Grand Sérail

He'll continue to live in this neighbourhood for ten more years – from 1976 onwards it is part of West Beirut. Teta Eva and he are the last Christians in the street; they live harmoniously with the Muslims. They'll endure everything that everyone, from our side to the Palestinian-leftists, will inflict on them. There is not only shelling, but also the terrible blockade of West Beirut by the Israeli army in 1982. Heartbroken, they decide to move to the Christian area at the end of the 1980s.

The disaster is complete, and in a few weeks nothing is left of all these little paradises that I loved going to with my mother when we went 'downtown'. We lived in the Ashrafieh neighbourhood, only a few streets away from the Borj, or Place des Martyrs (formerly the Place des Canons), but for me, going to the Borj, to Bab Idriss, to Souk al-Jamil, place Riad al-Solh or rue Allenby, was like going to Babylon. All of a sudden, Babylon has disappeared.

d

ablos

souk Jemil
souk Tawile
souk ayass

Rue Allenby

FOCH

Rue Weygand

Rivoli

Rue Byblos

place de l'étoile

Maarad

souk Nounzeh

place des Martyrs

Rue du PORT

Rue Pasteur

Rue émer Béchir

RUE GÖHRAUD

empire

Rue de Damas

place DEBBAS

N

E

Négib Trad

Samadi, the sweet shop across from *Mar Gerios*, the Maronite Cathedral of St George, and the pastry shop Bohsali have disappeared.

Gone is the Pâtisserie Suisse, across from the St Louis des Capucins church, that made the finest *palmiers* in Beirut.

Gone as well is the travel agency on rue Omar Daouk – I can't remember its name – that had the Pan Am aeroplane in the window.

Gone is the Kiriakos boutique on rue Allenby where my mother bought wool to knit us sweaters and Anny Blatt catalogues to be up to date on the latest fashion in knitwear.

Gone is the famous Ajami, right near the offices of *l'Orient* newspaper. My father often went there with journalist friends to discuss politics, and once took me there to eat *mouhalabieh*.* I'll remember it always.

My father's office in the al-Kamal building on rue de Damas, where he had just set up as a young lawyer, is gone as well.

Gone is a favourite stopping point, the Librairie Antoine on the rue du Patriarche Howayek, that sold children's magazines.

And the Rose du Liban, at the top of the Souk al-Jamil, where Jiddo would buy me a flower every time we went to see him in his shop. Gone, too.

Souk Ayyas, Souk al-Franj, Souk al-Nourieh, have disappeared.

Brahim, the *ghazl al banet*, candy-floss vendor, who also sold *kaak*† and Bonjus‡, moving around the downtown neighbourhoods according to the day of the week (in front of the great Al-Omari mosque on Fridays, or place Riad al-Solh on Tuesdays), and who we would run into on Sundays on the Corniche, gone, gone, gone.

And the cinemas: the Roxy, the Radio City, the Dunia, the Métropole, the Empire and the Rivoli, which already had me dreaming although I'd never been to any of them, gone.

Bye Bye my Babylon.

* flan made with milk
† ring-shaped bread covered in sesame seeds
‡ Lebanese brand of fruit juice

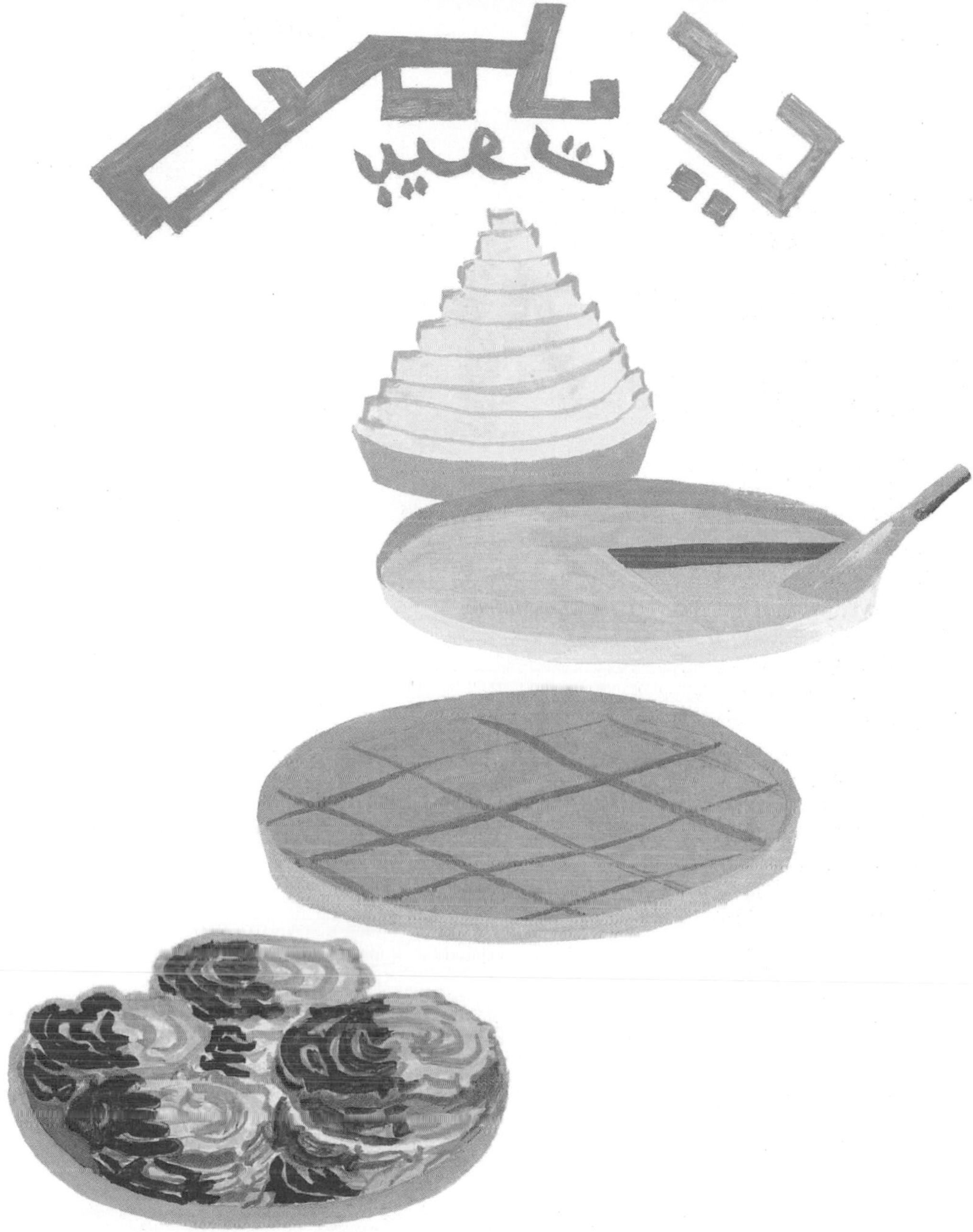

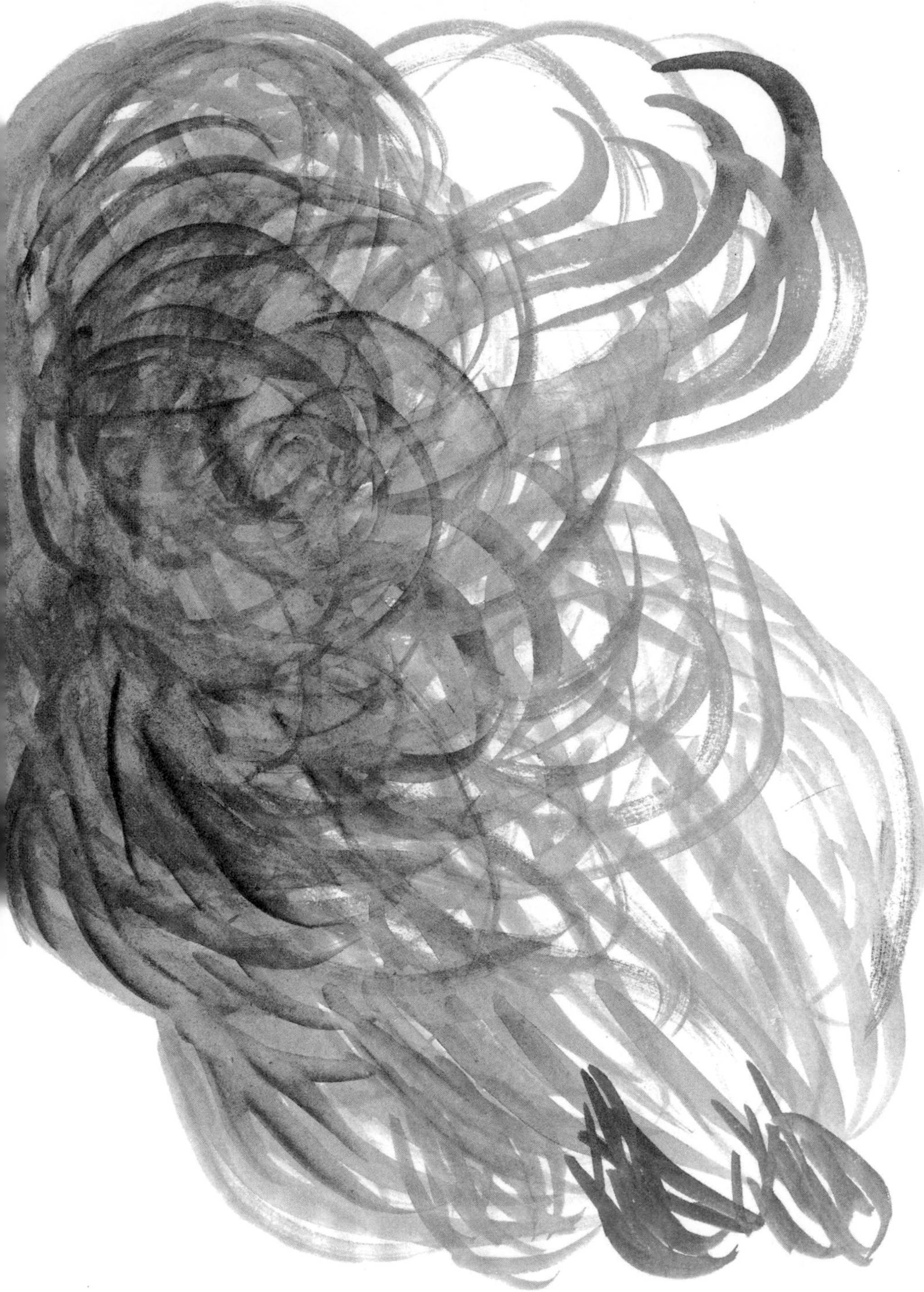

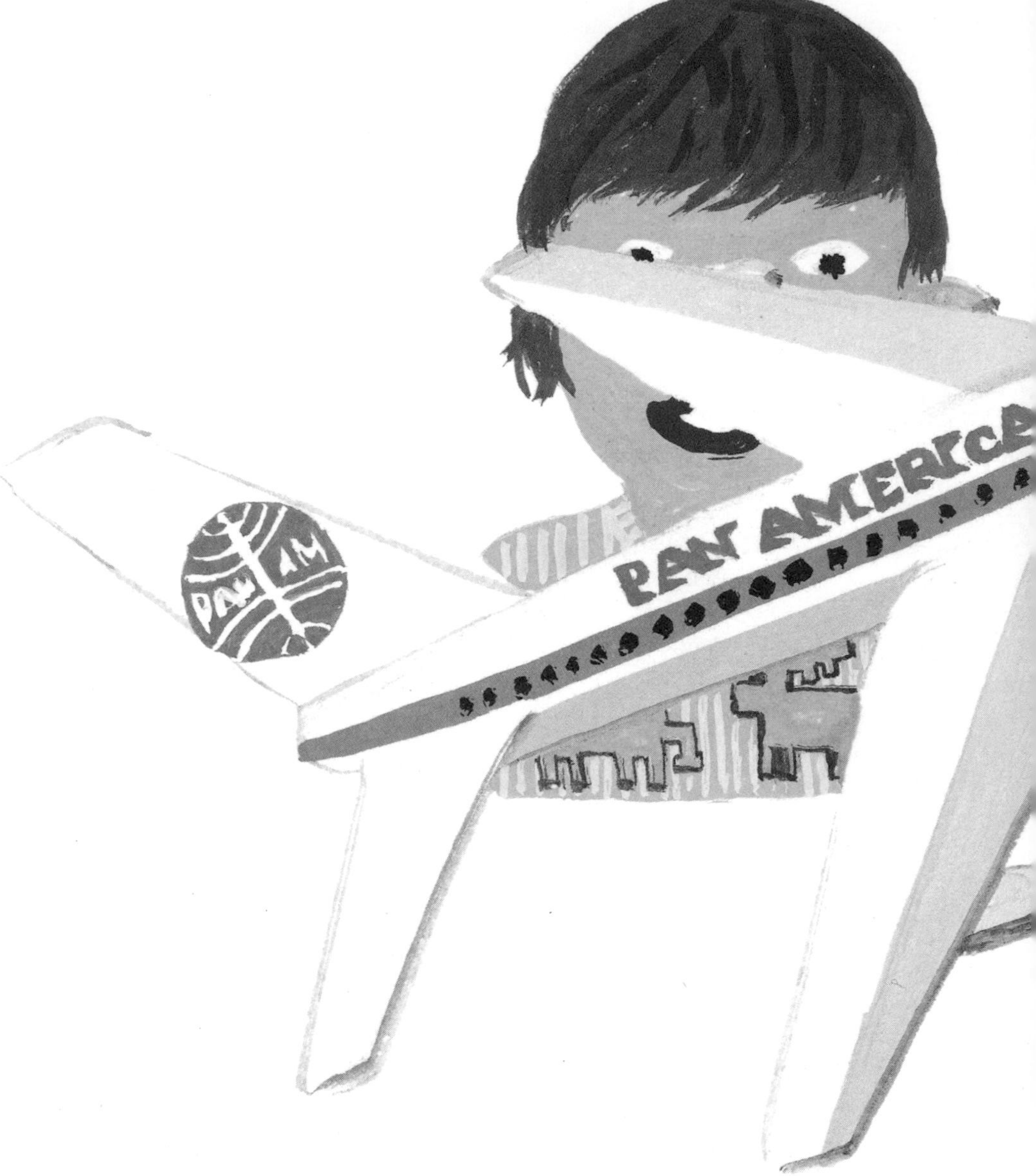
PAN AM
PAN AMERIC

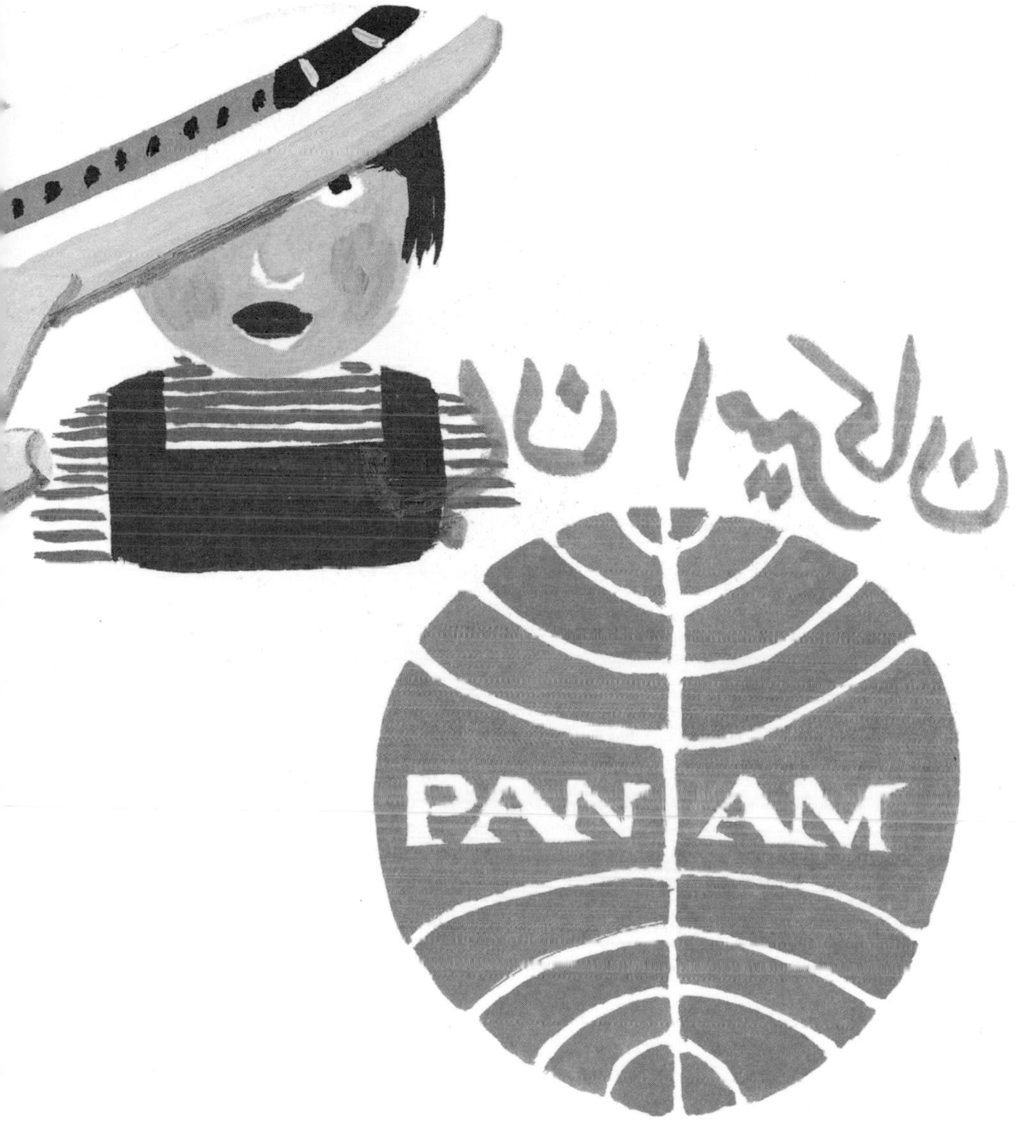
PAN AM

The travel agency on rue Omar Daouk

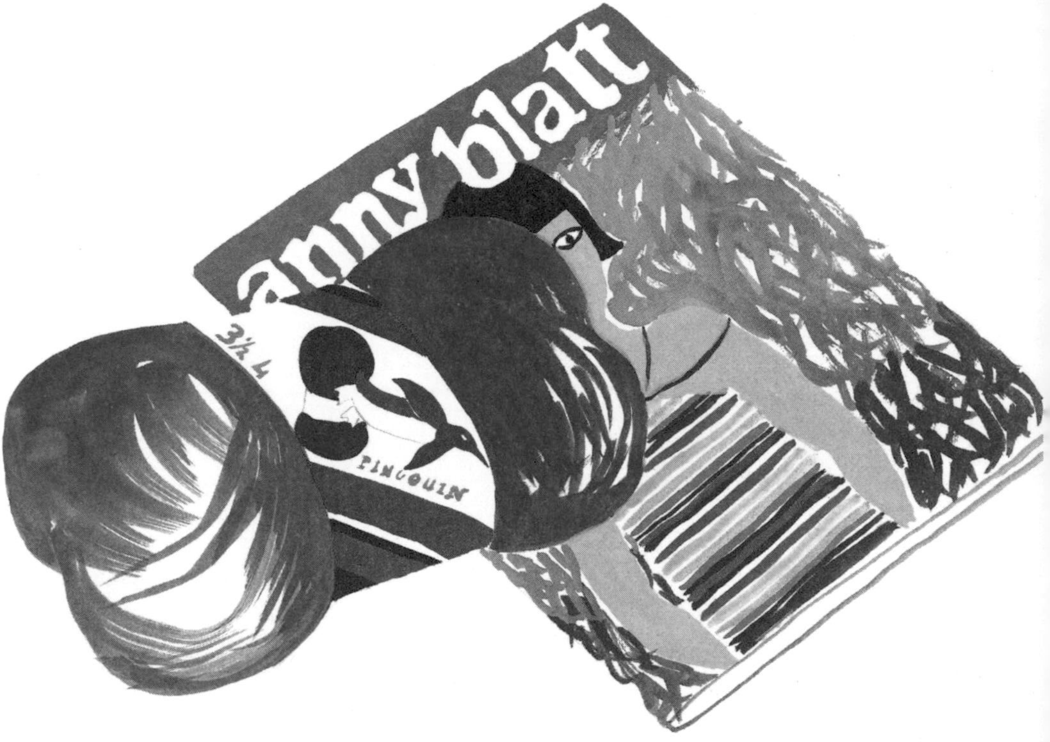
anny blatt
3½ 4
PINGOUIN

العجمي

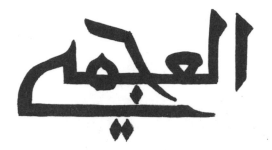

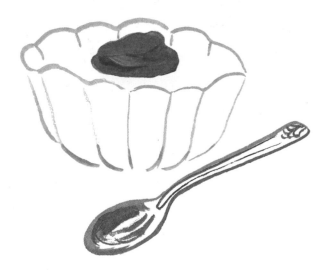

My father's office in the al-Kamal building

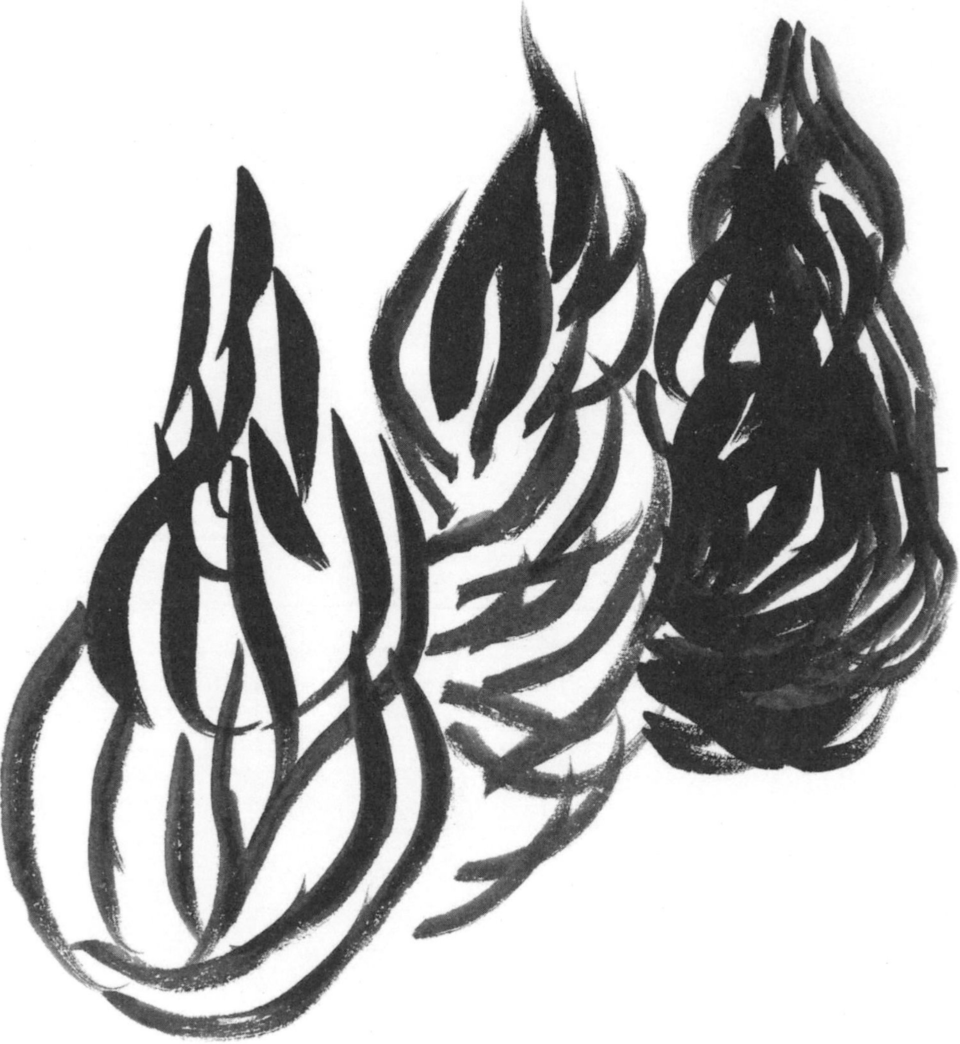

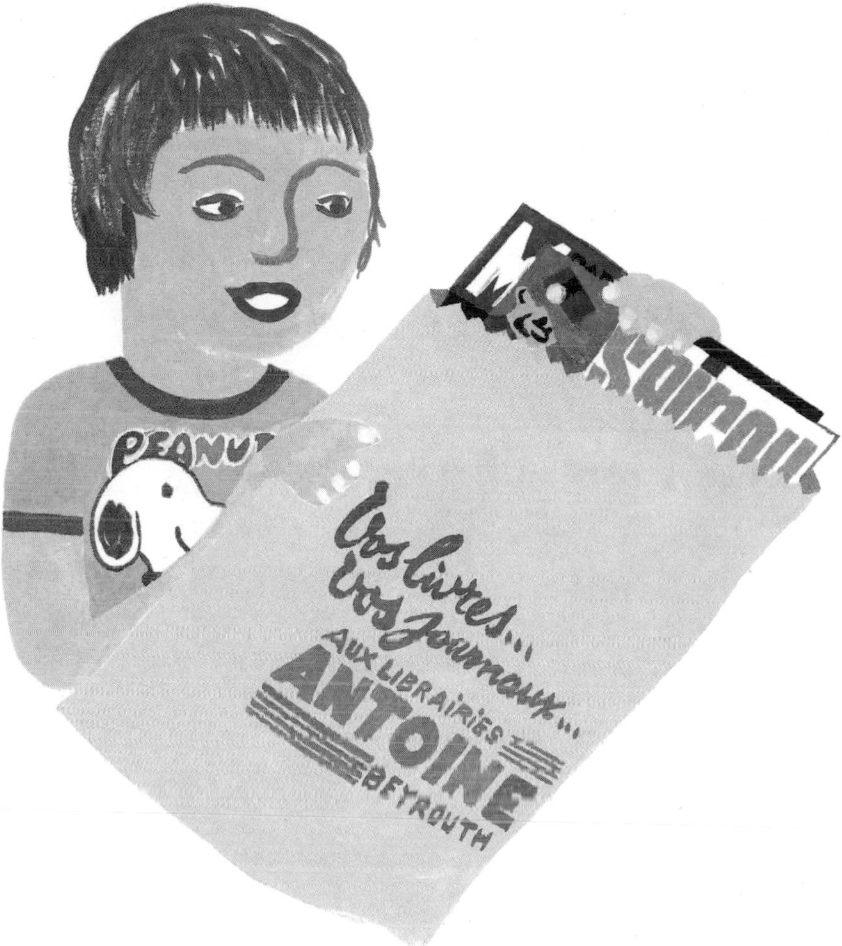
Vos livres...
Vos Journaux...
AUX LIBRAIRIES
ANTOINE
BEYROUTH

وردة لبنان

La Rose du Liban

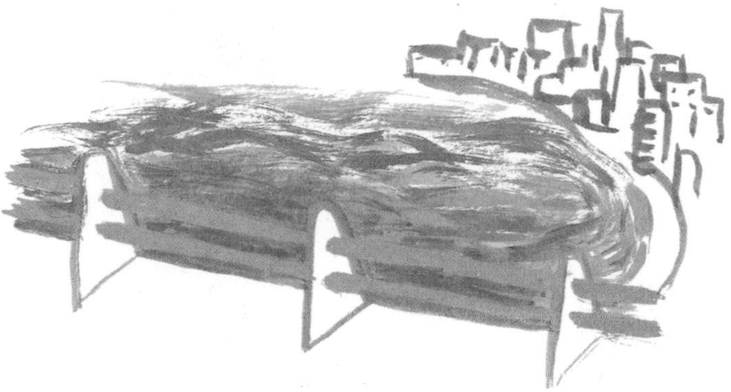

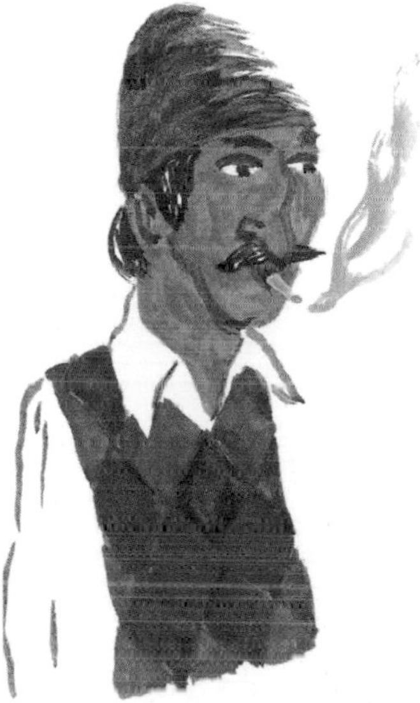

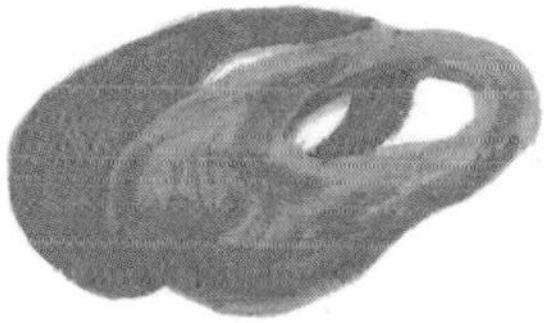

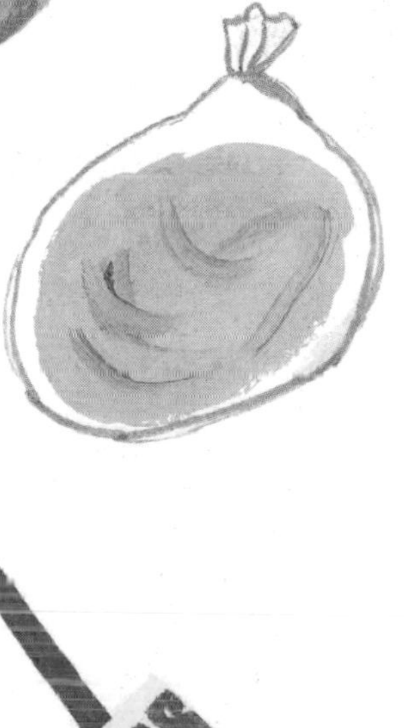

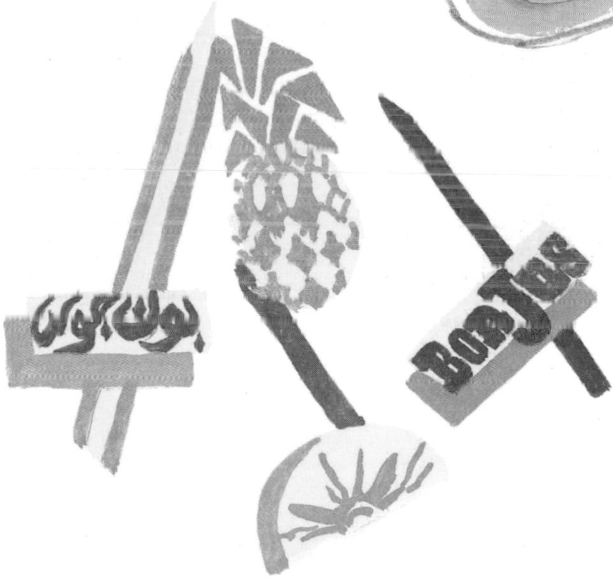
BONJUS

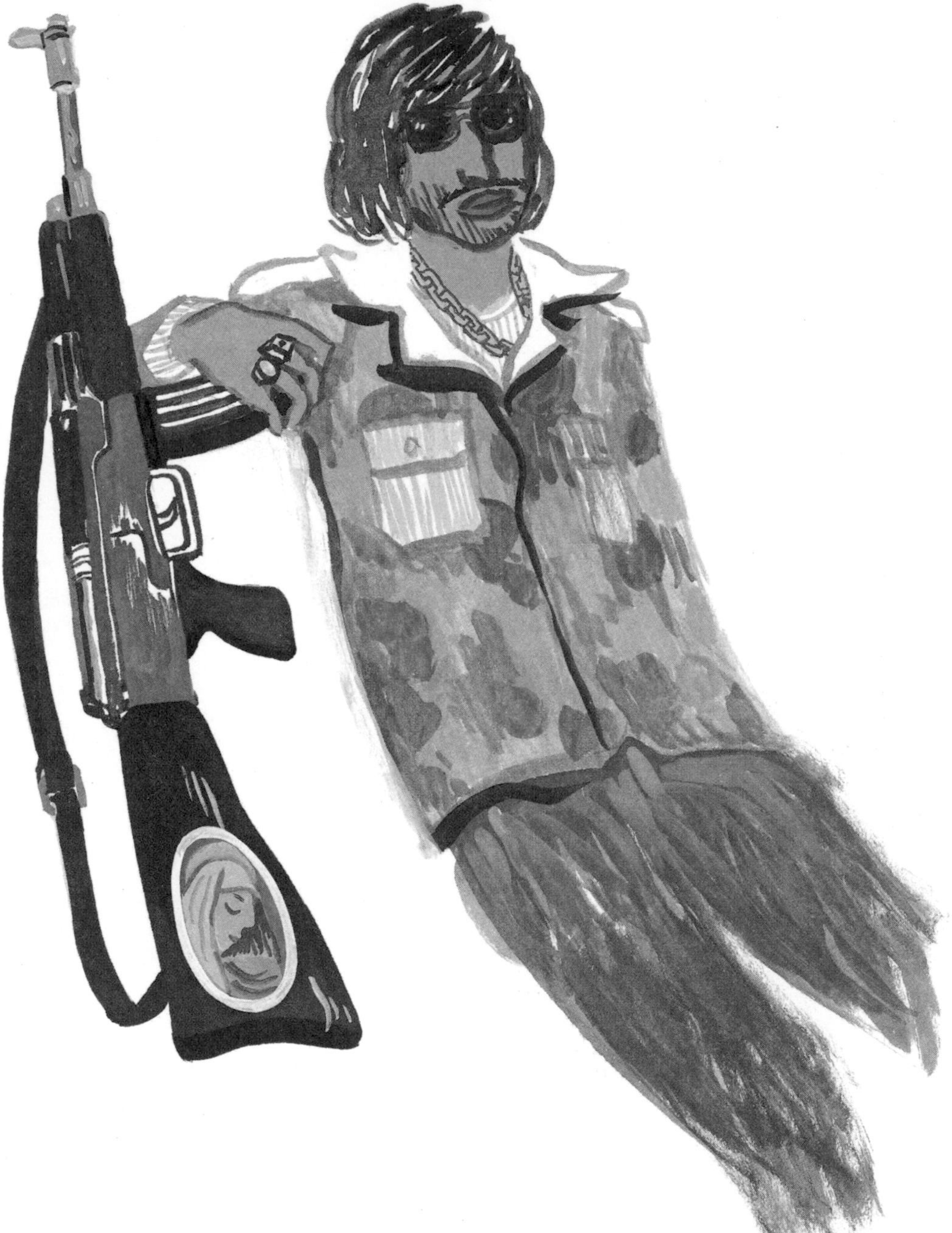

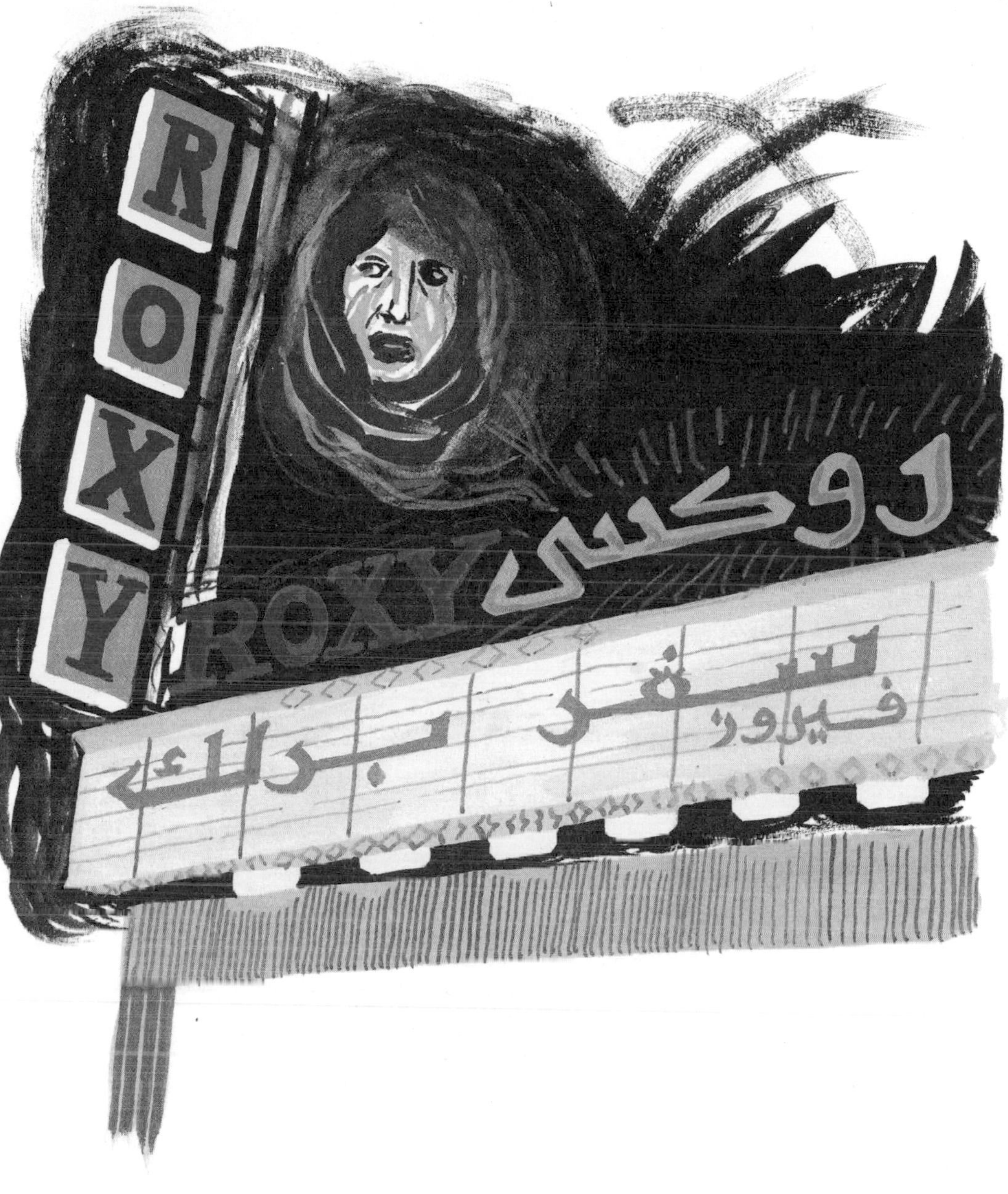
ROXY
روكسي
ROXY
فيروز
سفر برلك

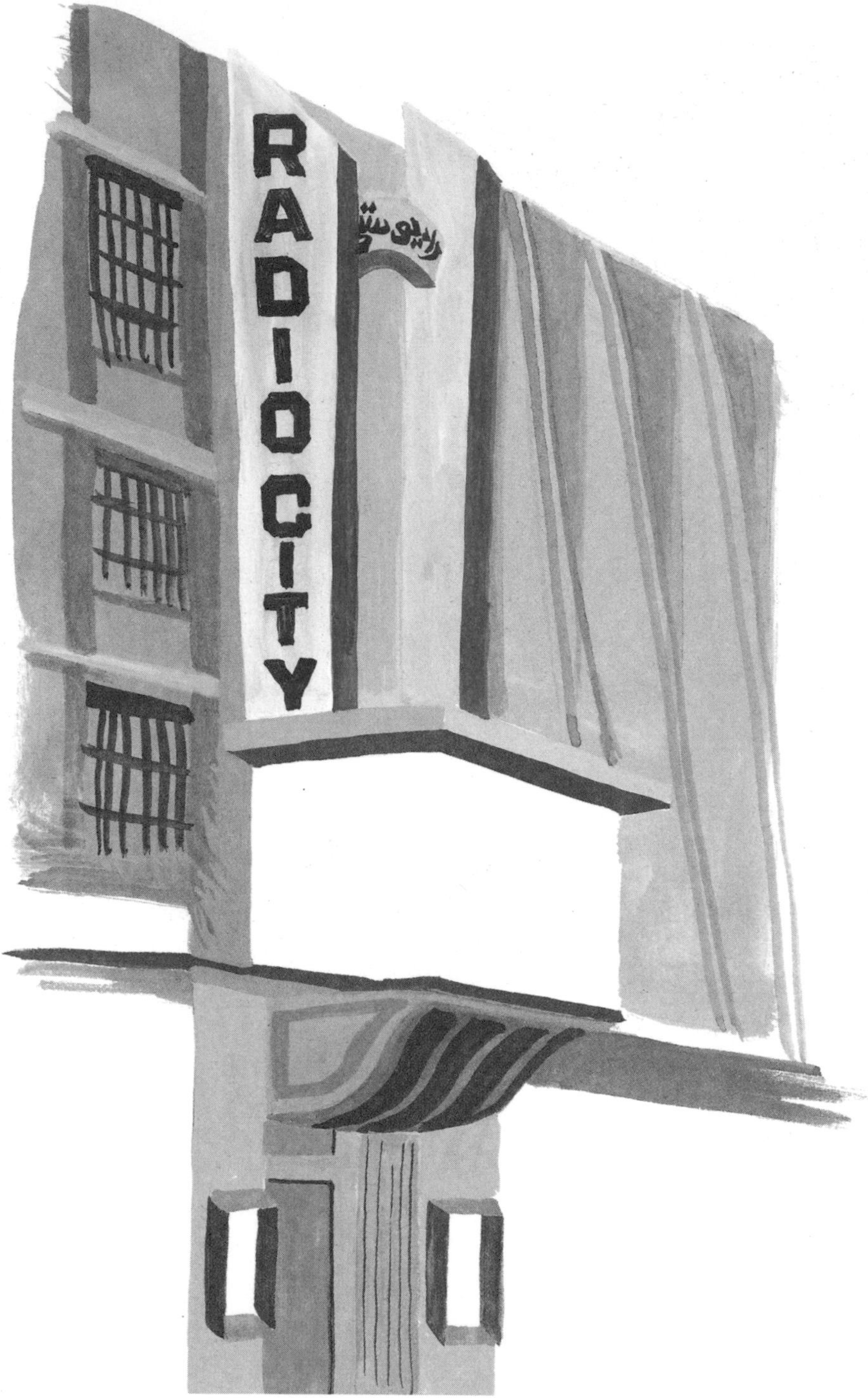
RADIO CITY

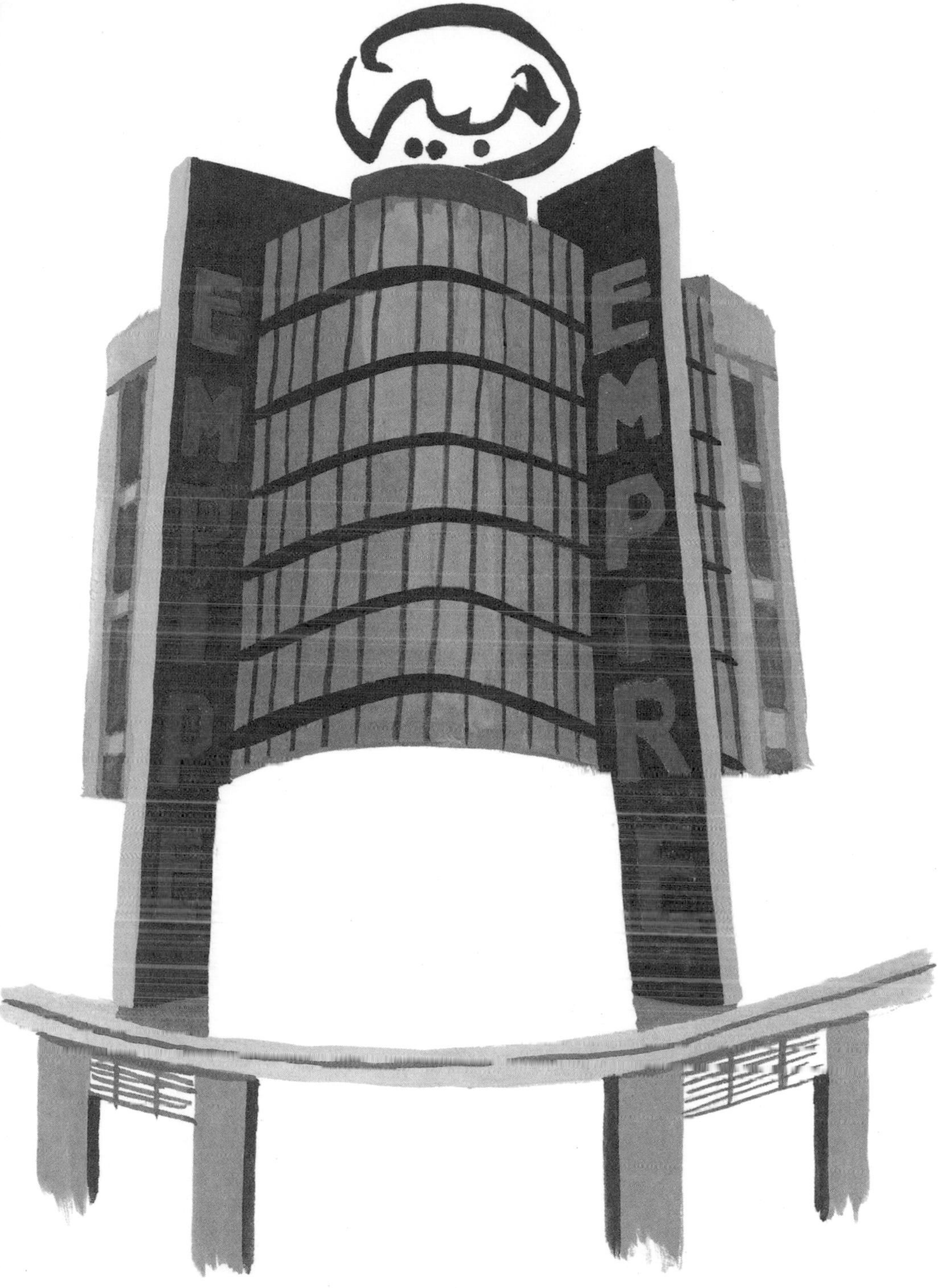
EMPIRE

On 8 December the Battle of the Hotels begins. Militiamen entrench themselves in the Saint-Georges, the Phoenicia, the Hilton and the Normandy. They are even in the Holiday Inn that I loved because my Uncle Ignace was the young director of the rooftop restaurant. They served the best hamburgers in the world and that's where I ate my first ever one.

On that day, when the employees in the various hotels see the militias arriving, they carefully roll up the carpets, afraid that they will get dirty. At this stage of the war they cannot imagine that three months later these glorious palaces will be charred shells.

While the battle rages, my Uncle Ignace will be stuck in the basement laundry with a few other employees.

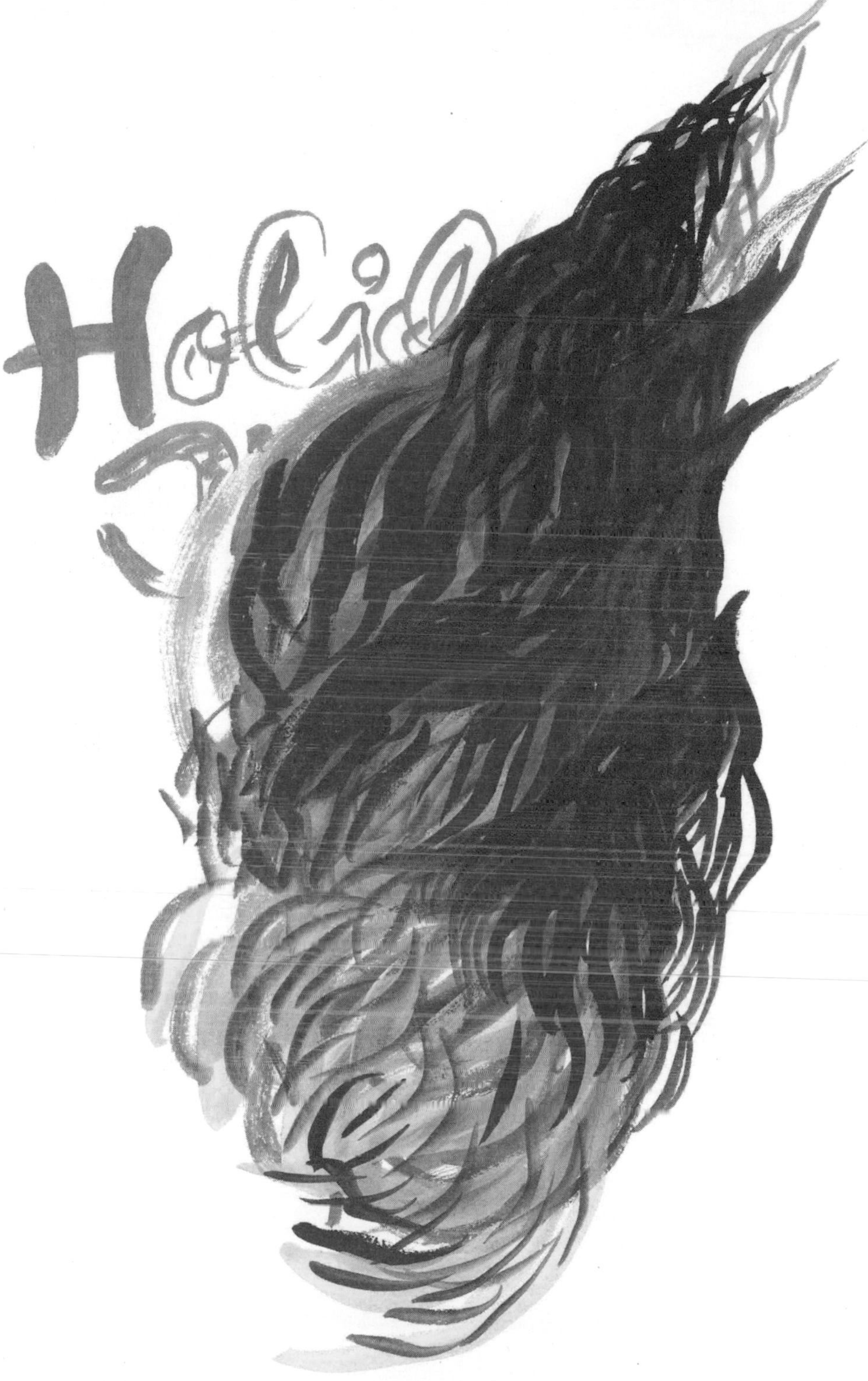

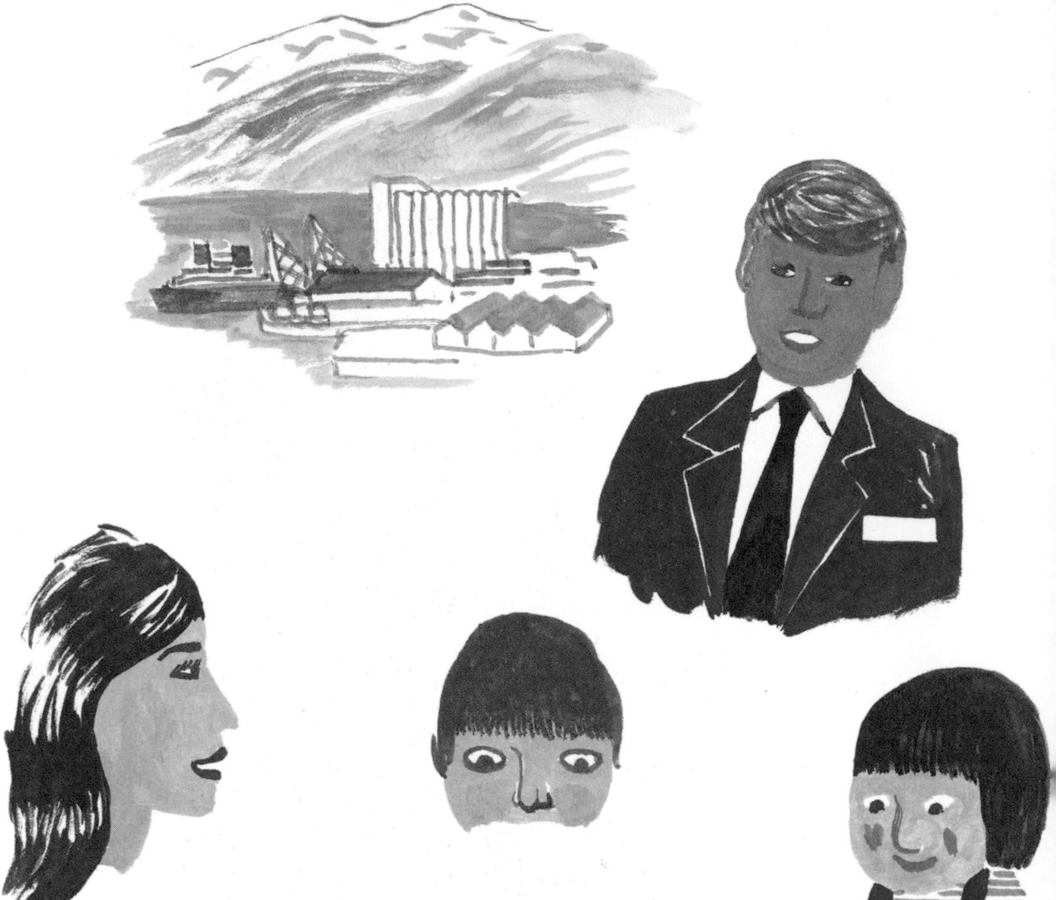

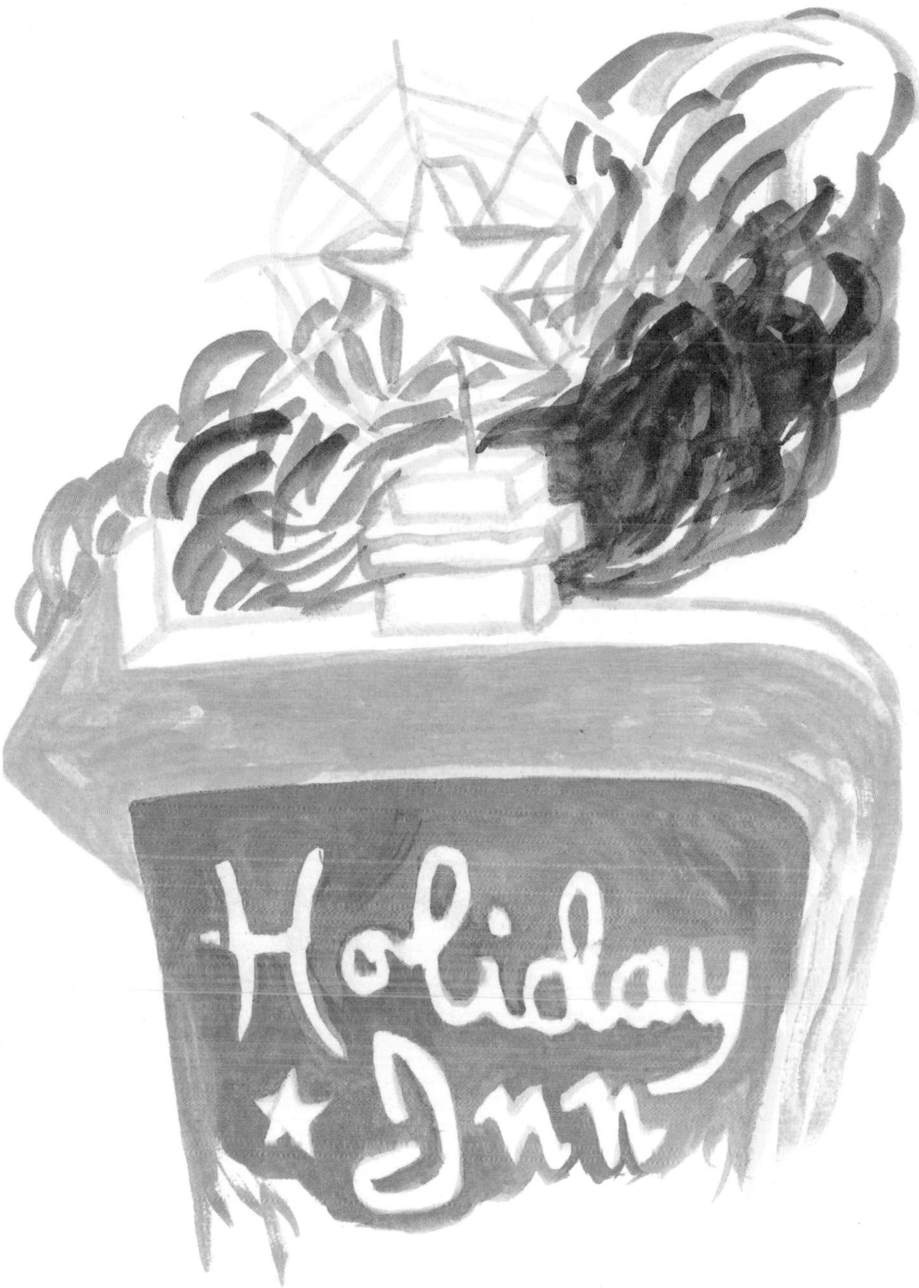
Holiday
Inn

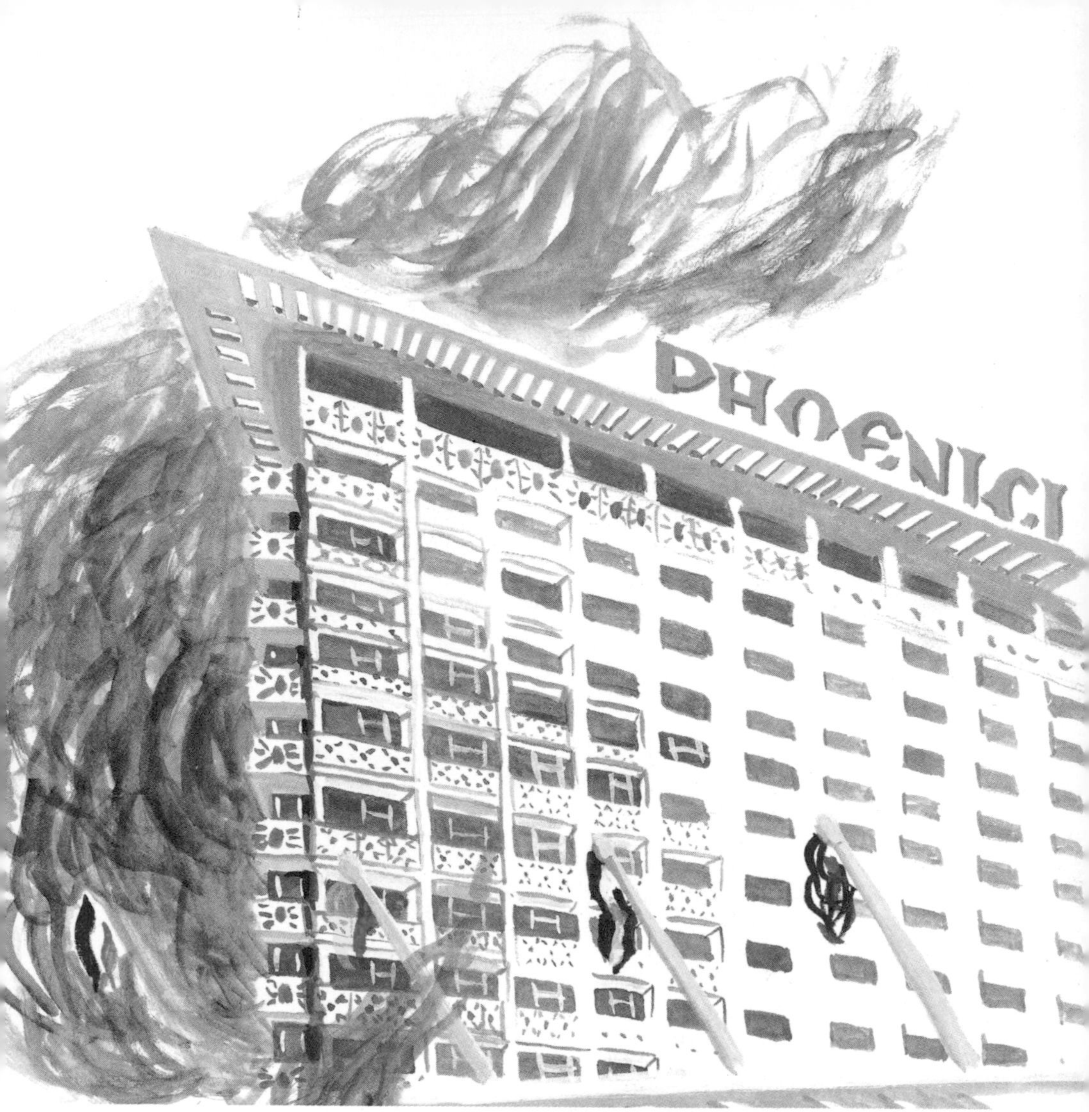
PHOENICI

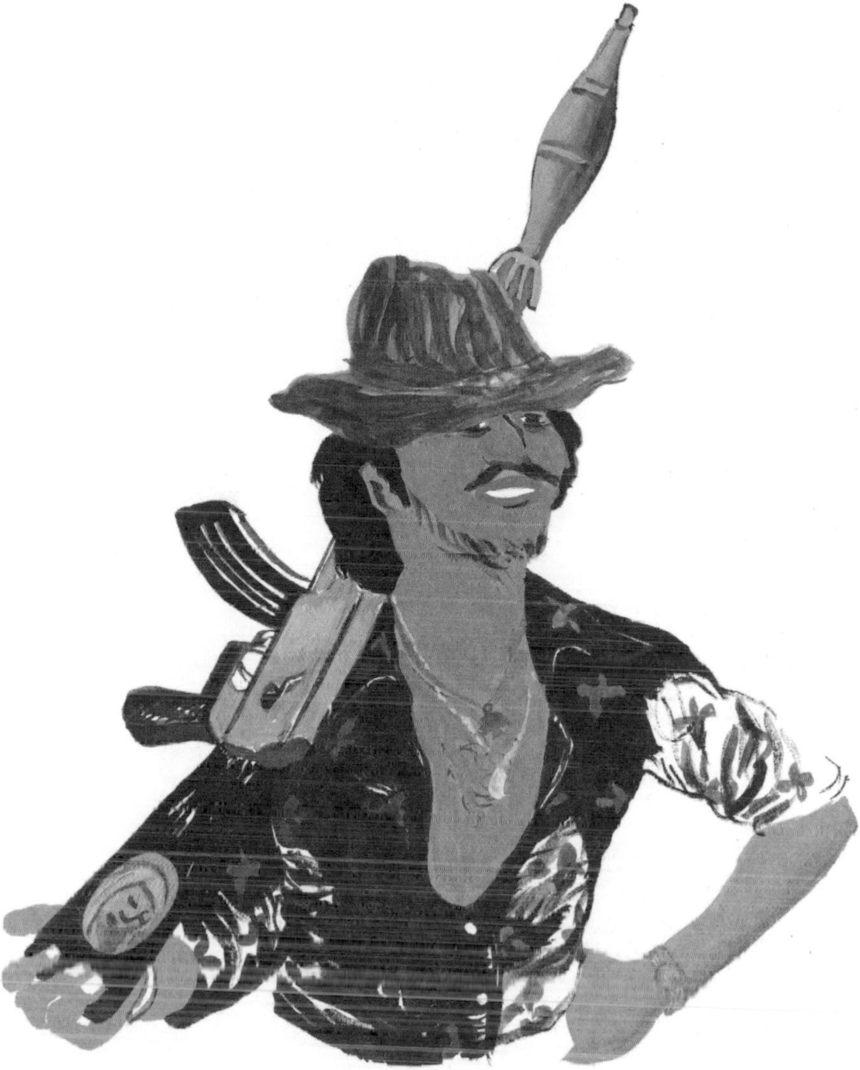

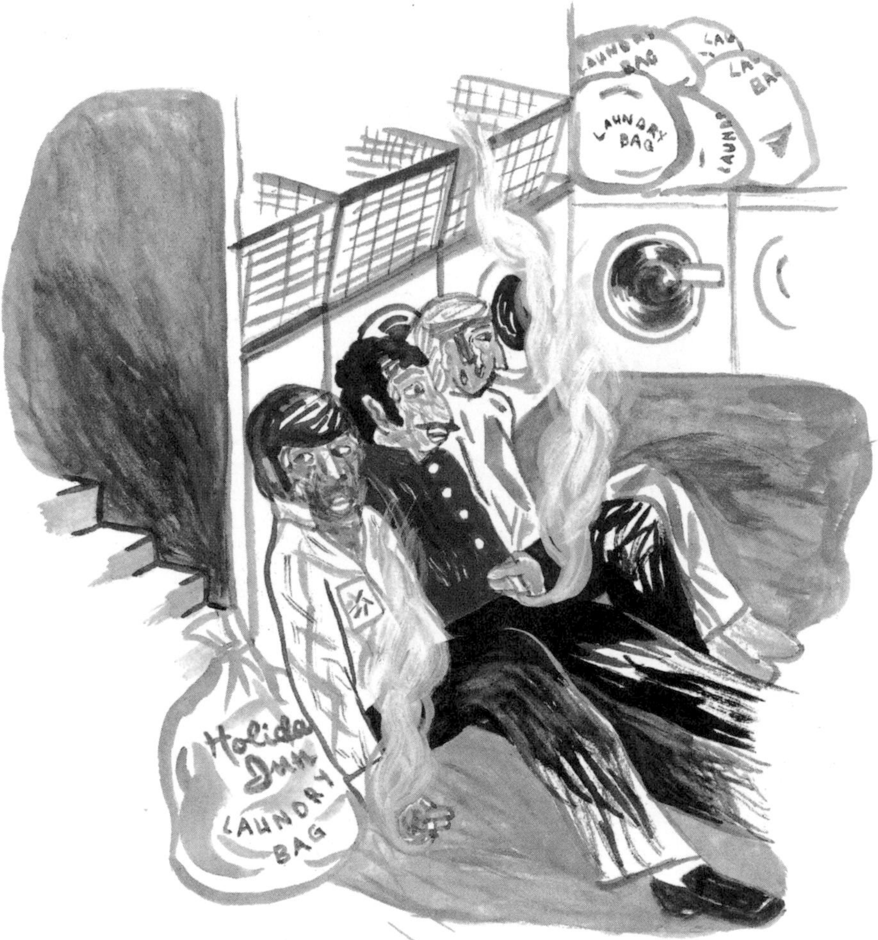
LAUNDRY BAG
LAUNDRY BAG
Holida Inn
LAUNDRY BAG

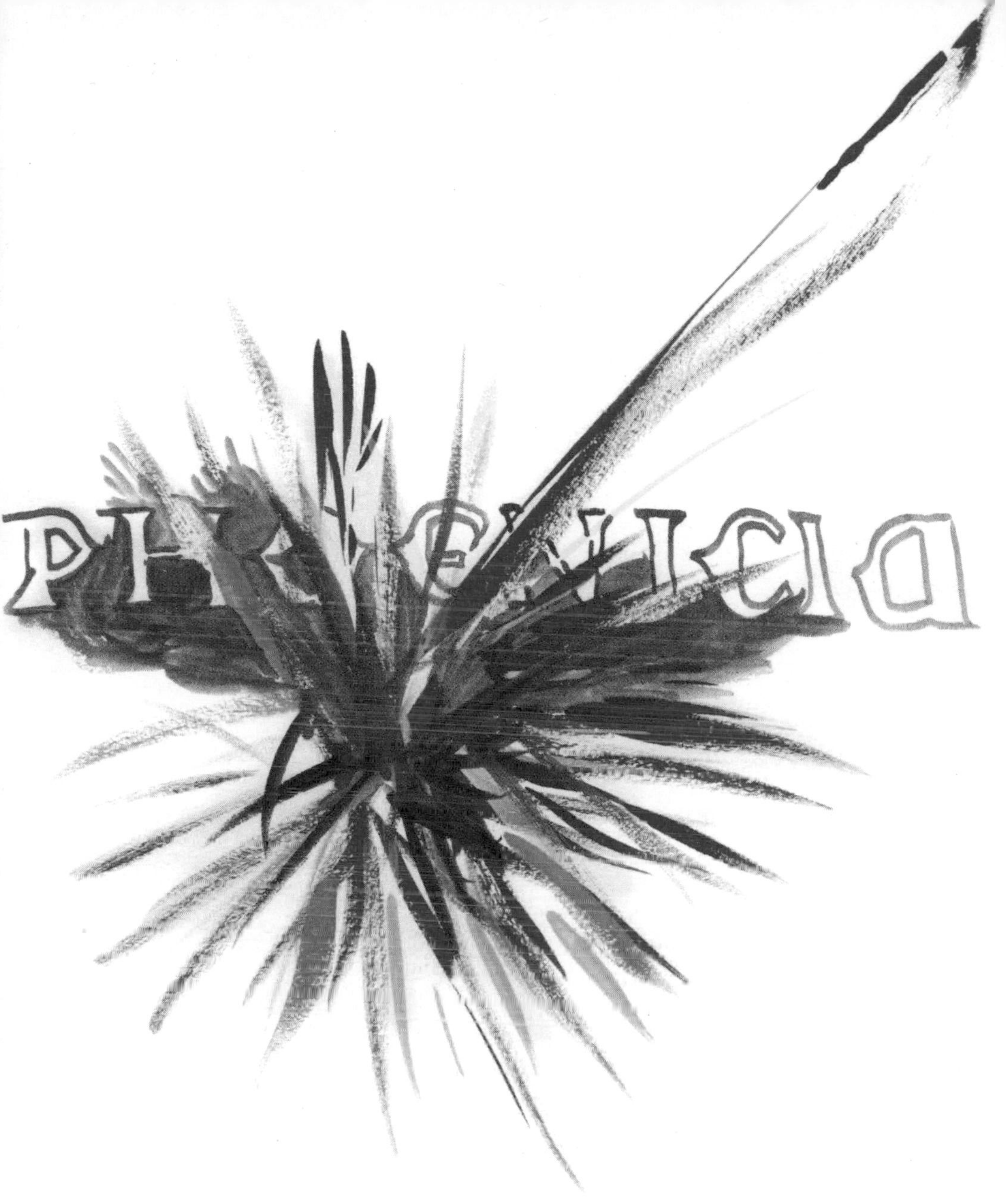

Three months later, on 21 March, 1976, the Holiday Inn falls to the Palestinian-leftists and the Battle of the Hotels is over. The ISF, *kouwa al-amn al-dakhili*,* evacuates Ignace, with the others, in armoured vehicles. His nightmare is not over: on the way to East Beirut, near the Rivoli, he hears bullets ricocheting off the side of the car and has a nervous breakdown. After a few hours of rest at the Maronite diocese of Beirut with his uncle, Monseigneur (*Sayyedna*) Ziadé, the bishop, he gets a ride with a paramedic friend in a Red Cross ambulance heading north, to get out of Beirut and seek refuge in the mountains. As they begin to cross the deserted Bourj Hammoud Bridge, they are shot at with machine guns near the Karantina district. They flatten themselves against their seats and cross the interminable bridge like a rocket, the paramedic's foot wedged against the accelerator. 'How can you see?' asks my uncle. 'I can't' is the reply he gets and that we still repeat when telling family stories, although we rarely talk about those early fear-filled days.
Uncle Ignace arrives safe and sound in our peaceful family village of Kattine where he remains shuttered in the house for a month without once stepping out onto the terrace.

During a ceasefire he finally makes it to the airport where he will take the first flight to Paris and then Nice, settling in Monaco, the real Monaco, a hotelier's paradise. He will never return to Lebanon.

* Internal security forces

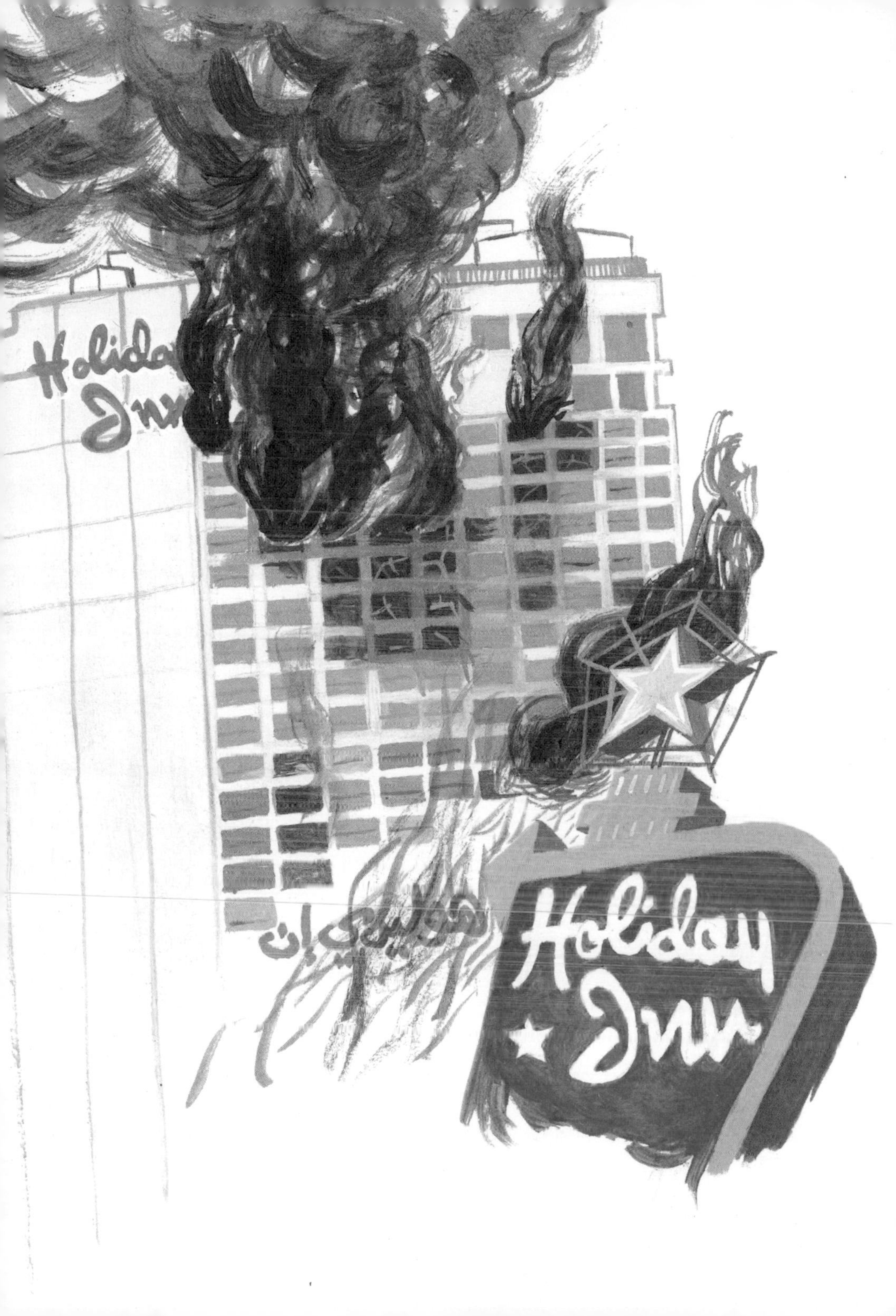

Holiday Inn

When he describes the days spent in the heart of the conflict I still think about the Holiday Inn hamburgers, and don't quite know how to link this to his story: he recounts how the enemy gangs engaged in fierce battles between one palace and another, using mortars and rockets, RPGs and dushkas. Then, during the occasional truce, the drugged-up *hashashin* militiamen sprawled in the red velvet armchairs of the plush bars and emptied bottles of Dom Perignon and Martini, gin and Chivas into crystal glasses, playing a few notes on the piano, their kalash always nearby, the bodies of their enemies at their feet.

It's a casual war. For us, what's important is doing it with style.

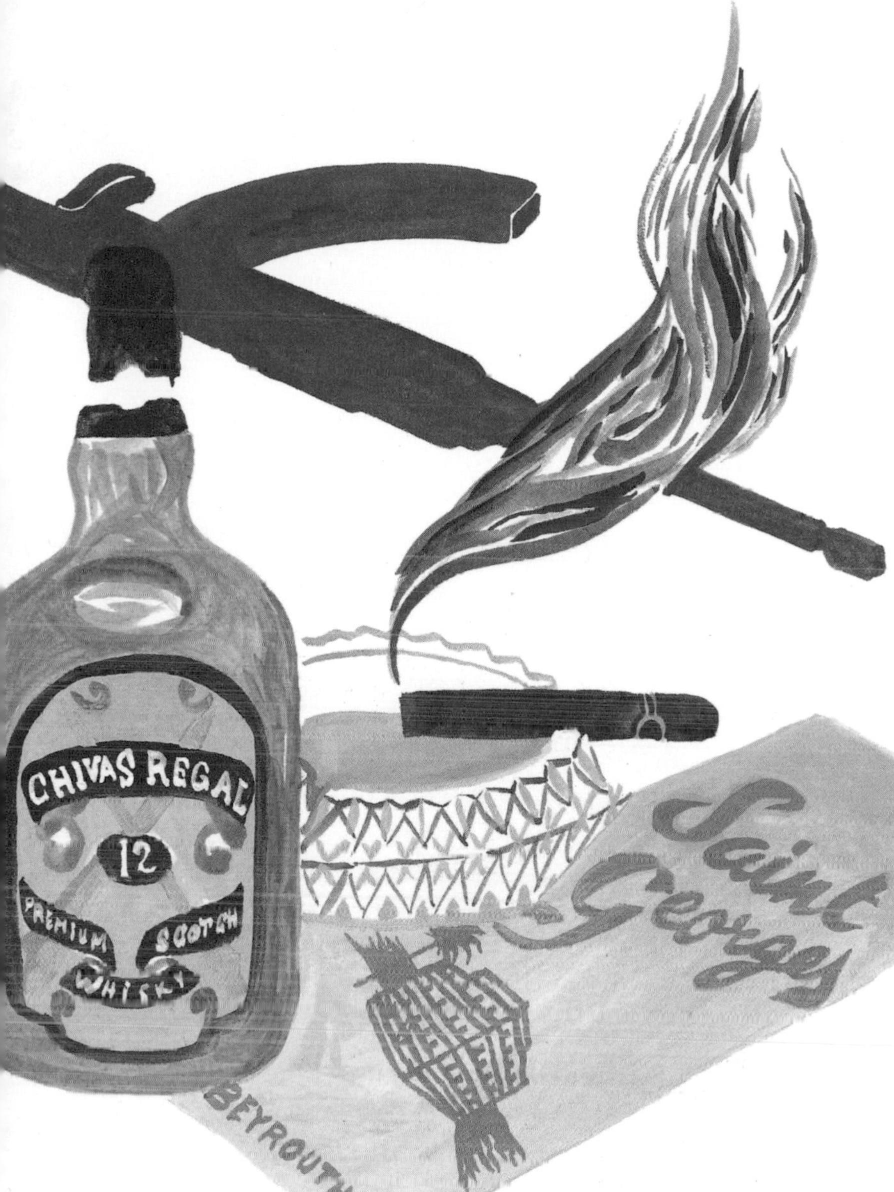
CHIVAS REGAL
12
PREMIUM SCOTCH
WHISKY
Saint Georges
BEYROUTH

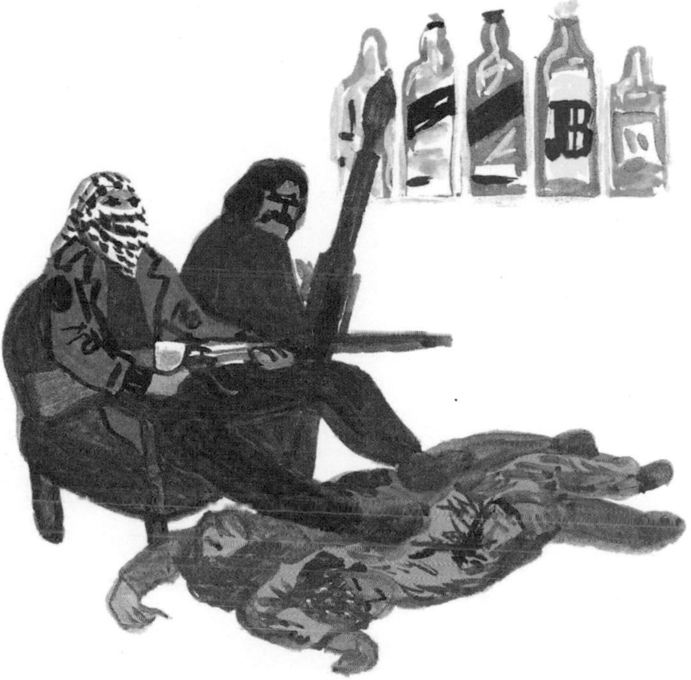
JB

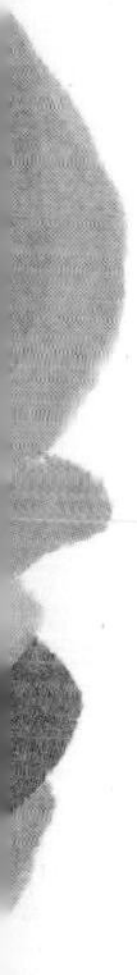

In Lebanon, the violence takes on legendary status. It's paramount as the war unfolds – during the first two years everyone is having so much fun: it becomes a ritual for fighters from both sides to drag their prisoners through the streets behind a car until they die.

Torture and mutilations are common practice.

The Phalangists carve crosses into their victims' skin while their opponents commit murder with axes. Both sides throw the bodies of their enemies from overpasses in the city or dump them on the coastal roads so that they can be seen by anyone around. Dozens of abandoned bodies are found; some with penises stuffed in mouths, others with ears or breasts chopped off. Often the enemy will be left alive but minus their index fingers (which are used to pull the trigger).

Walid and I hear these stories and other similar ones from Tamar, our nanny; from Salim, the grocer; or from neighbours gossiping in the kitchen. But I think they're wrong, as neither my mother nor my father ever talk about this sort of thing. I conclude that this information must fall into the category of *tofnis*, fabrications, and I don't dare speak to my parents about what I hear for fear of making a fool of myself.

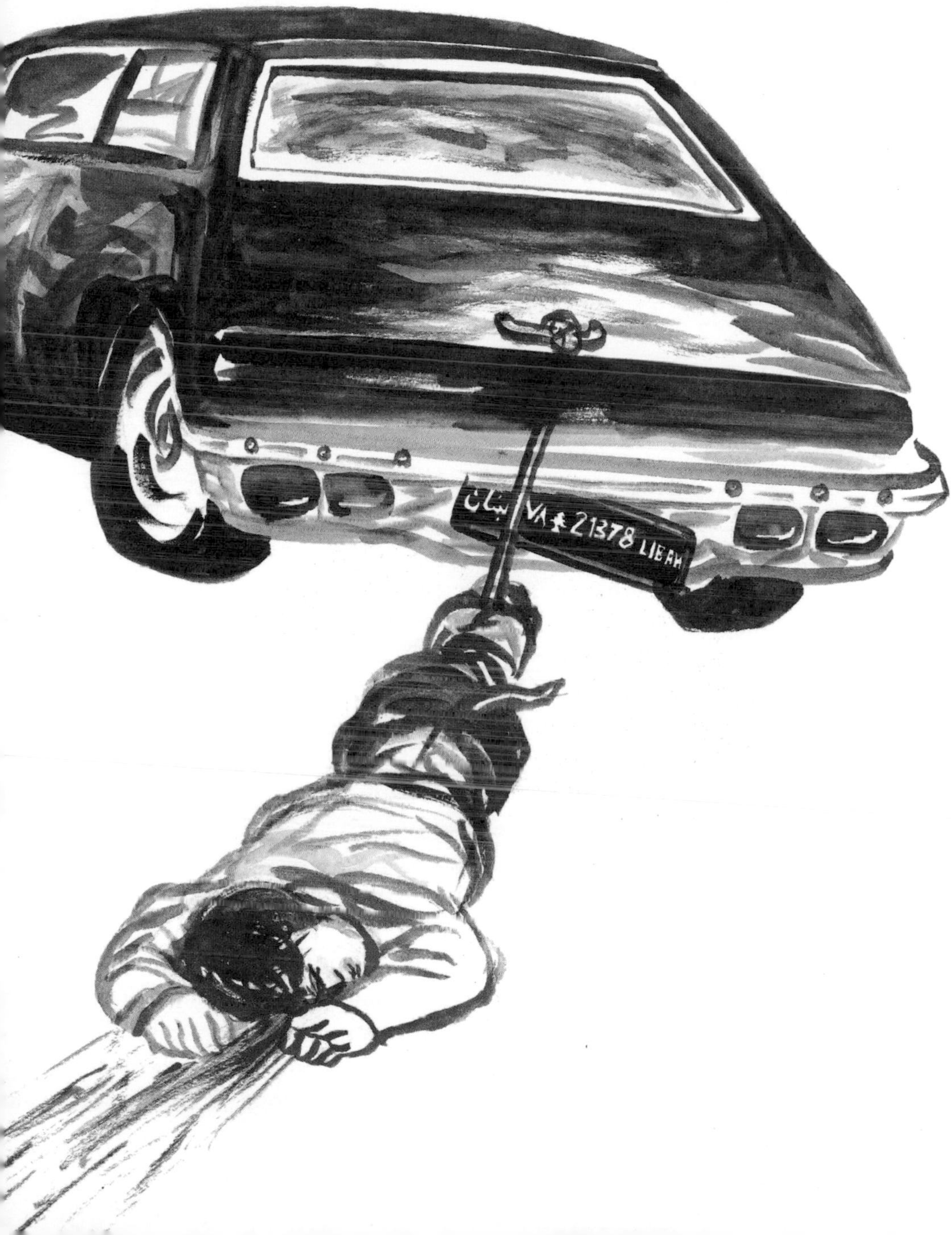
21378

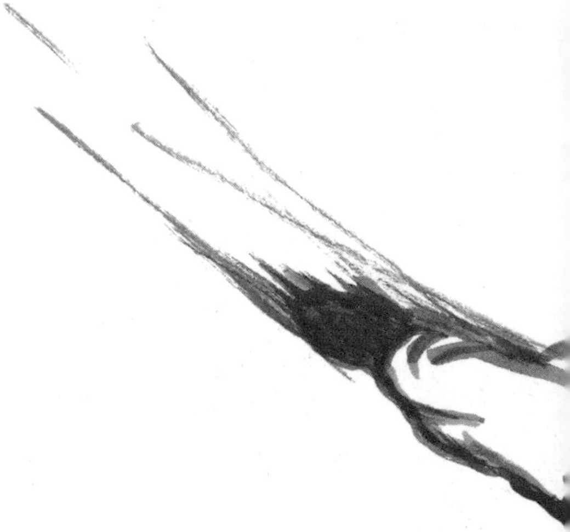

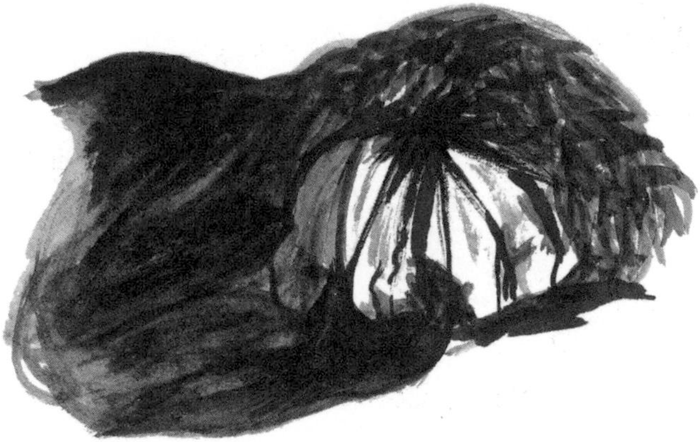

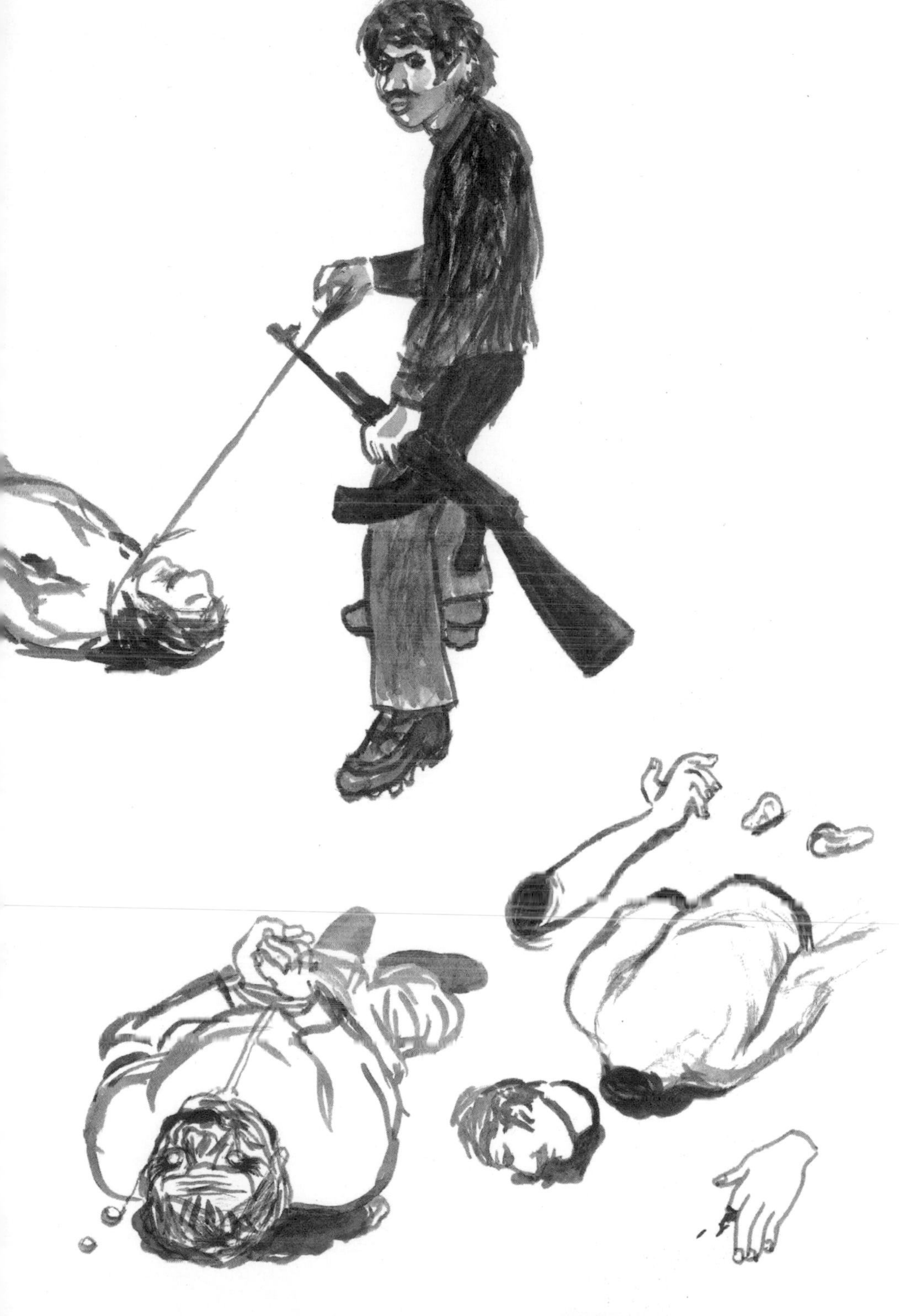

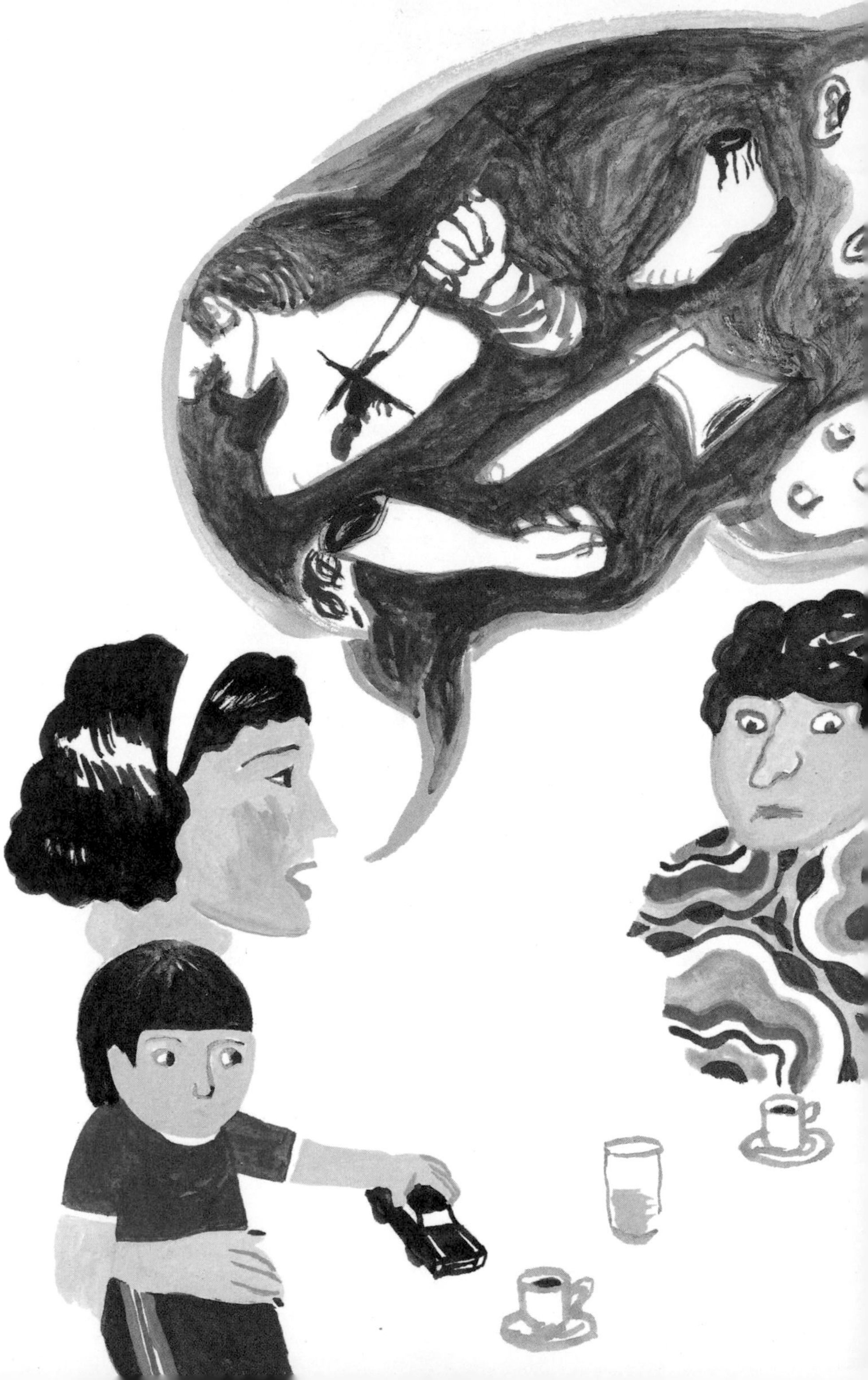

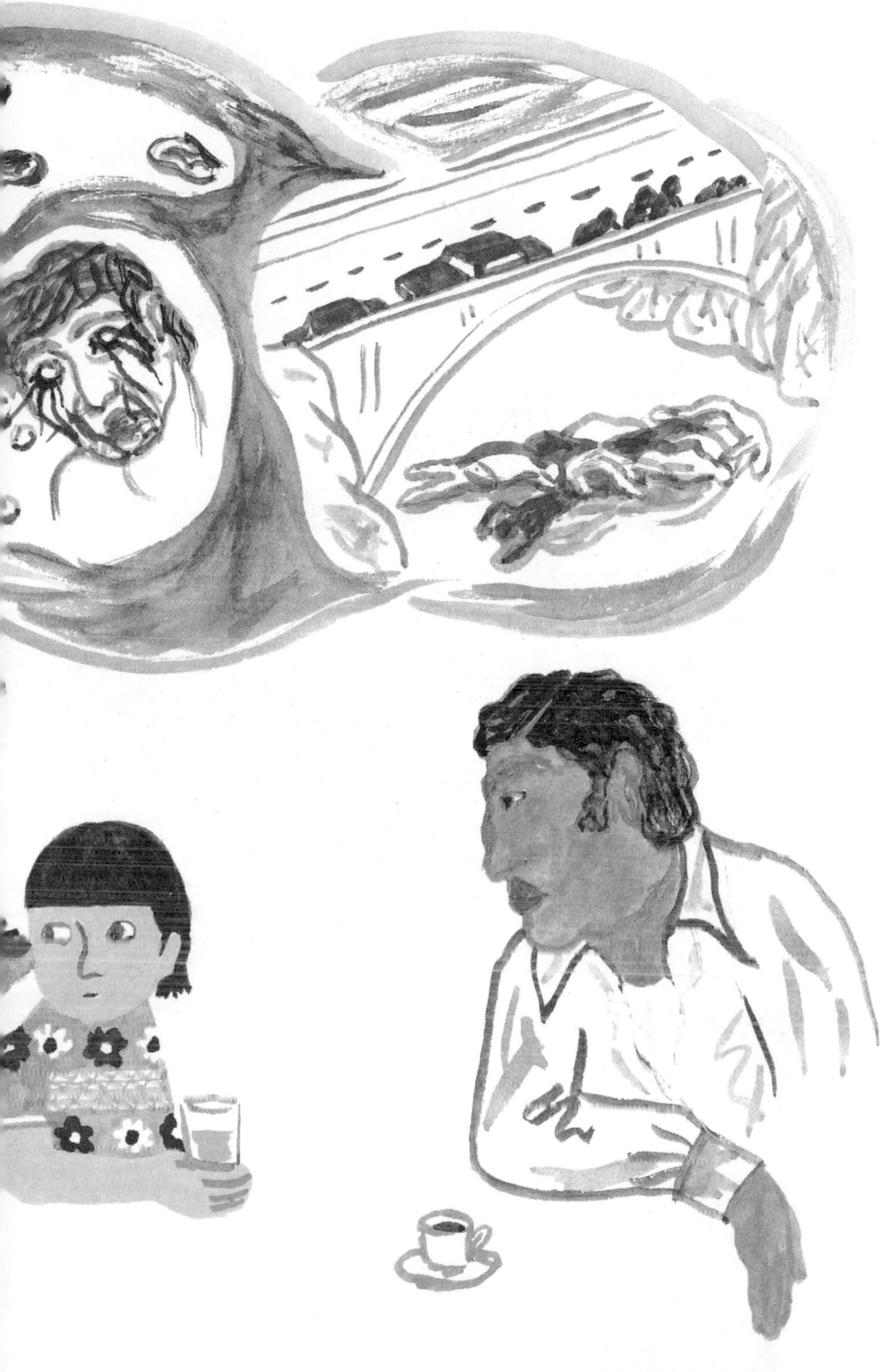

Of course my parents don't talk about all this in front of us. Only years later I find out that Charbel, a rowdy truck driver from Kattine, used to drag the bodies of Muslims behind his pick-up truck. He would proudly recount this to my despairing father, who would threaten him by saying he couldn't ensure his defence if he was arrested. (Before the war he had been imprisoned several times for being a troublemaker, or *abadays*, and my father had got him out.) '*Basita, estez* Kamil! It doesn't matter, Mister Kamil!' he would tell my father, to calm him down.

Charbel would also pillage the homes of well-to-do Muslims who had fled the Christian neighbourhoods of Beirut. He would offer my mother Persian carpets, Chinese vases and opaline glass. 'They're for you, *sitt* Leyla, since you love beautiful things.'

He would sell similar objects to others.

My mother always refused, scolding him, except once when he offered her a photograph album from the turn of the century with pictures taken with Jamal Bacha at the time of the Ottoman Empire, and others with High Commissioner Weygand or General Gouraud and President Habib Bacha el-Saad during the French mandate. There were also more recent photographs taken with the Shah of Iran, Camille Chamoun and Gamal Abdel Nasser. She kept the album, and gave it back to its owners fifteen years later when they returned from exile in Argentina.

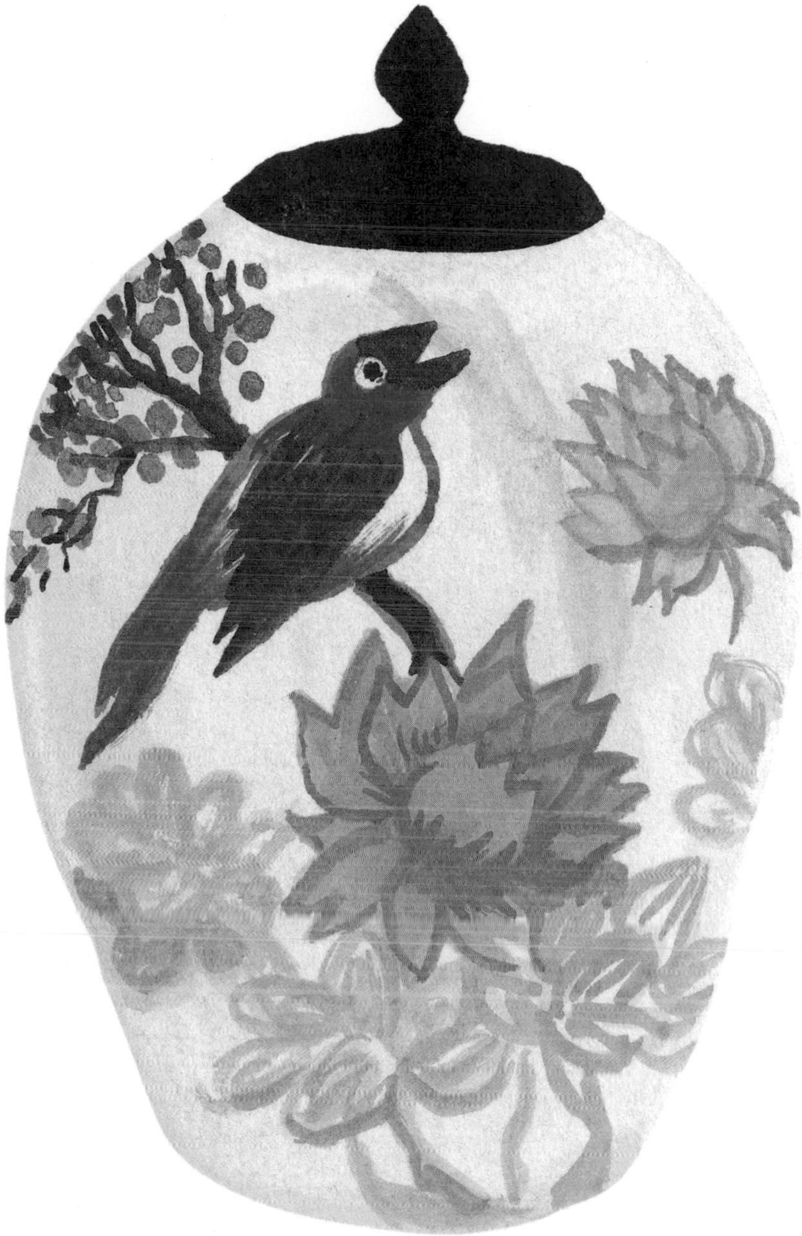

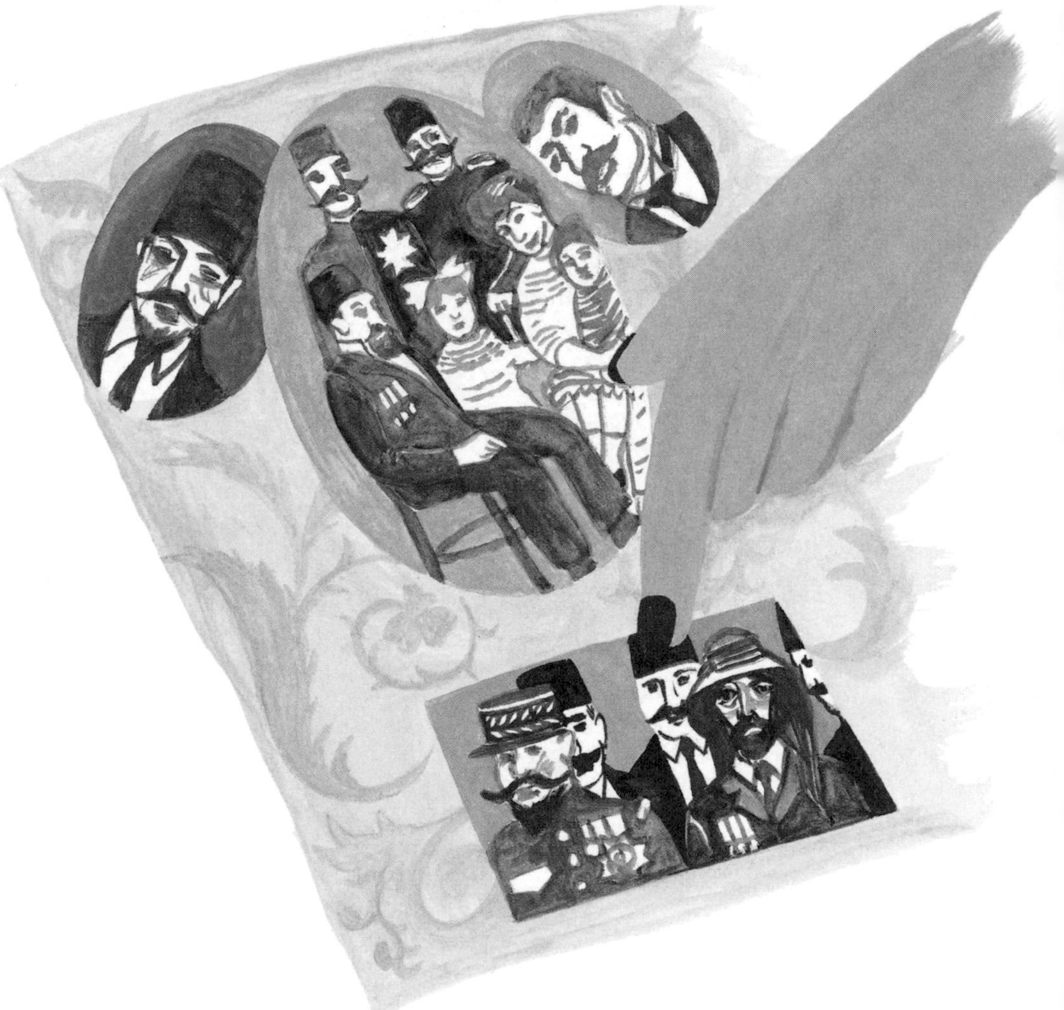

Panic-stricken, the Christian bourgeoisie also had to flee the lovely neighbourhood of Kantari, which had fallen into the hands of the Palestinian-leftists. They escaped from the backs of their houses and via the gardens, using ladders or ropes, or, like old aunt Honeiné, in a wicker basket that was lowered from a window. After its inhabitants fled, Kantari was looted.

Shortly afterwards, during a summer's evening under the arbour in Kattine, a friend of my parents who was an aesthete and a passionate collector of Sumerian art tells us a curious story about a little statuette. During the battles in Kantari he fled from his magnificent home. When he returned a little later, his family archives were smeared with excrement, the furniture and objects wrecked. Nothing was left of his splendid collection of Mesopotamian statuettes – everything had been stolen or was in pieces. But no, not everything: one little statuette had been spared the fury of the Mourabitoun. He picks it up; it is undamaged. Although it is priceless, he cannot enjoy the fact that it has been spared, he is so revolted by the extent of the disaster around him. He pledges never to want to own anything again. A nearby explosion startles him and he drops the statuette, which breaks.

Soon the looting and destruction of the souks, the ransacking and ruin of the luxury hotels and the befoulment and robbery of Kantari become almost trivial for militiamen from both sides. Then the Palestinians (mainly the Saiqa and the DFLP) carry out one of the biggest heists in banking history: they empty the safes on the rue des Banques, one of the wealthiest banking districts in the world, of millions of dollars, gold and jewellery.

Since the spring, control of the rue des Banques has changed hands several times. Two Christian militias even fought a battle for the privilege of robbing cash and traveller's cheques (easily accessible) from the British Bank of the Middle East. In the end they share the booty. But the Christians rapidly 'lose' the street. The Palestinians manage to hold out longer and penetrate the Banco di Roma and the British Bank, taking the time to hire mafia professionals from Europe who help them break open the safes.

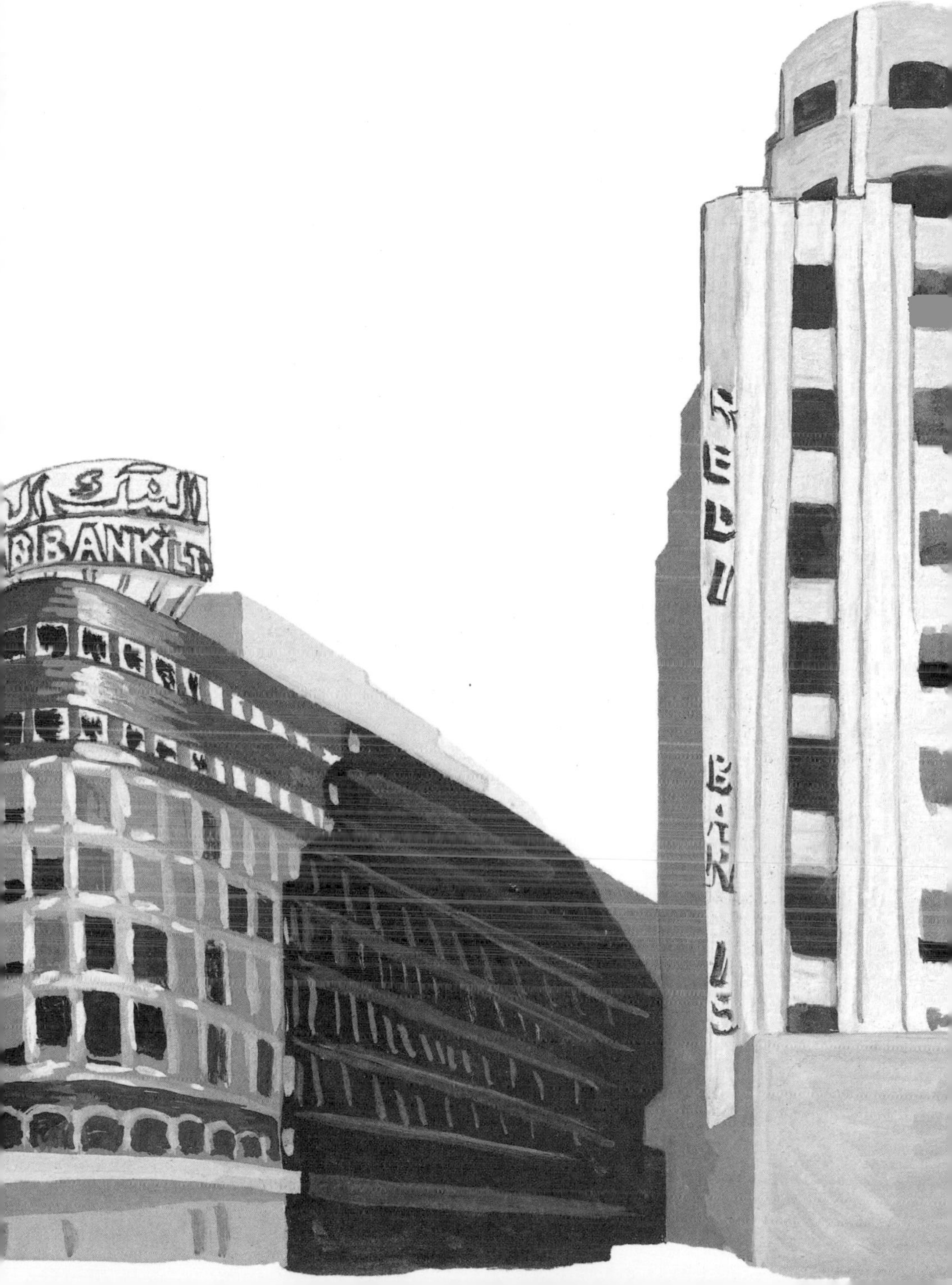
BANK

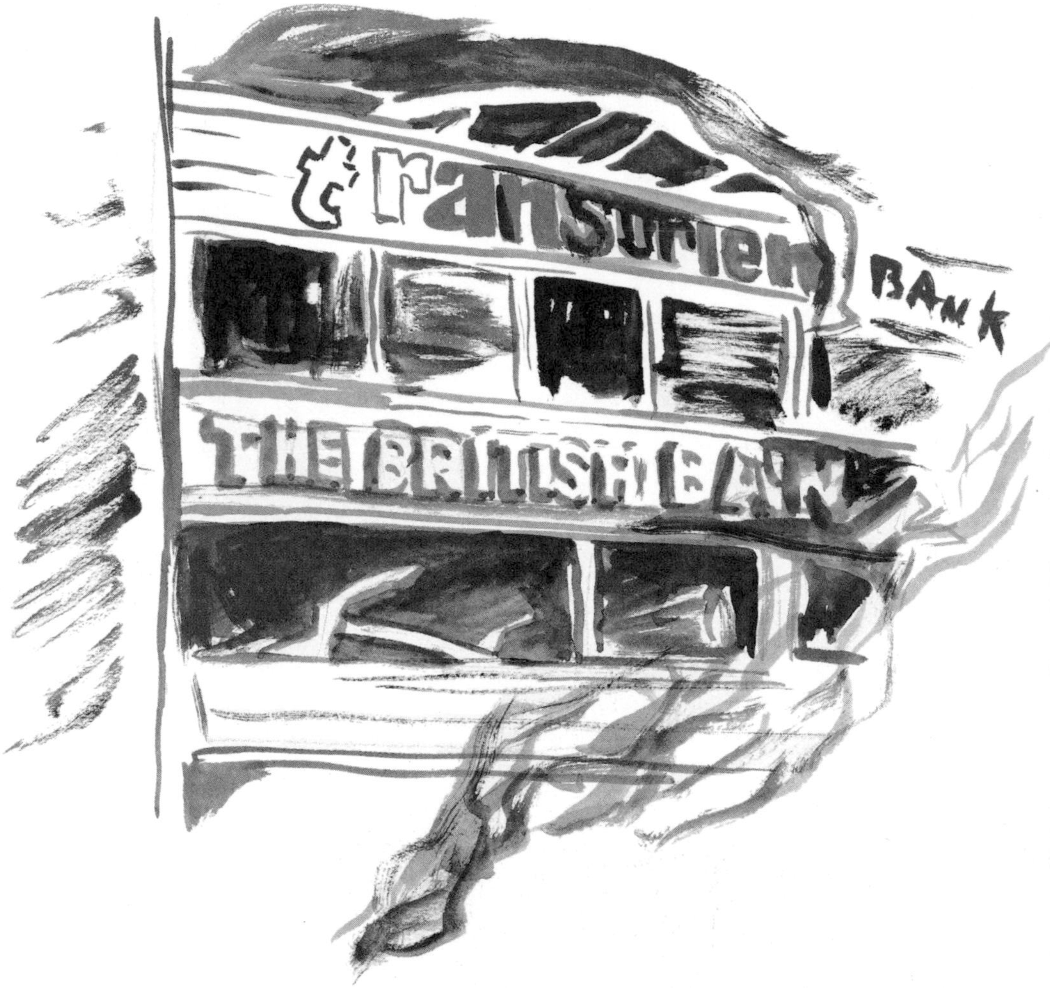
BANK
THE BRITISH

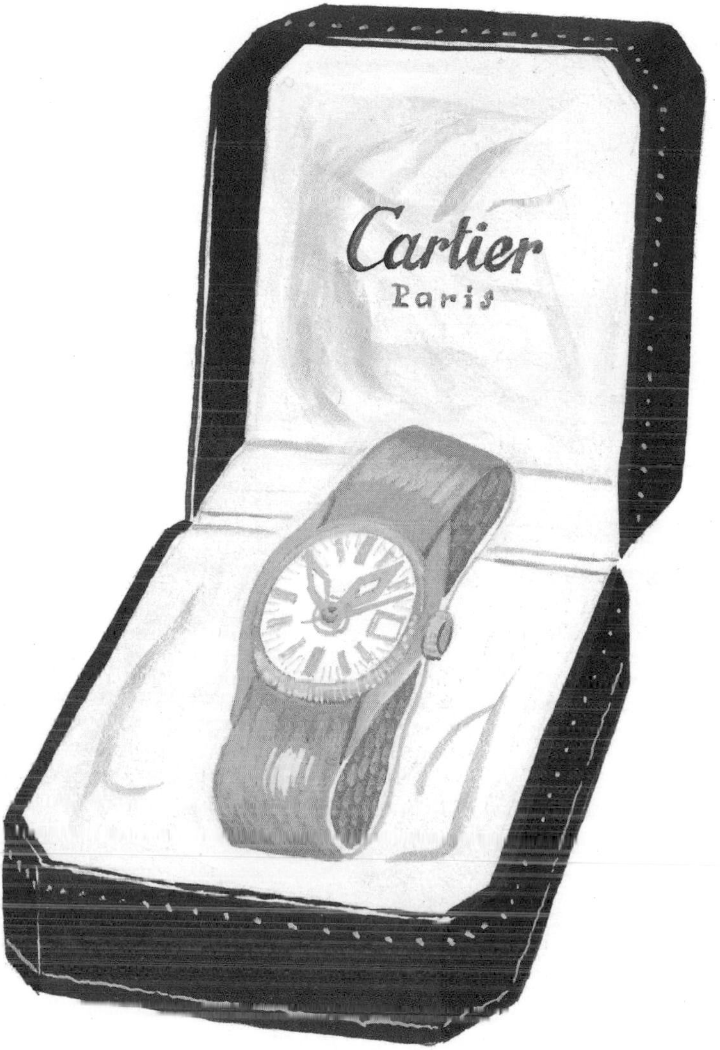
Cartier
Paris

The Phalangists loot and destroy the famous free zone in Beirut's port. For weeks, from the balcony of my grandmother's window overlooking the fifth basin, we observe the trucks going back and forth groaning under the weight of merchandise of all sorts.

Once the militia and their families have quenched their thirst for washing machines and fridges, Chryslers and Pontiacs, Swiss watches, Baccarat, Chopard and Nina Ricci, the remaining tonnes of merchandise are sold at auctions in the Collège des Frères school. When there is nothing left to take, they set fire to the empty warehouses to unsuccessfully camouflage their misdemeanours from the public eye. We watch Beirut's port burn senselessly for several days.

It is said that the Kataeb's pathetic defeat during the Battle of the Hotels was because they were too busy looting the port.

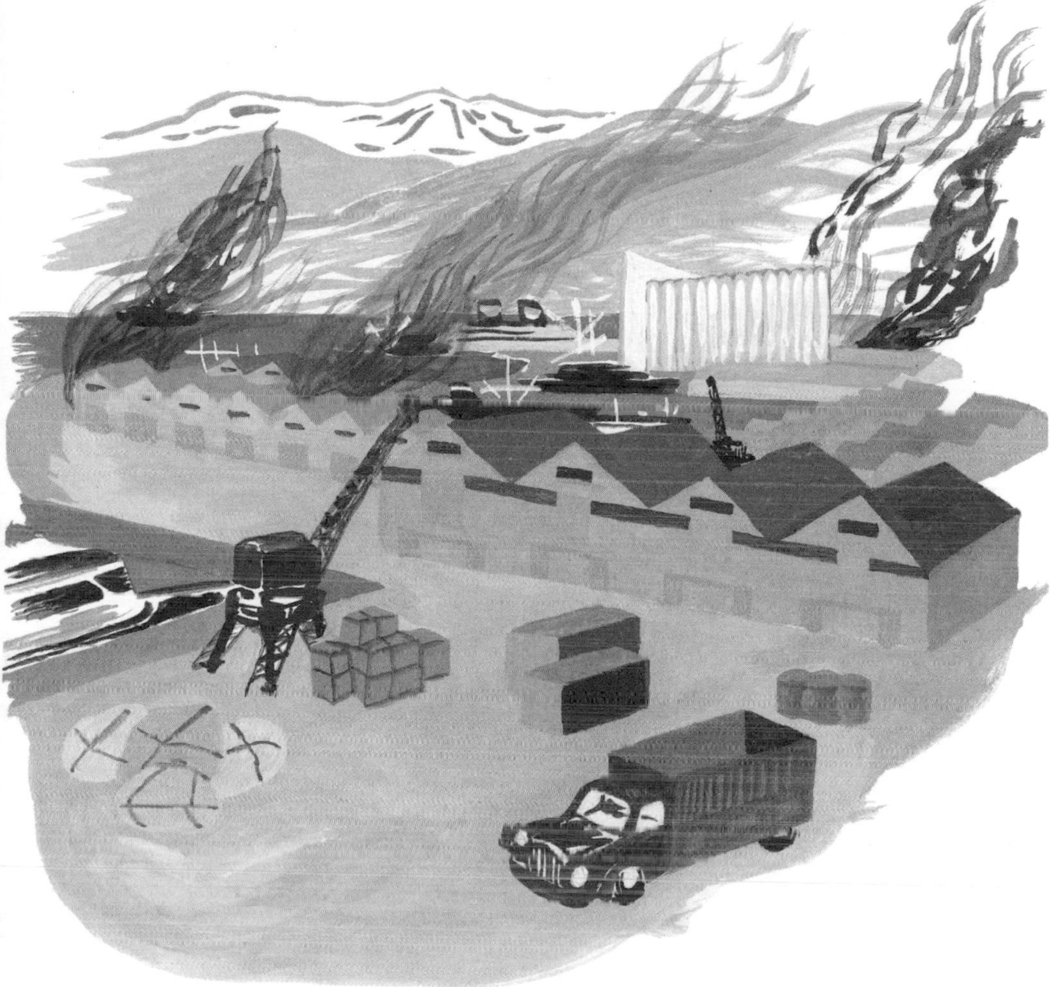

So in 1975 I'm seven years old and I'm in primary school at the Dames de Nazareth. After 13 April I will never see my school again, which is in a district named after it – *al-Nasra*. It is in one of the most explosive neighbourhoods of Beirut, right near *tarik al-cham*, rue de Damas, which has become the demarcation line between West Beirut, *Gharbieh*, and East Beirut, *Charkieh*, where we live. The division of Beirut is now well established. The entire downtown area (the Borj, Bab Idriss, the souks, place Debbas and place de l'Etoile) has become a gigantic no-man's-land, completely destroyed, where only militiamen and snipers venture.

As for us, we are now among Christians, with Virgins, crucifixes and geometric cedar trees* on our narrow horizon. A special tax is imposed on us by the SKS (Kataeb Security Sections).

For several months I don't go to school at all. Everything or almost everything has changed in my life as it has for all of Beirut's inhabitants.

An era of shortages, rationing and supplies begins.

* Symbol of the Kataeb party

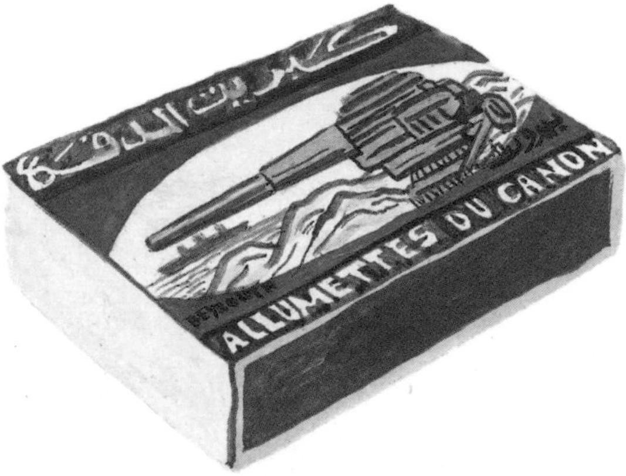
كبريت المدفع
ALLUMETTES DU CANON

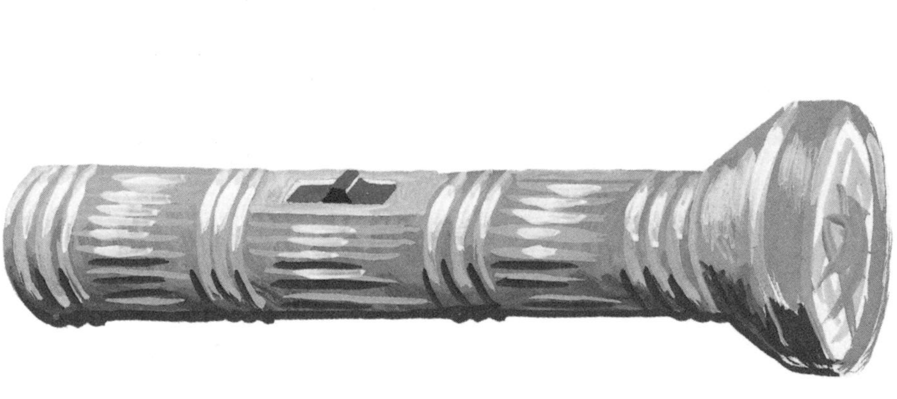

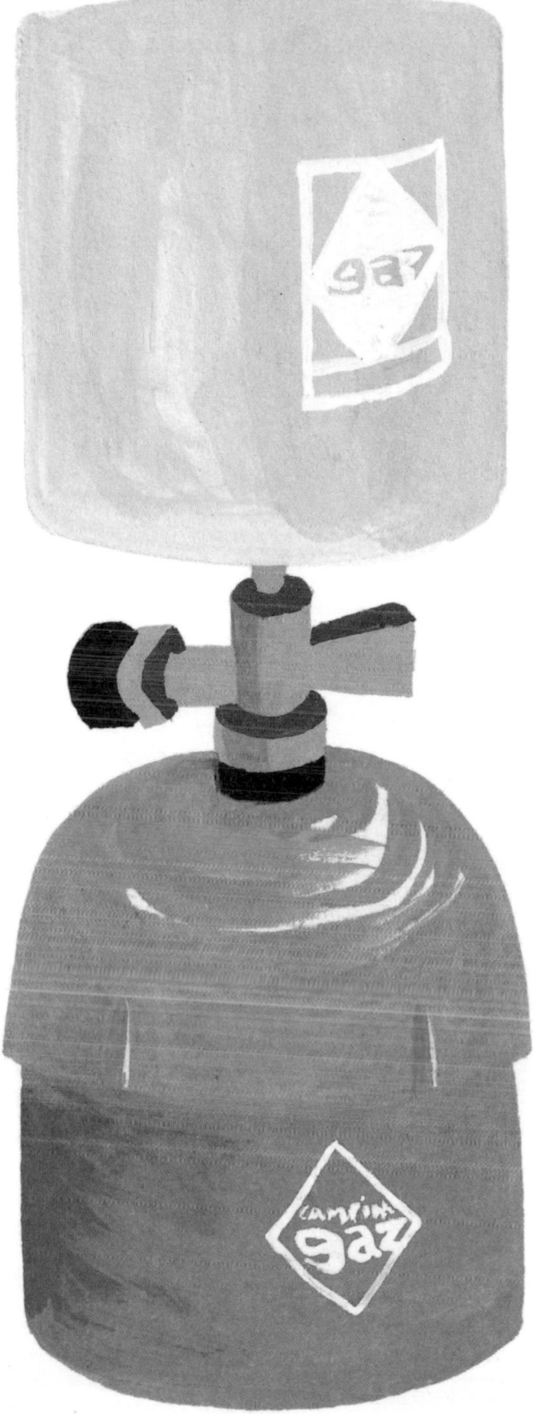
gaz
camping gaz

There is no more electricity so we use candles, torches, or the pale light of a Camping Gaz lantern.

We never take the lift any more, even when there is electricity, for fear of being stuck inside should there be a power cut.

The telephone works only rarely. It will get worse over the years. Hours can be spent waiting for a dialling tone, then one dials the number very carefully, as if treading on ice, on the alert for any sigh, breath or whistle in the receiver, like a doctor examining a patient, only to have one's hopes dashed with an engaged signal, *mashghoul*, and try again . . .

The miraculous phrase *'Fatah al-khat!'* 'There's a dialling tone!' is trumpeted all around and is met with exclamations of joy, bravos and hurrahs. It's an unmistakable sign that God has not completely abandoned us.

It's hard to be deprived of information in a country where regular news is vital. My Uncle Robert, always on the cutting edge of technology, brings back one of the first mobile phones from the US in 1977. He plugs it into his white Oldsmobile where it remains for several months, a genuine attraction for young and old. Telephoning from a car is as fantastic as walking on the moon. When, a year later, the use of these telephones becomes widespread, Robert will already be using individual electricity generators, which, as the conflict worsens, become an undeniable success.

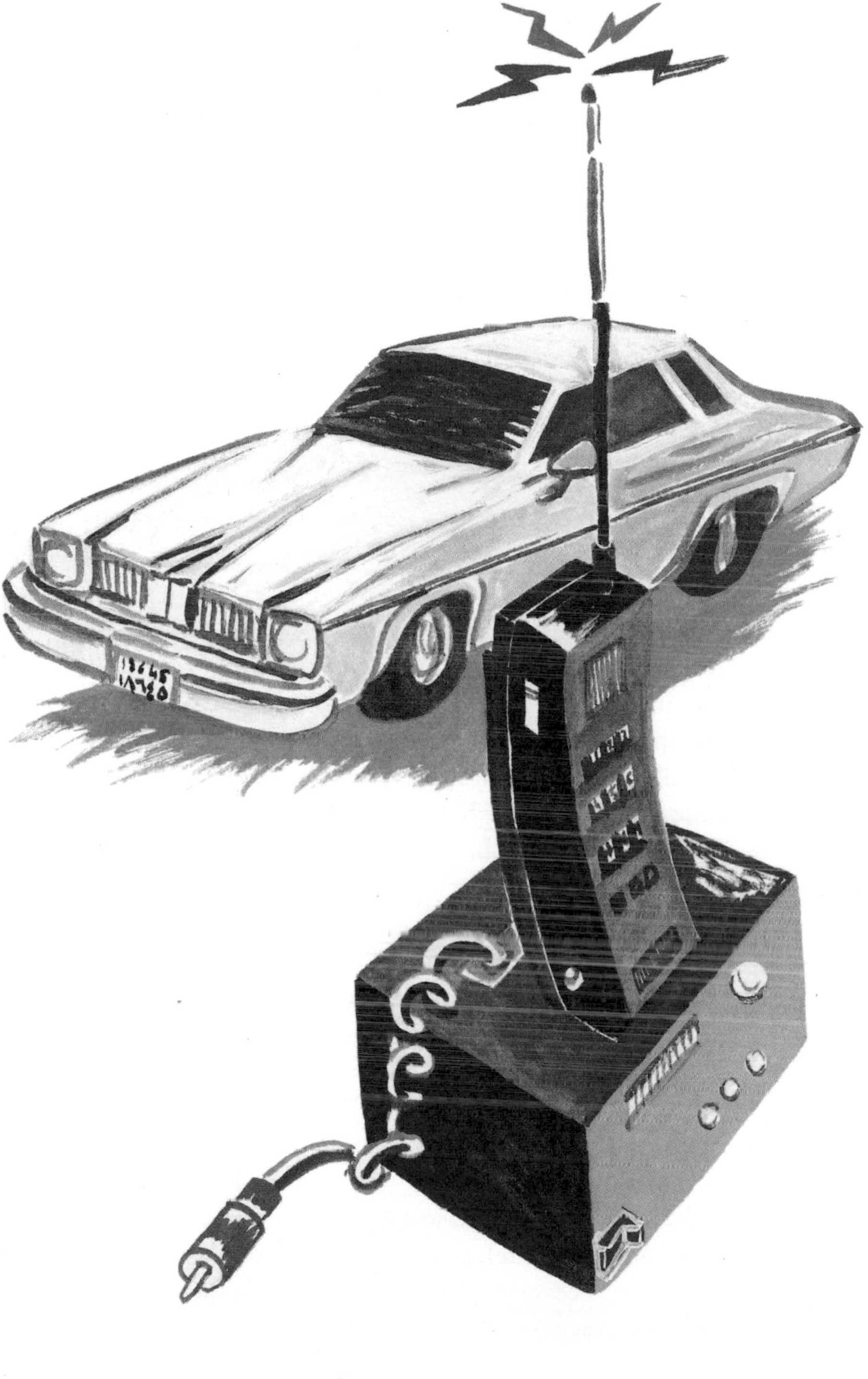

No more running water; we fill up at a fountain where we go armed with gallon containers and empty bottles. Daily showers become a luxury and flushing the toilet a real moral dilemma.

Water used for washing one's face and hands is carefully collected and recycled. To wash one's body, water heated in a cooking pot is mixed parsimoniously with cold for rinsing.

Petrol shortages . . .

Supplies of everything have to be stocked, as soon as possible, even if the Levantine attitude favours short-term planning.

Supplies of camping lanterns, Chiclets and Bomba*.

Of candles, matches and oil.

Of Zwan tinned pork and corned beef, magical food that doesn't need to be stored in the fridge.

Supplies of Gandour, Lucky 555 and *Dabké* biscuits, the latter are well named – 'fight'.

Supplies of Valium for those who can't sleep, and of Nivea for the soft face and hands of my nanny, Tamar. To my mother's consternation, she's in love with a Phalangist militiaman who drives a BMW.

* Lebanese chewing gum

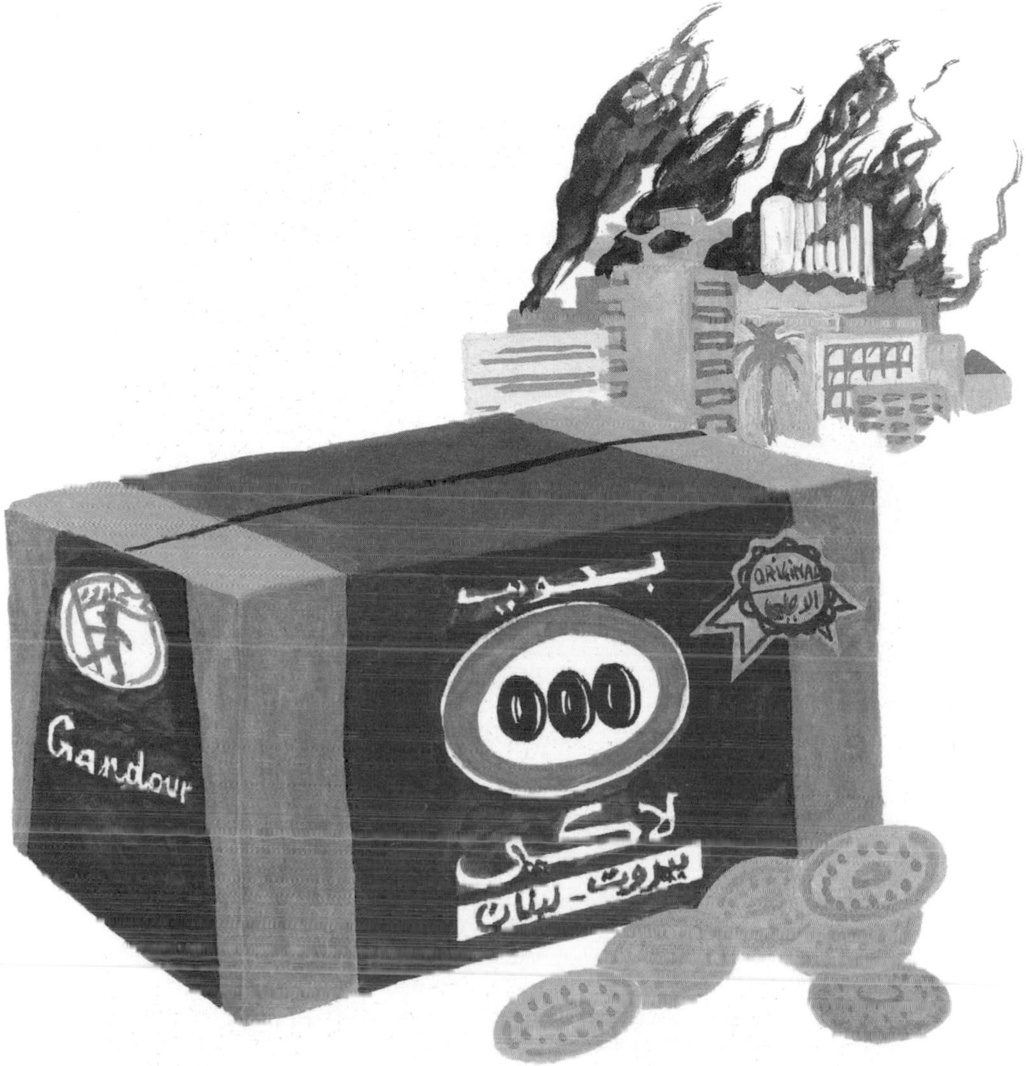
Gandour
بسكويت
ORIGINAL
لاكي
بيروت - لبنان

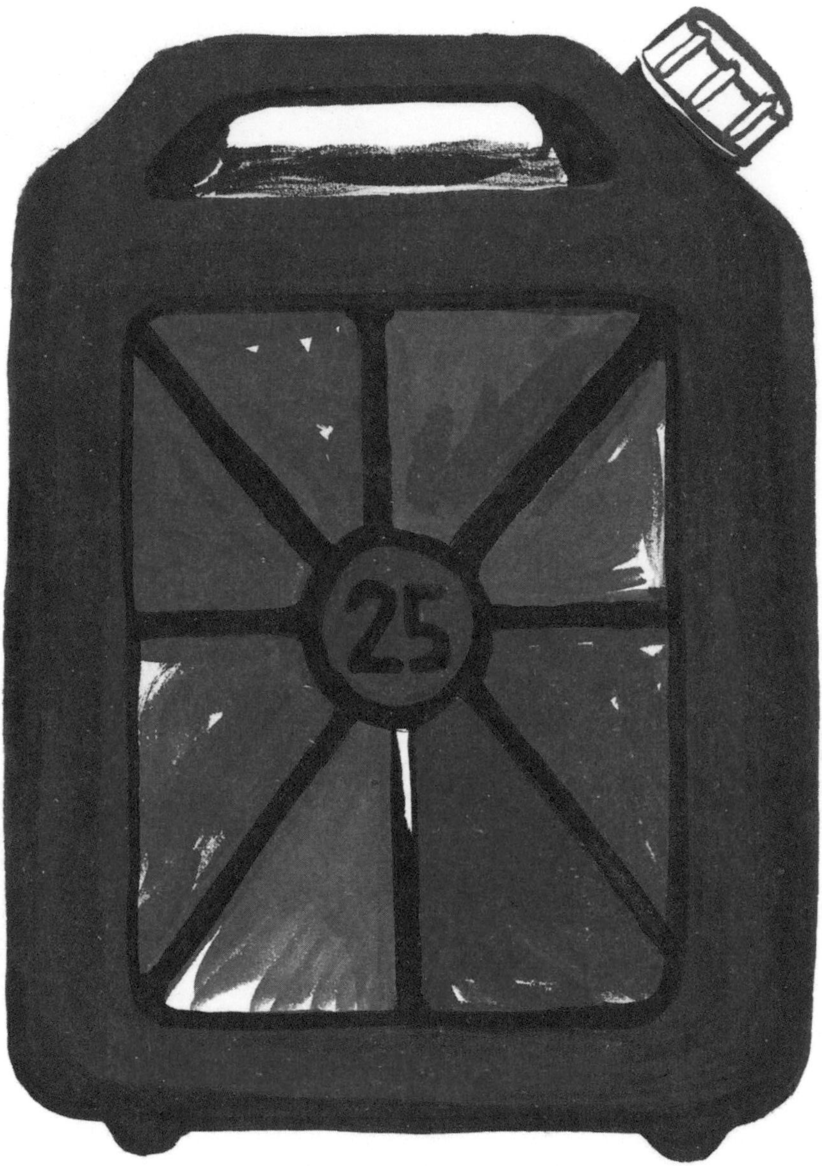
25

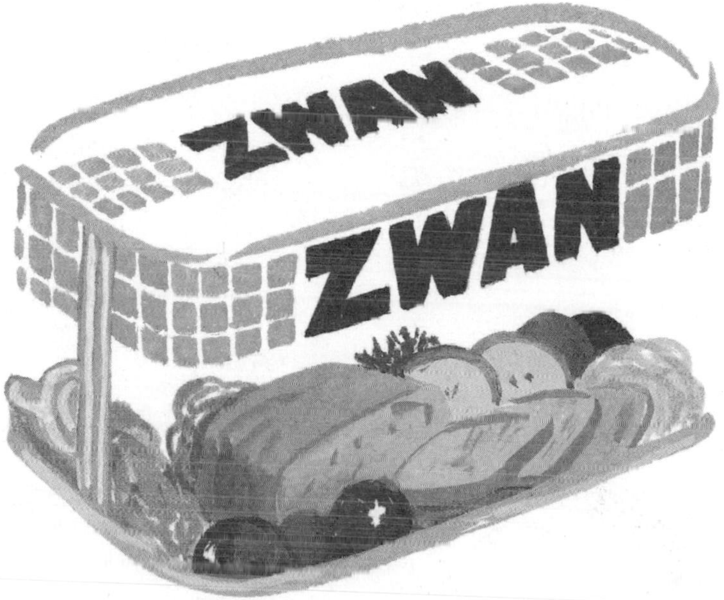
ZWAN
ZWAN

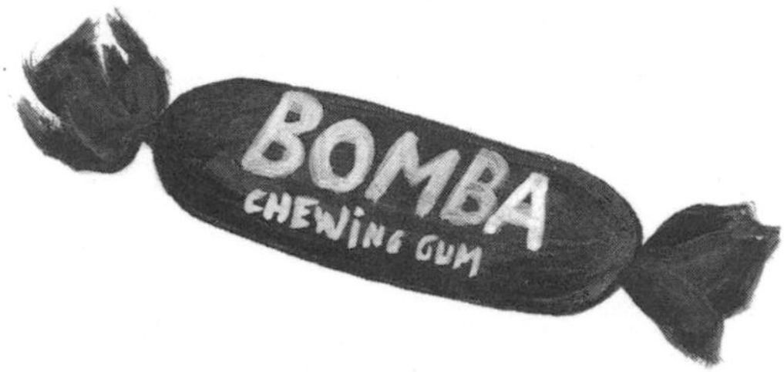
BOMBA
CHEWING GUM

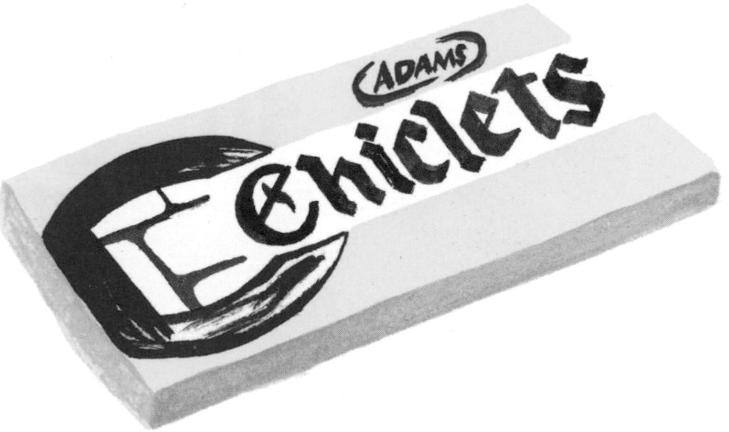
ADAMS
Chiclets

Valium
(Diazepam)
10

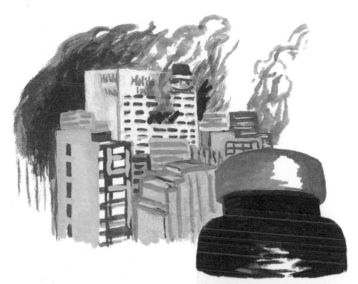

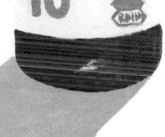

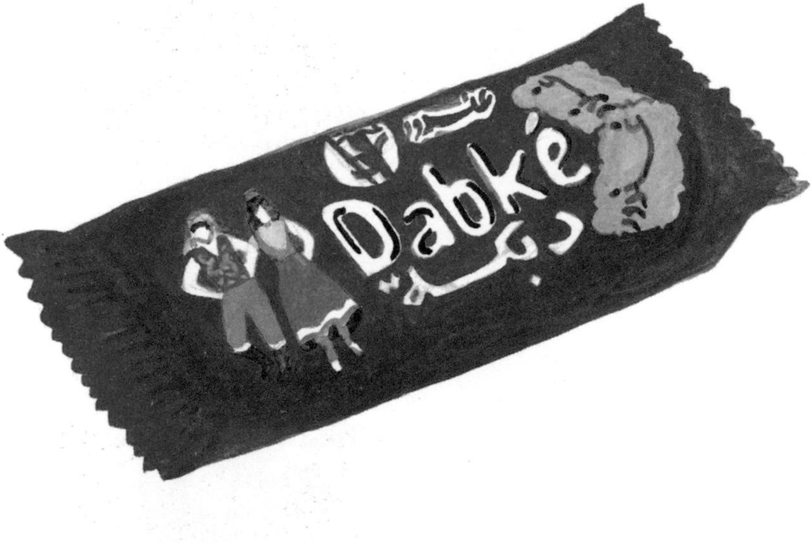
Dabké
دبكة

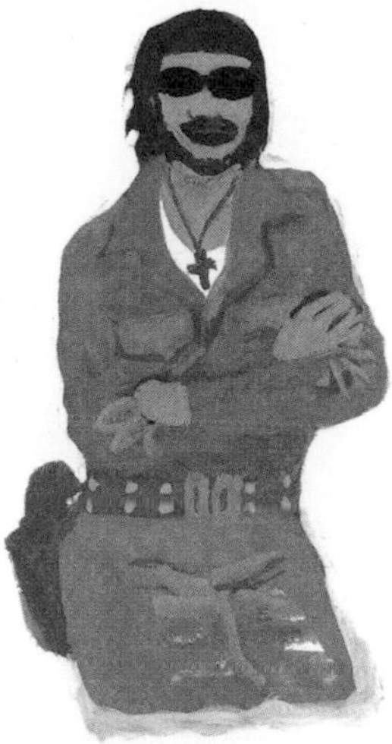

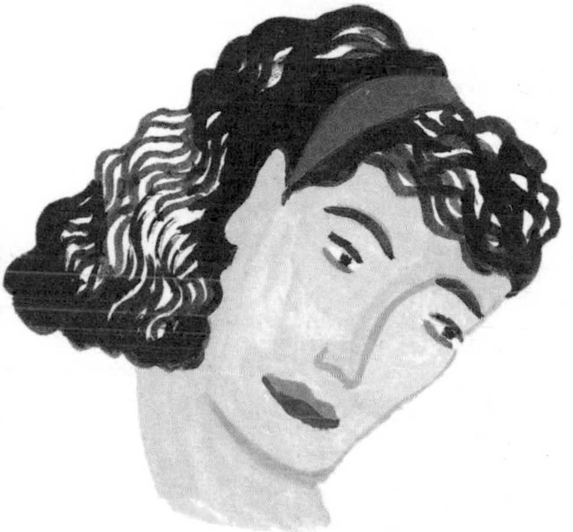

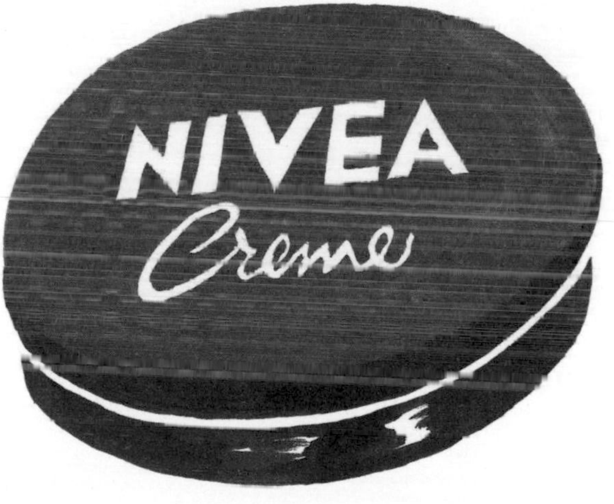
NIVEA
Creme

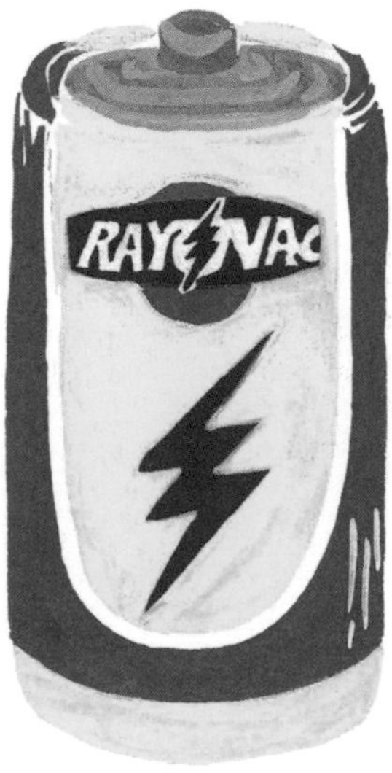
RAYOVAC

Stocks of batteries for torches, but above all for radios, which are switched on permanently for the *moulhaks*, or news flashes, that are broadcast continuously.

Small, battery-operated radios are widespread partly because there is no electricity but also because they can be easily carried around. My father will spend fifteen years with a radio stuck to his ear. (The volume on these little radios isn't very high and the roar of the shelling is loud . . .) Even today, twenty years after the end of the war, my father still listens to the news on a radio held to his ear.

Announced by an alarmist but enticing jingle, the danger zones are listed according to their location near well-known shops or cinemas – street names or squares had never been an efficient way of identifying an address in Beirut.

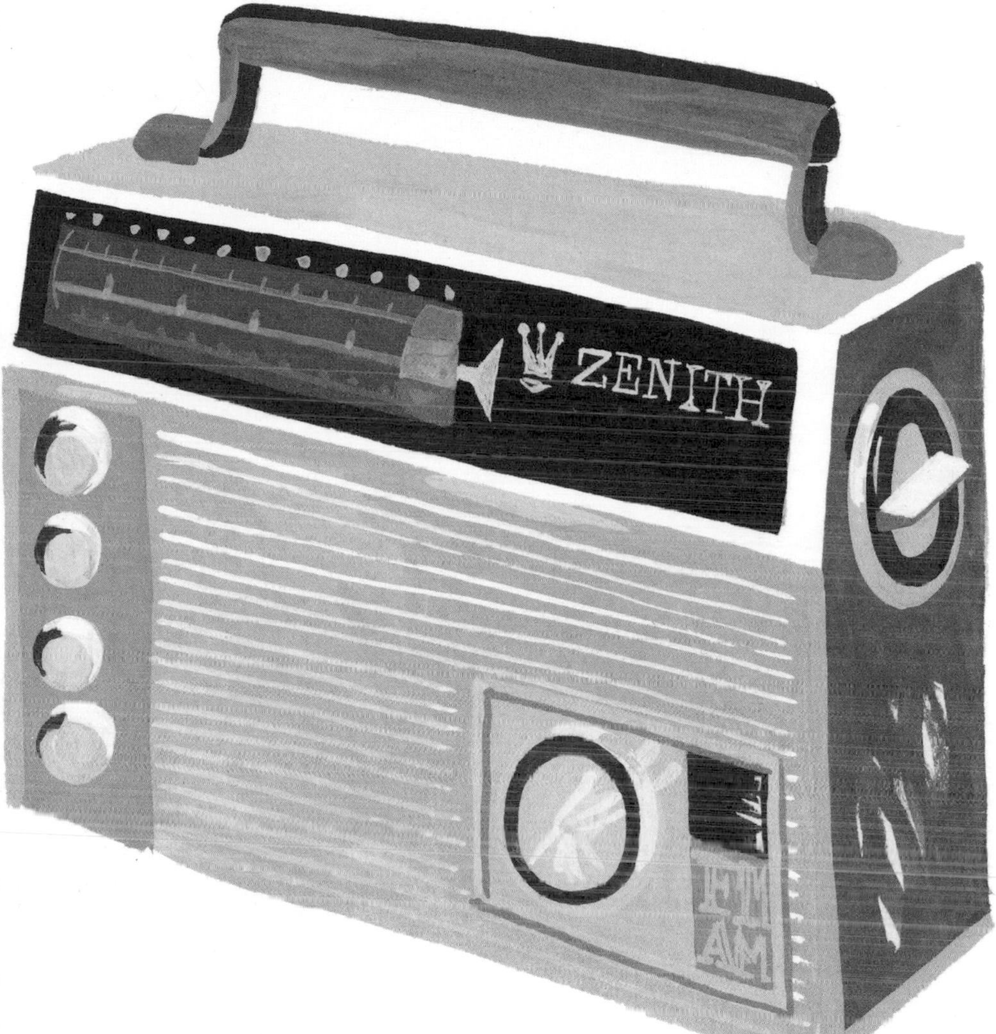
ZENITH
FM
AM

Mortar fire at Starco.
   Street battles at the Empire, the Rivoli,
the Regent and the Automatic.
   Random checkpoints at Sodéco.
   Abductions at Galerie Semaan.
   Mutilated bodies at Azarieh.
   Snipers at Souliers Gérard.
   Artillery fire at the Cola and the Chevrolet crossroads.
   Bloody clashes at *Binayat al-Kamal*, the al-Kamal building.
   Fire at Spinney's . . .

We also stock up on cigarettes . . .

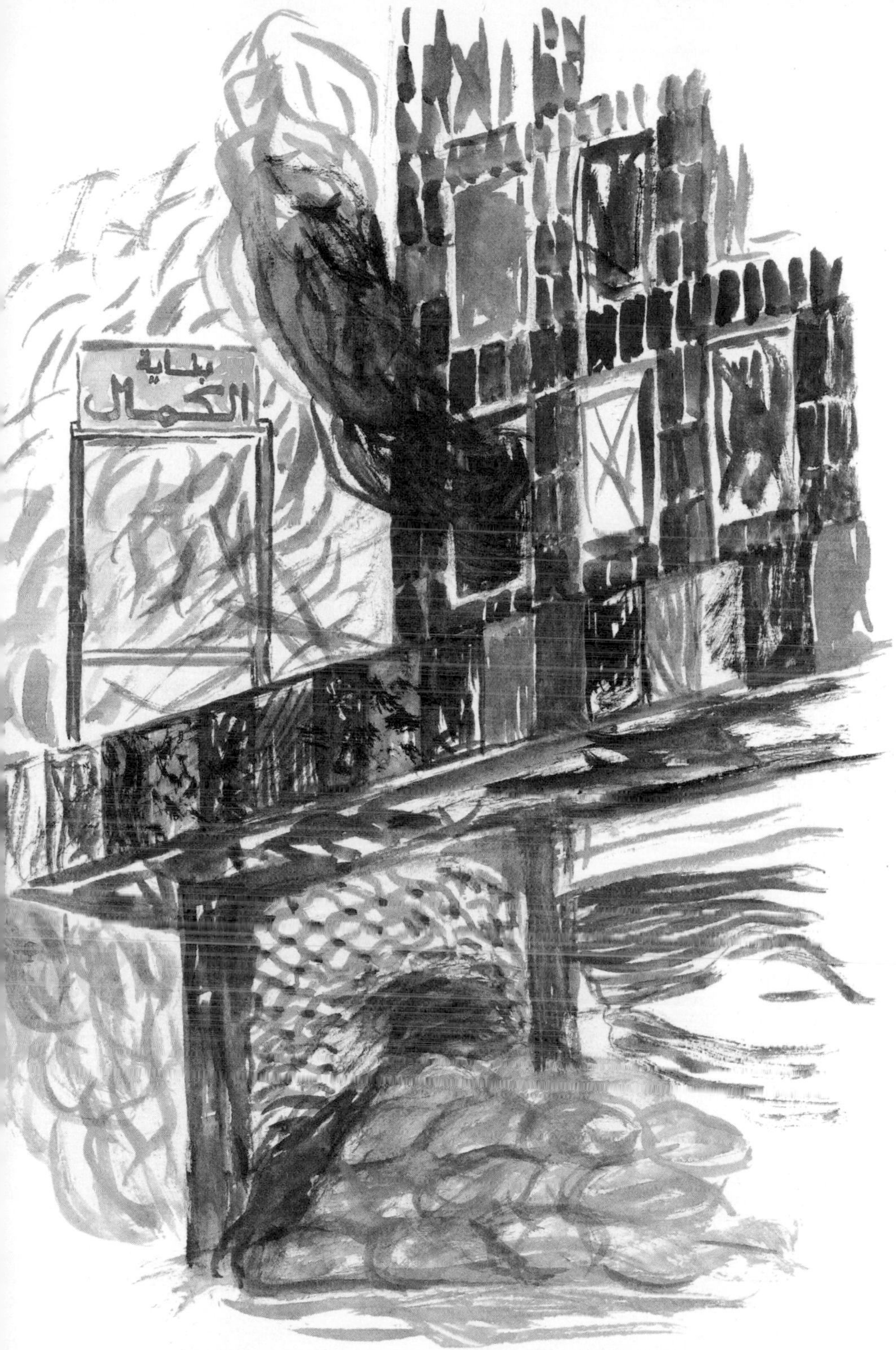
بناية
الكمال

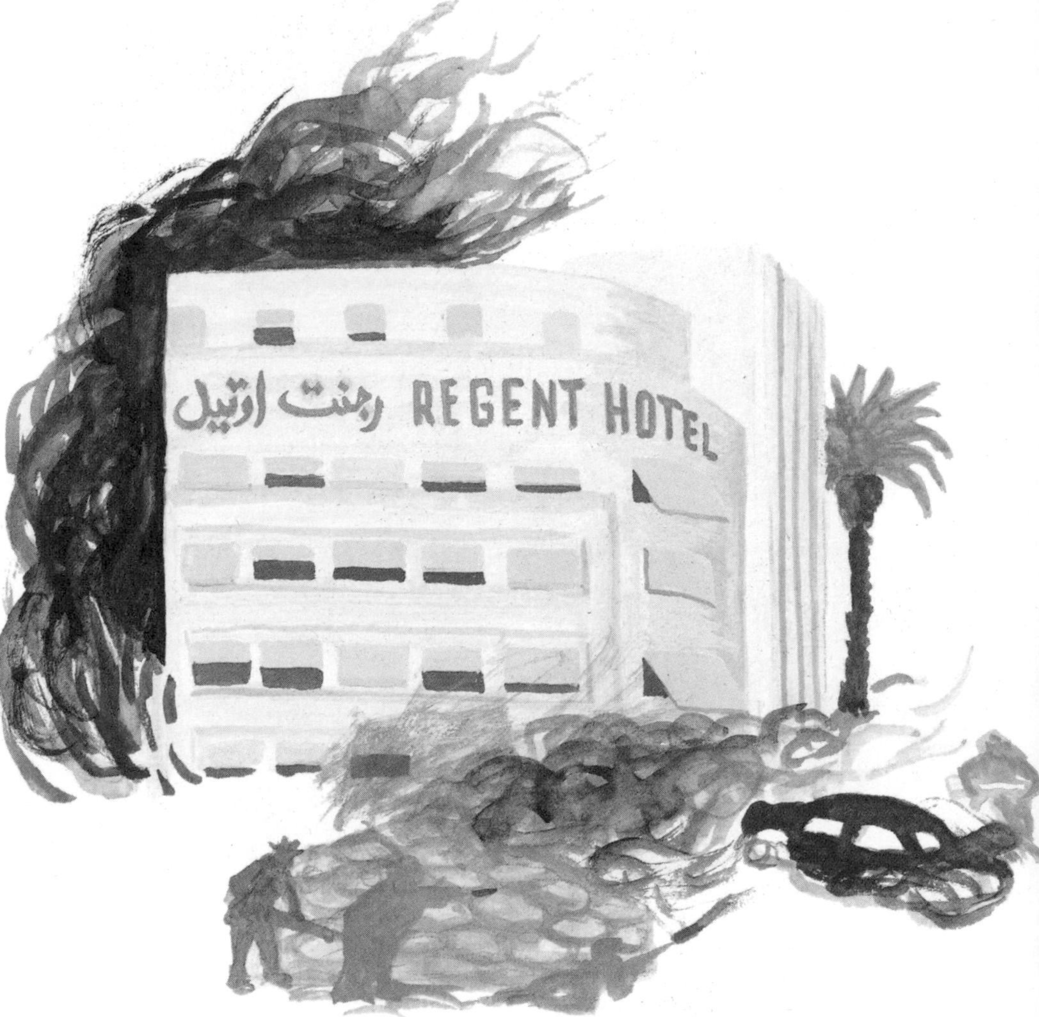
رجنت اوتيل REGENT HOTEL

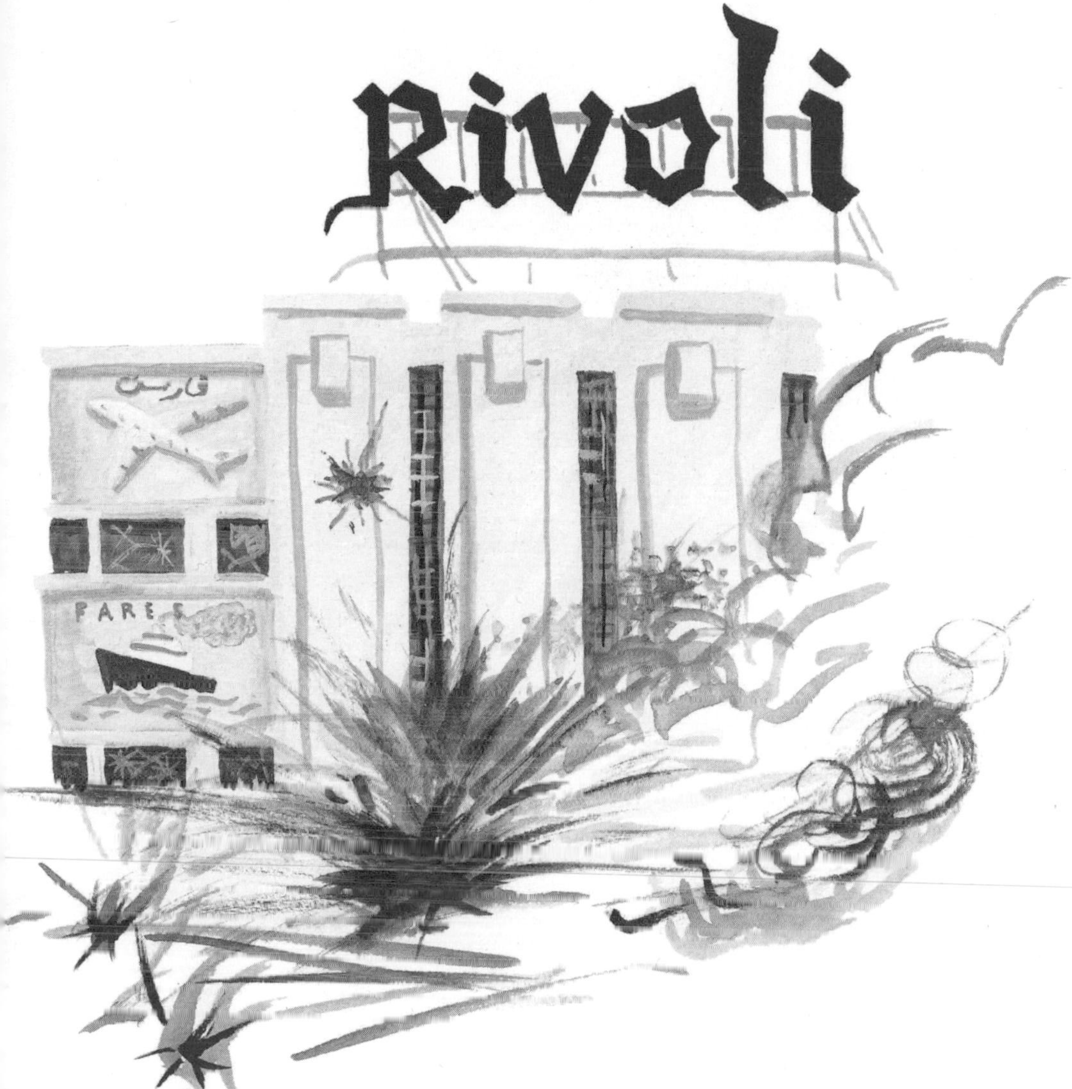
Rivoli
FARES

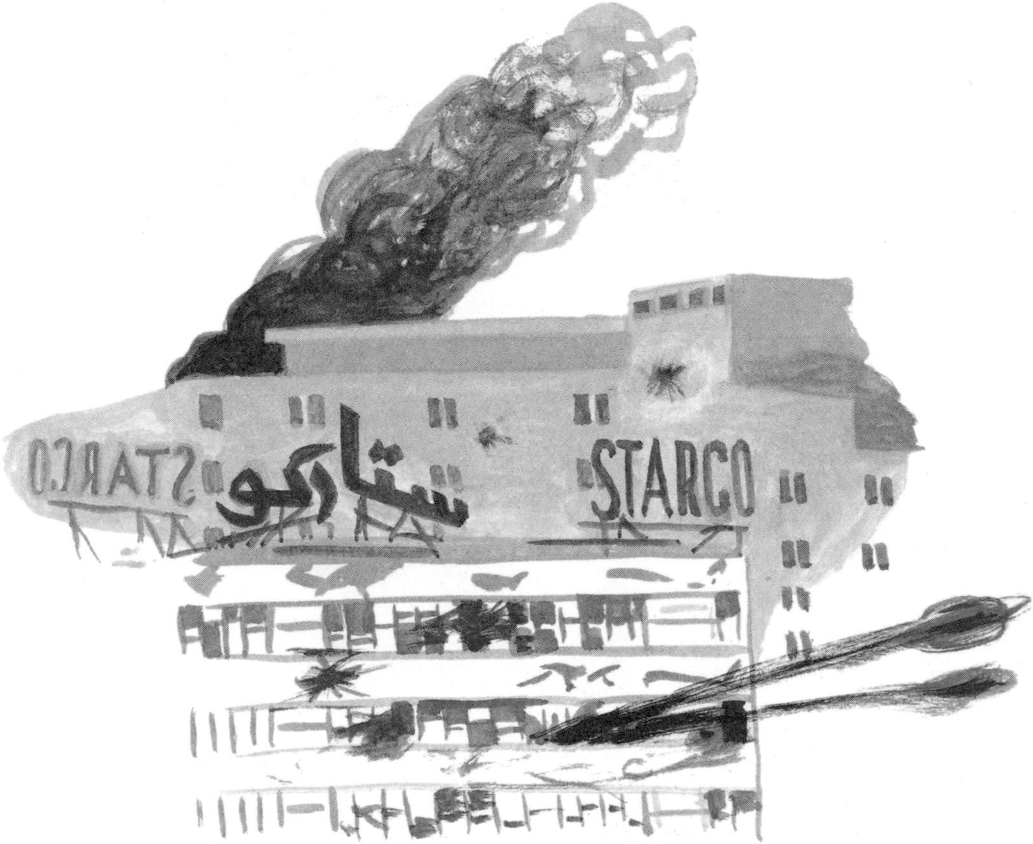
ستاركو
STARCO

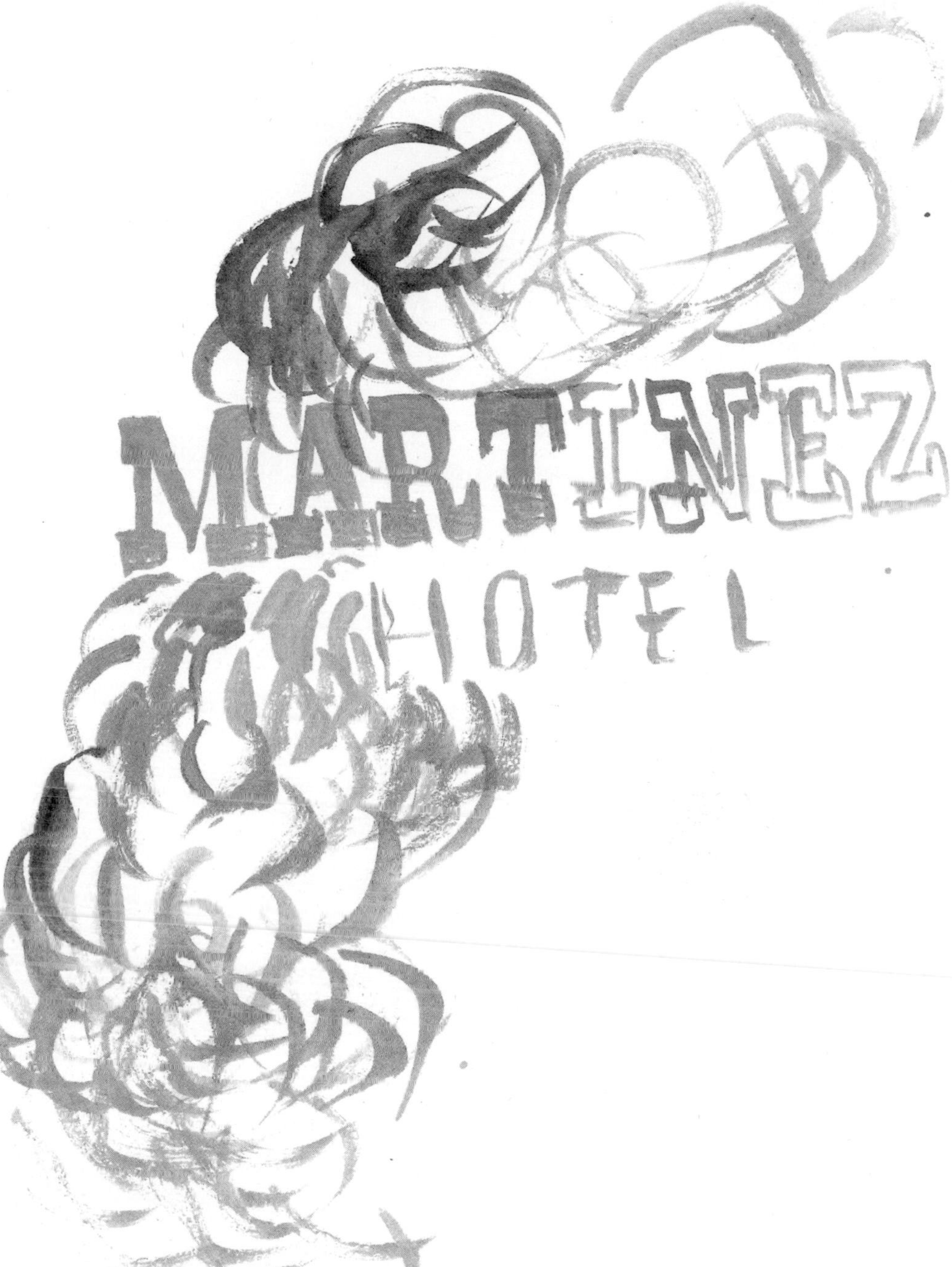
MARTINEZ
HOTEL

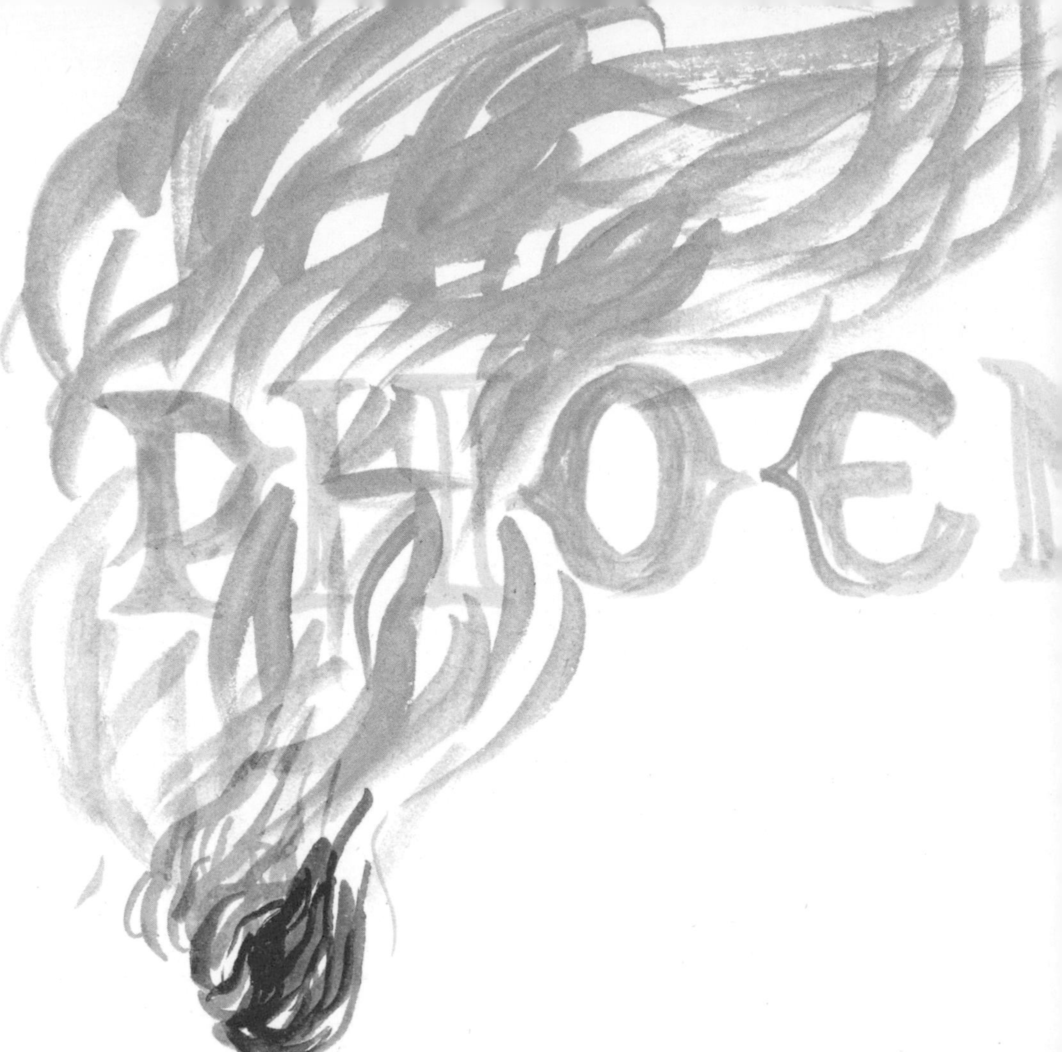
PHOE

IX

الكازار

ALCAZAR

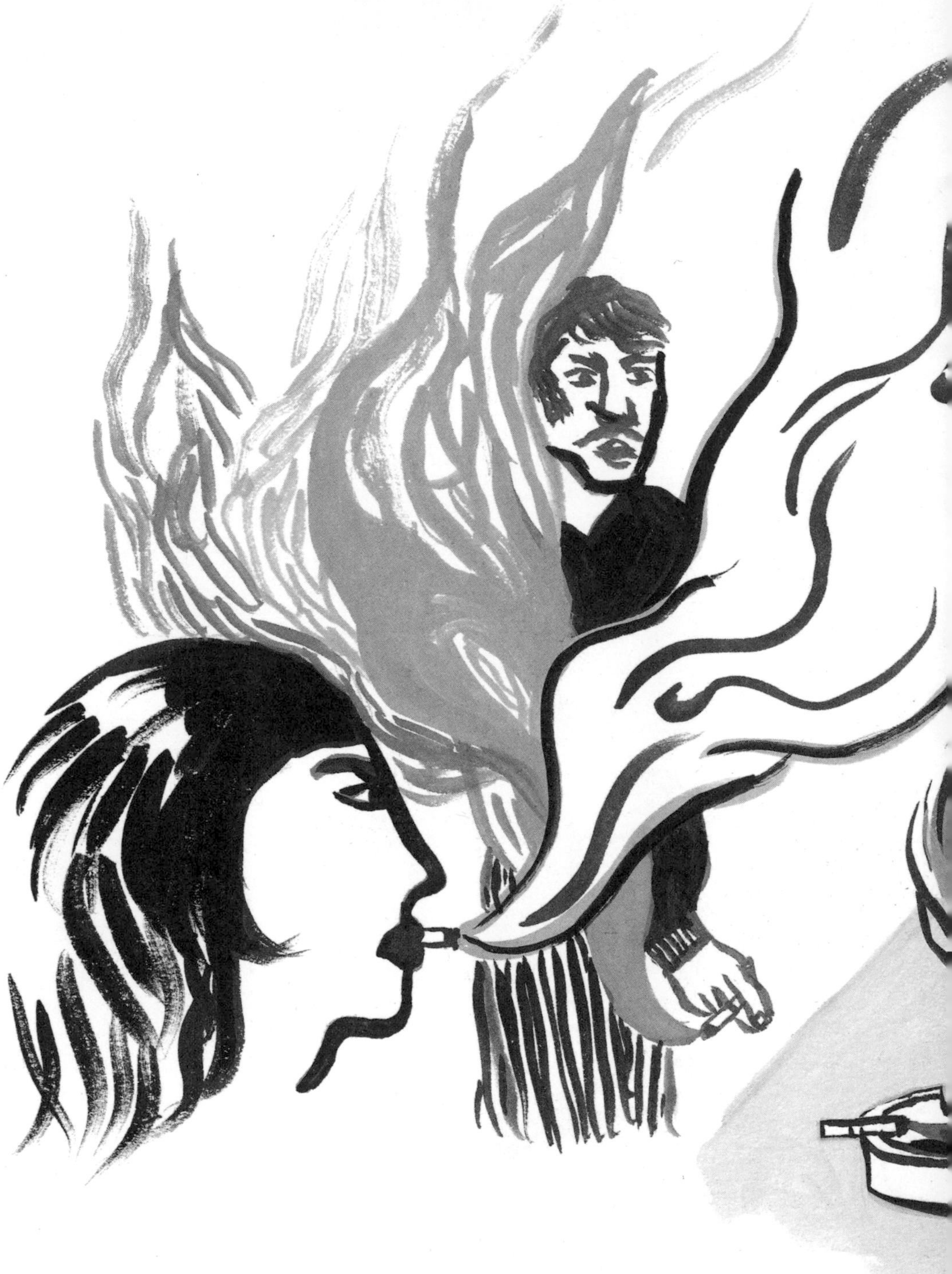

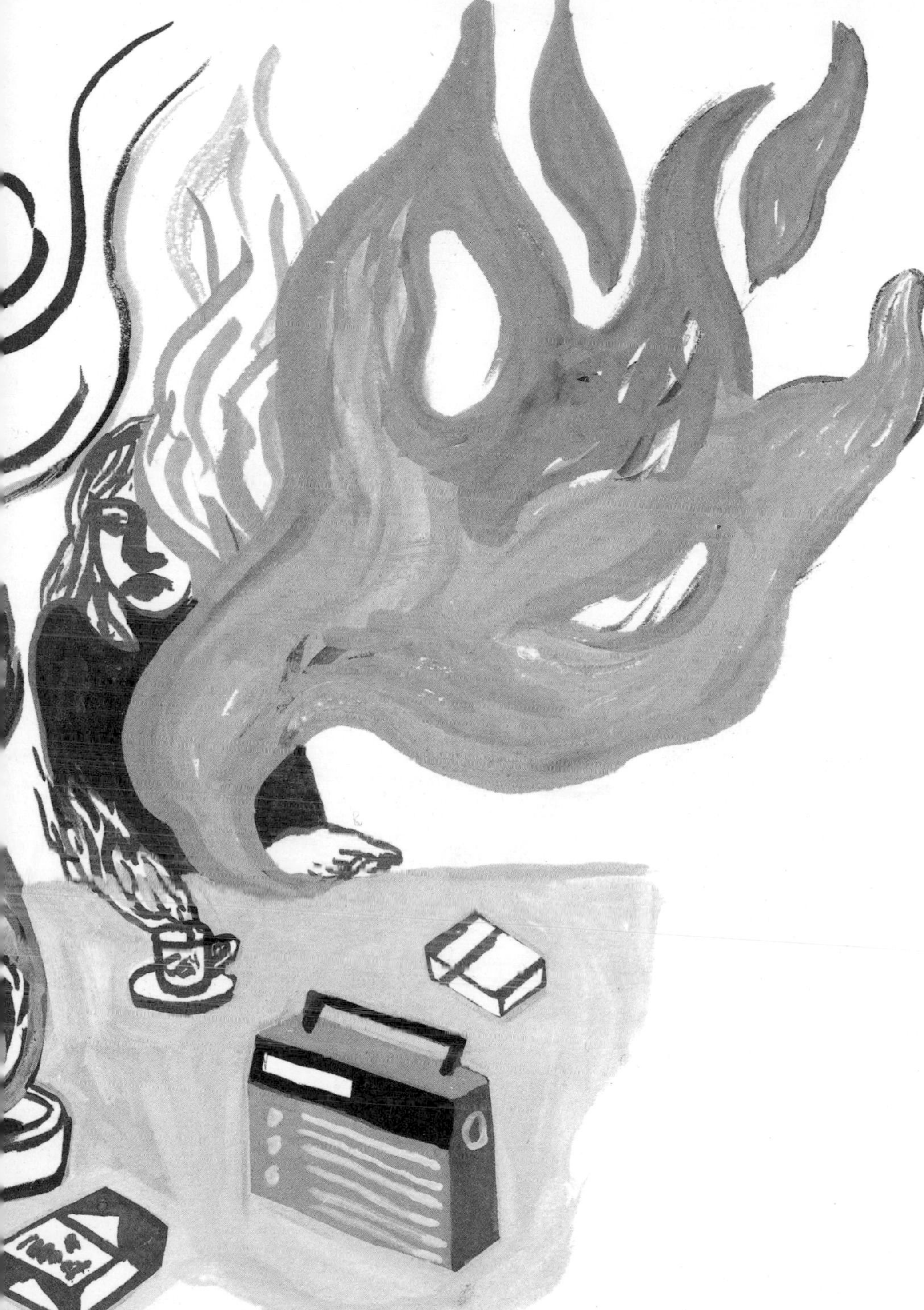

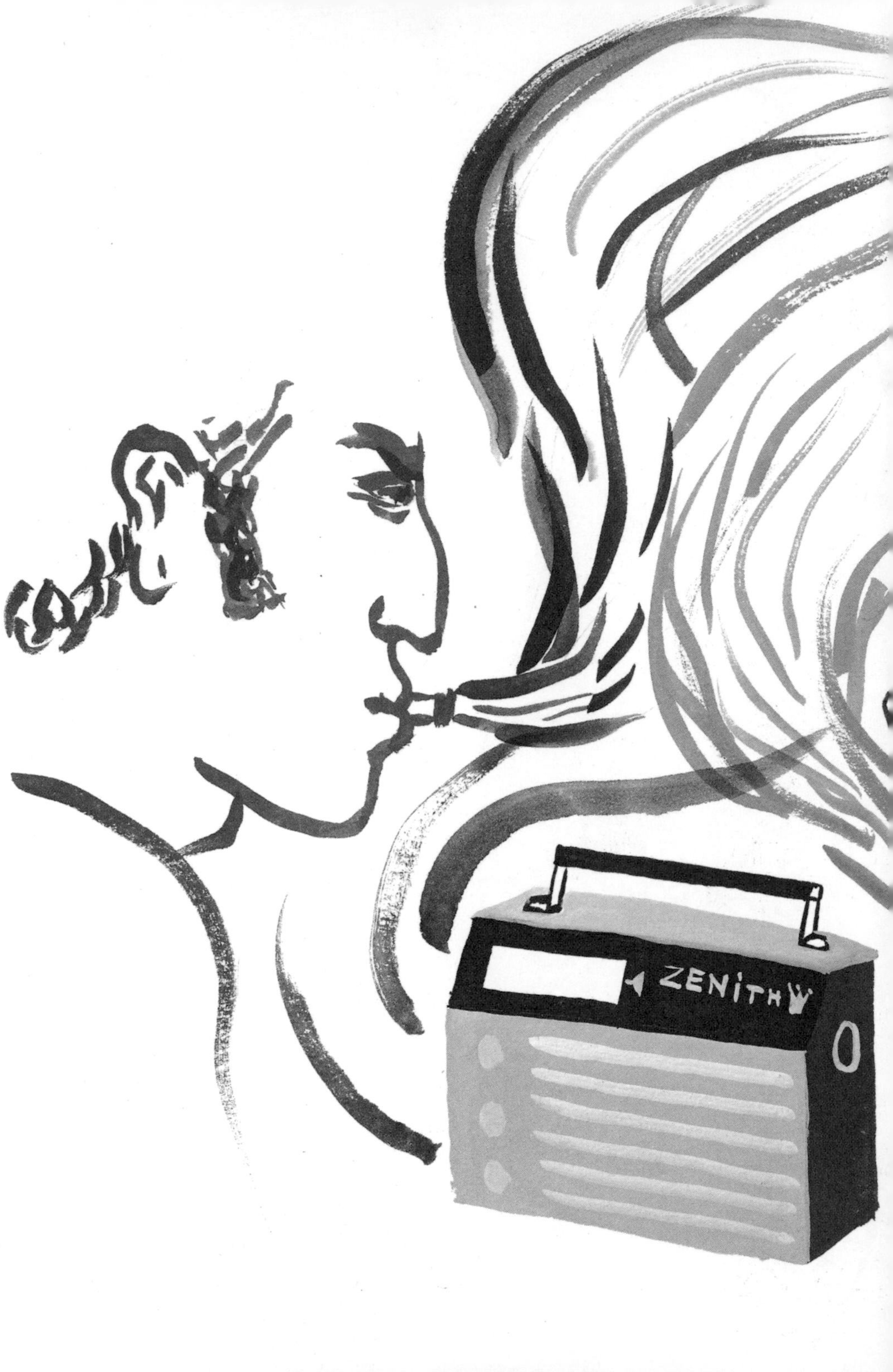
ZENITH

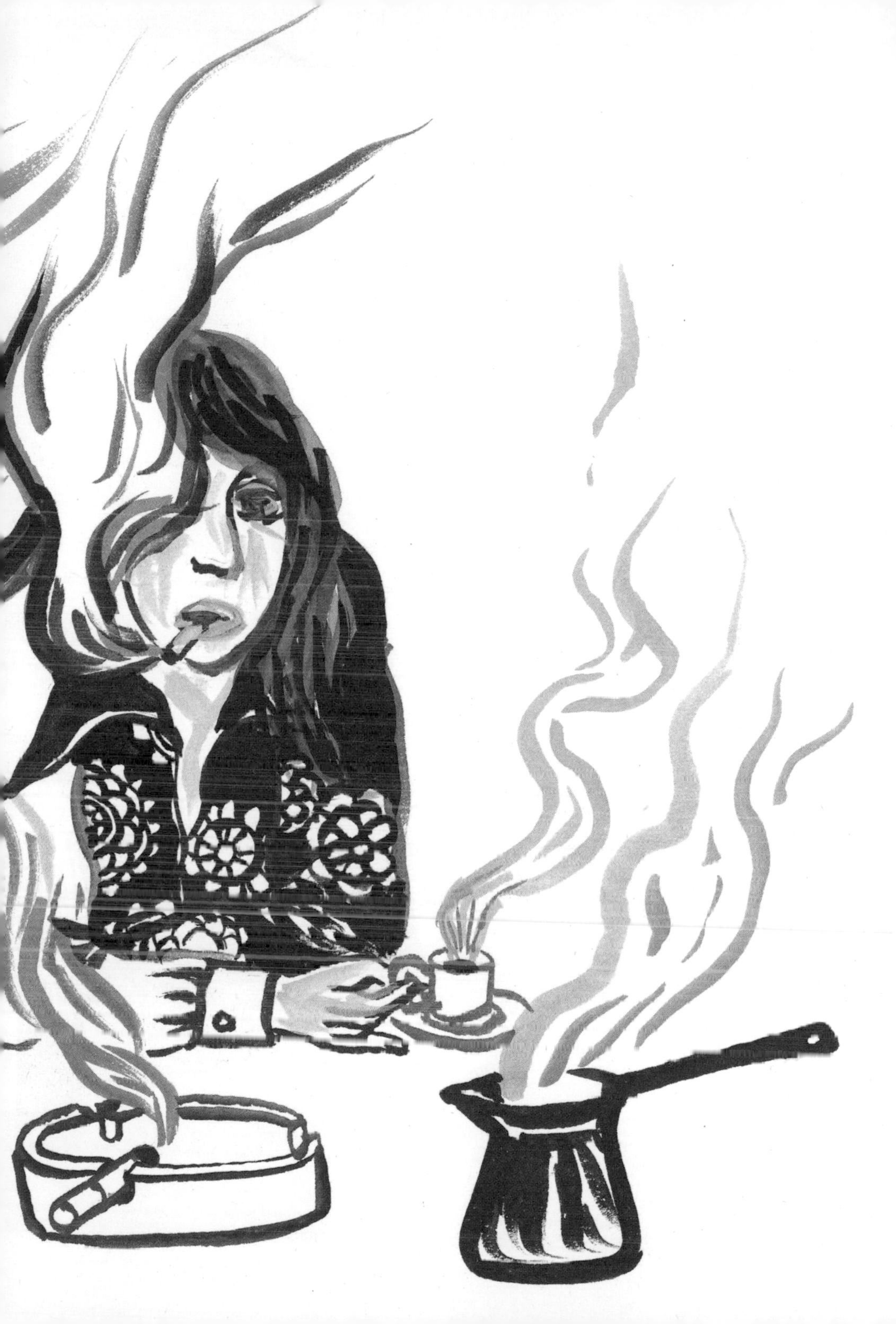

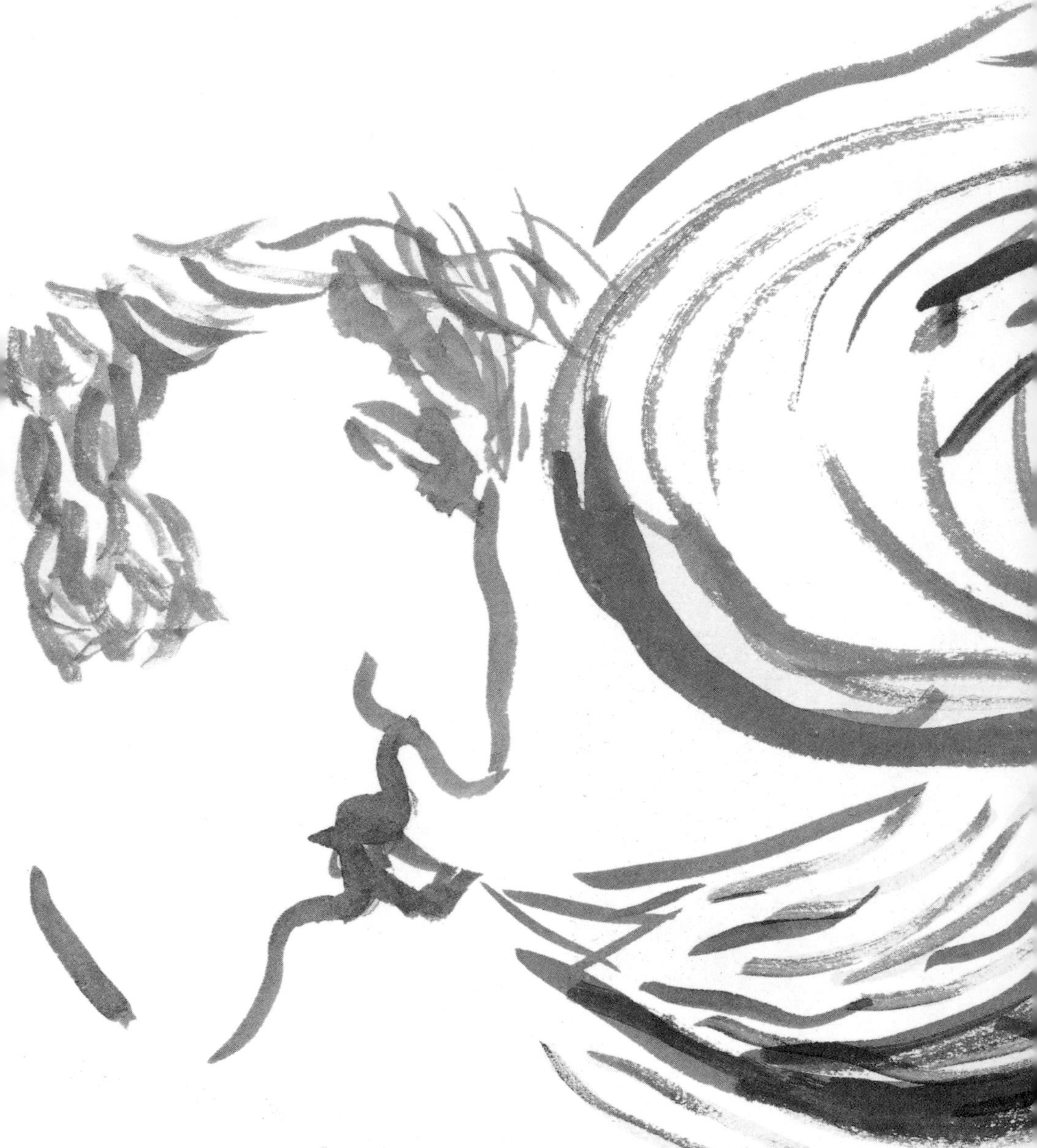

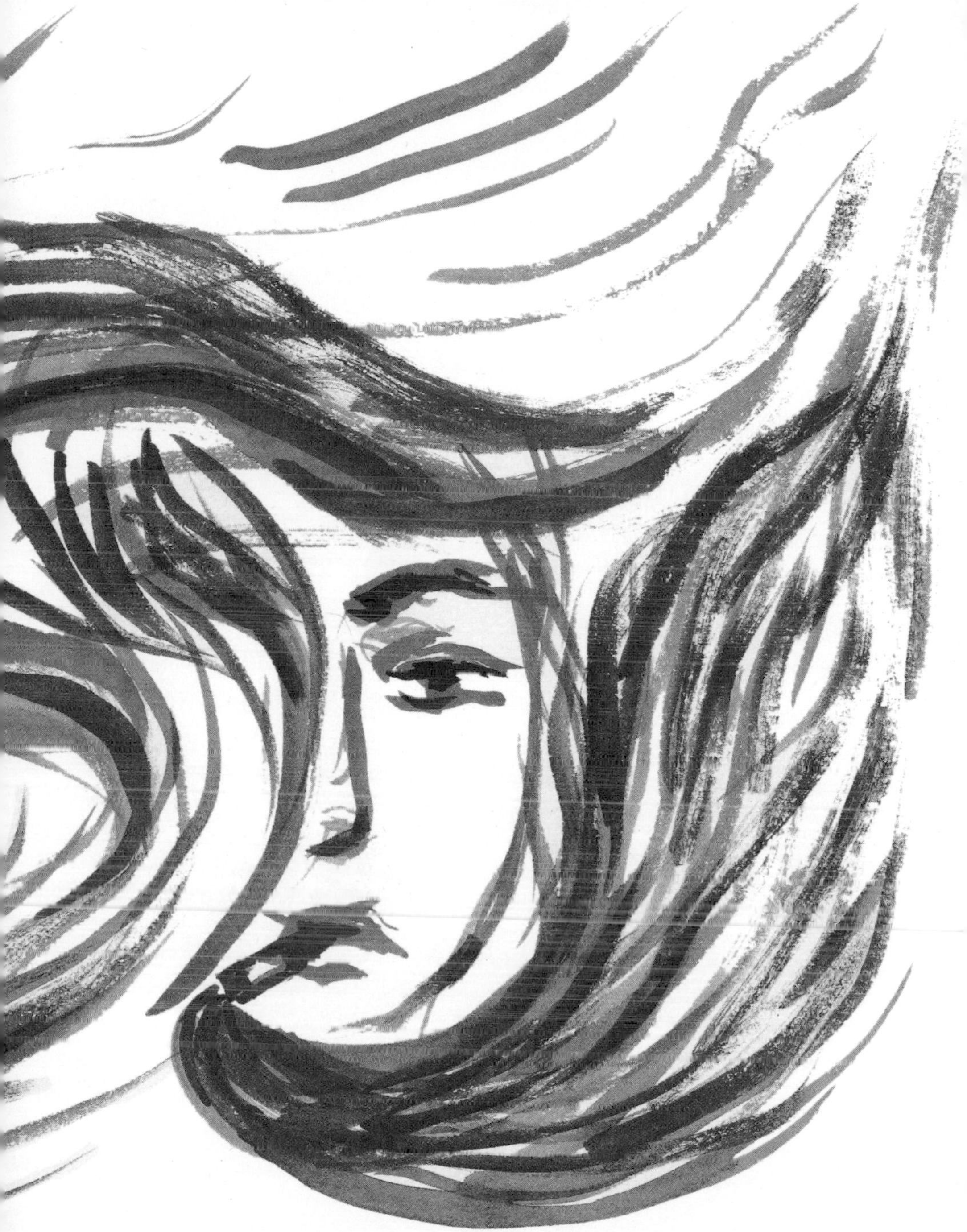

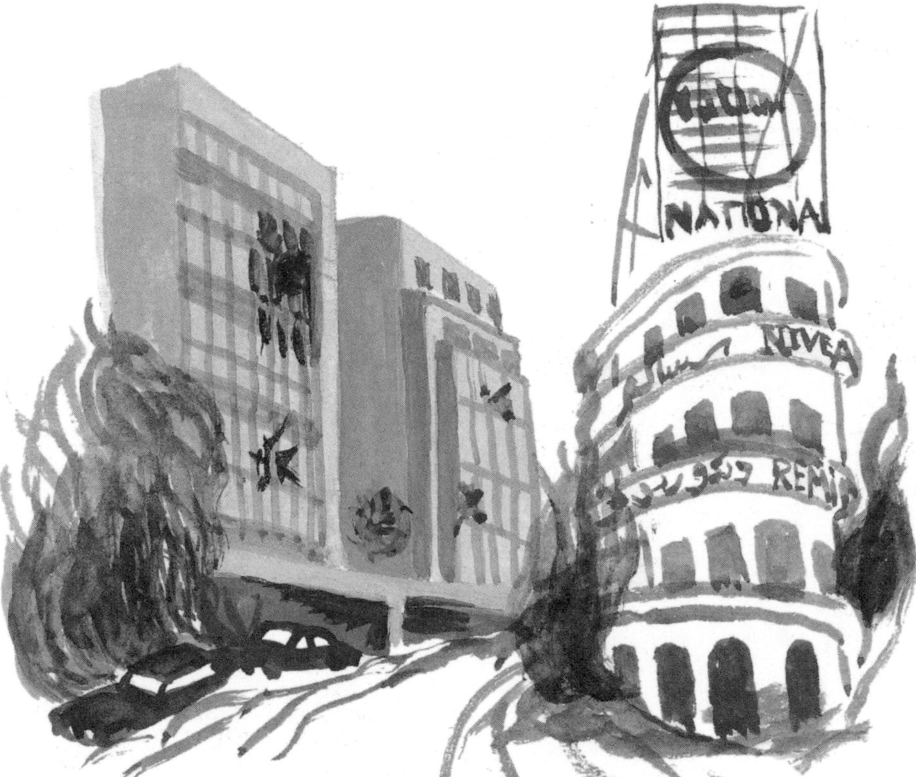
NATIONAL
NIVEA

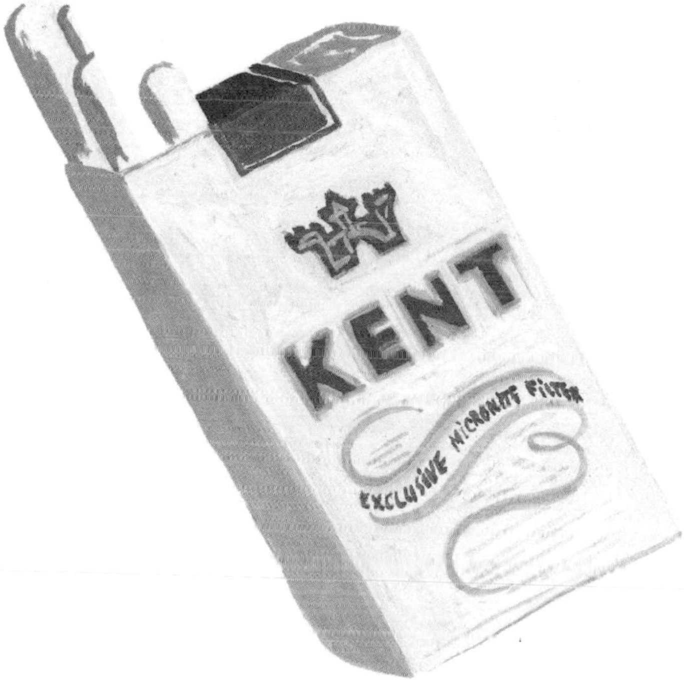
KENT
EXCLUSIVE MICRONITE FILTER

Henri has disappeared! He hasn't come home!

Arrested? Kidnapped? Executed?

Henri has left our house in Ashrafieh, where he often comes to launch into political discussions with my father, and he has not yet arrived home in Zarif, West Beirut, where Aunt Marcelle is waiting for him.

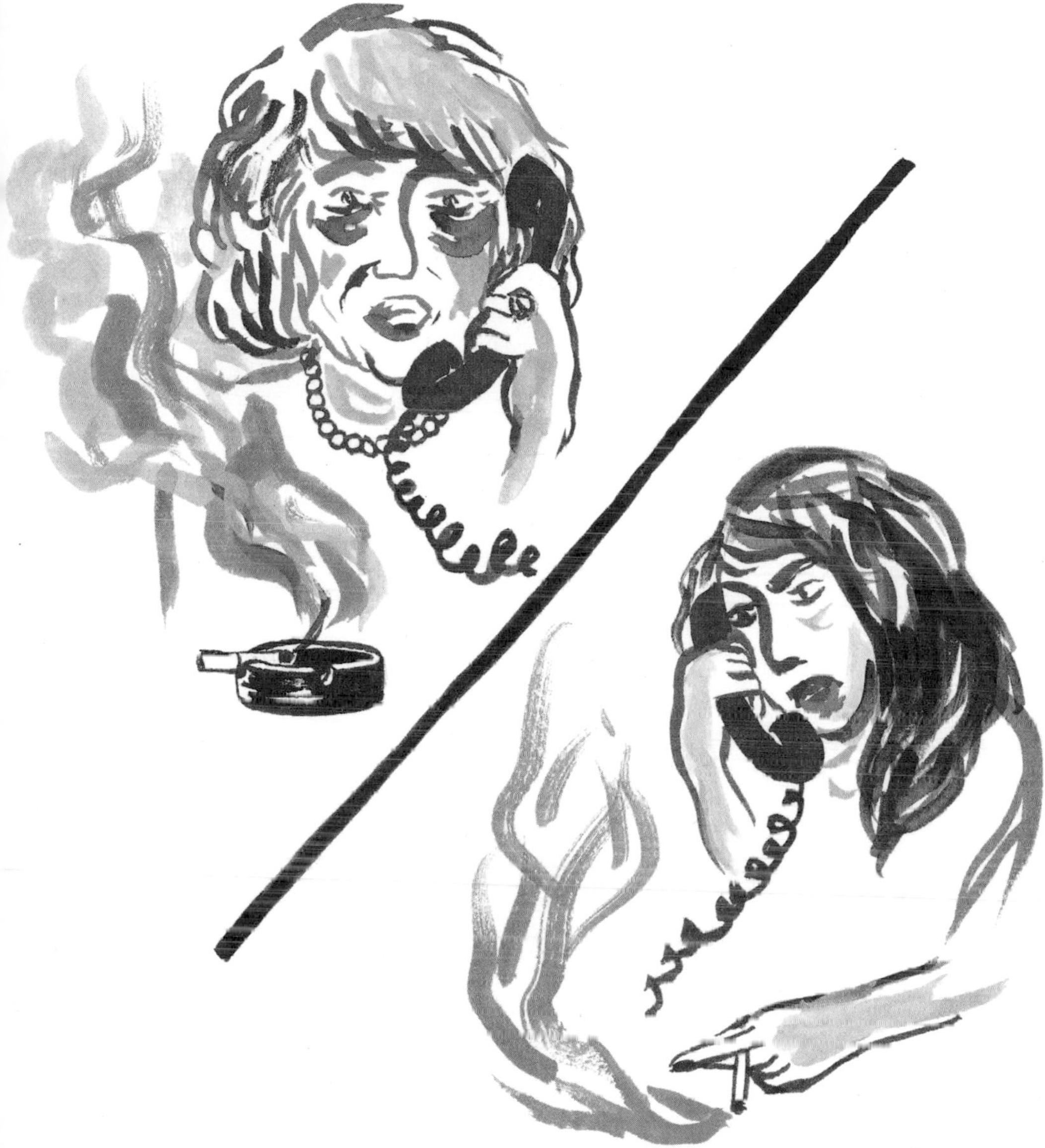

We are worried because for several months now abductions and summary executions have become a national pastime between Christians and Muslims.

Different militias, or 'uncontrollable elements' stop civilians at flying checkpoints and carry out executions after checking people's religions on their identity cards, or *tézékra*.* Some are luckier than others and are kept alive to be used as bargaining chips.

Uncle Zouzou (Ignace's brother) was stopped in front of the Soeurs de Besançon school a few weeks earlier in this sort of situation as he came out of the Central Bank where he worked as a civil servant. Held for several hours while interventions in his favour were worked out (my father and Monseigneur Ziadé, my great-uncle the bishop, were quickly alerted and got in touch with their contacts in West Beirut), he was lucky to be traded for a Muslim.

* Until 2009 Lebanese were required to have their religion listed on their ID cards

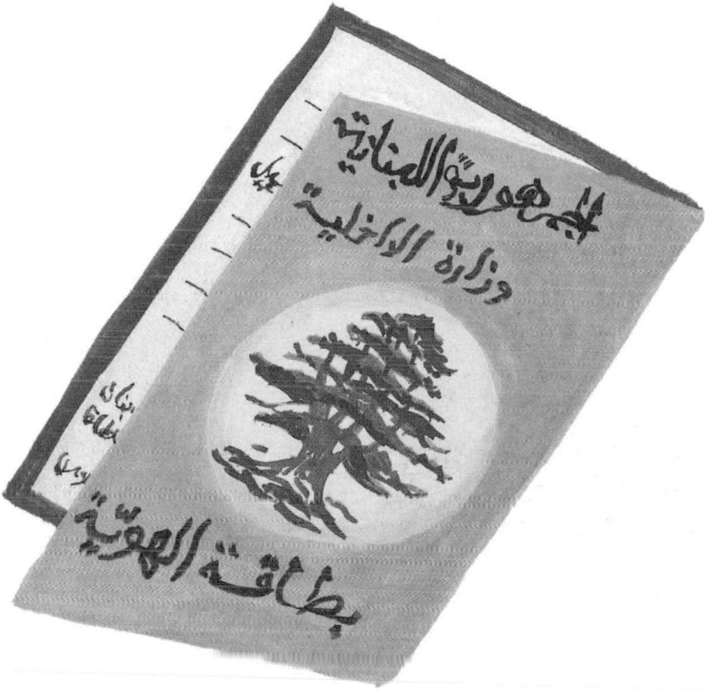
الجمهورية اللبنانية
وزارة الداخلية
بطاقة الهوية

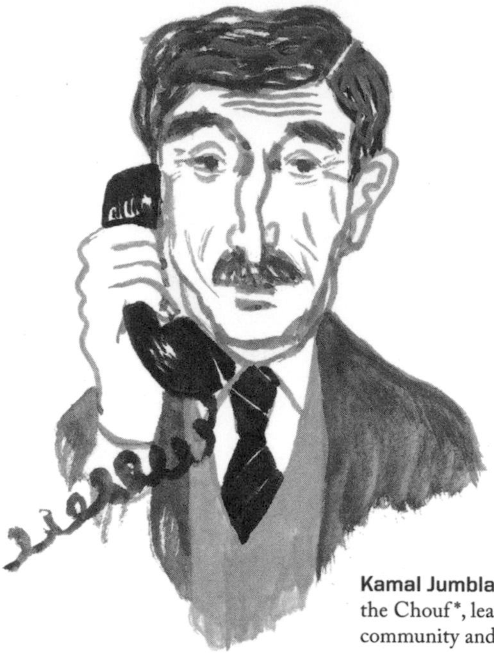

Kamal Jumblatt, Deputy for the Chouf*, leader of the Druze community and of the PSP party.

* Druze area in the mountains

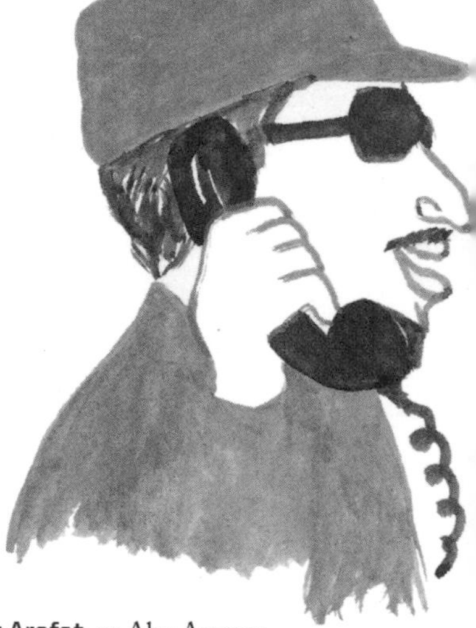

Yasser Arafat, or Abu Ammar, head of Fatah and the PLO.

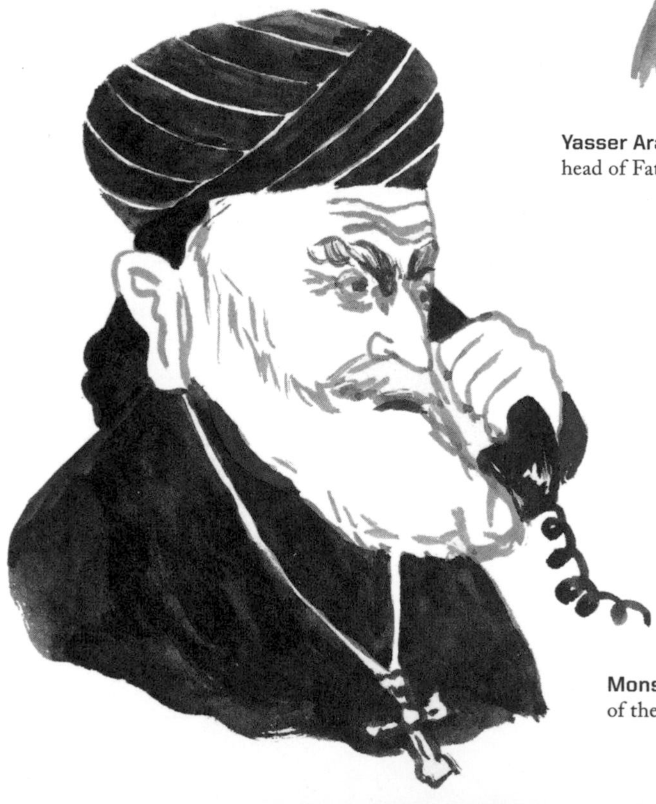

Monseigneur Ziadé, bishop of the Maronite Church of Beirut.

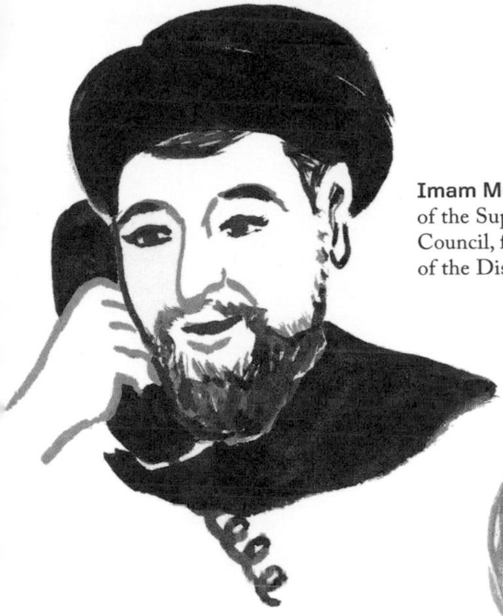

Imam Musa Sadr, head of the Supreme Islamic Shiite Council, founder of Movement of the Disinherited.

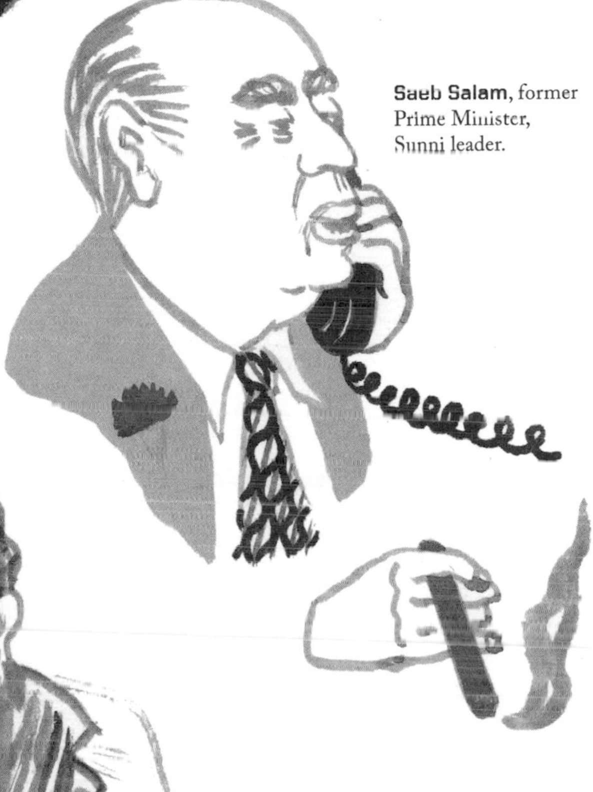

Saeb Salam, former Prime Minister, Sunni leader.

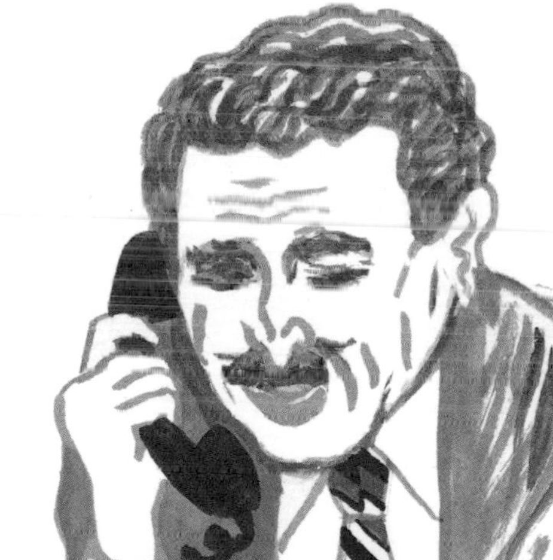

Rashid Karami, MP from Tripoli and Prime Minister.

We are right to be worried about Henri . . . Henri is listed as a Maronite (Christian) on his identity card, but he's really an atheist. Politically left wing – *yassaré* – he is actually closer to his friend Kamal Jumblatt (leader of the progressive socialist forces and a Palestinian ally) than to the right-wing Christians. The 'uncontrollable elements' that drag him out of his car on a lovely afternoon in March 1976 can't be bothered with these nuances.

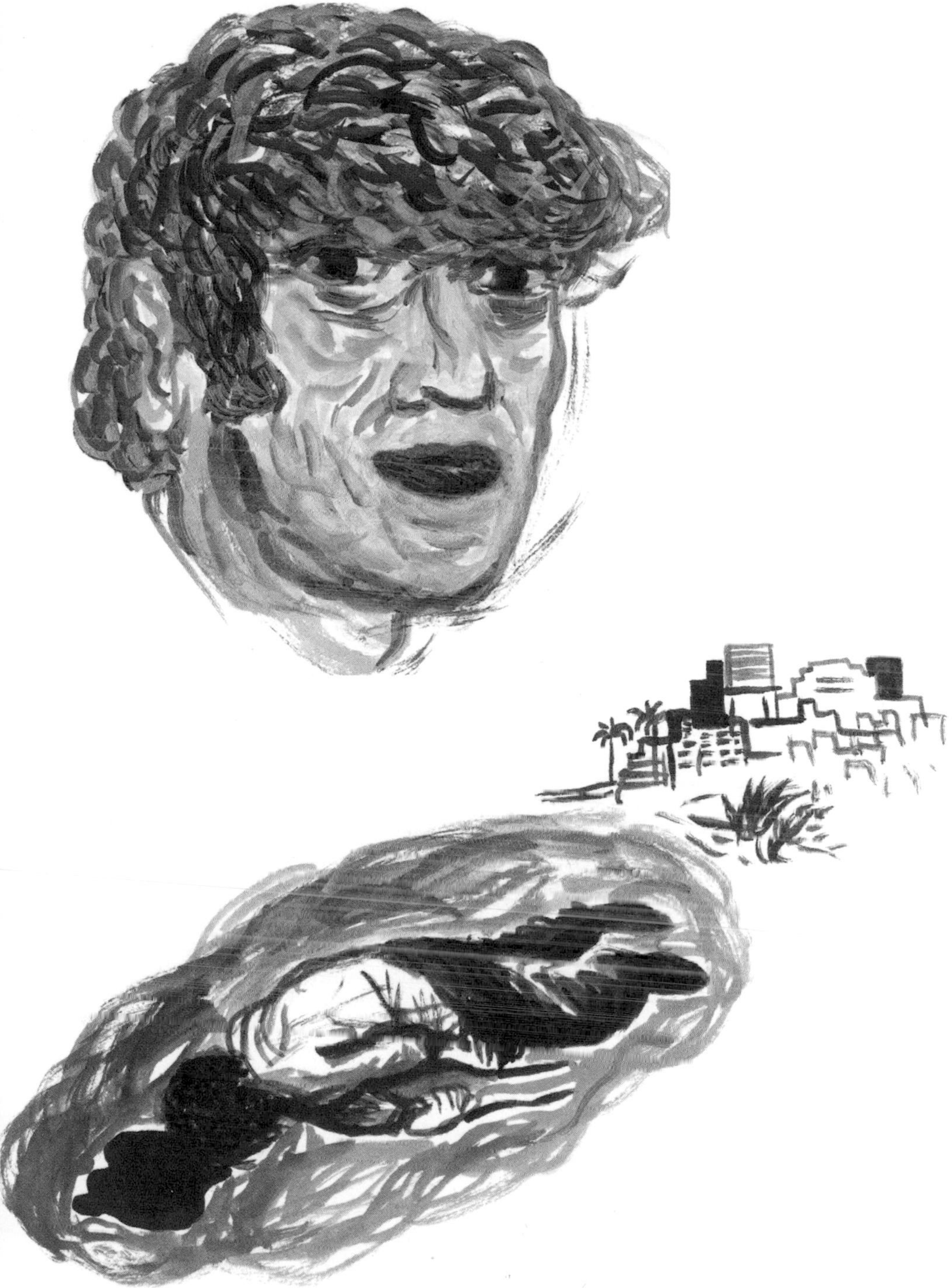

It's during this period that my parents go to spend a few days at the Cavalier Hotel where they will get stuck for several weeks. I think they're the worst weeks of my life.

HC

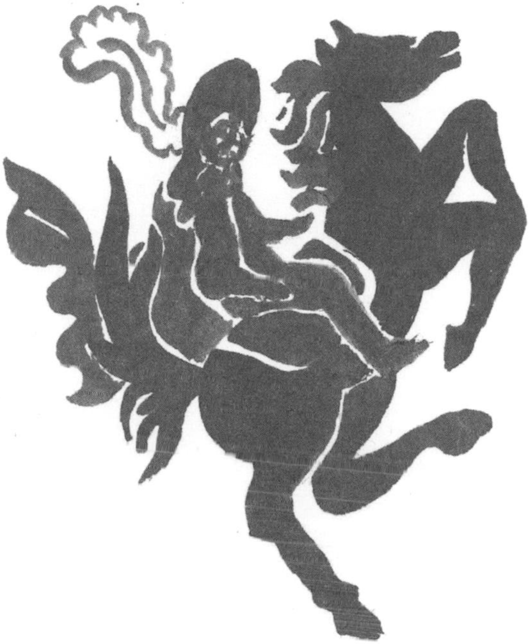

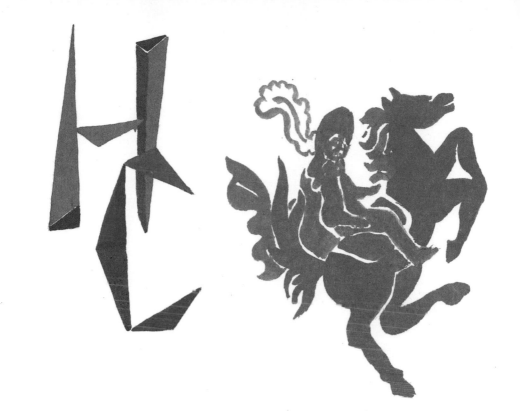

HOTEL CAVALIER

The Cavalier is in the vicinity of Hamra, in Gharbieh near *Al-Nahar*, the prestigious newspaper (Beirut has the reputation of having the freest and best-informed press in the Arab world). The paper's journalists, publisher Ghassan Tuéni and politician Raymond Eddé make the hotel their headquarters; it's the city's nerve centre for political analysis, the centre of the world. My parents have gone there to help Aunt Marcelle who is investigating Henri's disappearance. While they are there, it rapidly becomes an act of suicide to attempt crossing from Gharbieh to Charkieh and my parents are forced to stay longer than expected. They are, it must be said, at the heart of where the information is, and at Raymond Eddé's side. My father is close to Eddé, who is a Presidential candidate.

C

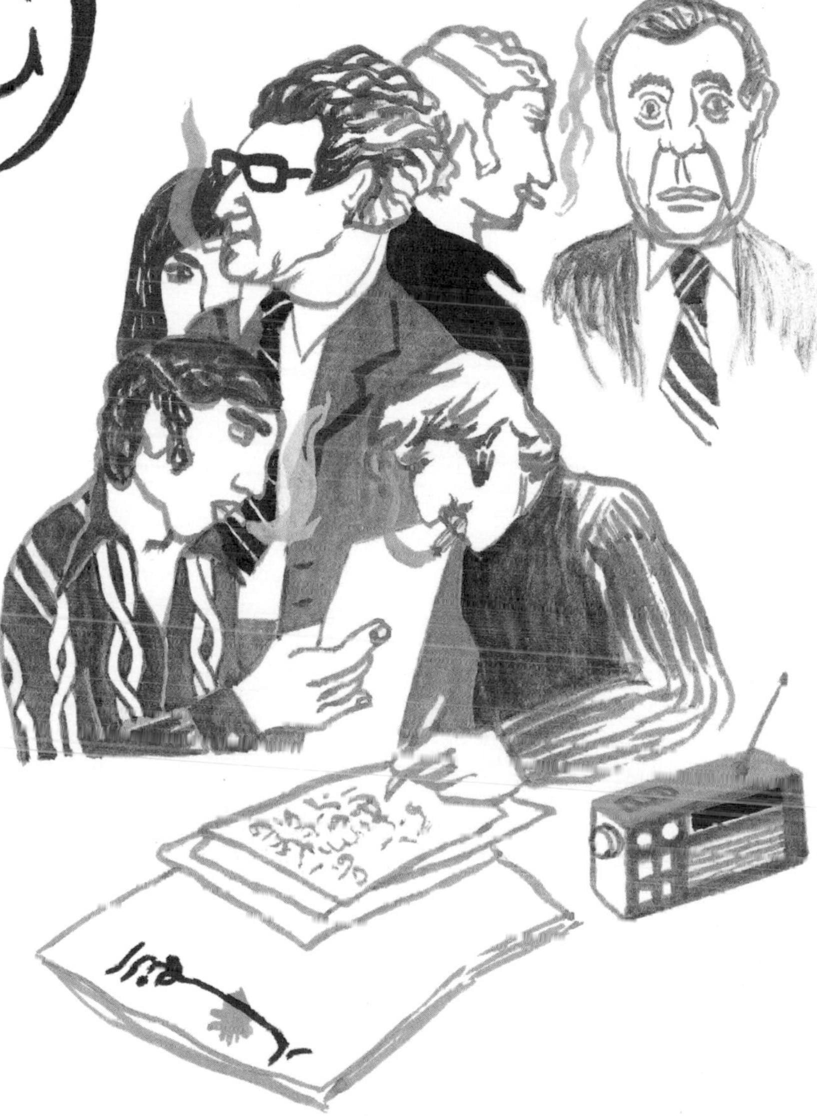

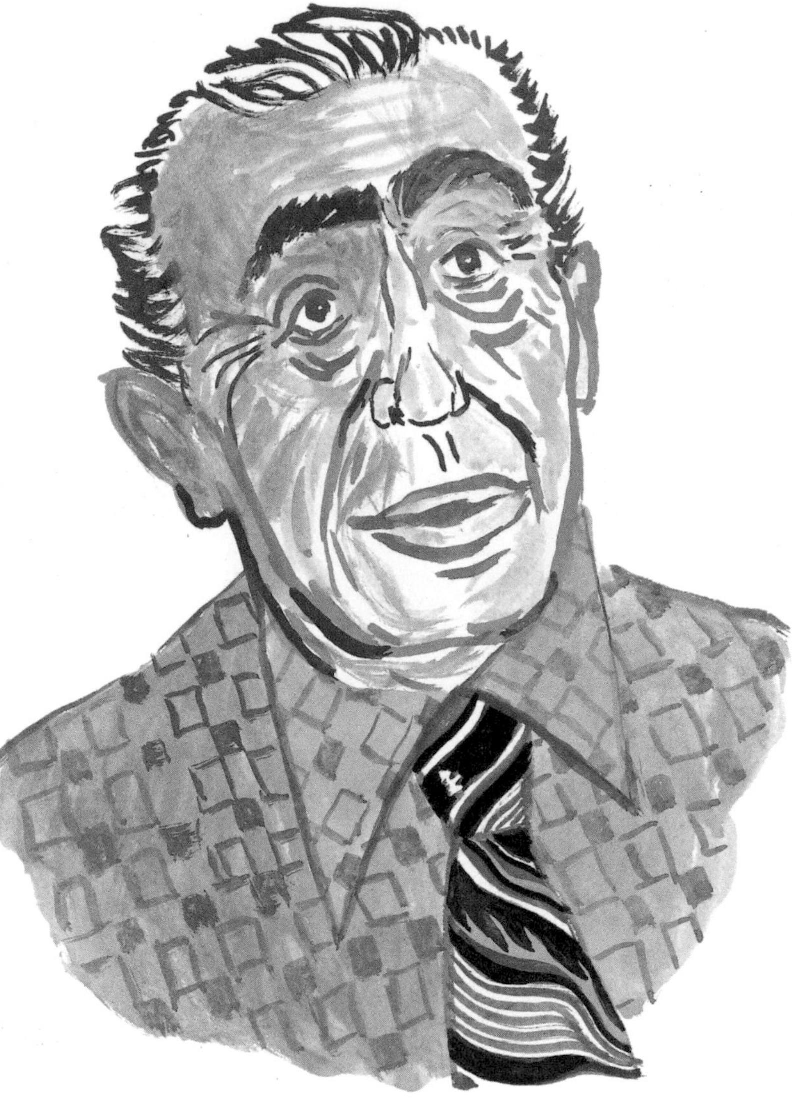

Lebanese voters who think that a political solution can be found without using weapons – in other words, not very many Lebanese – back Raymond Eddé. He is the only major Christian leader who doesn't have his own militia, or an organised system of racketeering. He is on good terms with Muslims, the left wing and the Palestinians. He will go into exile several months after losing the elections and escape three assassination attempts in the Christian region.

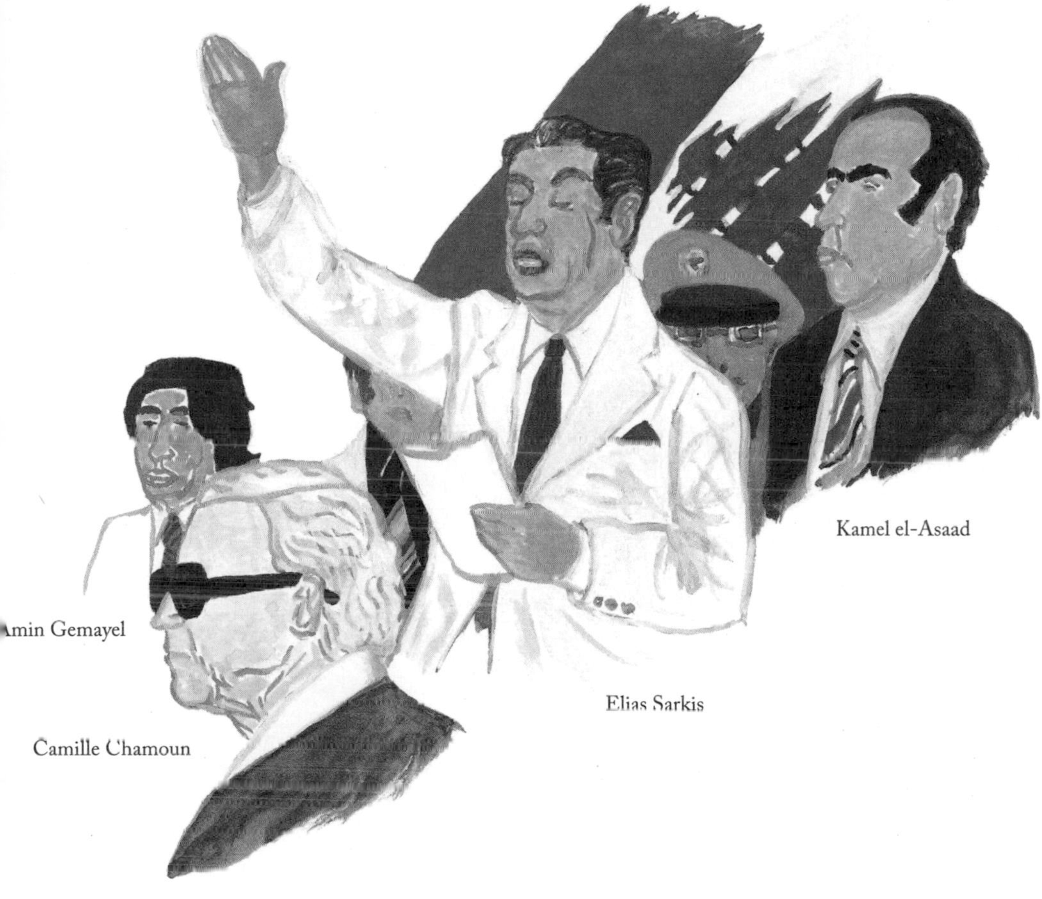
Kamel el-Asaad
Amin Gemayel
Elias Sarkis
Camille Chamoun

The new president, Elias Sarkis (at the time, governor of the Central Bank), will be elected in twenty minutes by a fraction of deputies at the Villa Mansour with rockets raining down around them. While everyone hopes this might be the beginning of the end of the 'crisis', I can still hear my Uncle Zouzou's sceptical sigh as he watches Sarkis on television taking his oath at the Park Hotel in Chtaura. Yet another hotel!

But I'm getting ahead of myself. My parents are still at the Cavalier Hotel, and I'm angry with them. I hate this hotel that has separated me from them in such an awful world. I hate them for having left Walid and me alone in Kattine with my grandmother and Tamar. While the country is ravaged by war they are enjoying themselves at the Cavalier.

Yes, that's what I believe. In my overactive imagination, I am sure that the Cavalier, in the wicked Hamra neighbourhood, is a sort of brothel or a cabaret where people are making merry: dancing, kissing, laughing, feasting and drinking. They've abandoned us and are having fun, forgetting the war, giving us only a passing thought.

I think that their recklessness will be their downfall and that they'll die like Henri – the Cavalier is located in what is hell for me – on the other side of the demarcation line. I'm horribly tormented and unhappy, and am convinced that I will soon become an orphan. New accounts of massacres reach me such as those at Karantina and Damour. Not to mention the famous Battle of the Hotels that is raging at the same time. The Cavalier Hotel isn't in the same neighbourhood (just a few streets away), but at the time, even the word 'hotel' is explosive for me.

There hasn't been a phone call in weeks.

What are Walid and I to become if they never come home?

I can already imagine myself, twenty years later, a tragic beauty like the Egyptian soap-opera actresses that I follow zealously on TV in Tamar's room, returning to the Cavalier to find out what became of them.

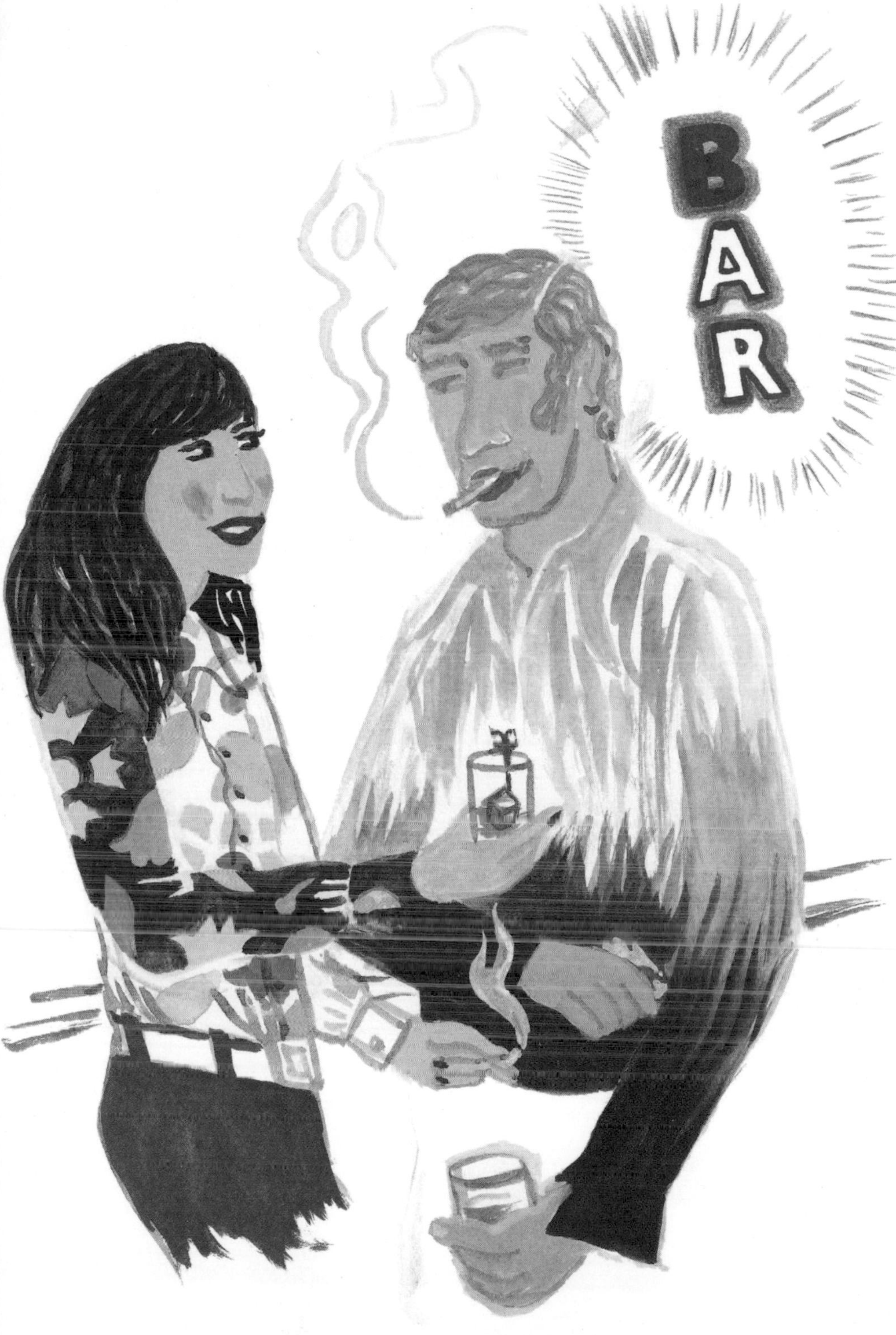
BAR

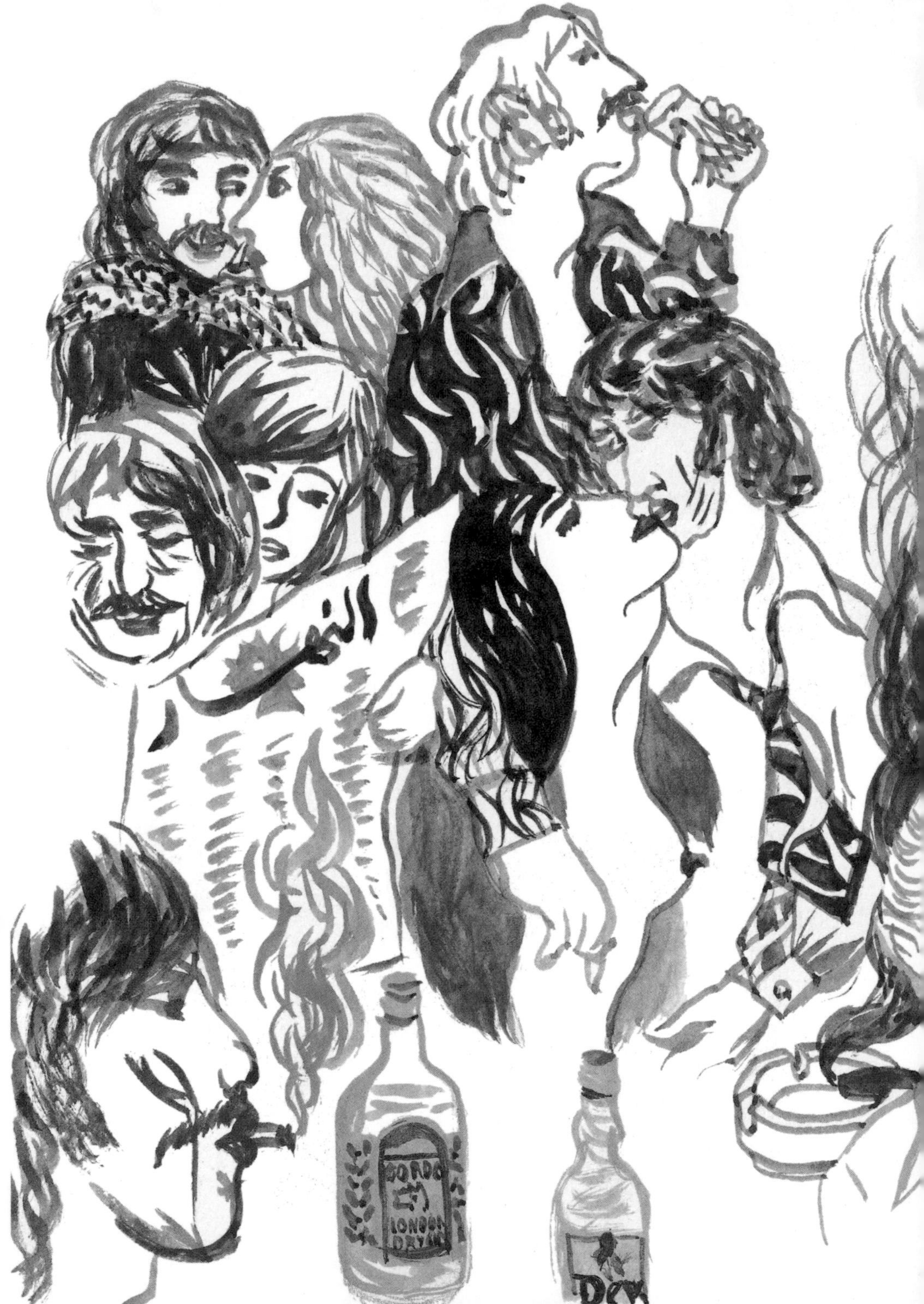
GORDO
LONDON
Dew

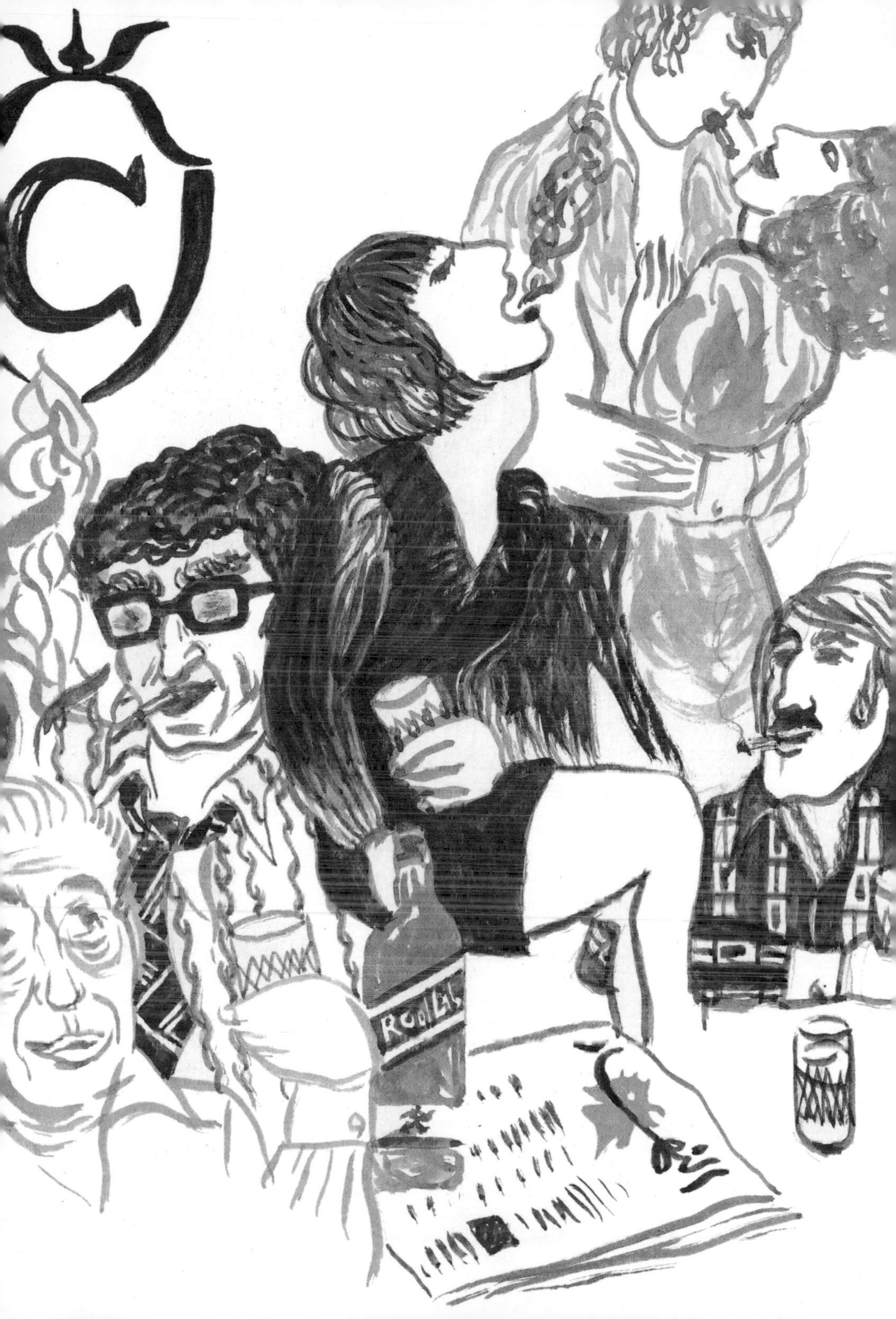

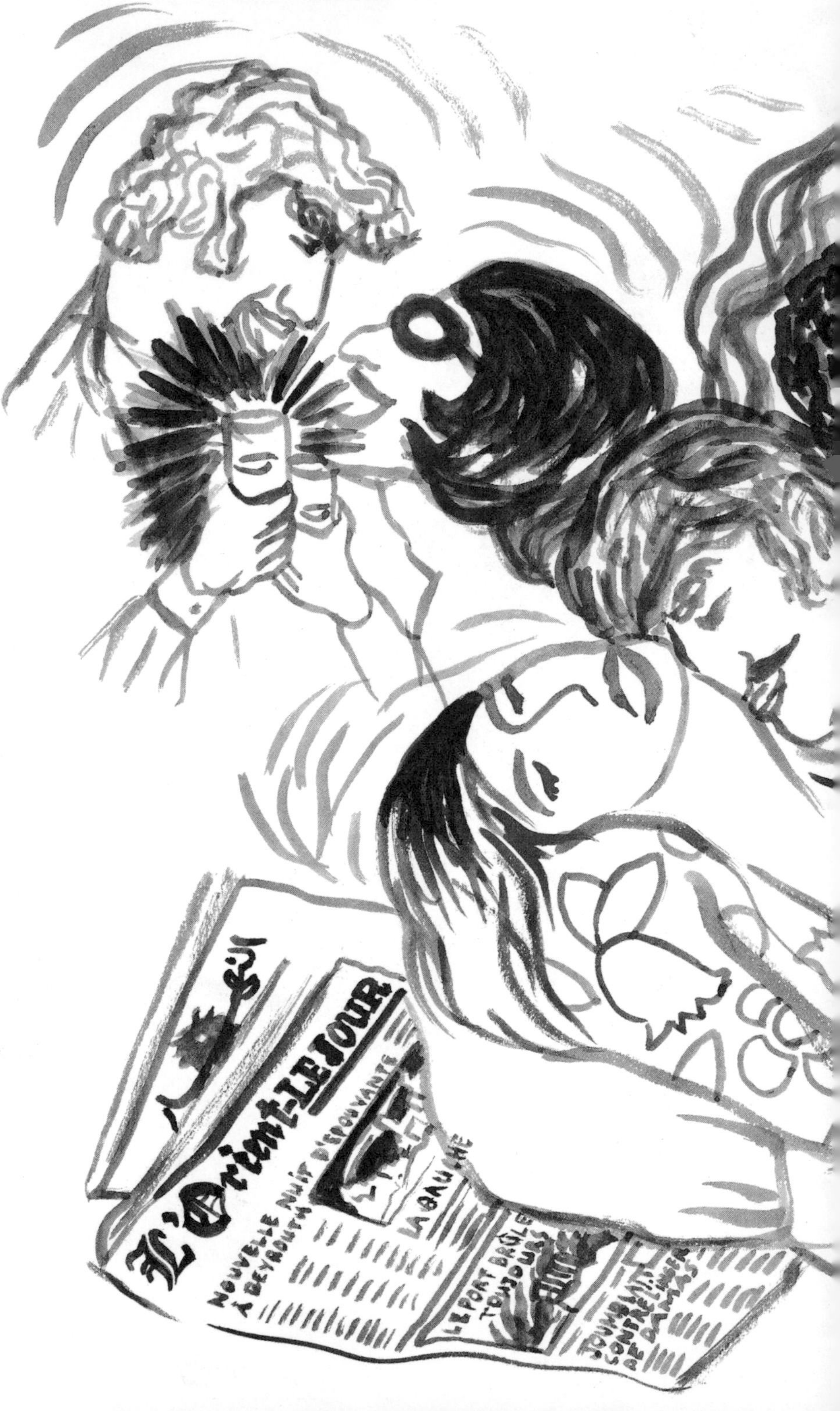
L'Orient-LE JOUR
NOUVELLE NUIT D'ÉPOUVANTE
À BEYROUTH
LE PORT BRÛLE TOUJOURS

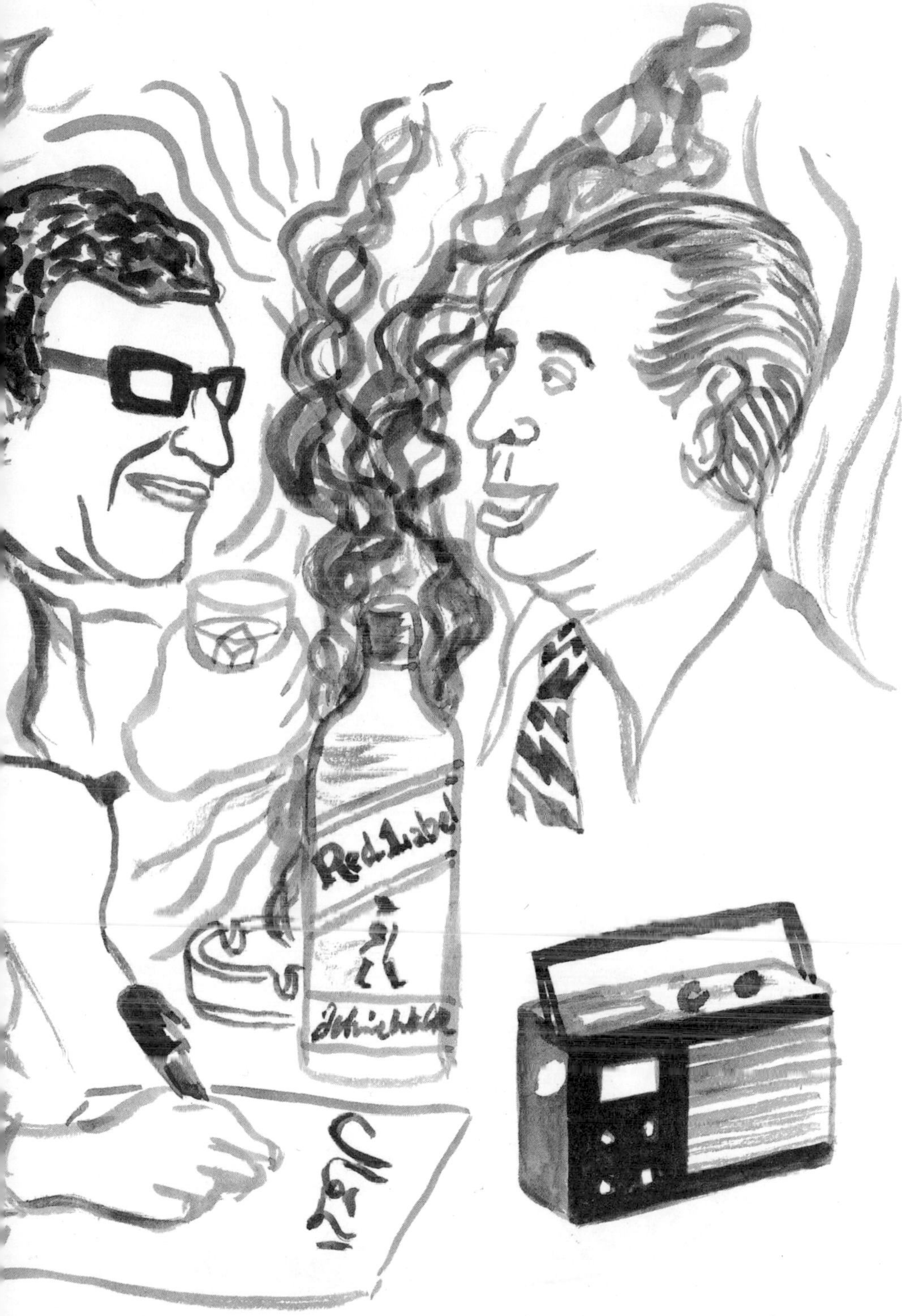
Red Label

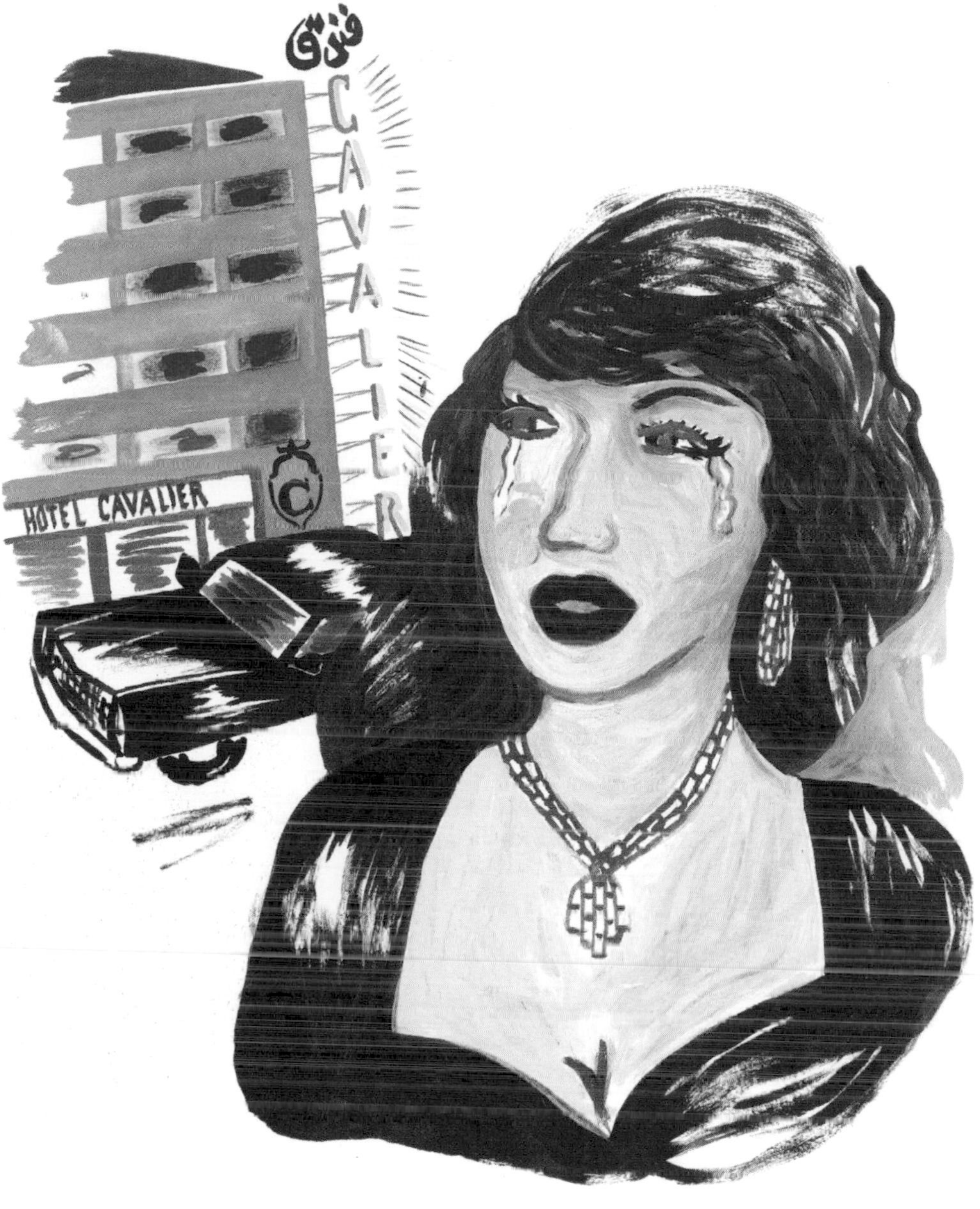
فندق
CAVALIER
HOTEL CAVALIER
C

The era of massacres and terror takes on a new meaning with Black Saturday. Each wave of horror is surpassed by the next. As the months go by, the Lebanese lose hope that all this will one day end. They pack up their bags and depart, leaving the country to the warlords, to the bloodthirsty, and to traffickers of all sorts.

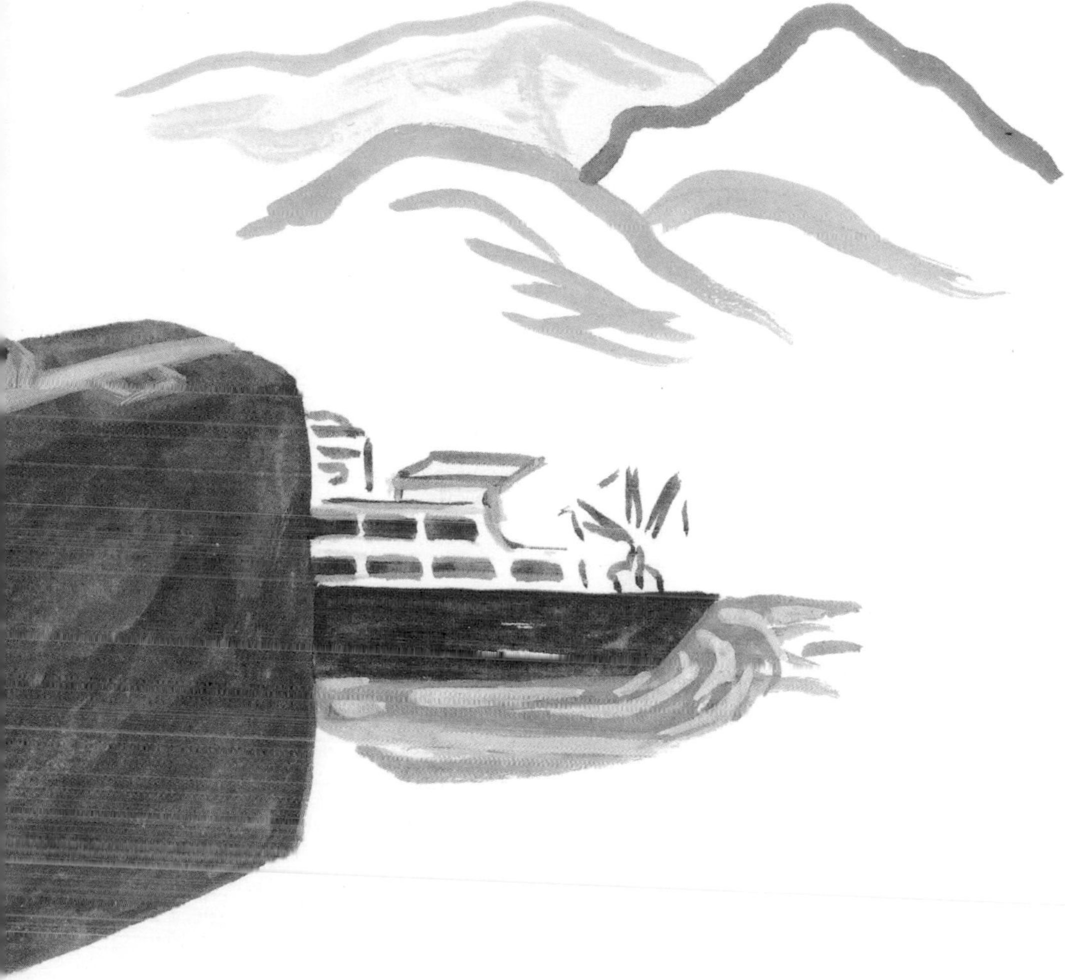

My parents, who have never wanted to emigrate, have finally returned from the Cavalier Hotel. They don't belong to any of the categories mentioned above but to another: suicidal Middle Easterners.

This means that my childhood will be regulated by a pattern of dreadful events, the most memorable being Black Saturday, *El-sabt-al-Aswad*, 6 December, 1975.

In response to the axe murder of four Phalangists the night before, two hundred Muslims are slaughtered by the Kataeb in the Christian area of Beirut.

This particular Saturday is qualified as black because it happens at the beginning of the war and is the first massacre of this type and magnitude. Later, there will be far more dismal days but they'll no longer be called 'black'.

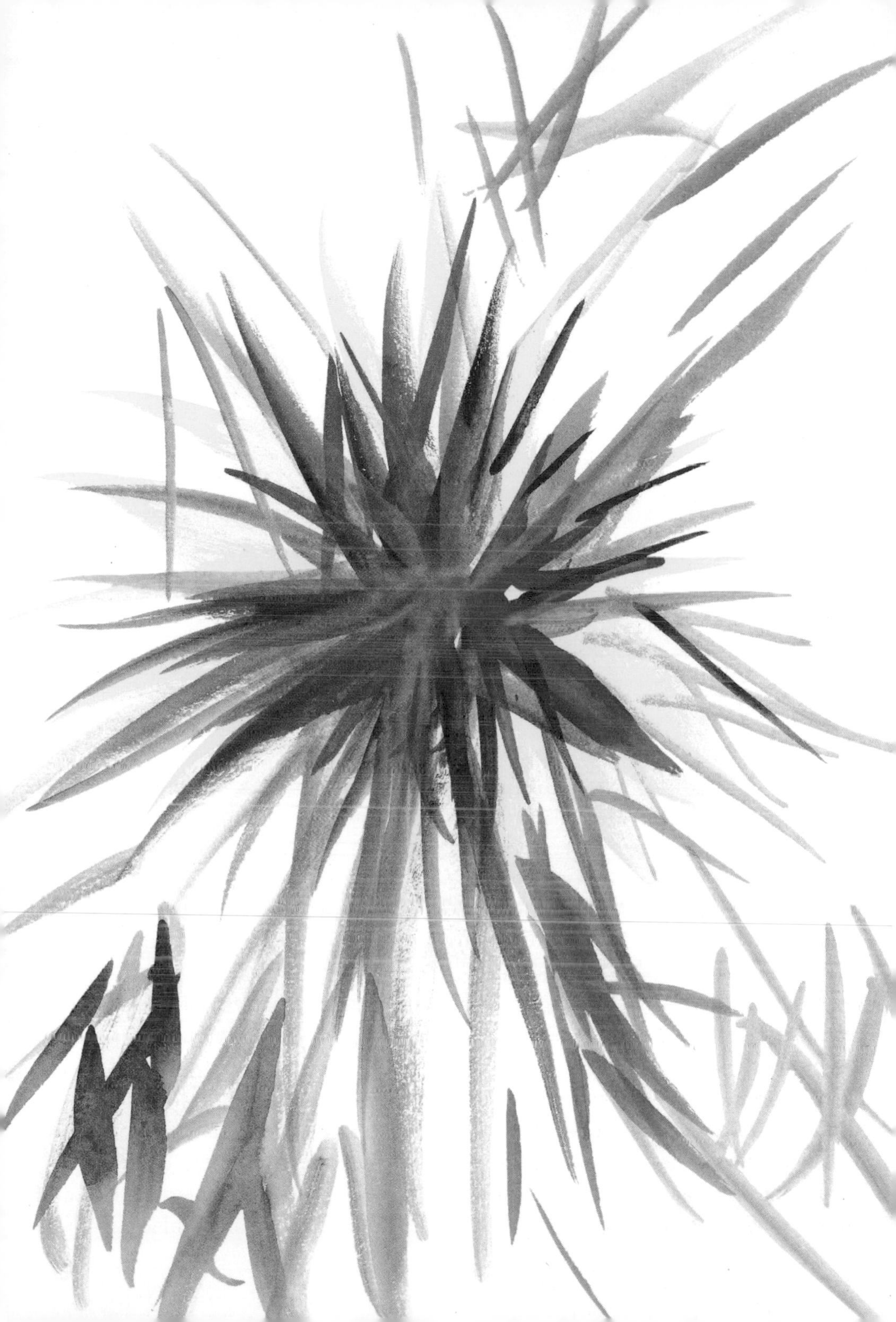

The *Karantina* (Quarantine) massacre, 19 January, 1976.

The Kataeb burn and raze the Karantina camp then break out the champagne. 1000 people are massacred. 25,000 become refugees. This squalid, poverty-stricken slum, infiltrated by the *Fedayeen,* is located on the northern outskirts of Beirut along the coastal road we take to go to our house in Kattine. *Krad* (Kurds), Palestinian and Lebanese refugees from the south live here.

This Palestinian-held bastion in an exclusively Christian region had become a threat and a problem for the Kataeb, which could not effectively control the northern passage out of Beirut.

It's my favourite part of the journey on the way to Kattine. I like the fluorescent colours of the women's headscarves, the sweet and acid colours of the children's T-shirts, the sheets and towels drying in the sun, the children playing barefoot whom I envy, the young girls who look like heroines out of a romantic novel, the eucalyptus trees that cast gigantic shadows onto shacks made of wood, cinderblocks and corrugated sheet metal, where I would have loved to play hide-and-seek.

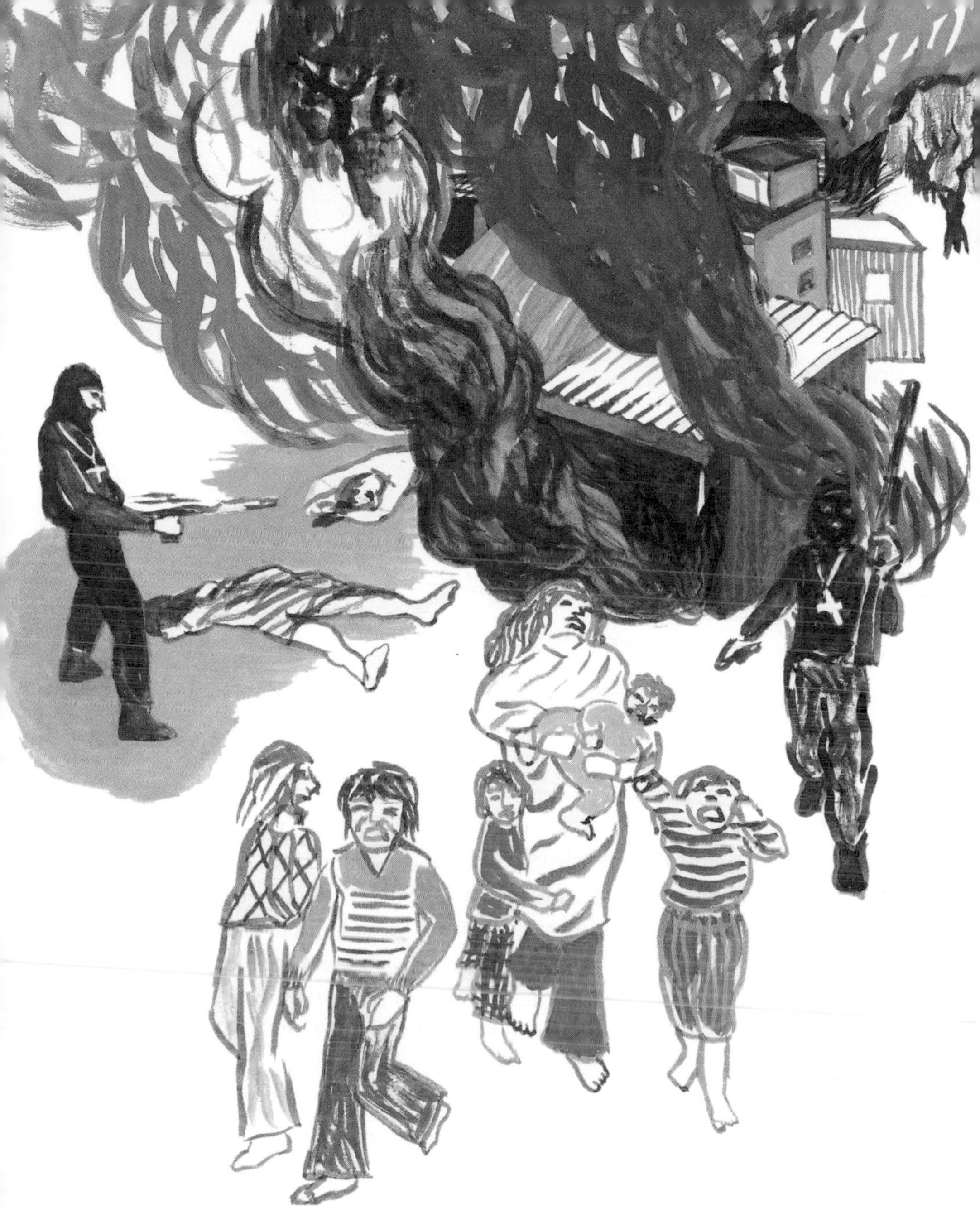

When we return to Beirut after the massacre, driving past the razed camp that has become an immense wasteland, I feel heartbroken and ashamed, ignorant little rich girl that I am, to have envied the lives of those poor children.

Then Tamar says: 'The Kataeb finally cleaned out the Palestinian riff-raff from Karantina!'

I'm overwhelmed, and don't know what to think.

Maybe I've got it all wrong. Are the bad people the children wearing the multi-coloured clothes and the good people the armed, hooded militia?

Snuggled in the back seat of the car with my eyes glued to the lifeless, empty expanse of land, for the first time I want someone to explain things to me. But I don't ask Tamar.

As soon as I get to Beirut, where my parents have already arrived, I rush into my father's office. 'Is it true that the Palestinians in Karantina were scum? And what are Palestinians anyway?'

He closes the door and right then and there I get a short, age-appropriate geopolitical class on the Middle East. Palestine, the English bastards, Balfour, Zionism, Jerusalem, the King David Hotel, David Ben-Gurion, the state of Israel, refugees, the Israeli bastards, the settlers, the camps, Gamal Abdel Nasser, the Six-Day War, Moshe Dayan, the Yom Kippur War, Hussein of Jordan, Black September, the PLO, the American bastards, terrorism, armed struggle, the weakness of Lebanon, the mistakes the Palestinians made, the Christian fears, the beginning of the war . . .

I would have loved to learn that the Palestinians were actually the bad guys; it would have been so much easier. At eight I had entered a complex world filled with contradictions and nuances, Lebanon being one of the best examples on the planet of this.

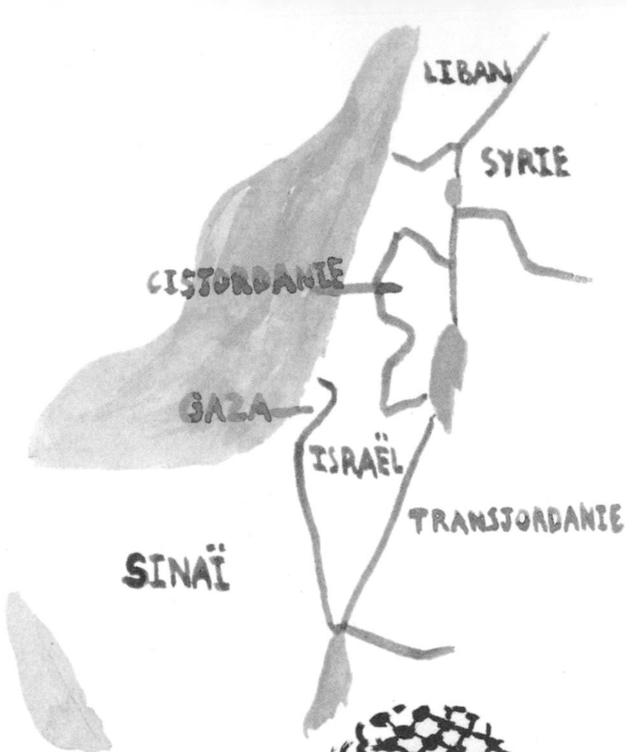
LIBAN
SYRIE
CISJORDANIE
GAZA
ISRAËL
TRANSJORDANIE
SINAÏ

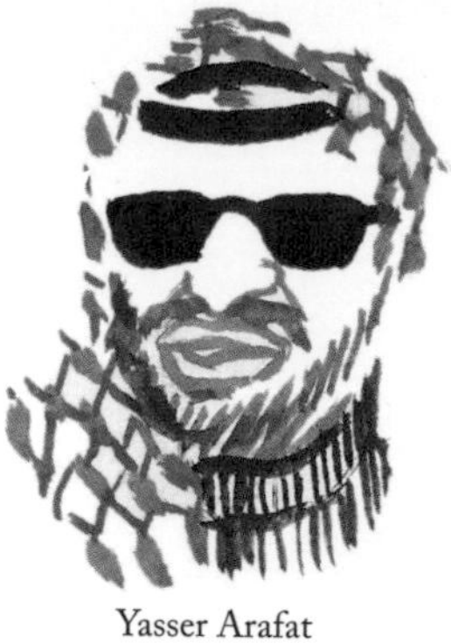
Yasser Arafat

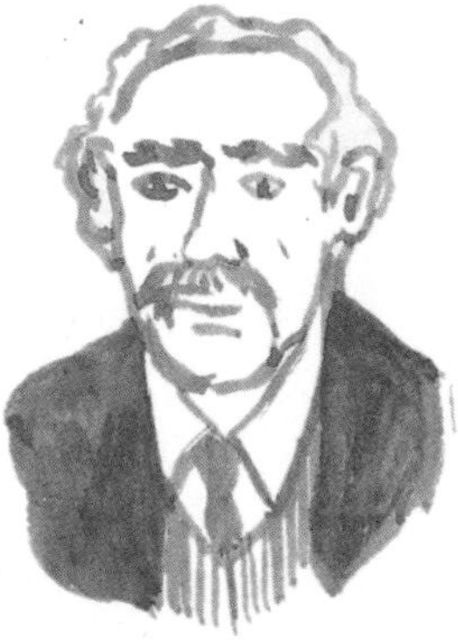
Arthur Balfour

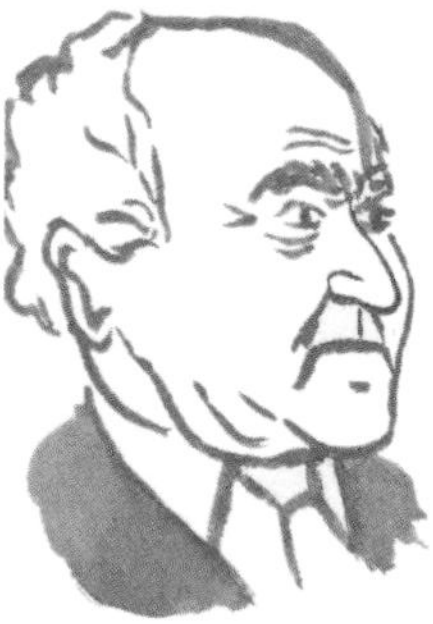
David Ben Gurion

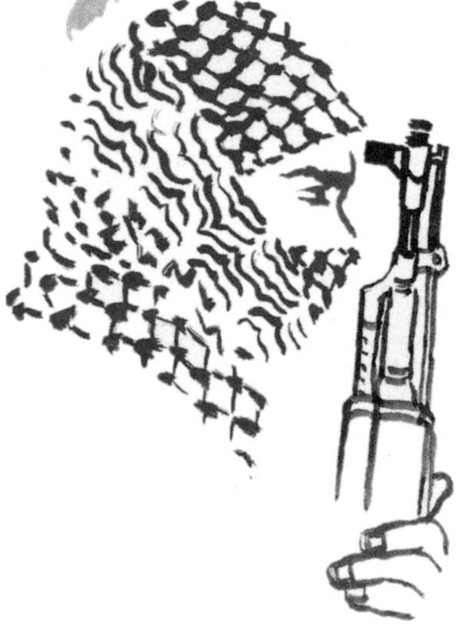

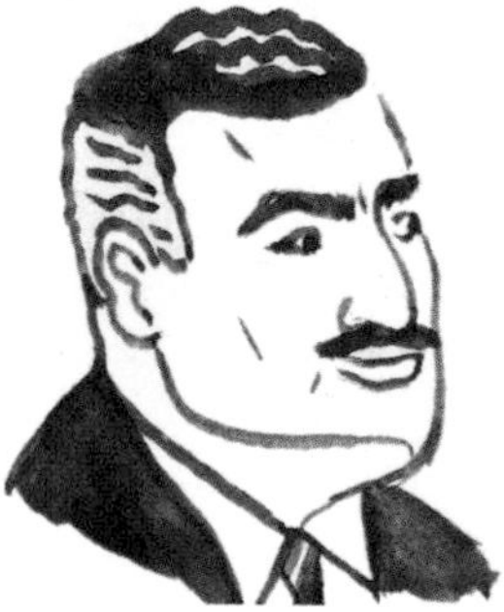
Gamal Abdel Nasser

فَلِسْطِين

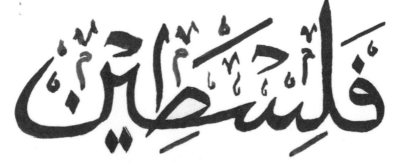

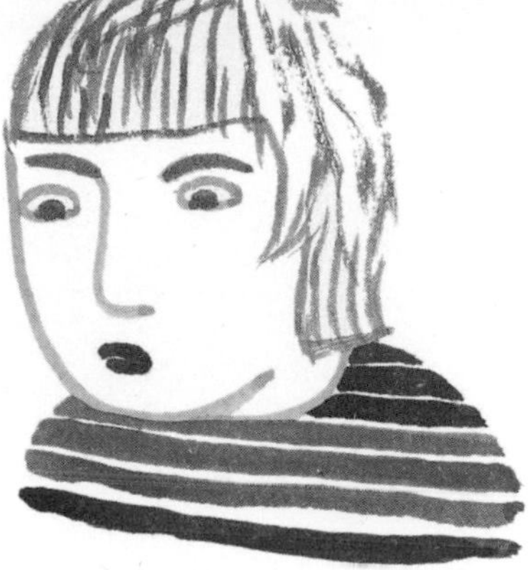

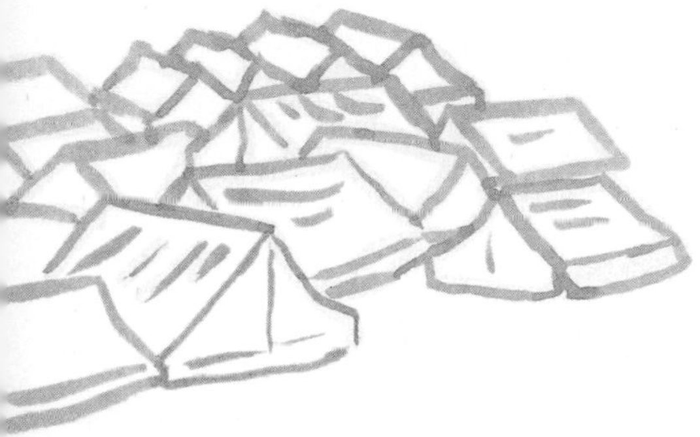

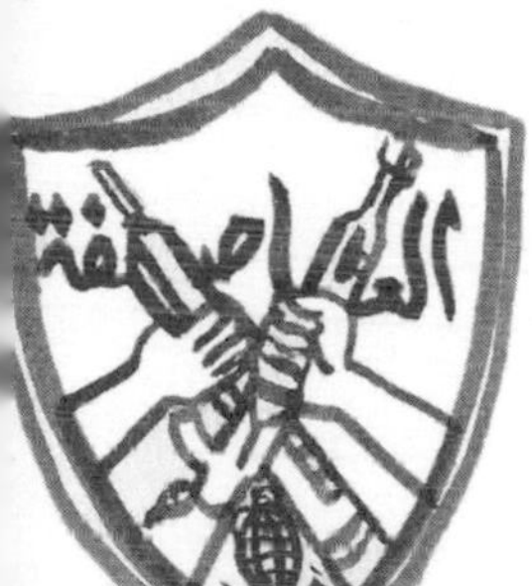
العاصفة

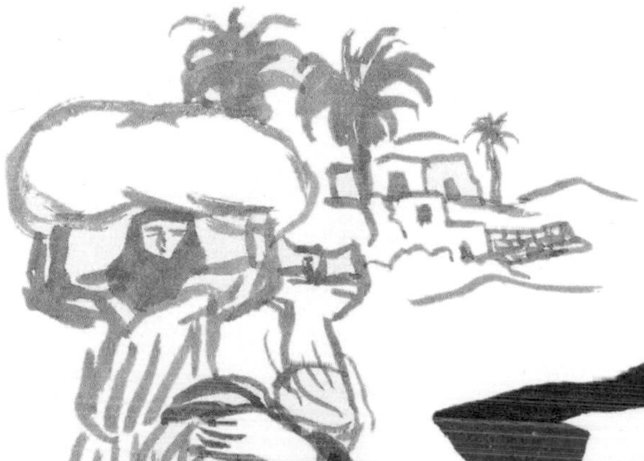

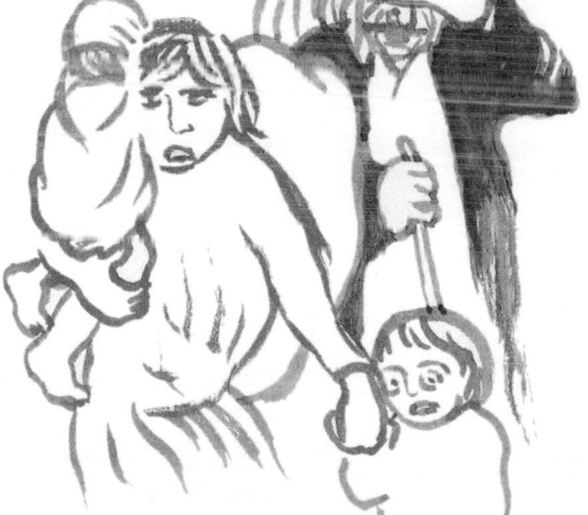

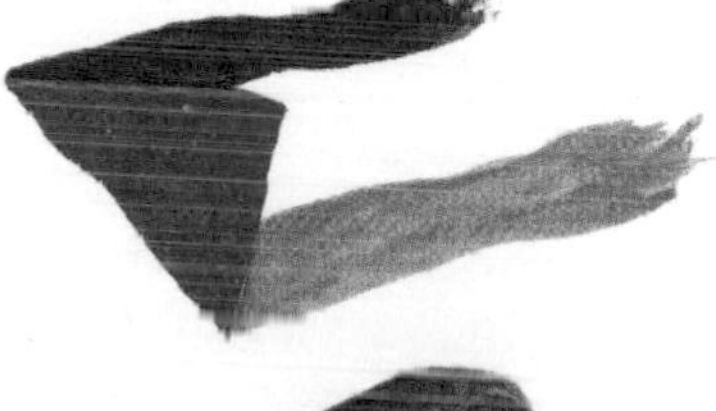

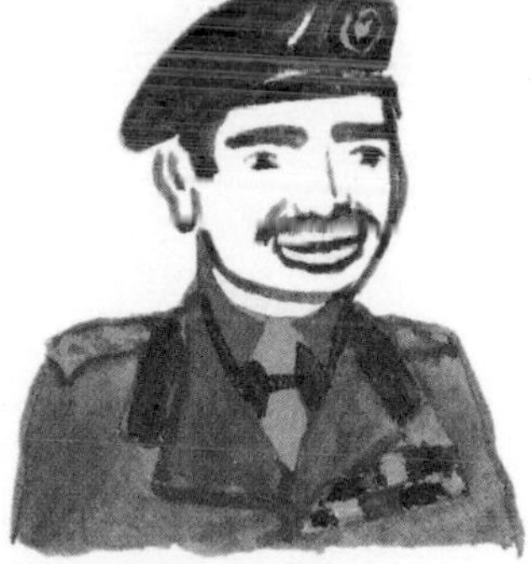

King Hussein of Jordan

20 January, 1976, two days after *Karantina*, there's the Damour massacre: retaliation.

The Palestinian-leftists and mostly the Saiqa sack and destroy the affluent Christian village of Damour, south of Beirut, massacring 500 people. My father's cousins, whom I know only by their surname, Chkaibane, are alive but have lost everything else: their beautiful houses, their orange groves, thousands of banana trees. They flee towards Saida, travelling across Lebanon (Saadiiat, Jezzine, the Bekaa valley, the Cedars, Batroun . . .) Two or three families arrive in Kattine one morning and stay with us for several months.

They're like refugees from the camps; everything that they have left is packed on the roof of their car. It's April and my parents are still at the Cavalier. When I see all these fleeing strangers arrive I am frantic. If everyone is escaping from the dangerous areas to come take refuge in Kattine, why aren't my parents doing the same? Are they already dead or are they having too much fun in Hamra?

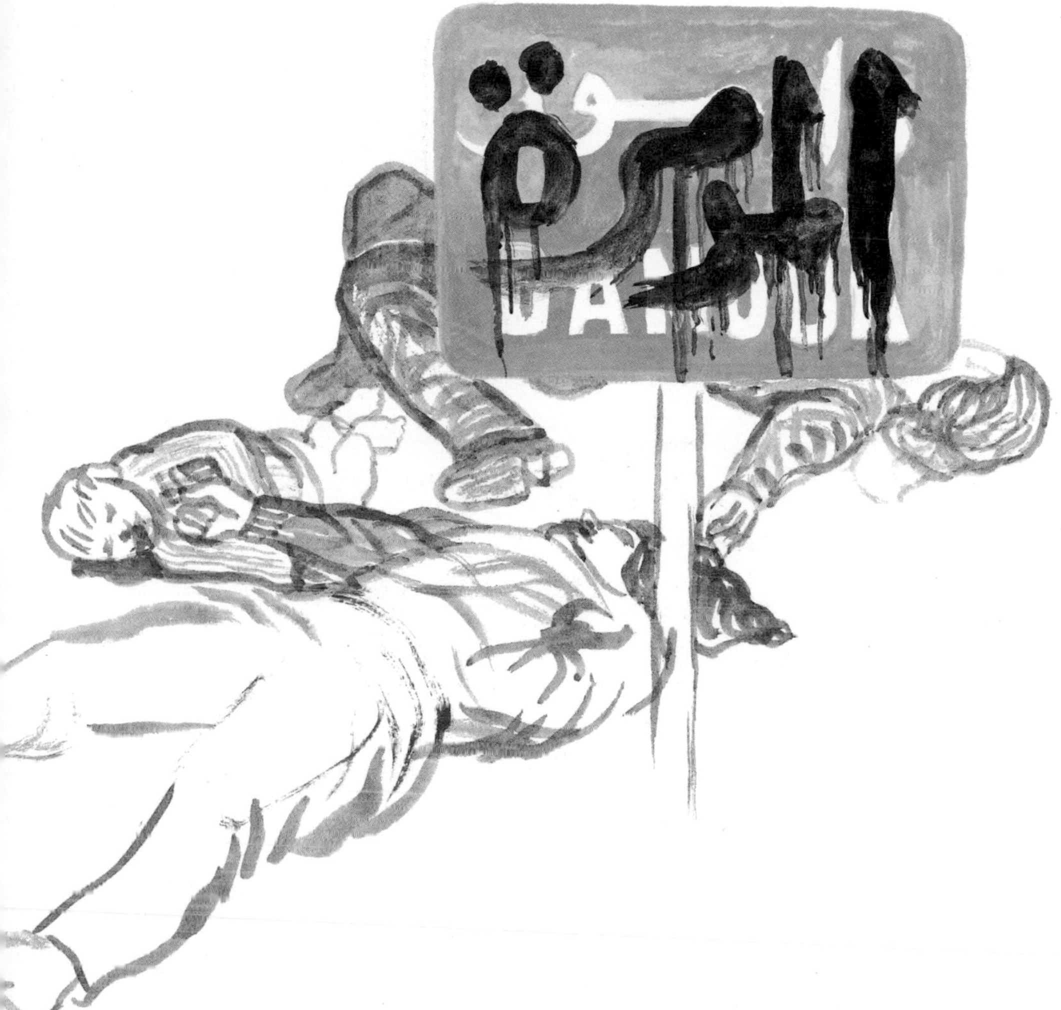

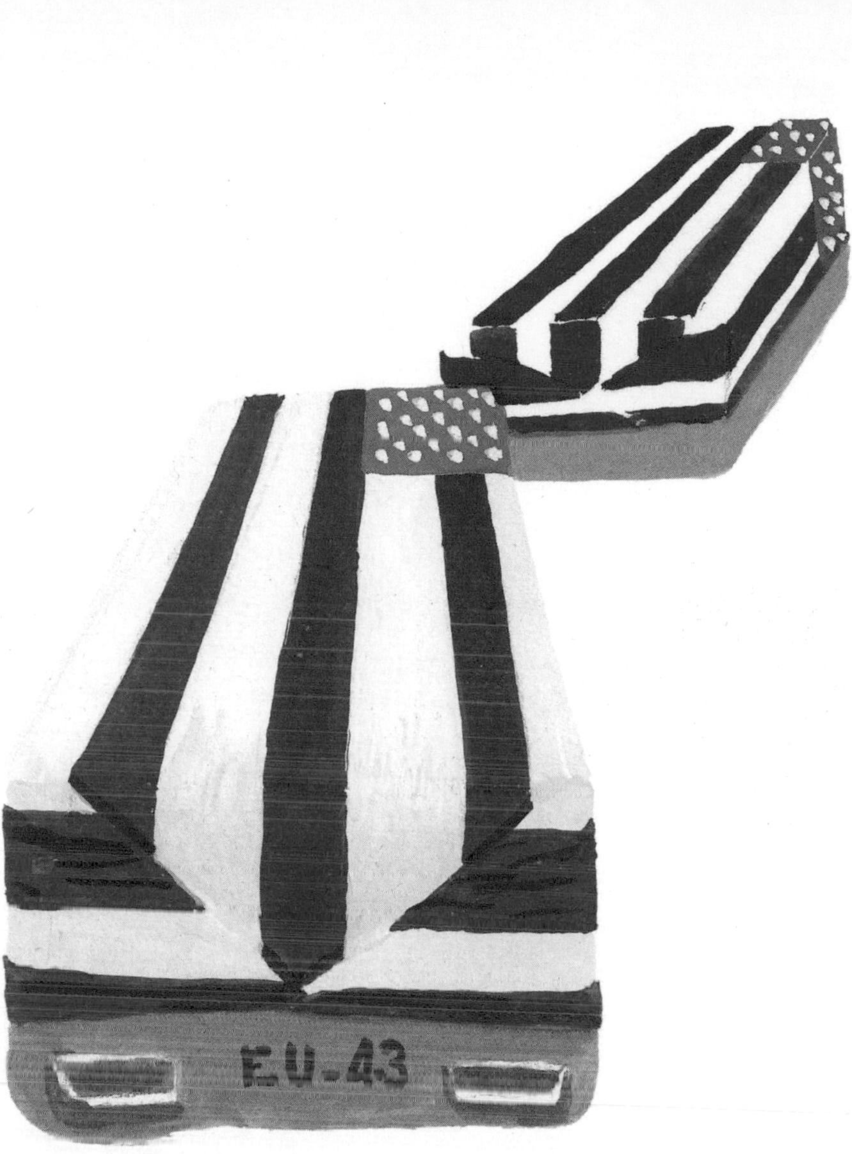
EU-43

27 May, 1976: the assassination of Kamal Jumblatt's sister, Linda al-Atrache, at her home in the Christian area.

16 June,1976: the assassination of US Ambassador Francis Meloy, his economics counsellor and his chauffeur, slaughtered at the 'Museum Crossing' – the passage between east and west.

The list of assassinated dignitaries will be long. Journalists, ambassadors, Lebanese politicians, Palestinian officials . . .

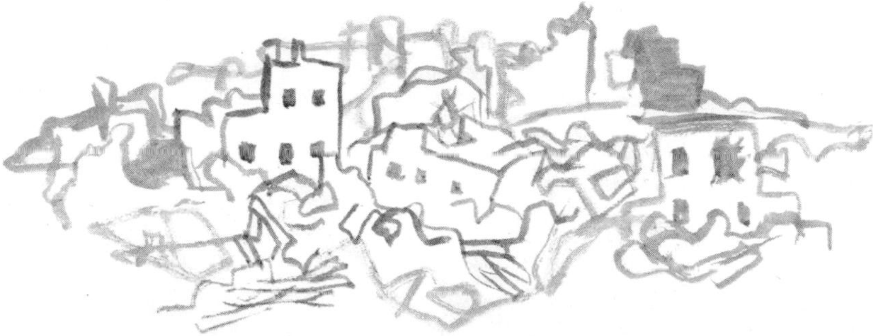

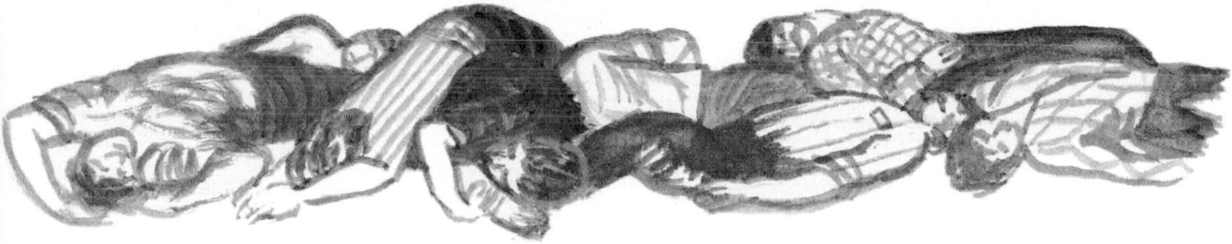

The day after my ninth birthday, on 12 August, 1976, the Palestinian camp Tal al-Zaatar falls, after a terrible, fifty-three-day siege. 2,500 are killed.

None of my school friends can come over but my mother still wants to have a little party and invites stupid children that I don't know, the daughters of her friends or other exiles in the Kattine area. Since then I have always hated my birthday.

On 16 March, 1977, a few days before I go through the motions of my first communion, Kamal Jumblatt is assassinated in the Chouf region. No one in my family circle feels obliged to impress upon me the existence of God (except the priest, perhaps, but I can't remember).

The ceremony takes place in the underground parking lot of an abandoned building used by my substitute school, the Athénée – we can no longer get to Nazareth. It's the type of place where little girls get raped, not where they meet the good Lord.

On 14 March, 1978 more than 20,000 Israeli soldiers, supported by planes, land and marine artillery as well as tanks, occupy one-tenth of Lebanon in less than twenty-four hours. Hundreds of Palestinians and Lebanese are killed and thousands are wounded. The destruction is enormous and 120,000 refugees stream towards the north where they end up in tents and on the pavement in Saida or west Beirut.

The tragedy in the south continues, Menachem Begin is hell-bent on his mission. My parents seem panic-stricken but I don't really understand why. These days it's calm in our area and the south seems so far away, we hardly hear the bombings, just the fighter jets in the sky . . .

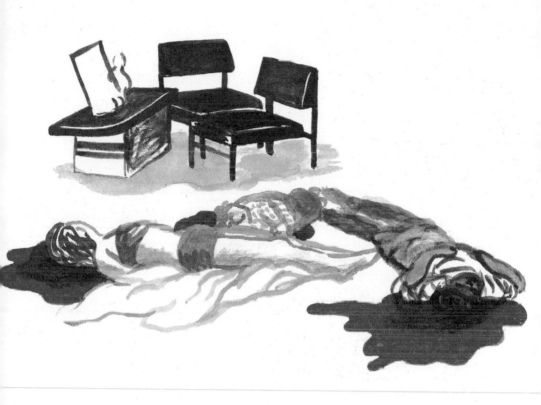

*Majzaret Ehden.** On 13 June, 1978, Tony Frangieh (the son of President Frangieh), his wife, his daughter, his henchmen and his dog are assassinated in Ehden. A new development has begun – from now on Christians massacre each other. The Christian region is divided into two enemy camps.

* Ehden massacre

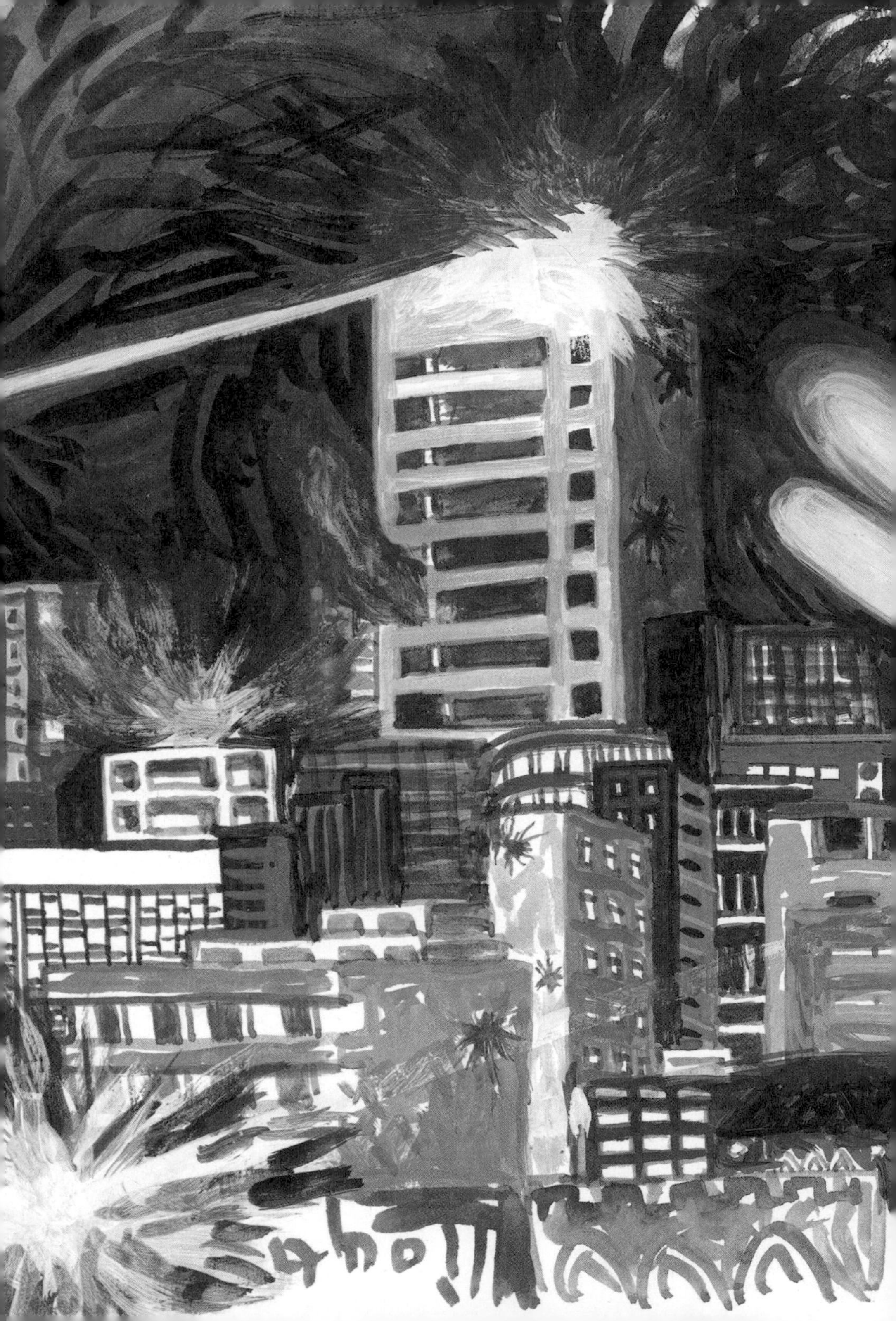

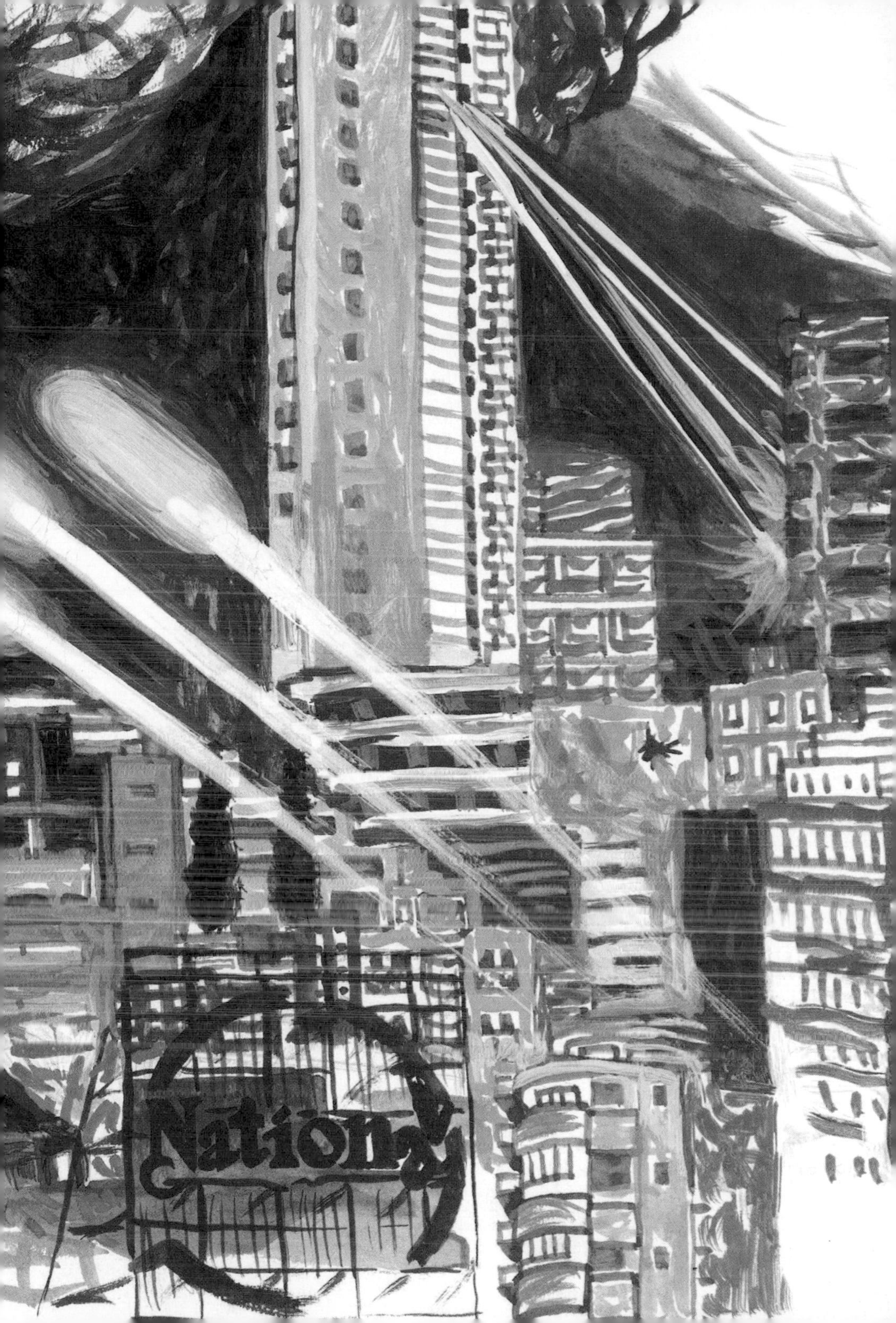
National

The list of assassinations and massacres is long, still very long. It creates an atmosphere of dread and anguish that we live with daily. But for me what is most traumatic is the shelling – the indiscriminate shelling of the city. I can't even recover between ceasefires.

Like everyone else, I am now able to decrypt the 'departure' and 'arrival' blasts that leave us shaken each time and that terrify me. So too the ear-splitting whistle that accompanies the trajectory of a shell, which is supposed to be reassuring because it means the shell has passed over you and will therefore not fall on top of you. Even though I know this, I'm petrified; jelly-legs and dry-mouth at each whistle. I'm goosepimpled, my stomach tied into knots, my heart in my throat and my feet like lead. For sure, it's more 'comforting' to hear the muffled blast of a 'departure' since these are the shells our side is firing at the others. The explosions of the 'arrivals' are the worst since these are the shells fired by those just across the way, shells that land right next to us..

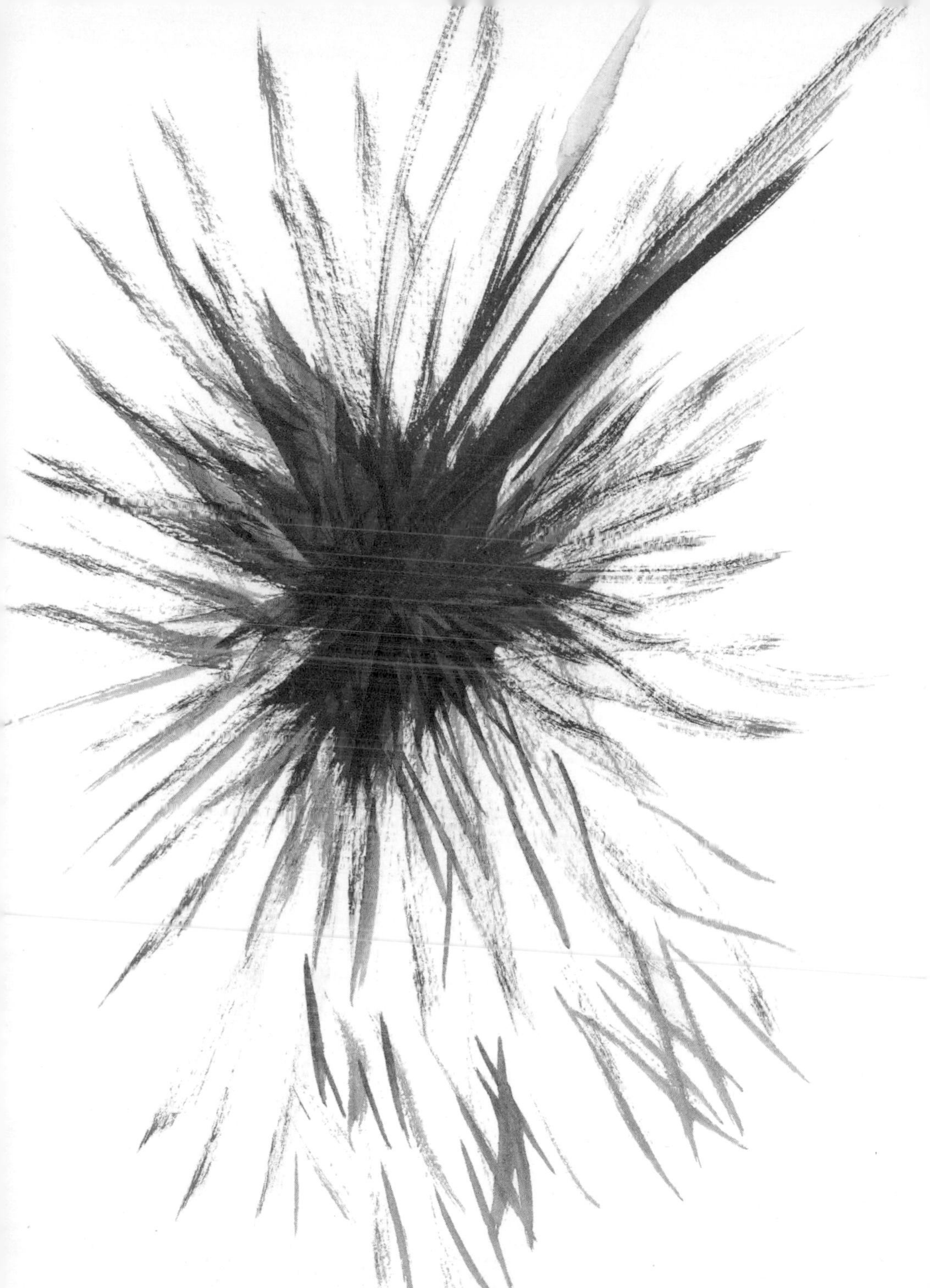

Of course, sometimes we hear the departures and arrivals of the same shell, usually when it's a little farther away and just an 'artillery exchange' that we're not directly involved in.

That said, the departure noise that 'our' artillery makes isn't necessarily reassuring. If it's too close, then the others will be able to locate where the firing is coming from and will be able to retaliate. For example: if the shells that are meant to land in West Beirut are fired from the parking lot next to our building or from the empty lot just behind, then we will have a real reason to be worried since those just opposite us will 'send it back on top of us'.

Another logical way of thinking is that when one hears the departure of an enemy shell it cannot be dangerous, because the shells travel faster than the speed of sound. When one hears it depart, it has already landed, and is not 'on top of us' since we are still alive and can hear it.

In the end, one might think that all these noises we hear are more or less reassuring as long as we can hear them, and that there's really no reason to worry.

Then there are those, like Walid, a good little boy, 'hal azaar, rascal', says Tamar, who can recognise and name, simply from the sound, the different pieces of artillery that are being used – It's a *Haouen*, a *155*, a *Dushka* – the way one might recognise flowers by their smell: jasmine, marigolds, snapdragons or chrysanthemums.

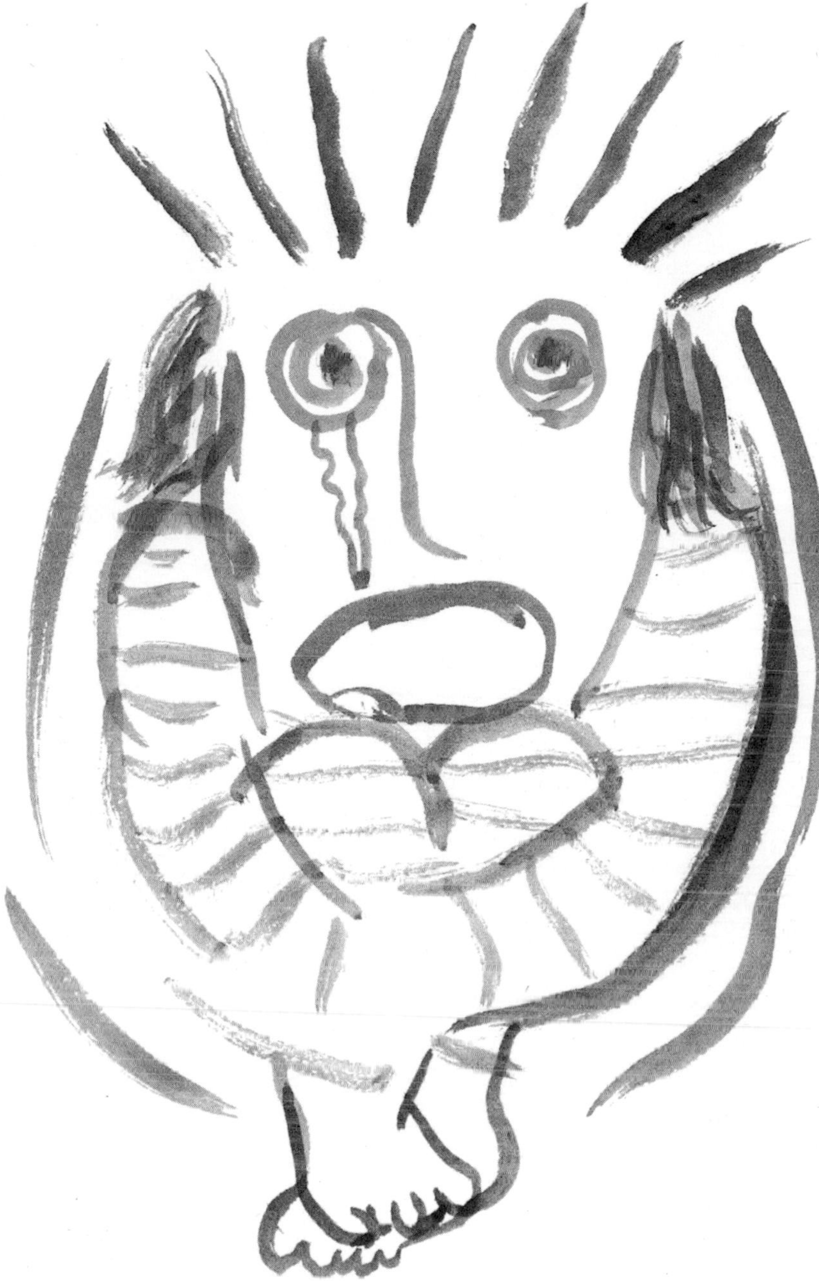

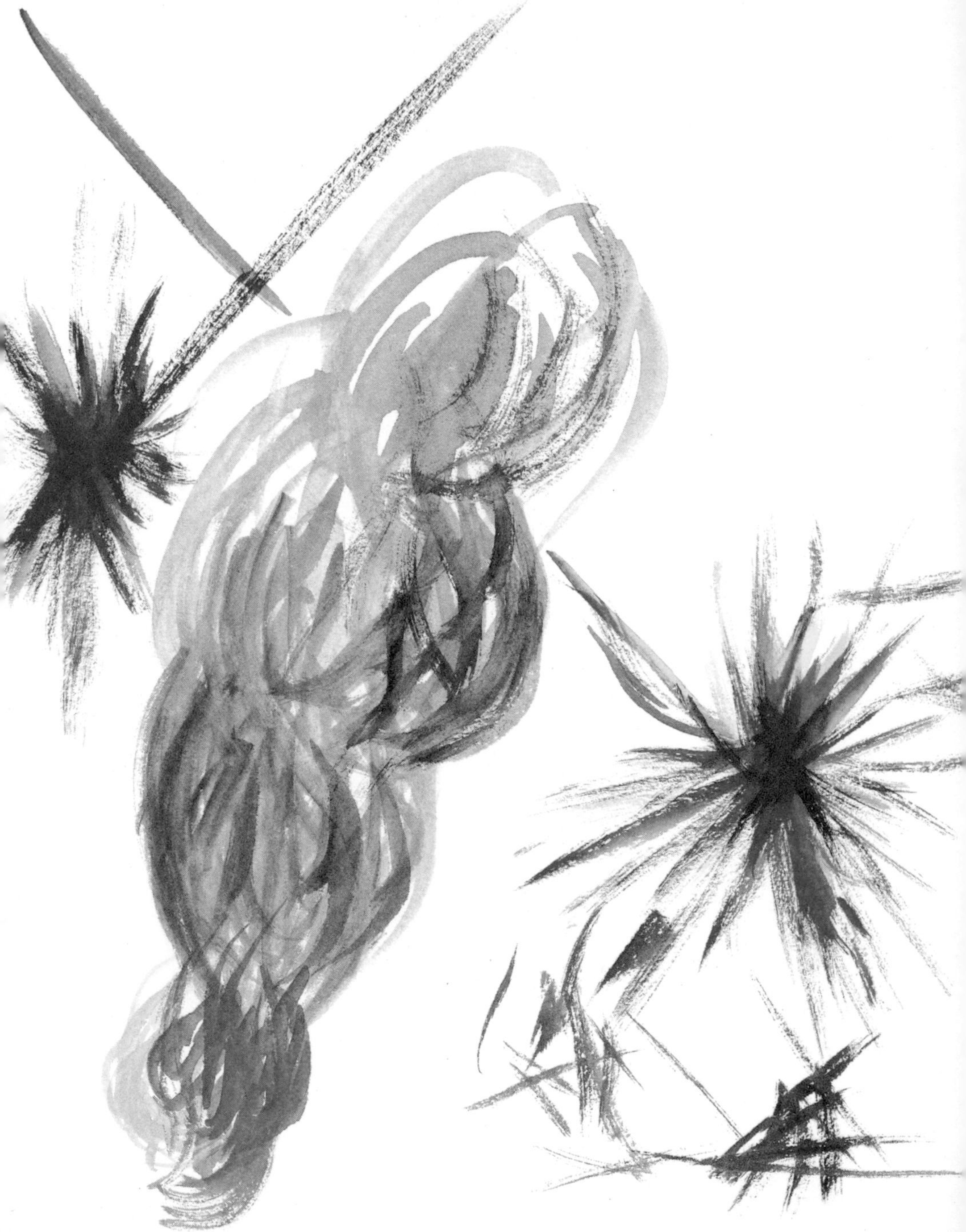

For lots of people, counting the explosions, trying to locate where shells have landed, guessing their calibre and commenting on the evolution of the shelling and the logic behind it is a good way to overcome their fear and makes the interminable nights seem shorter. But for me, everything is frightening, including the rumbling of a storm, a metal blind being lowered, a door slamming.

On one particularly dreadful night spent in the corridor of the apartment (the only space without external walls that we use as a shelter), I develop such terrible stomach cramps that I scream in agony over the noise of the shelling. The next morning as soon as the ceasefire is in place my mother takes me, still doubled over with pain, to the Orthodox Hospital (the closest to home). She's sure it's appendicitis. Doctor Fayez Bitar, exhausted by his night spent in the operating theatre, but still capable of making a diagnosis, examines me carefully and says, smiling: nothing is wrong with her, she was just very frightened. I leave with a few pills feeling a little ashamed.

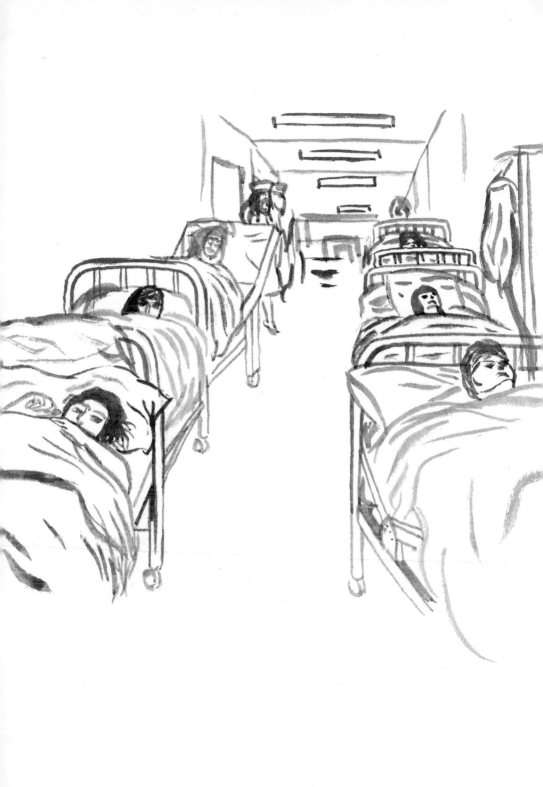

The nights there is shelling I go to sleep in my parents' bed or in Tamar's. If the shelling is too intense and too close then we all take shelter in the corridor, which is by now equipped with permanent makeshift beds. With time, we have stopped going down to the shelter in the cellar unless the shelling is really apocalyptic. Even on calm nights I keep myself awake and read in my bed as long as possible. My fear is that if I fall asleep I won't hear the beginnings of far-off shelling and won't be able to warn everyone to take shelter in time. I think that my parents and Tamar are sleeping soundly and aren't afraid because they are adults. I only recently discovered in a conversation with my mother that I did not have a monopoly on insomnia during those days.

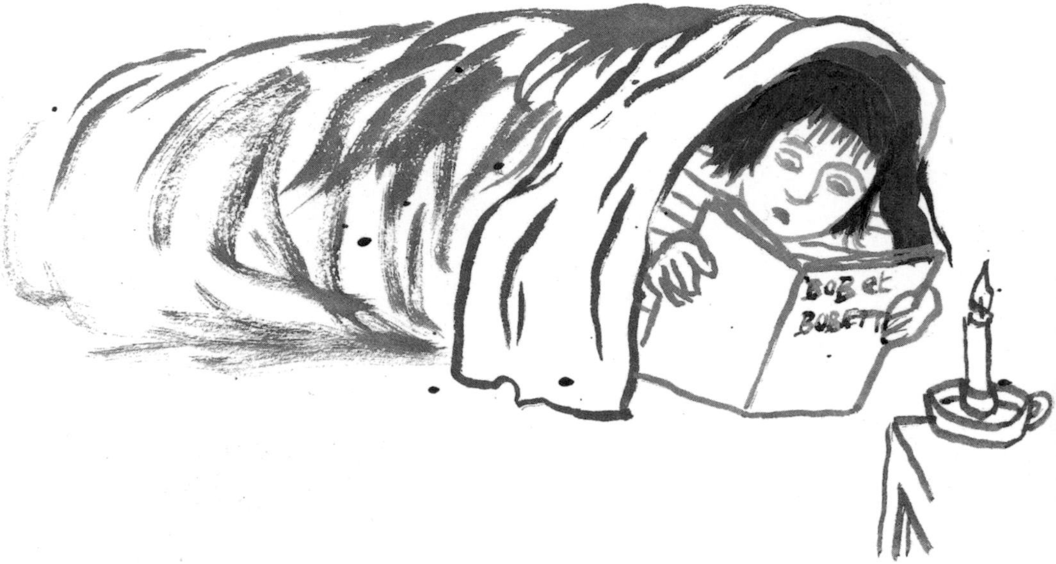
BOB et
BOBETTE

So I read. With fear in my gut, I devour all the Enid Blyton books and comics to keep me awake just in case . . .

My sleepless nights are filled with heroes that I love.

They are my friends.

They protect me.

Other, more sinister characters float above the city.

Wearing *keffiyehs*, safari jackets, white suits and patent leather shoes or combat uniforms.

They frighten me.

They are monsters and I hate them.

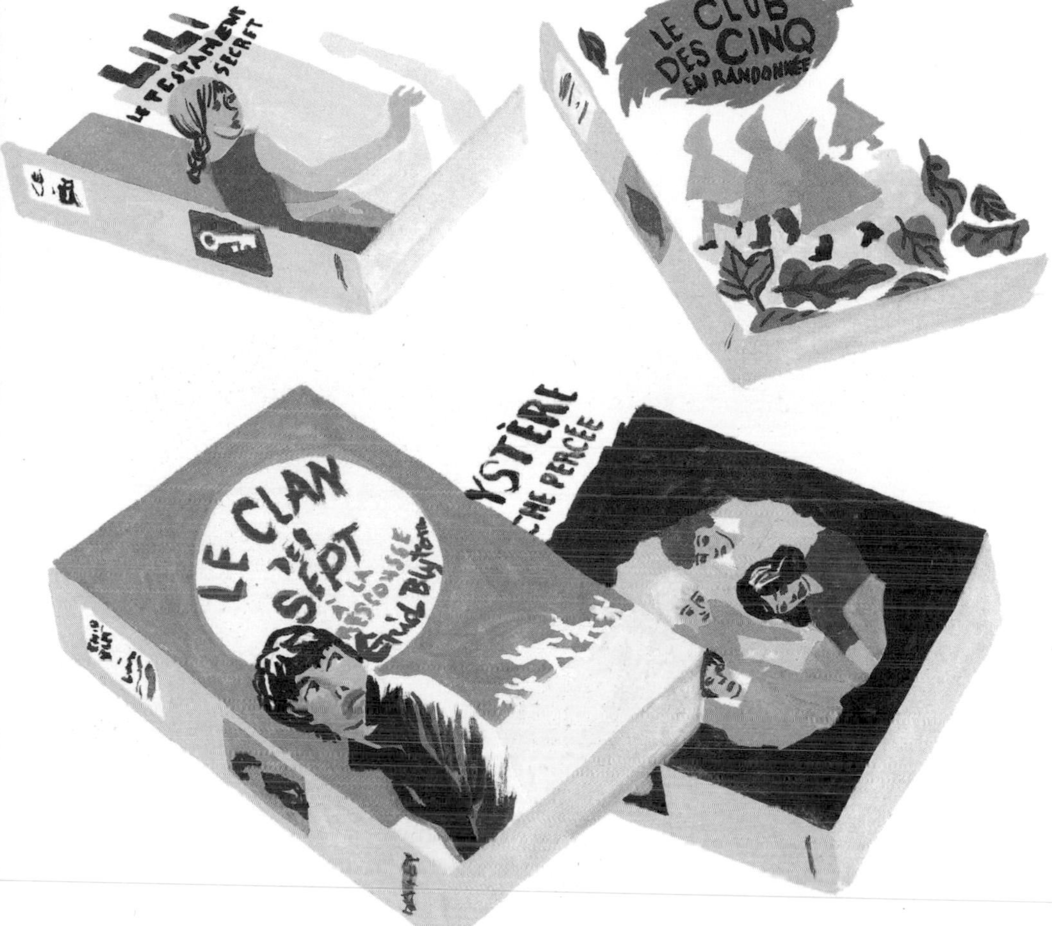
LILI
LE TESTAMENT SECRET
LE CLUB DES CINQ
EN RANDONNÉE
LE CLAN DES SEPT
À LA RESCOUSSE
Enid Blyton

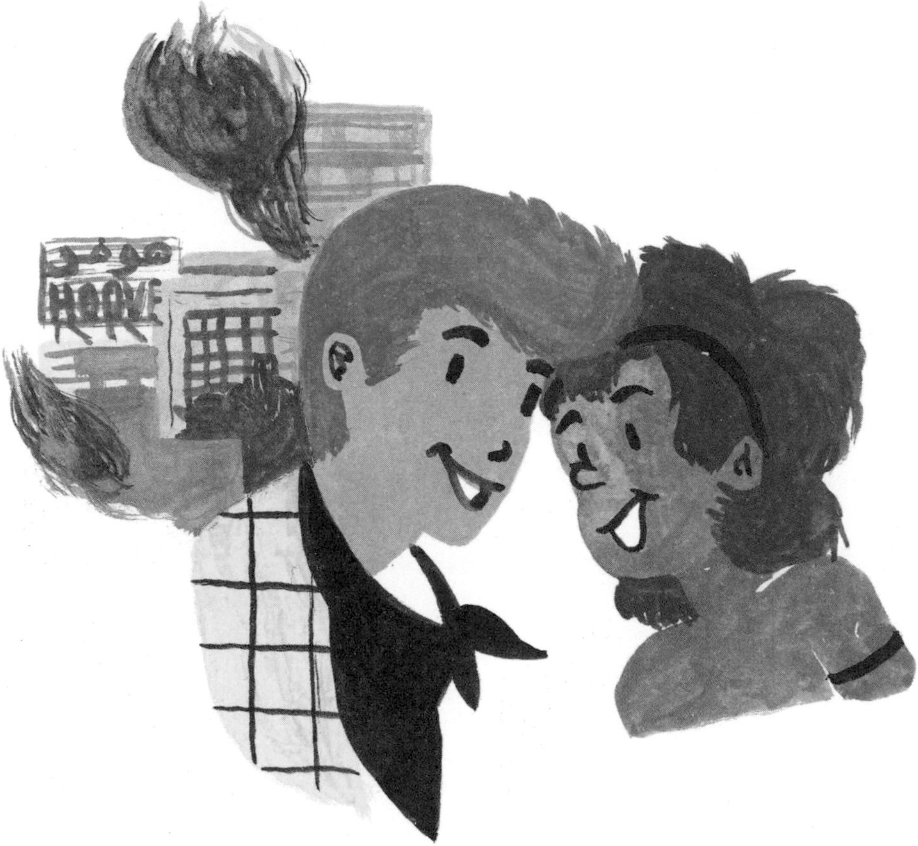
HOOVE

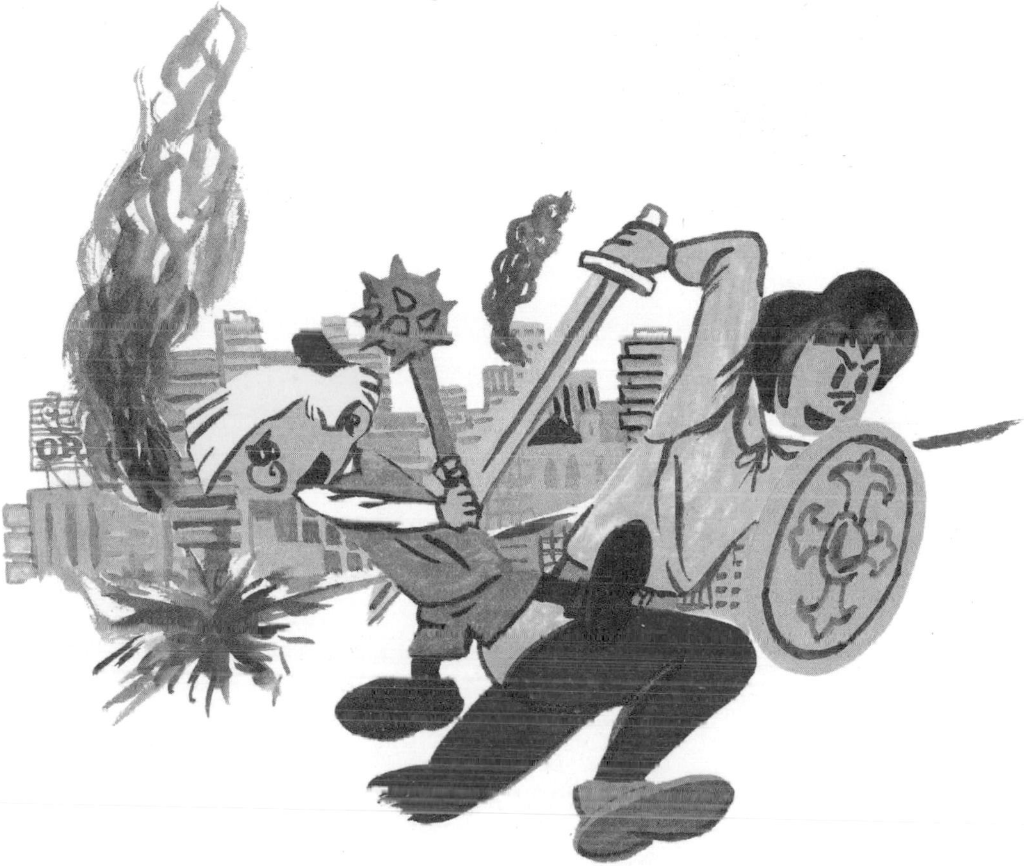

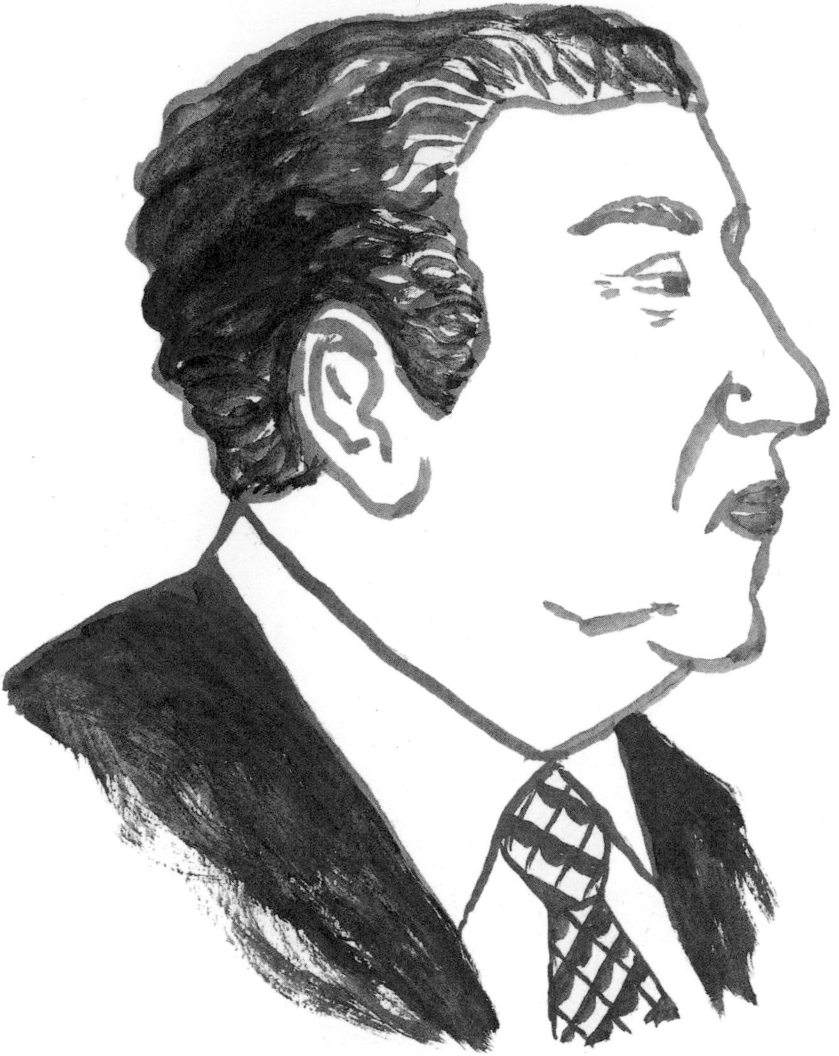

Elias Sarkis, the new President of the Republic

Hafez al-Assad, the Syrian president

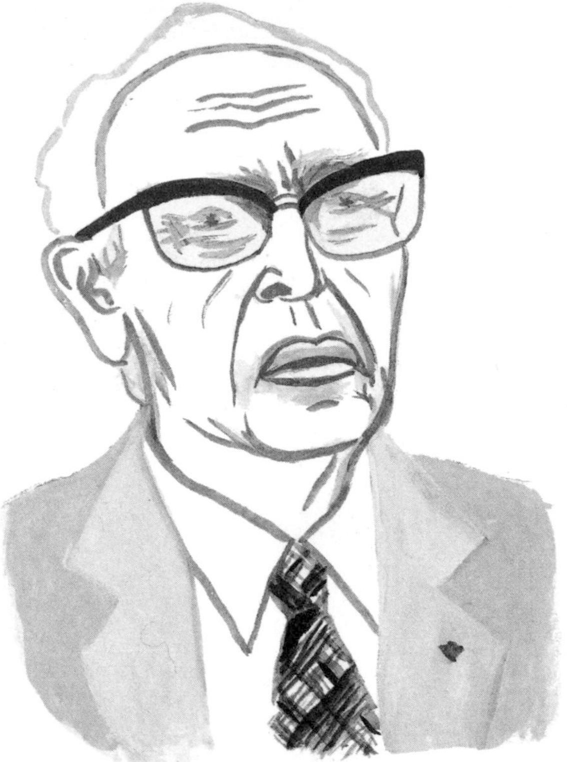

Suleiman Frangieh,
former President of the Republic,
Maronite Christian chief

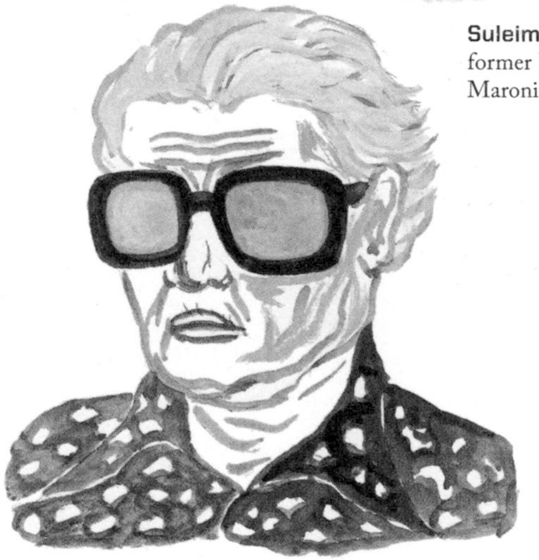

Camille Chamoun,
former President of the Republic,
Maronite Christian chief

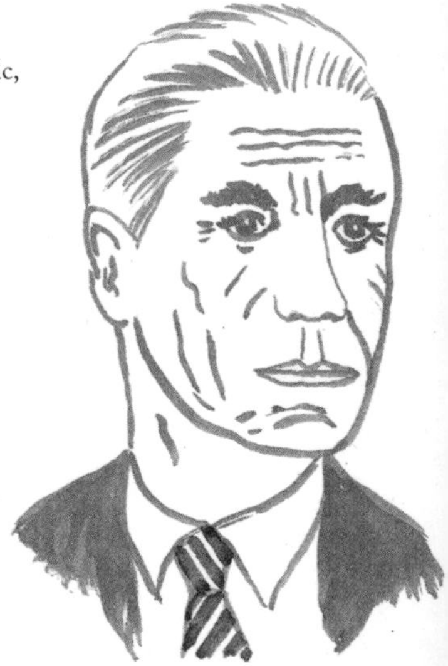

Pierre Gemayel,
founder and president of the Kataeb,
Maronite Christian chief

Rashid Karami,
Prime Minister,
Sunni leader

Kamel al-Assaad,
president of the Lebanese
parliament, Shiite leader

Bashir Gemayel,
son of Pierre Gemayel,
Maronite leader of Kataeb militia

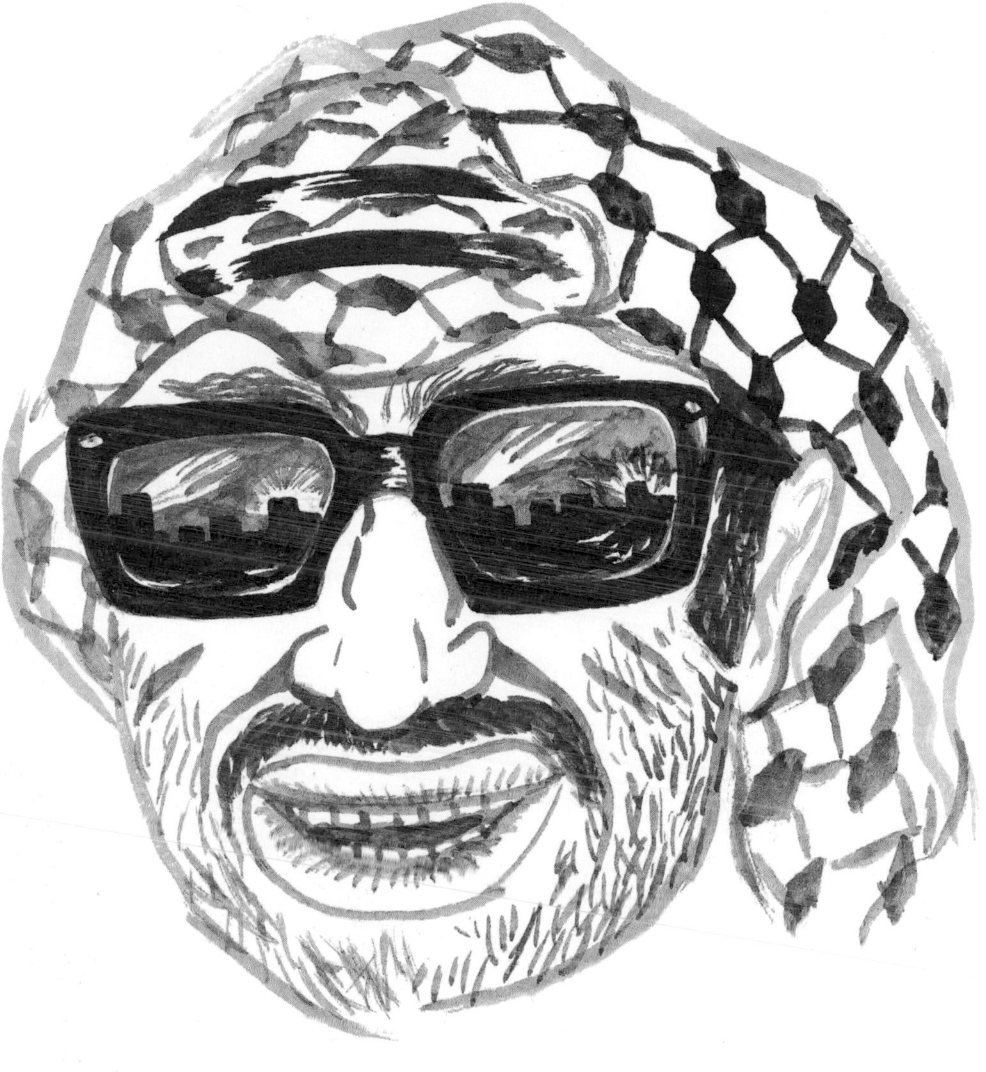

Yasser Arafat,
'Abu Ammar', Palestinian leader
of Fatah and the PLO

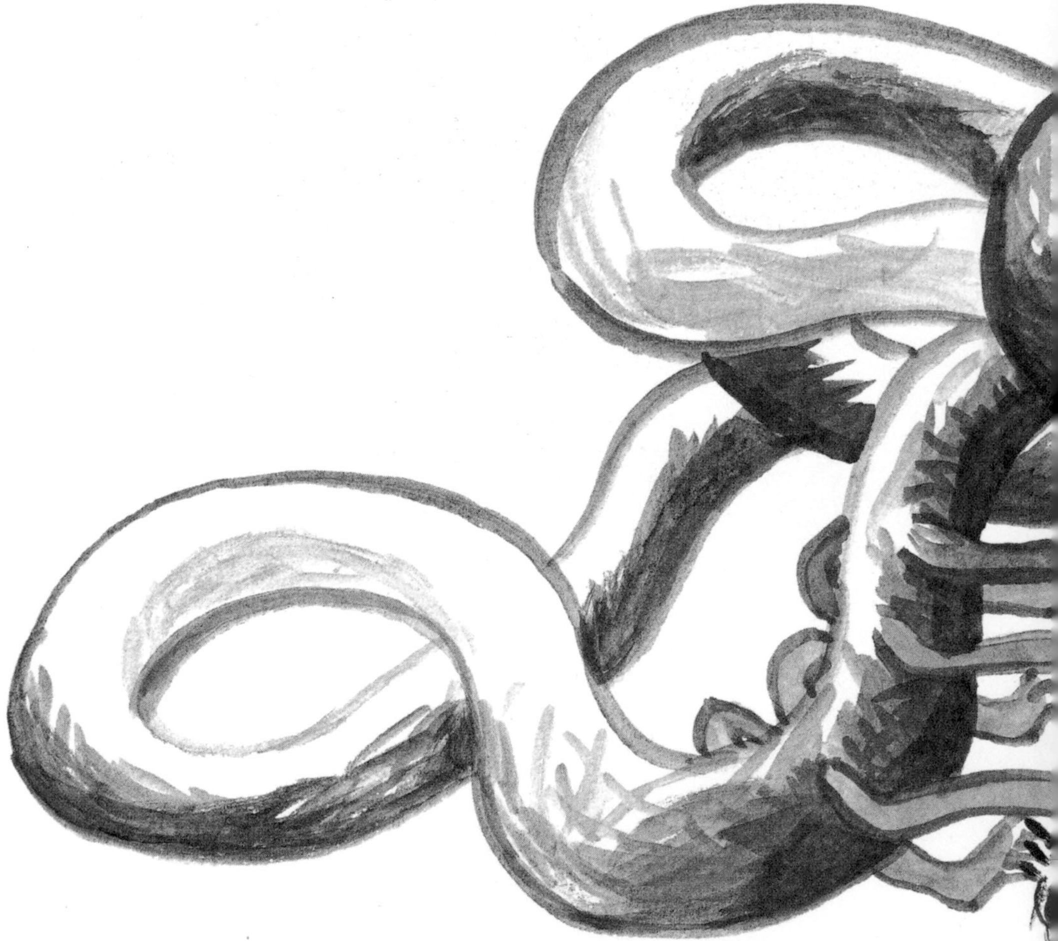

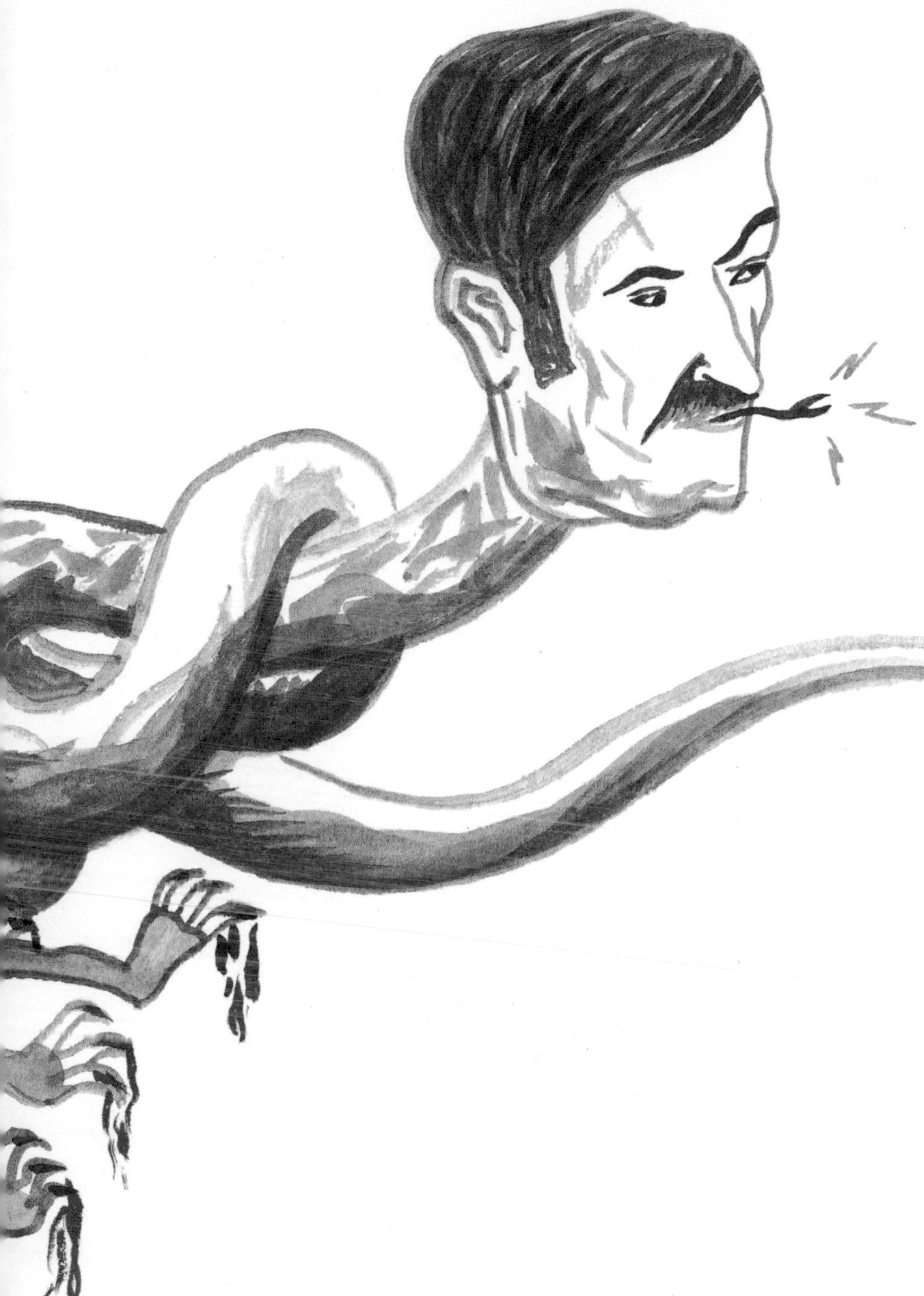

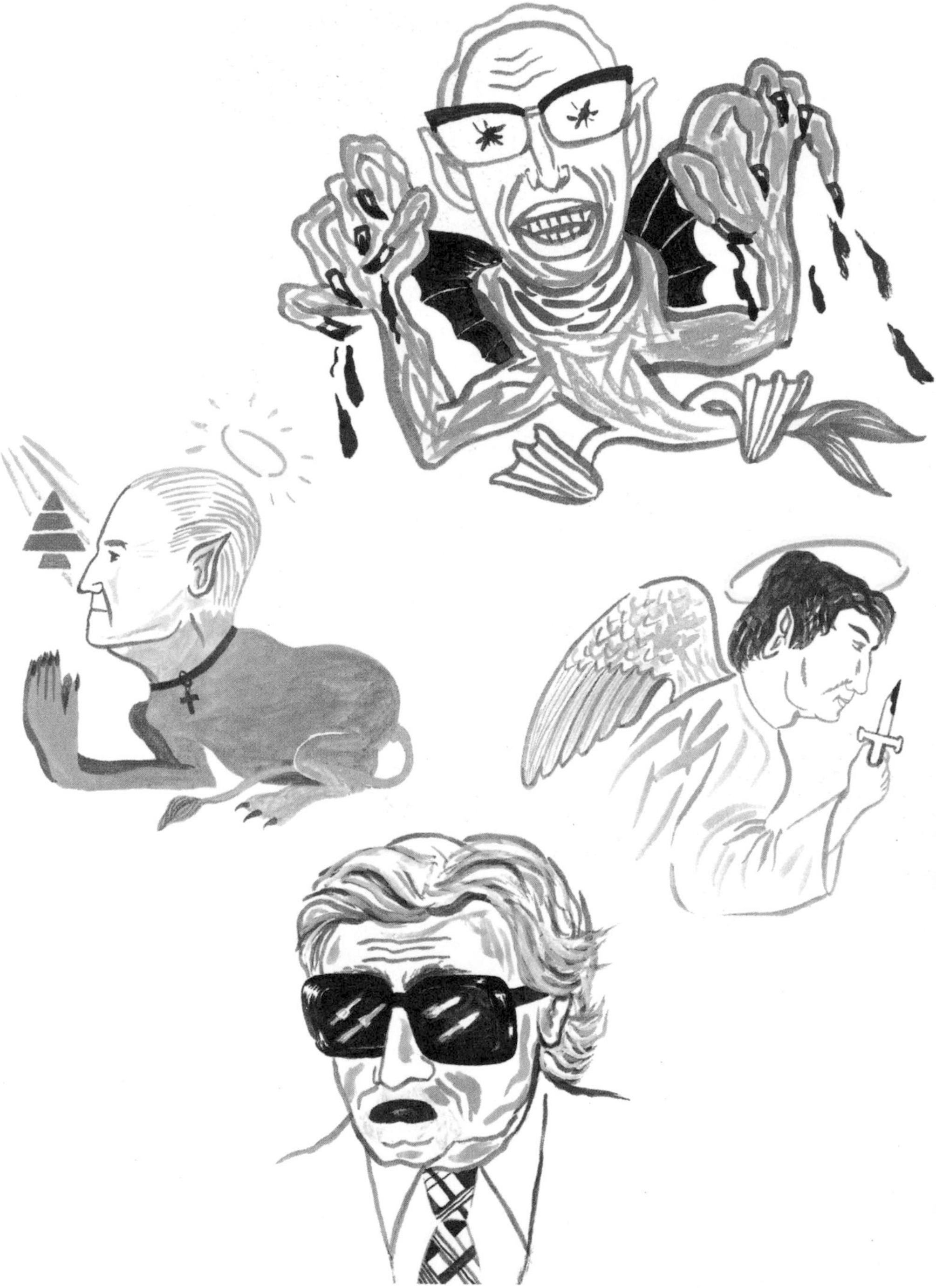

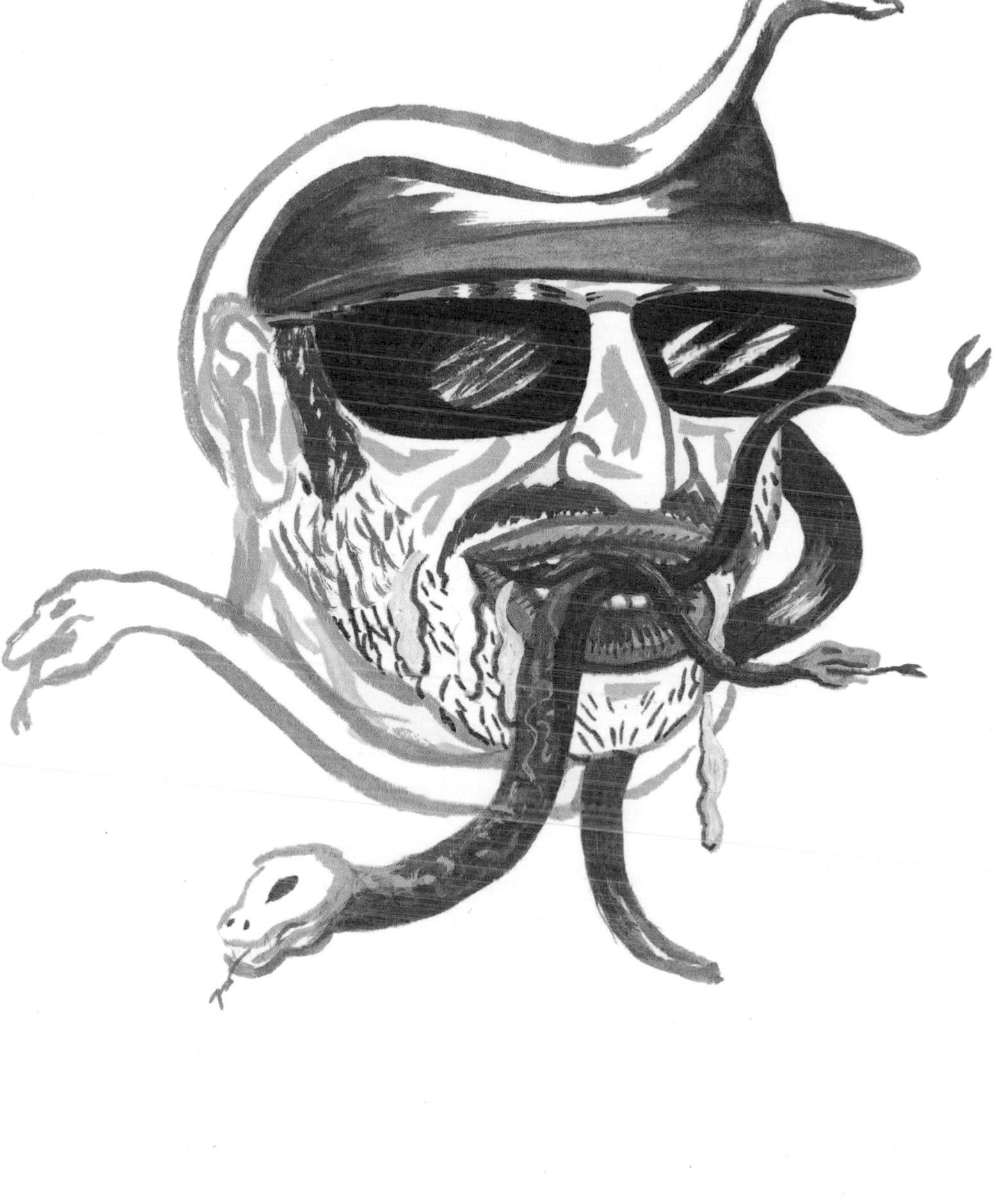

There's reading, and television provides another source of bliss. Egyptian and American TV series, Lebanese comedies, cartoons . . .

But these pleasures are numbered. We have to wait for the electricity to come back on before we can rush to the TV – *al Dunia heyk** can't be watched by candlelight . . .

Anything is possible on television; we even see Sadat in Jerusalem, and that's real. Dumbfounded, we watch him address the Knesset! The Israelis also make a political gesture towards the Arab leader: they play Egyptian-born singer Dalida's *Salma ya Salma* on the radio, a nostalgic poem put to music.

* *Such is the World*, a Lebanese comedy series

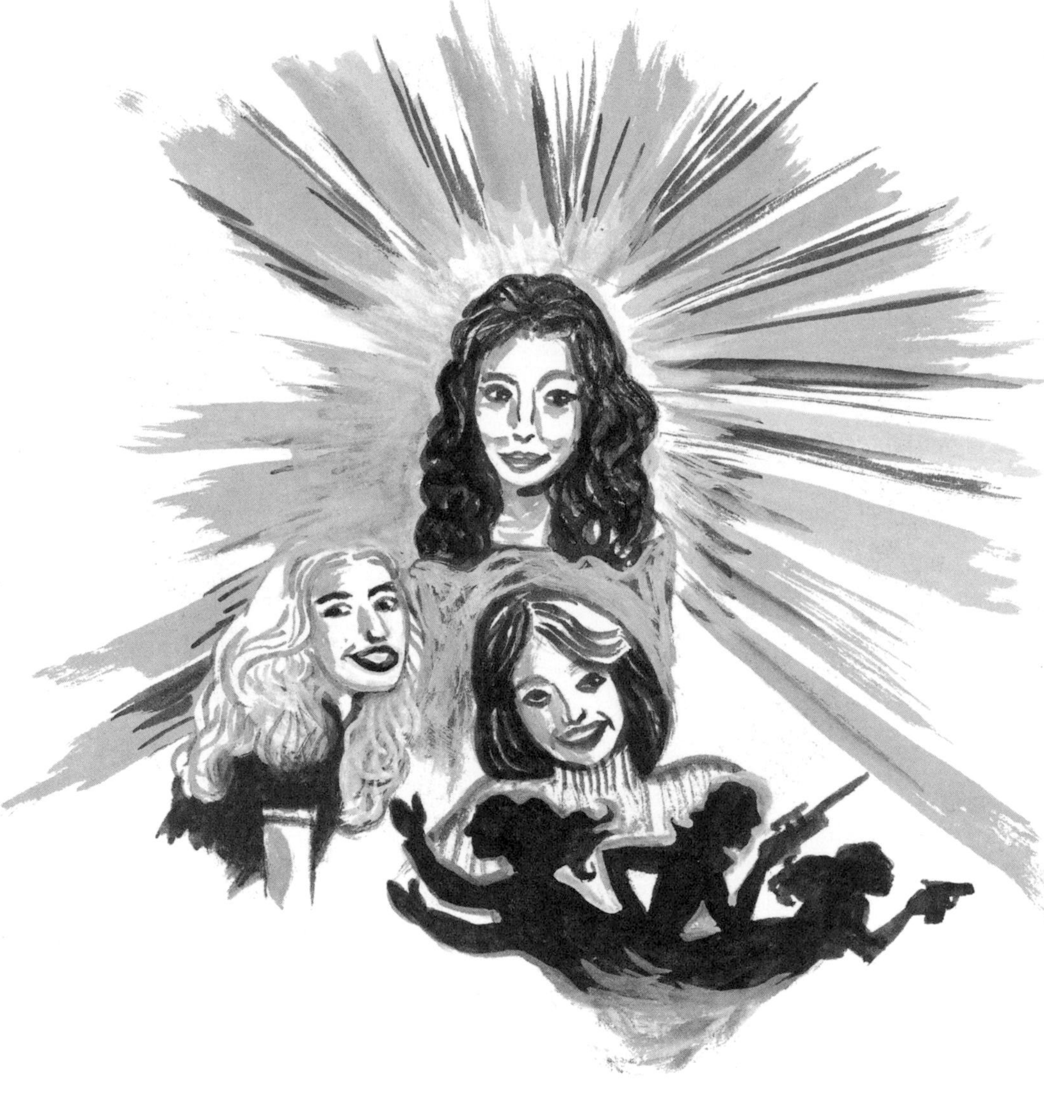

Then the Hundred-Day War breaks out. It pits the Christian militias against their former Syrian friends.

As the Syrians blindly bombard our neighbourhood, Ashrafieh, our apartment burns while we take refuge in Kattine.

That summer the relentless shelling lasts for three months.

The nature of the Hundred-Day War is particularly murderous and destructive.

The Syrians hammer away at Ashrafieh from one building to another using weapons that are supposed to be used to attack entire cities. The *rejmé*, or 'Stalin's organs', installed in the Syrian-held Rizk tower, the highest building in Charkieh, disgorges up to one hundred rockets an hour onto the neighbouring buildings.

Tragic news reaches Kattine each day: destruction and spectacular fires in the oil storage tanks of Dawra. Severe shortages of water, wheat, petrol, gas. And, above all, of electricity, even in hospitals. Doctor Pierre Farah, my mother's cousin who is a surgeon at the Hôtel-Dieu hospital, operates by candlelight. Sami Haddad dies from shrapnel in his skull. Nayla Asfar is found under the rubble of her house. Our apartment goes up in flames . . .

That summer, amid the TV series, we also dully witness the signature of the Camp David accords. Smiles, satisfaction, peace, love . . . Beirut is in agony but we're happy for them over there in Camp David. We're even moved to tears. Above all, in Sabra Camp, Shatila Camp and Burj el-Barajneh Camp, where we're literally crying. We don't know it yet, but the crying won't be over for a while.

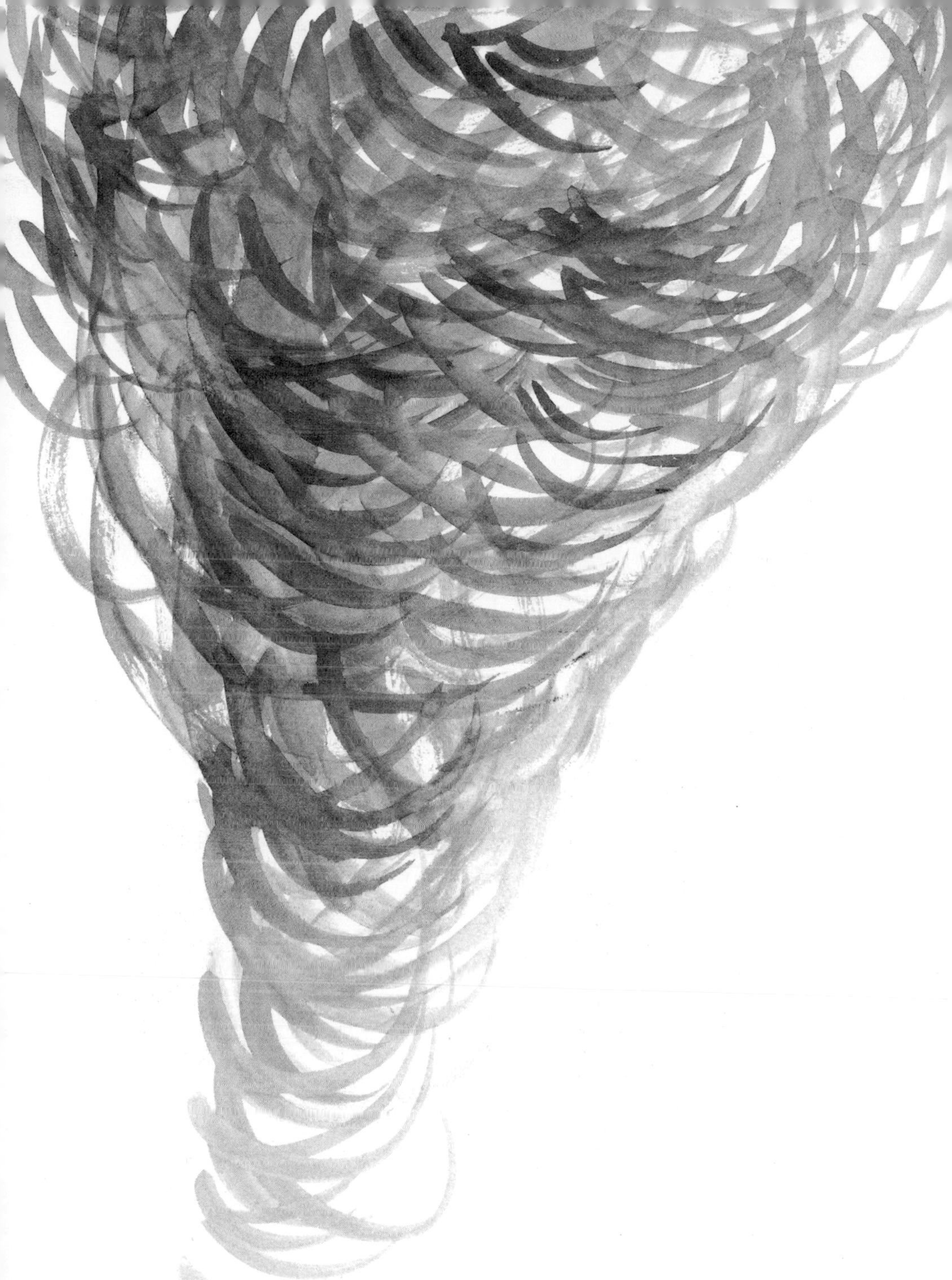

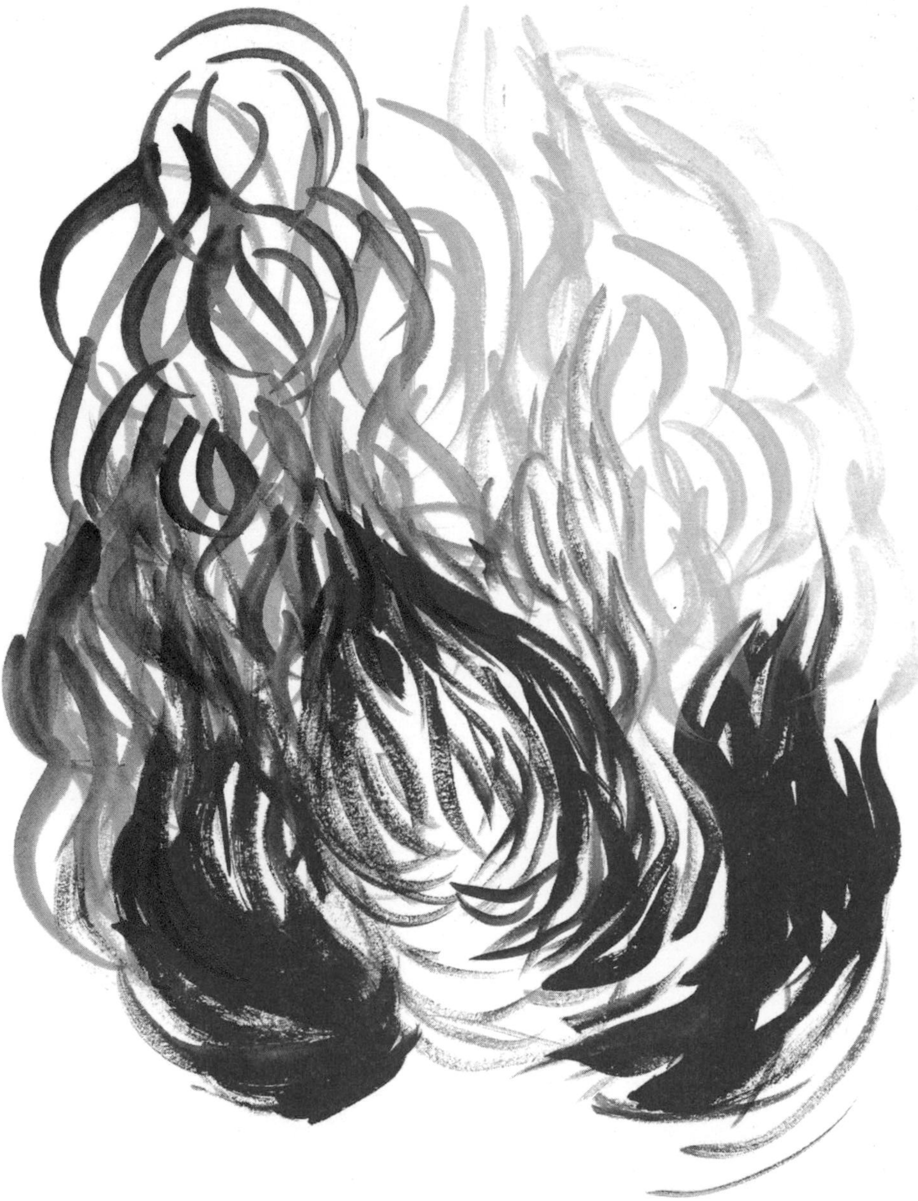

Jimmy Carter

Anwar Sadat   Menahem Begin

l

Then it's the end of the Hundred-Day War. After three months spent in Kattine, our return to Beirut during the October ceasefire is awful.

This time it's not the souks and the Borj that have been hit. (We haven't been back since.) Our neighbourhood, our streets and our building have been transformed into an apocalyptic scene. Buildings collapsed or reduced to ashes, burnt or exploded cars, crushed roads, and black smoke rising from pretty much everywhere.

From the back window of my father's car this end-of-the-world vision gives me a stomach ache; I feel like vomiting and have a lump in my throat. I could cry, but I don't, and don't know why. My mother tells my grandmother over the phone a few hours later: 'Oh don't worry about the children, they haven't realised what it means!'

Six out of ten floors of our building are charred while the others are gutted.

The Syrian forces responsible for hammering our building were based in the Abuhamad building, just a few streets away.

When I see our apartment I feel as if I've been reborn for a third time. Things will never be the same again.

My mother is far more upset about the loss of her photograph albums than anything else – the jewellery, clothing, furniture, objects and paintings. Luckily my favourite doll was with me in Kattine.

We go to live with my grandmother for a year while our apartment is being repaired.

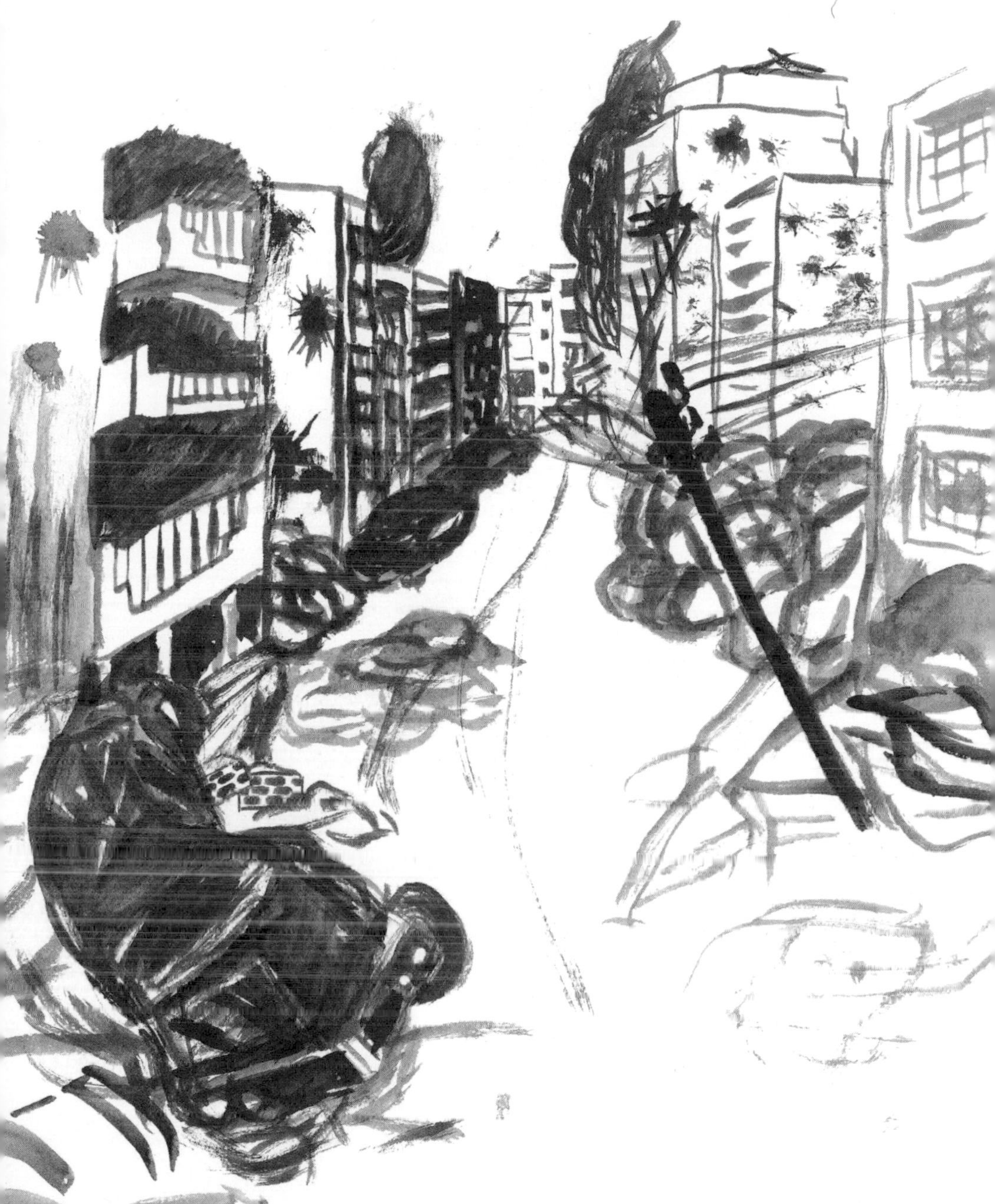

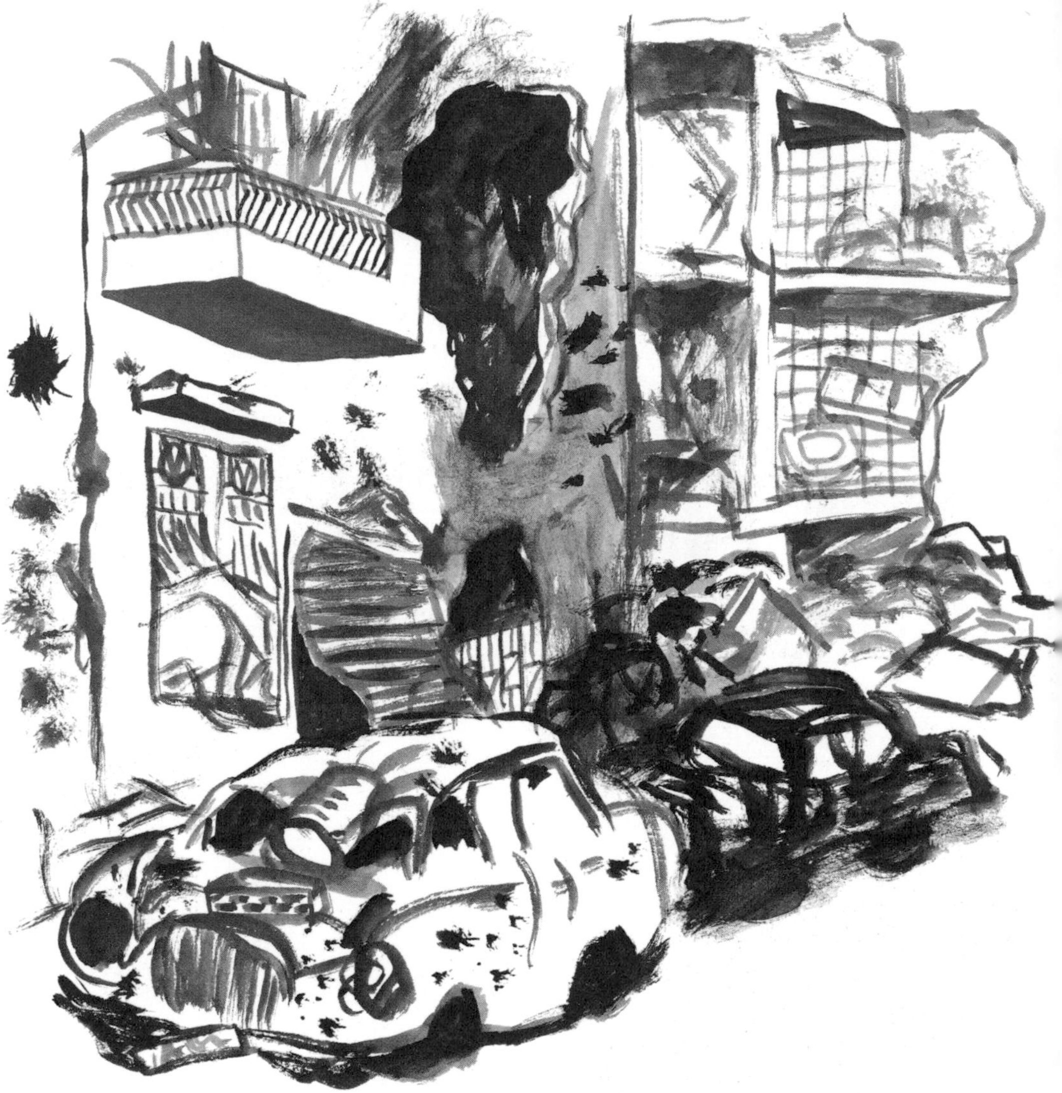

Teta Simone lives on rue Pasteur, in Gemmayzeh, in an old Lebanese house overlooking the port, and several hundred metres from the demarcation line. (Place des Martyrs is at the end of rue Pasteur.) To indicate where one should stop in order to stay out of the line of fire, tyres, sandbags, a container stolen from the port, and a Beirut city bus close off the middle of the street. Teta's house is located just before these warning signs.

Some days bullets fly by this border and ricochet off the wall surrounding the garden on the west side, near the main entrance of the house. Accordingly we never use it but enter and exit via the kitchen, five metres further away.

For the last three years we've known that the shortest distance between one point and another is meaningless. It isn't unusual to take a ten-minute detour between two places only several metres away from each other on the same street. For this same reason, one-way streets no longer exist in the demarcation line neighbourhoods.

Teta's bathroom is also a dangerous place. It benefits from an improbable series of openings and angles between nearby buildings and has an almost unobstructed view of the Place des Martyrs. To her despair, Teta has no choice but to use the shower in the other bathroom; she considers that we are all infested with germs that she doesn't want to be exposed to.

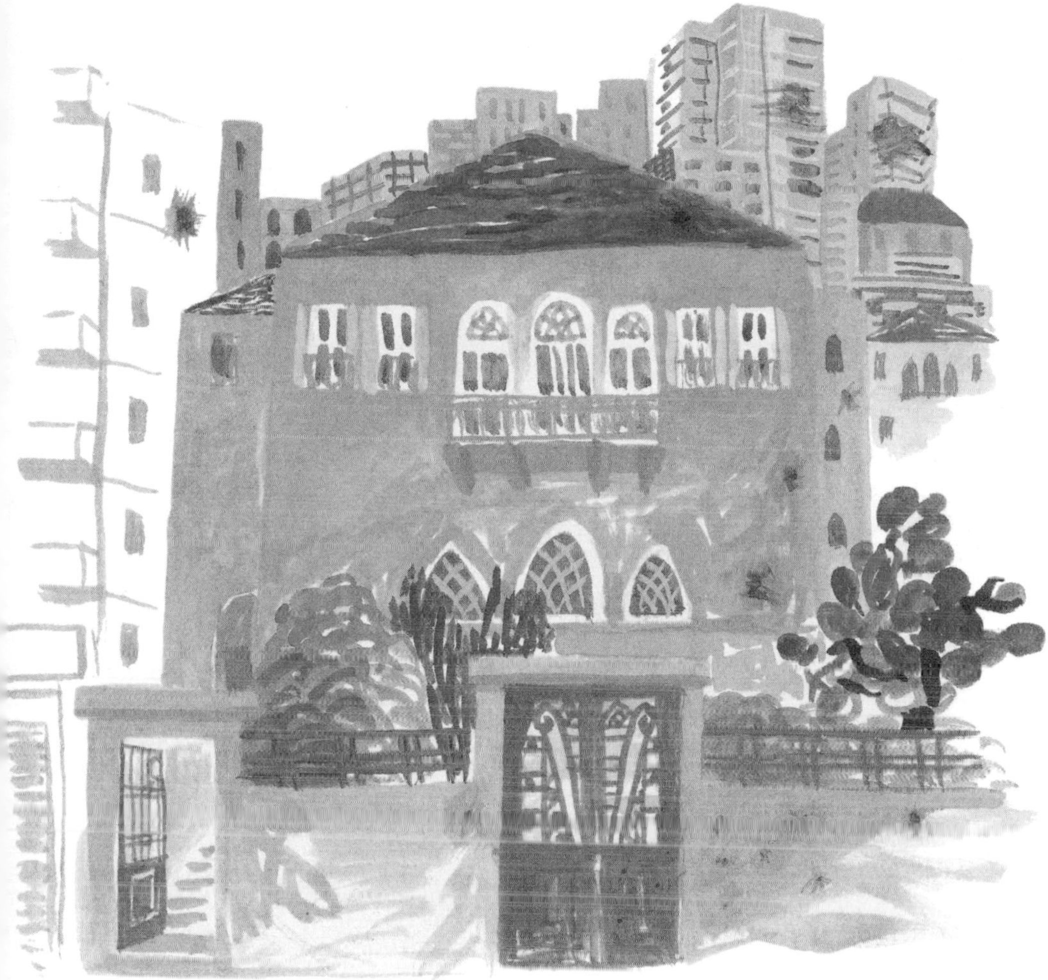

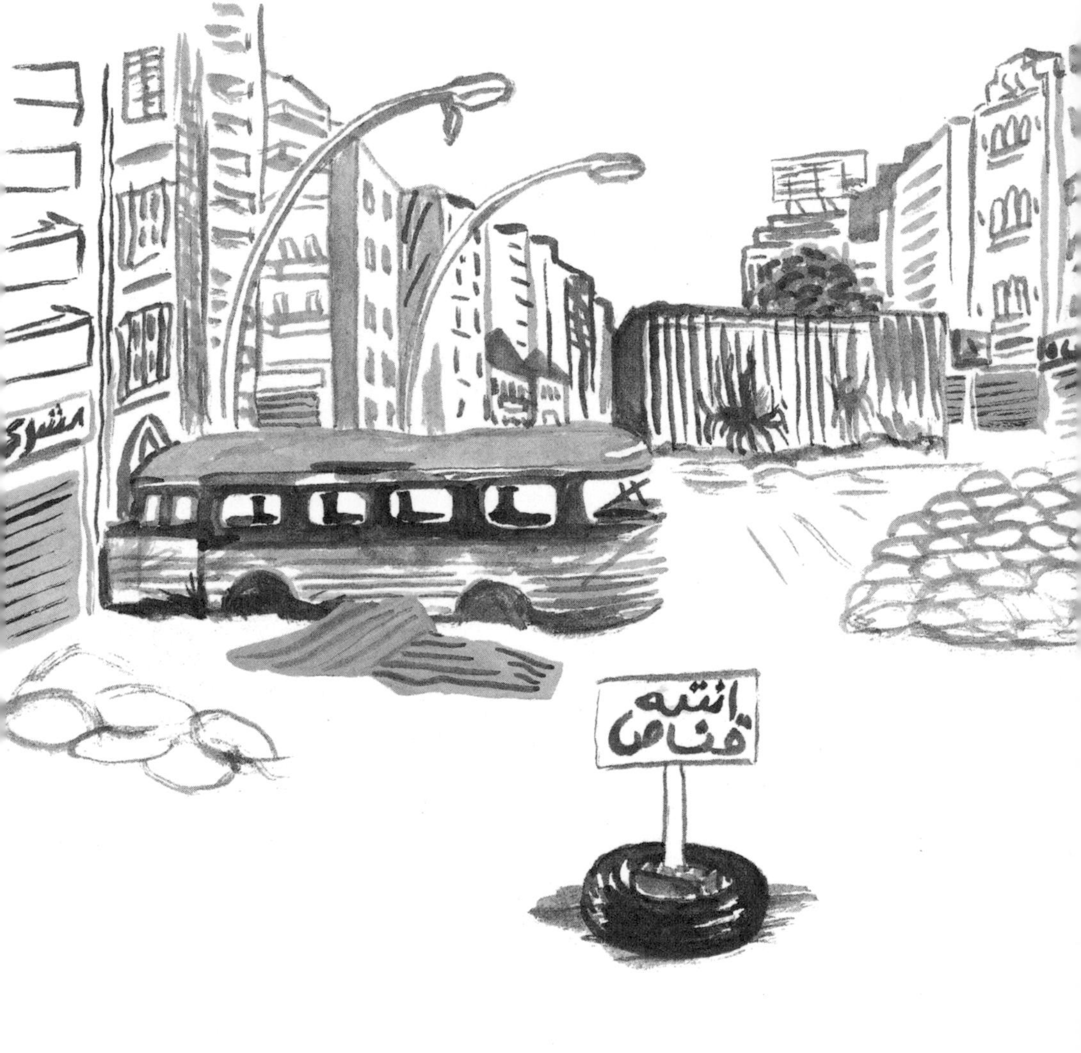

انتبه
قناص

Teta lives on the top floor. Her chauffeur Bechara and his family live on the ground floor.

These days everyone covets the ground-floor rooms. When the night shelling is particularly intense we go down to 'Bish's'. We are: my father, his radio held to his ear, my mother, my grandmother, Tamar, Walid and I, Bechara, his wife Nada and their two children, Fadi and Fadia. Nada spends the night preparing and serving coffee to the adults, as if the shelling isn't enough to keep them awake.

There's Thérèse as well, but we have to beg her to come downstairs, and before she does she declares that she would rather die up above, than to hide away like a rat, and Abu Ammar (Arafat), *hal kalb, yrouh aa jhanam*, that dog, he can go to hell. Actually, she is so fat that the idea of climbing up the stairs in the morning once it's calm is more trying than dying heroically. She usually ends up following us for the simple reason that Walid refuses to go without her, but she always waddles down ten minutes after the rest of us, cursing everyone across the way, as well as the *shabeb* (ruffians) in our street, *kellon ekhwet sharmouta*, all sons of bitches.

Come morning when the battles have ceased, Walid and me go upstairs to the roof of Thérèse's room (the only one to have a flat roof above it) and pick up stray bullets, shell casings and shrapnel for our collection.

The *chazaya* have a variety of odd shapes, like Rorschach test inkblots. Madonna, rabbit, motorcycle . . . Some bullets are precious and dangerous as they haven't yet exploded. The star attraction of our collection is the base of a 50 mm mortar casing.

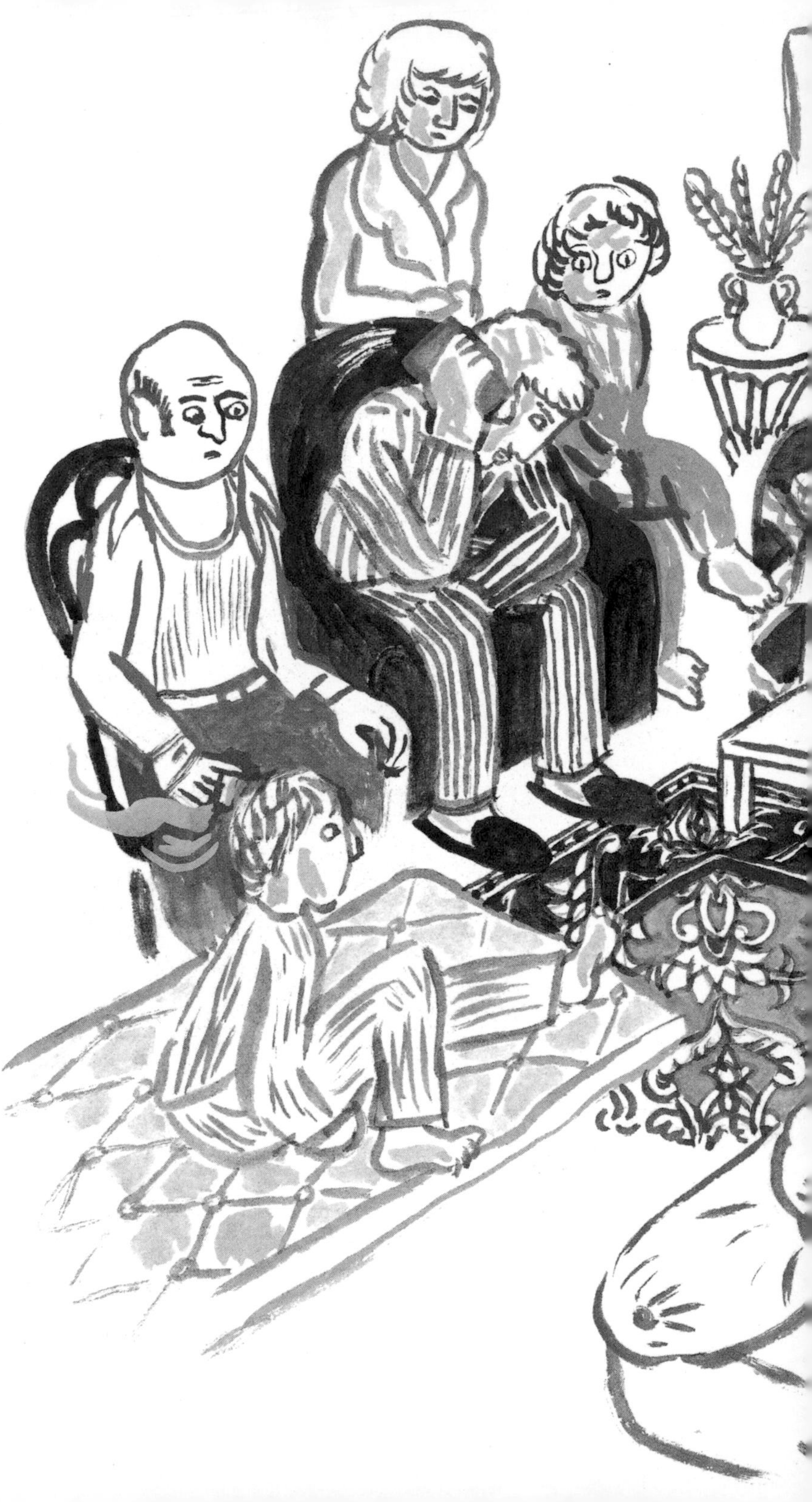

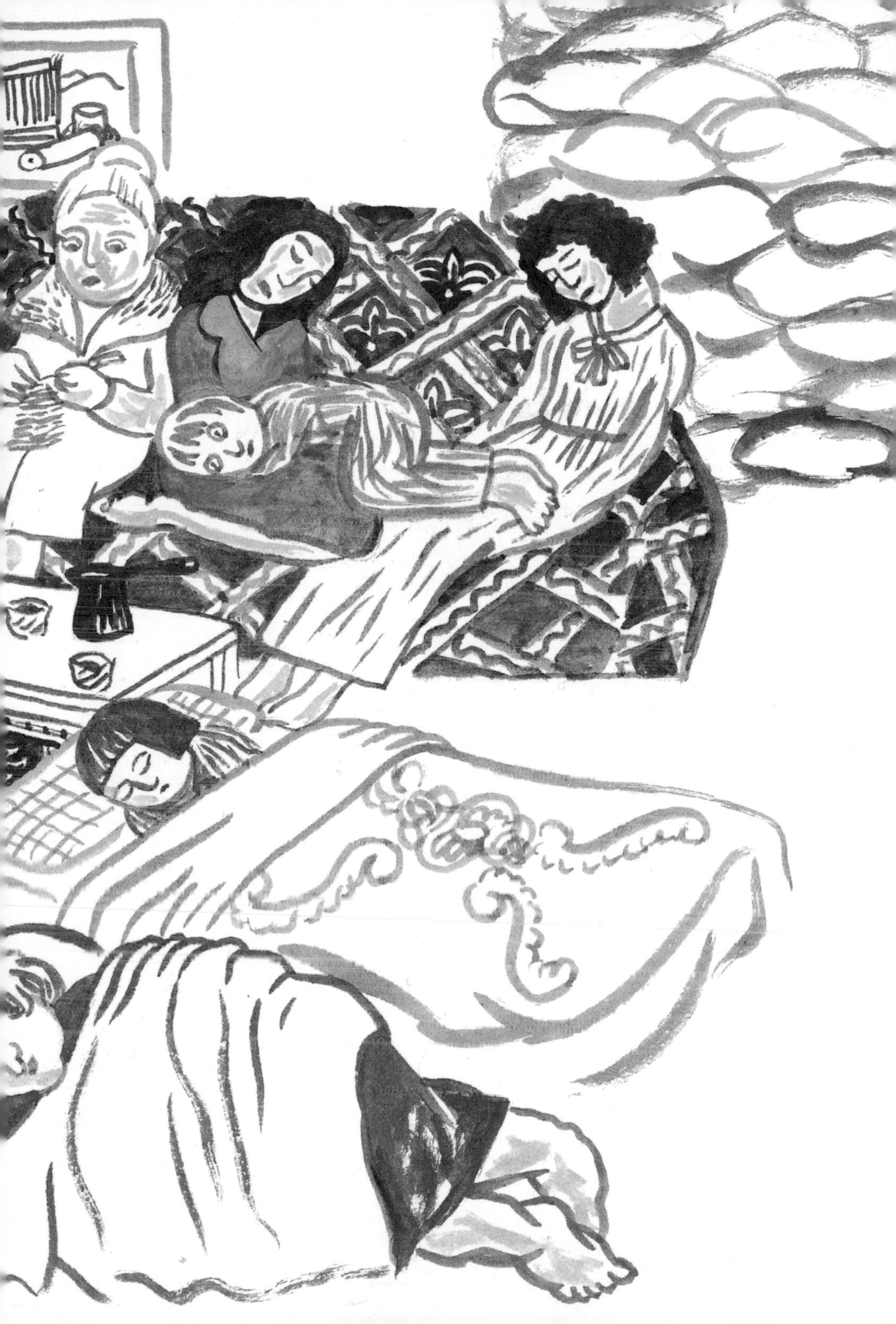

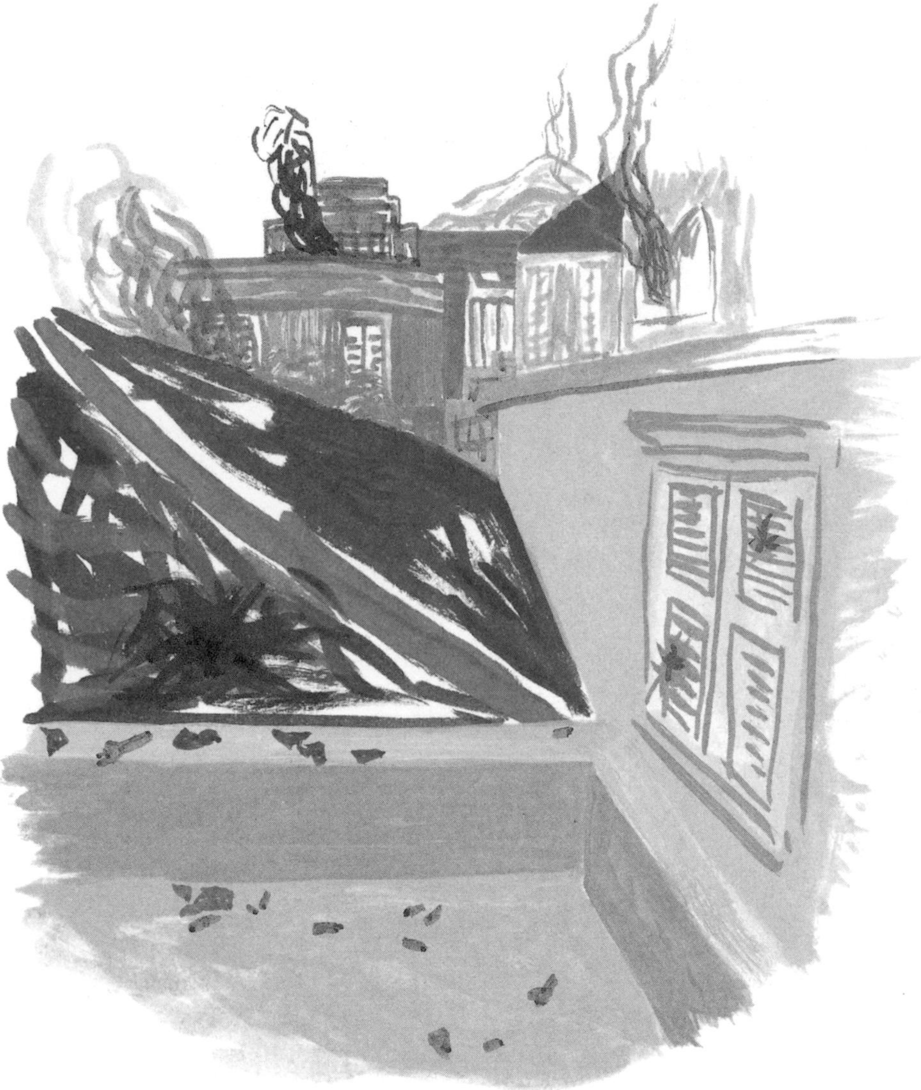

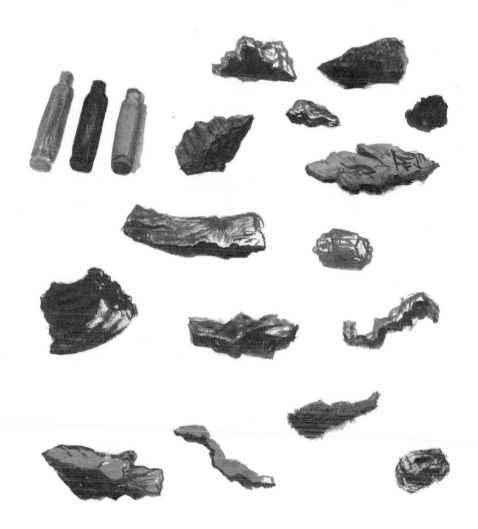

Teta piles up two or three mattresses under her magnificent Baccarat crystal chandeliers to cushion the fall (7 metres) in case a shell should come too close. Nothing can be done about the plaster mouldings on the ceiling; since the autumn of 1975 not much is left anyway.

But the mouldings aren't important. The roof tiles are more of a problem. If the tiles aren't replaced each time they are broken, it rains inside the house, and in Beirut the rain is torrential. Teta has found Toni, the only man in the neighbourhood who will venture onto her roof. Teta gives him a glass of whisky for bravery before he goes up. It's more like an entire bottle of whisky, which she lets him empty at his leisure. Teta feels guilty about encouraging alcoholism but it's necessary, she says understandingly, for Toni to summon enough courage to be in the line of sight of an *annas*, a sniper.

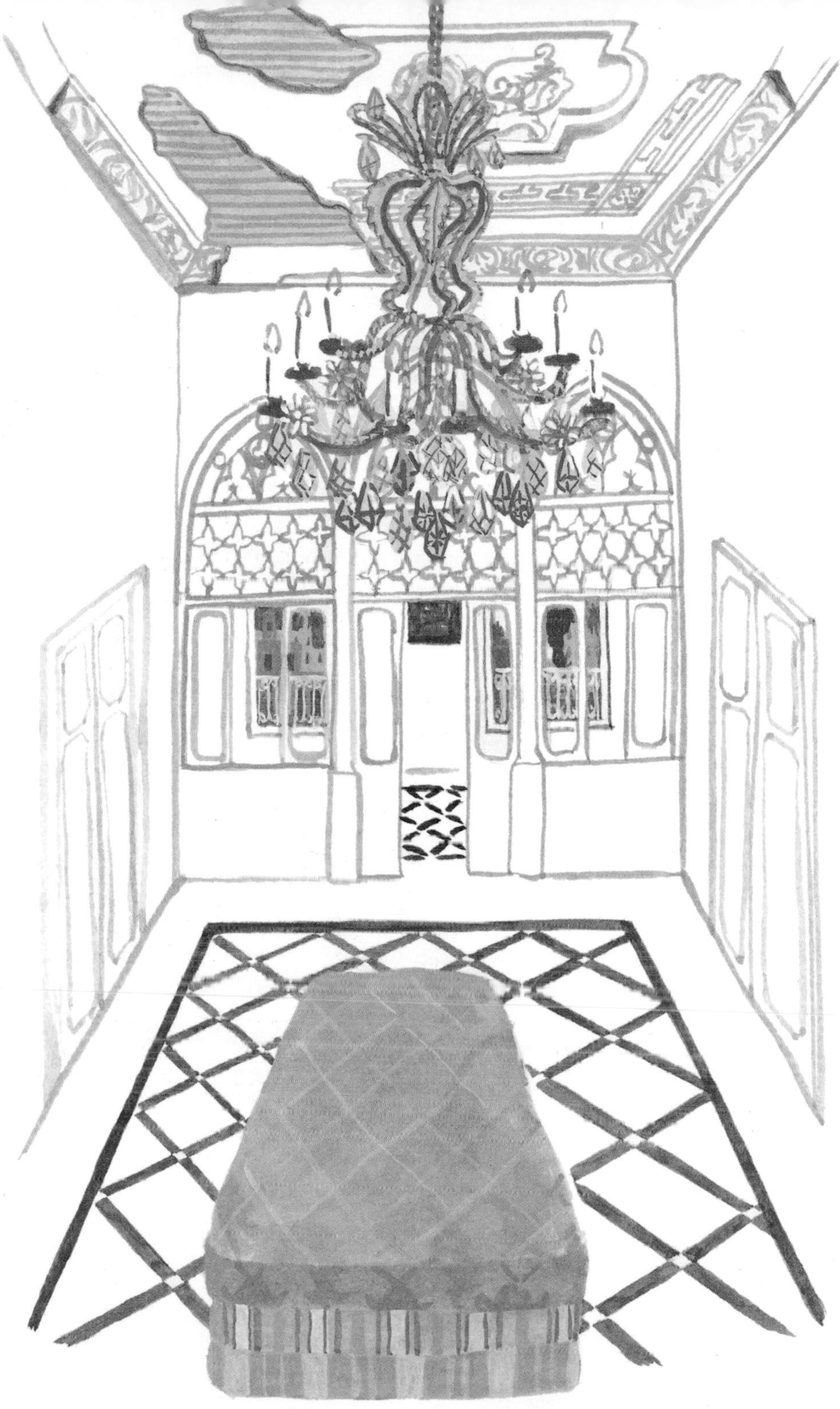

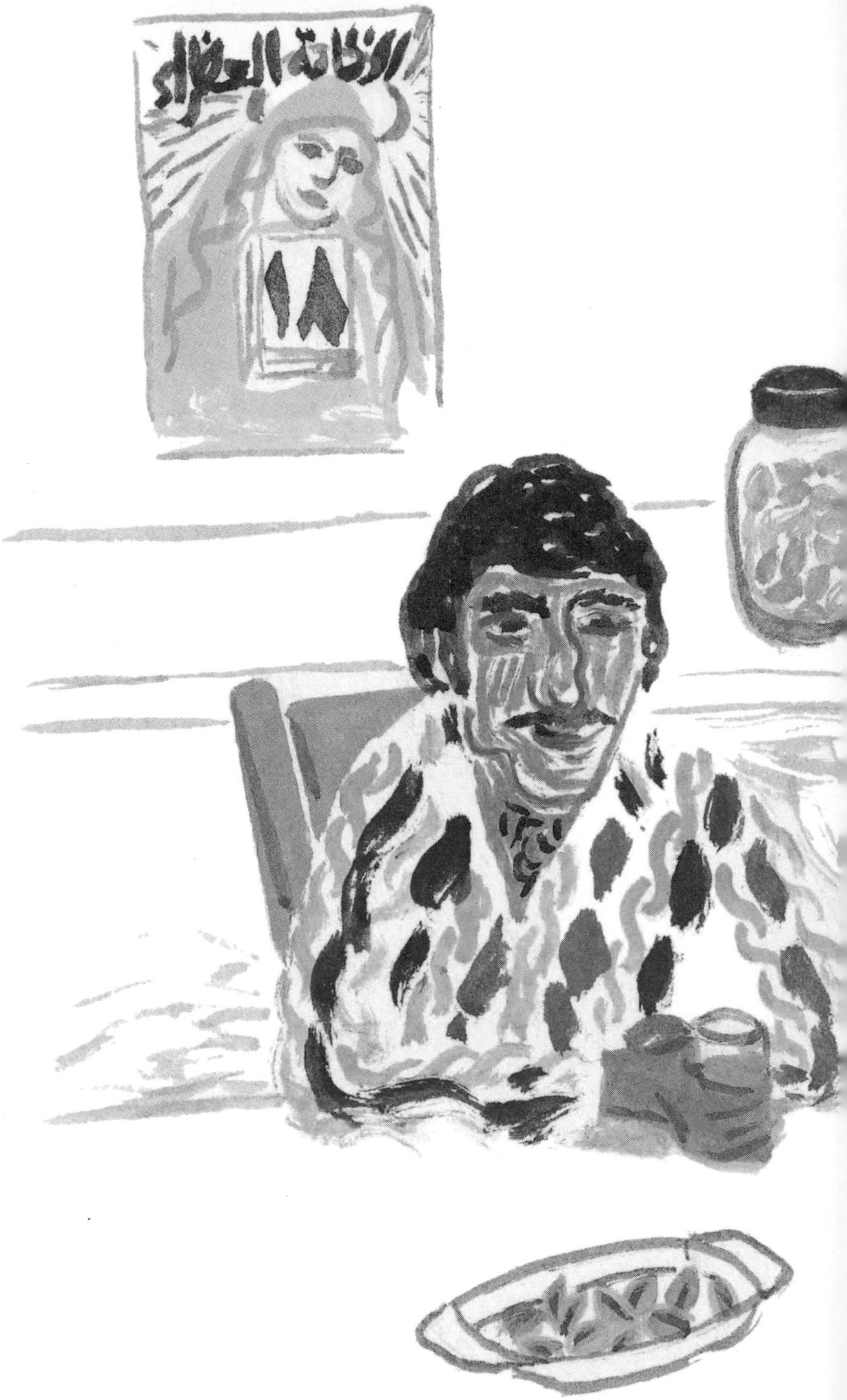
١٨

Although the war continues, I have happy and sweet memories of 1979. Probably because it's not the most terrifying year of the war, but also because we spend it at Teta's house. There is an atmosphere of irresistible charm in her home, filled with Lebanese myths, family lore and aromas.

The scent of jasmine that wafts through the window, the smell of Thérèse's cake coming from the kitchen, the aroma of *marsaben*, the marzipan flowers made by Greek Catholic nuns in their convent in Zouk, the fragrance of the rosewater syrup that we drink each day with our afternoon snack . . .

The smell of cold coffee, when Marie Abdallah comes to 'read' the future in the grounds that collect on the side of the cup once she has turned it upside down for a few minutes.

'Sitt Simone, the good Lord loves you, your granddaughter (not me, my cousin) is going to have a big wedding, I see a huge diamond ring at the bottom of the cup', or else '*Allah ynaijina*, God save us, sitt Simone, be careful, a handsome Palestinian is going to seduce your granddaughter, this overturned shoe in the middle of a path in a valley is a sure sign.'

It would have been just as easy to say 'My poor sitt Simone, Menachem Begin's last statement, *hal kalb*, doesn't bode well for us, *Allah ysaidna*, God help us, I see a black dog at the bottom of the valley.'

There's also the smell of Eight Hour Cream that Teta puts on her lips three times a day, and the aroma of chocolates from Attié that we continue to buy even though most Beirutis have given up.

Attié, the city's best chocolate maker, was the official supplier to the presidential palace before the war. Today few make the trip to the neighbourhood where he has his shop. But we do, although we can't take much credit for it – the shop is on rue Pasteur, smack next to the house!

You might say we are in the same boat.

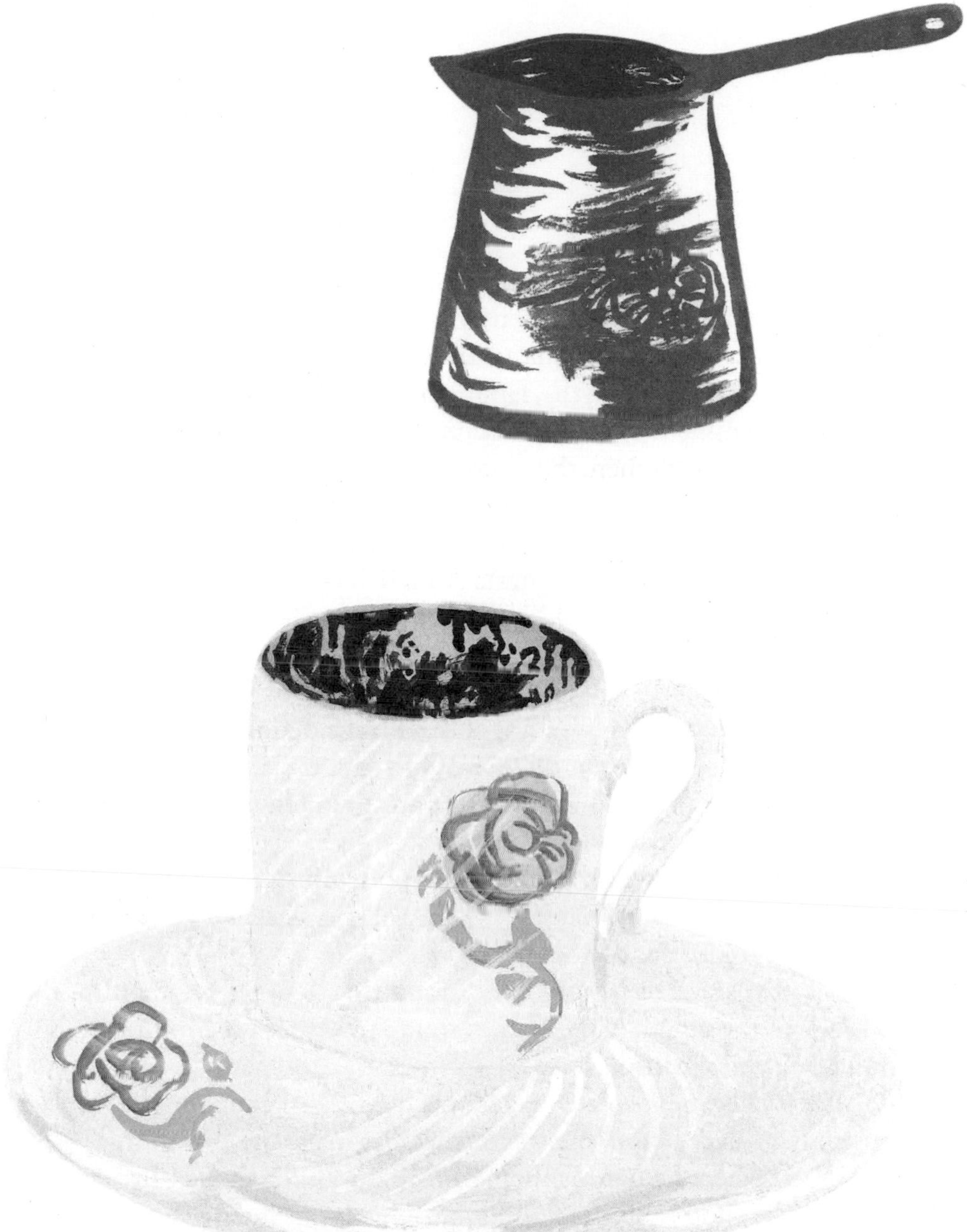

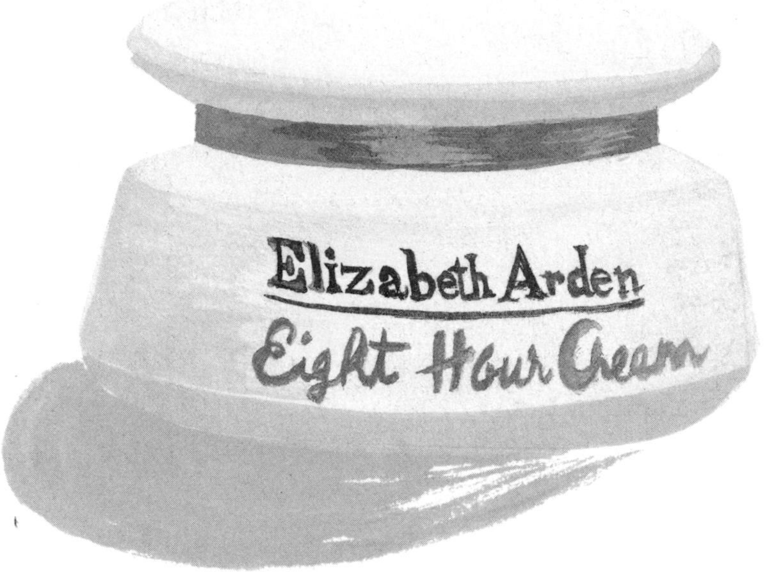
Elizabeth Arden
Eight Hour Cream

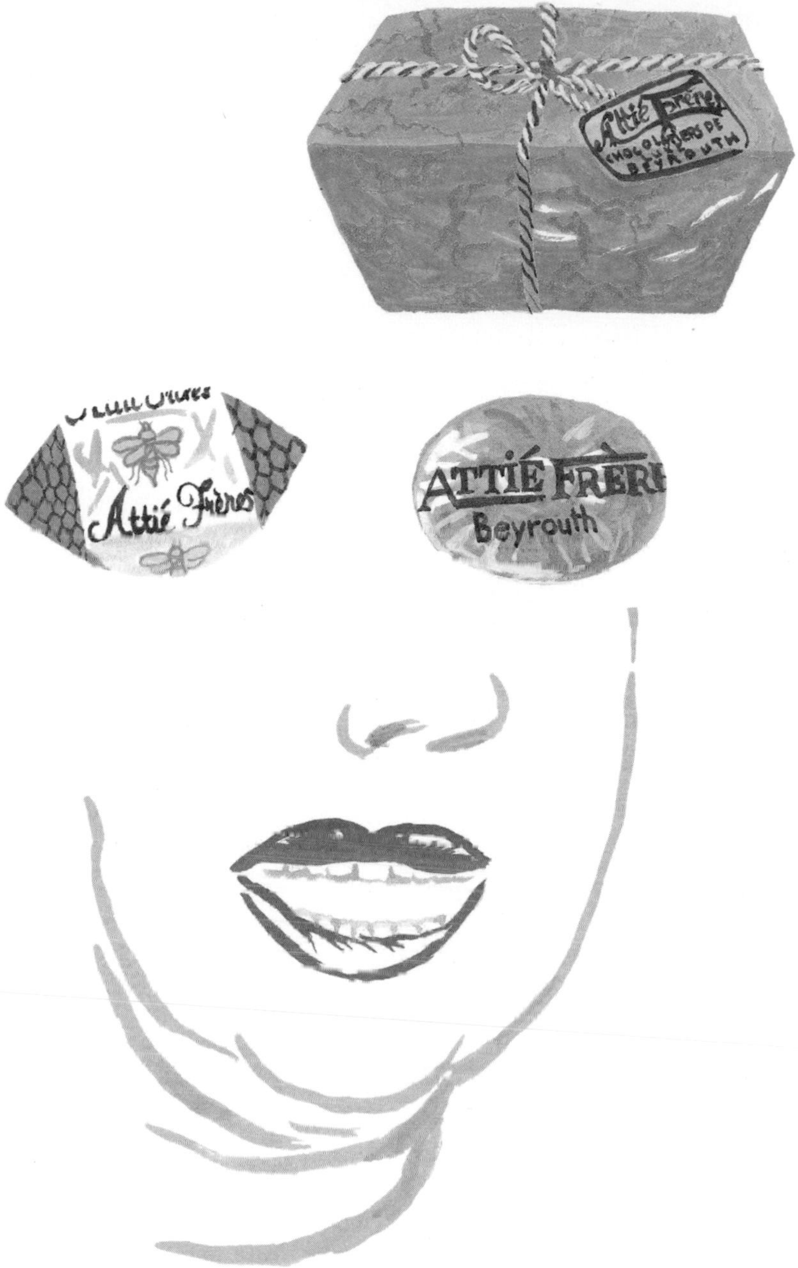

Attié Frères
Attié Frères
ATTIÉ FRÈRE
Beyrouth

The scent of *bakhour*, Father Kebbé's incense. Each year during Epiphany he comes to bless the house. Teta makes him walk through every single room; she holds the Holy Spirit in high regard and can't imagine that he would be annoyed, given the circumstances.

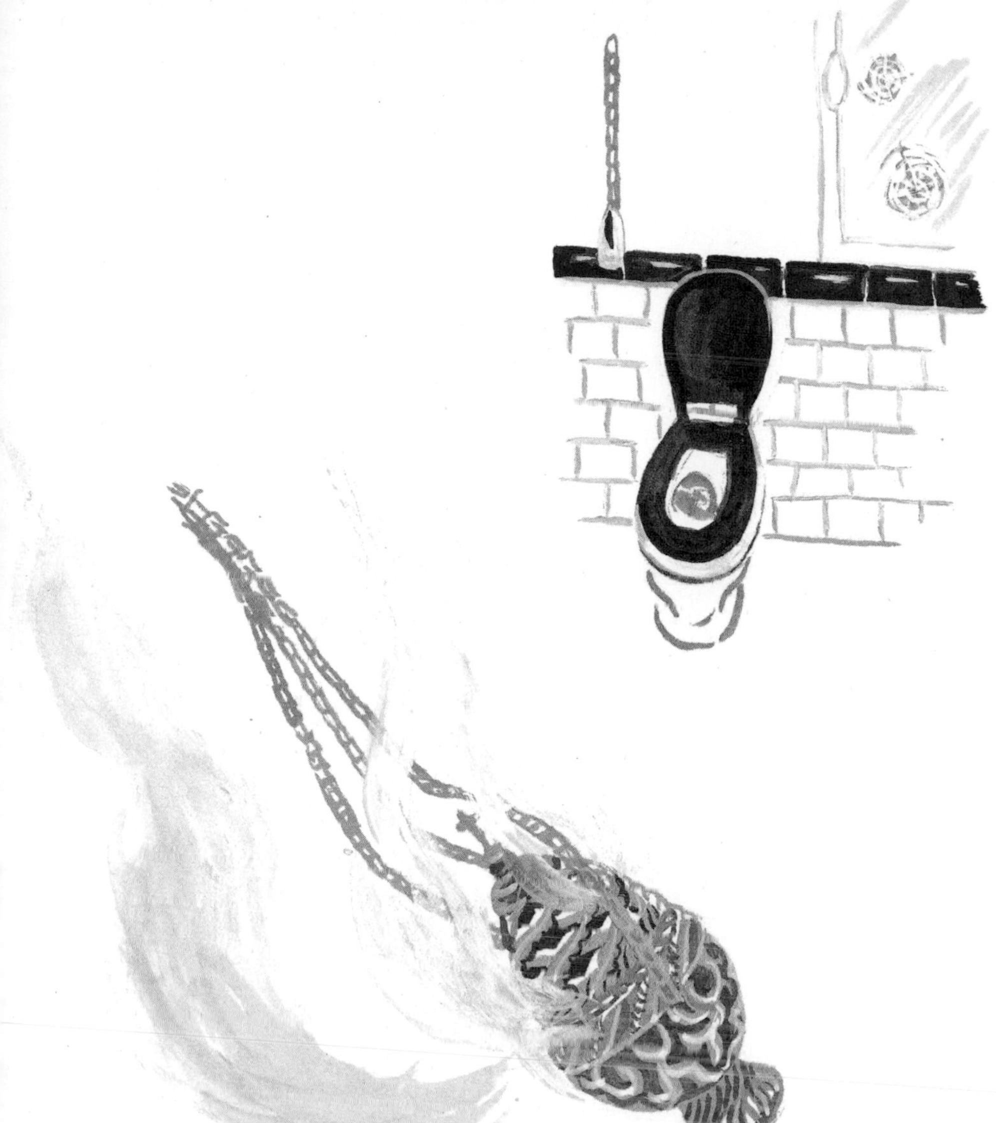

Then there are all the people who live in the house with us: the Virgin Mary in her alcove in the back of the blue room, with its paraphernalia of rosaries, flowers and candles; the bronze statue of the little mermaid of Copenhagen which has a place of honour on the dining-room radiator; Mitri and Michel in their silver frames, long dead. Teta stills shuts herself into her room twice a day to think about her husband Mitri and her son Michel. She has been in mourning for fifteen years and still dresses in black, with only a black, white and grey foulard or five strands of pearls as accessories.

Although she insists on wearing black, she is neither gloomy nor melancholy. She's the most joyous person in the world.

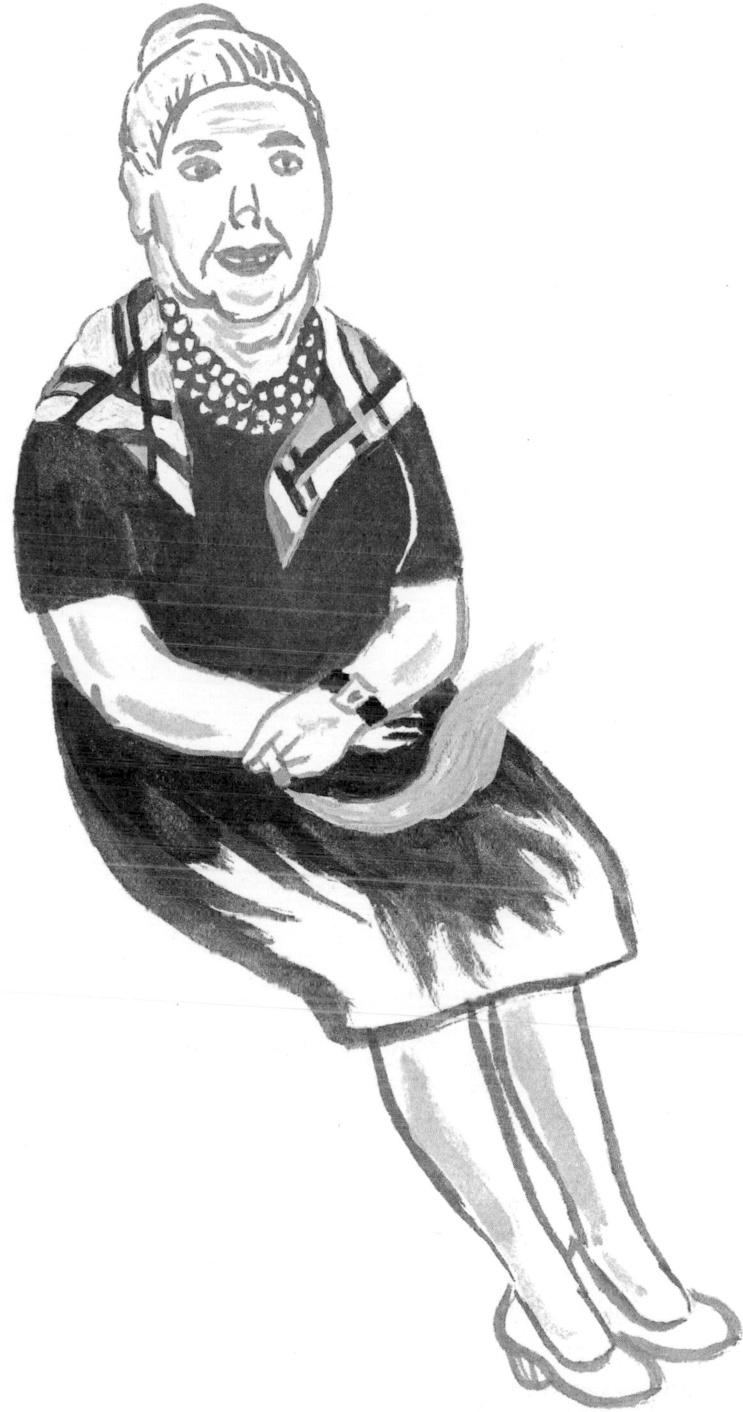

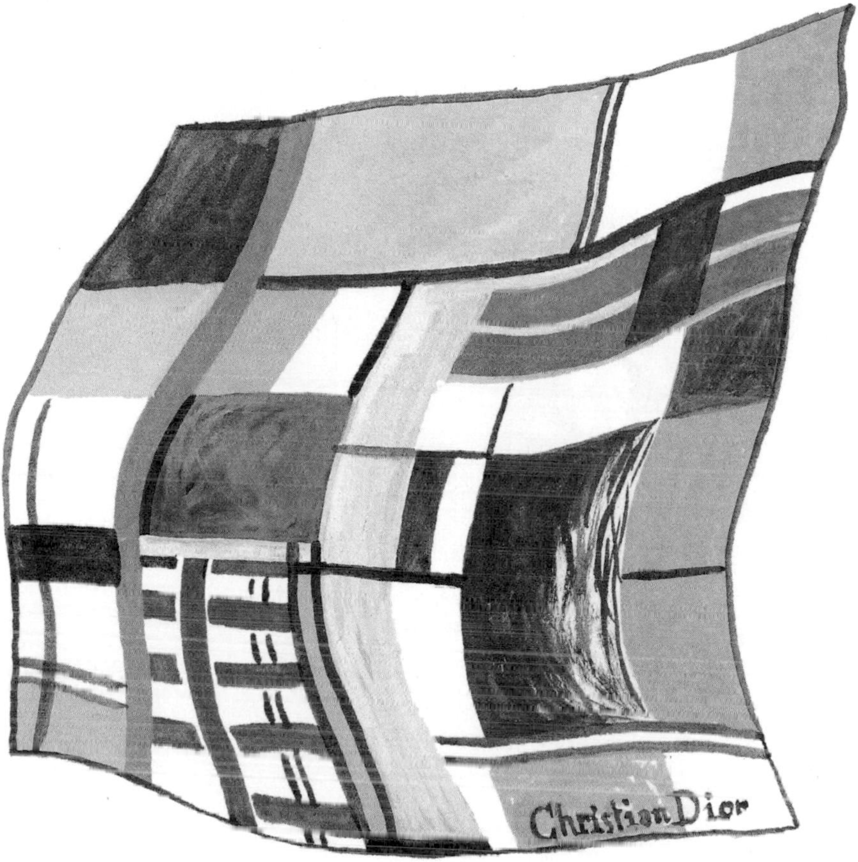
Christian Dior

Above all there is Thérèse. Thérèse weighs 180 kilos. Family legend has it that she, who was once slim and pretty, gained the weight in one night – the night my uncle Michel died.

It is said that she is the best cook in Beirut. At fourteen she came down from the mountains to work for Madame Eddé, who taught her everything. Madame Eddé was President Emile Eddé's wife during the French mandate. Thérèse knows all the secrets of French gastronomy. Boeuf Stroganoff, Veal Marengo, Tournedos Rossini, Savarin Chantilly or Tarte Pompadour hold no mystery for her. Her name, too, comes from that time; Madame Eddé changed the Arabic names of her domestic help to names of saints. Thérèse used to be called Wadiha or Salwa, I can't remember any more.

Thérèse knows the lines from *Ben Hur* by heart; each year she goes to see it at the Rivoli during Holy Week. Well, she did until 1974 . . . She always says that France would not be France without the Mont Saint-Michel. I think she says that because of my uncle Michel, whom she venerated. She also claims to have worked in the 1950s for a certain Mr Smith, a British banker she suspected of being a spy, *jesous*, and moreover that she herself was a spy for then president Camille Chamoun (who never knew about it).

Like all women, she was crazy about Camille Chamoun.

When he narrowly escaped an assassination attempt she had a gargantuan candle made especially to size (he was very tall!) to thank the Virgin Mary, *Saydet Harissa.*

Thérèse's stories delight me. When her memory (or her imagination) fails her for new stories I make her repeat my favourites that she has already told me hundreds of times. But after a few months, when the first colour television arrives – what bliss – she has serious competition.

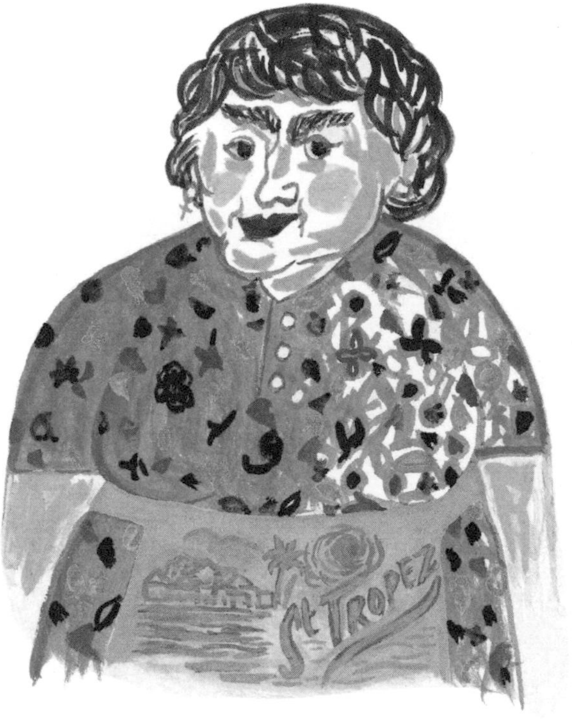
St TROPEZ

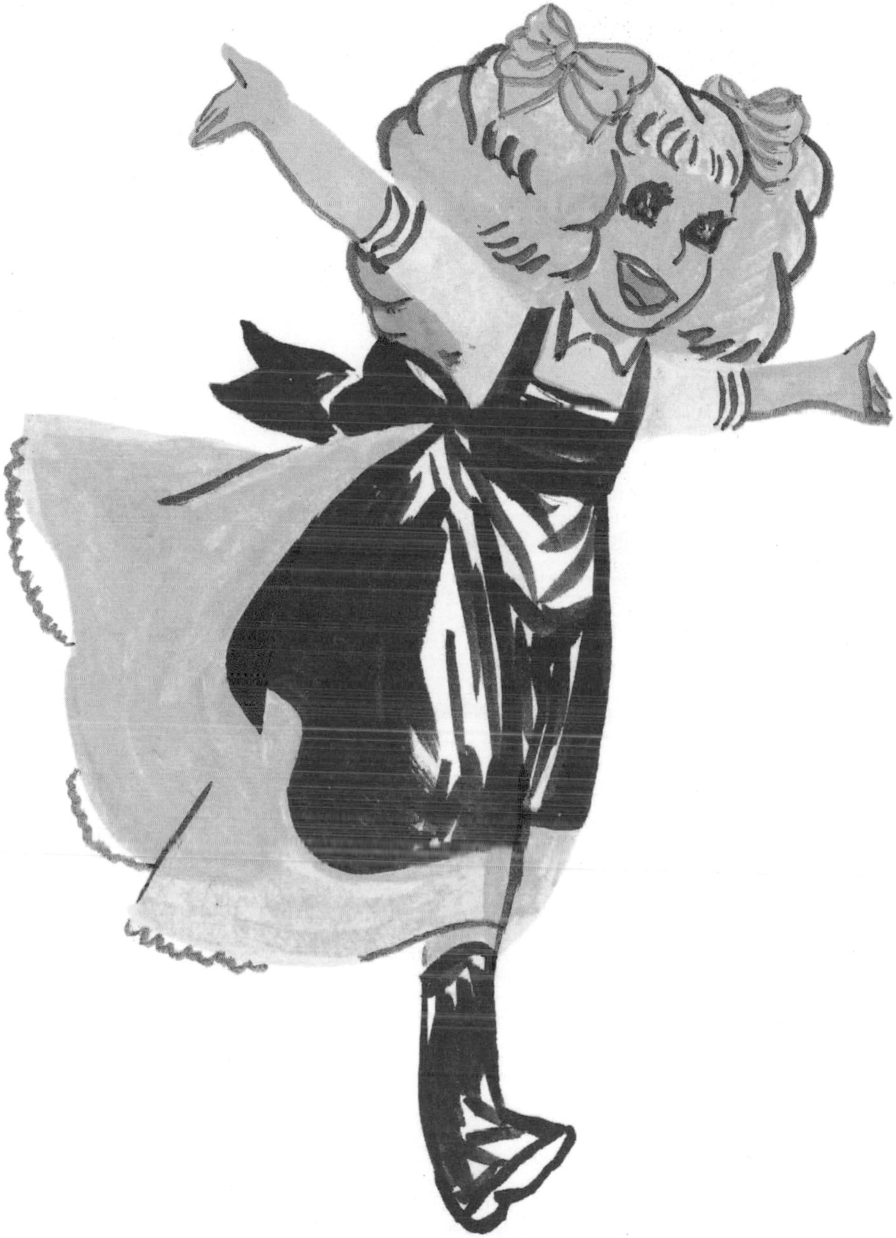

It's around this time that my mother and I begin to visit Elie. Elie is handicapped. He has opened a small chocolate factory in a cellar under the demarcation line! His mother and sister are the only employees. To get there without being shot at by a sniper one has to be taken by a trusted guide through a maze of houses, garages, stairways, gardens, deserted cellars connected by demolished walls with gaping holes, and alleyways lined with sandbags.

It's a dangerous adventure.

We go not only to help Elie and his little enterprise but also because his chocolate is so good. At first my mother (and Walid and I) began to make the journey just for chocolate Easter eggs, then little by little, for different occasions during the year. At the time, it seemed normal to me to buy chocolate underneath the demarcation line. In hindsight I think it was madness, and that the taste for risk and a certain *frisson* were also ingredients that explained the astonishing infatuation that the ladies from Ashrafieh had for Elie's date-filled chocolates. This was their war too, and they had to find some way to get to the frontline, *aal jabha*.

Another dangerous place that we continue to visit is la Santa church. But not on Maundy Thursday, the day when Christ washed his apostles' feet and when the priests in Beirut churches wash twelve of their parishioners' feet. That day, all good Christians must visit seven churches to admire the decorations on the temporary altar where the Holy Sacrament is displayed for the occasion. Since Teta is a very good Christian that's what she, Walid and I do, accompanied by Bich. Before getting to la Santa, we start out on our tour; first going to St-Antoine-des-Grecs-Catholiques church, *Mar Mtanios al-kouatlé*. My grandfather had this church built and Teta gets a queen's welcome from Father Kebbé. Next we go to St Demetrius, *Mar Mitr* (Greek Orthodox), to Notre-Dame-de-l'Annonciation, *Saydet al-Bechara*, rue du Liban, then to the St Saveur church, *Kniset al-Mkhaless*, Walid's favourite because of the great black veil pulled over the façade to represent the utensils used to torture Christ.

We continue our circuit via Notre-Dame-des-Dons, *Saydet al-Ataya* and St-Antoine-le-Grand, *Mar Mtanios al-kbir*, home to Maronite monks, on rue Abdelwahab al-Inglisi in front of the PNL's headquarters. Walid grumbles, while I could visit twenty churches! The smell of incense, the decorative iconostases, the bouquets of gladiolas and calla lilies, the beautiful Byzantine or Syriac chants, sung in Arabic by nasal voices, little girls all dressed up, veiled old ladies, the *zaatar*, or thyme *kaak* that we buy on the square, the Virgin Marys with neon halos and thousand-light-bulb chandeliers, all this keeps me enraptured for days.

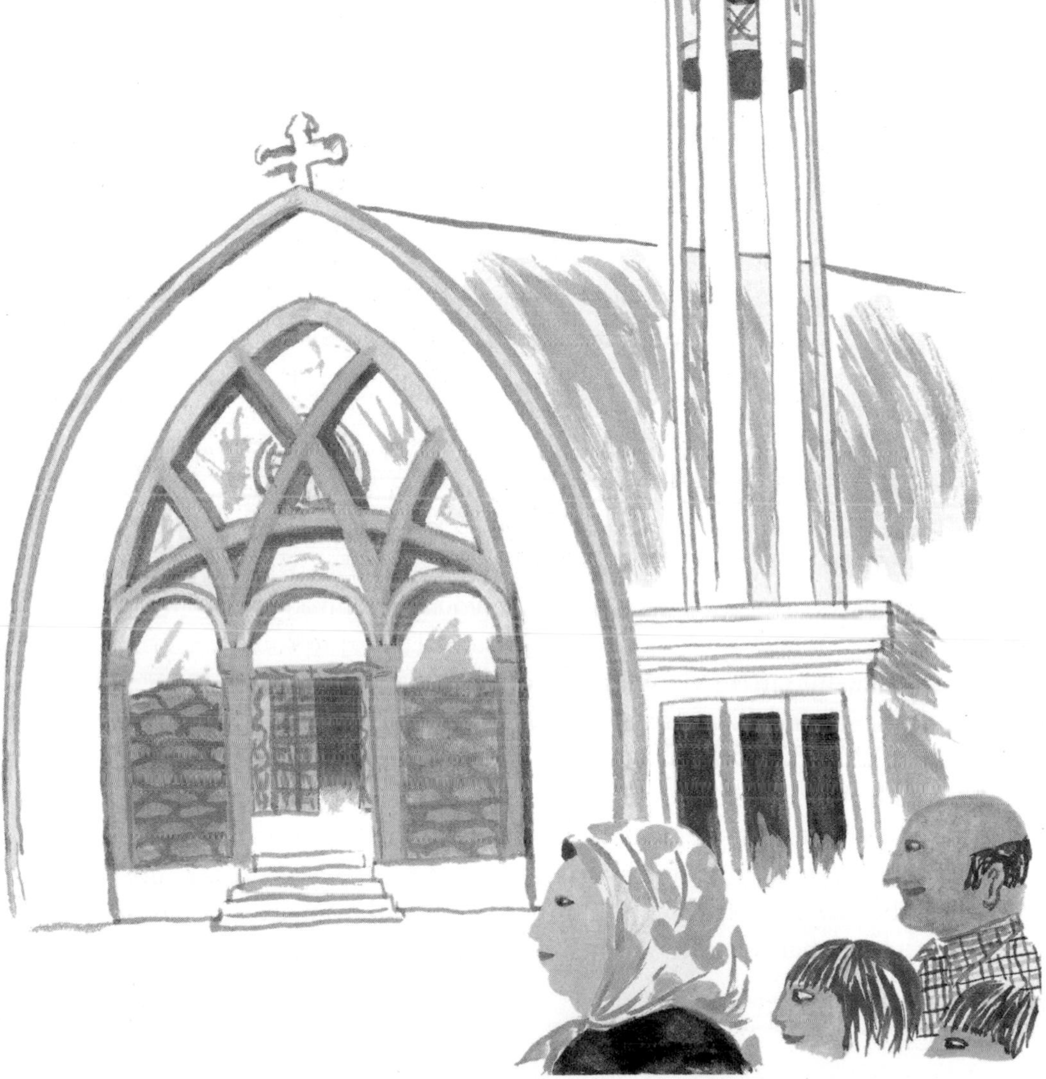

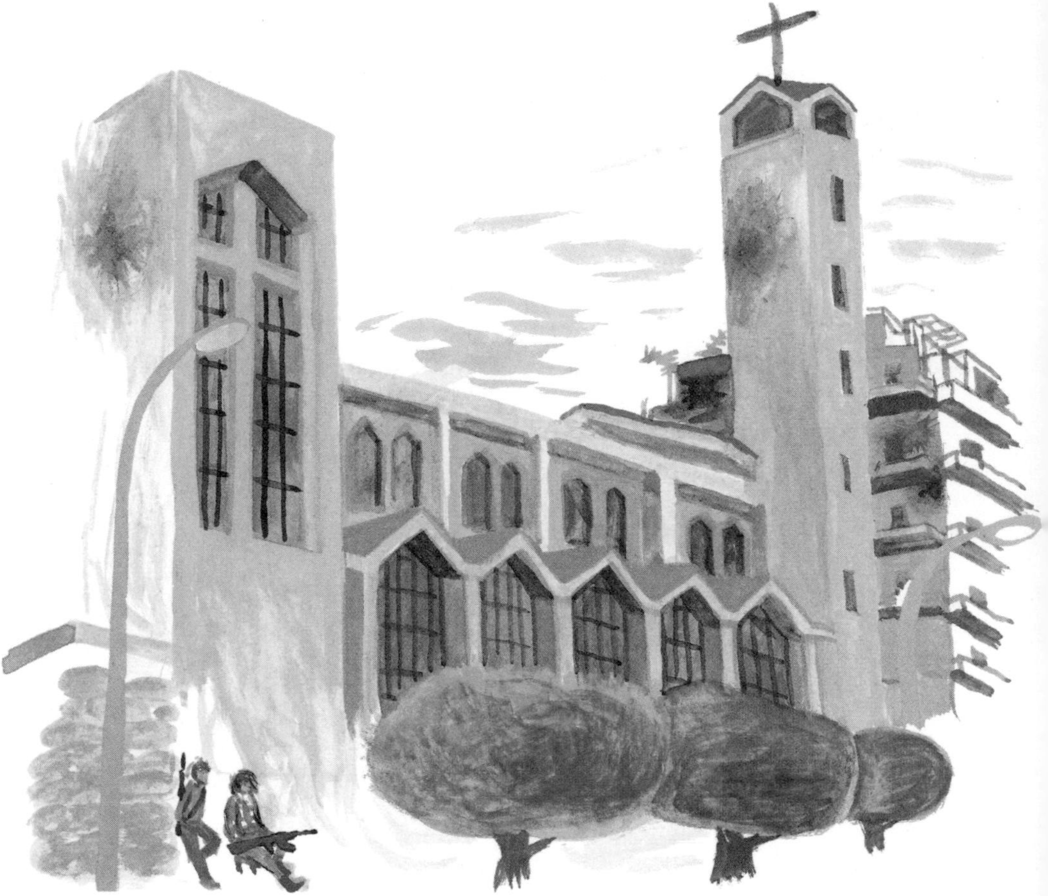

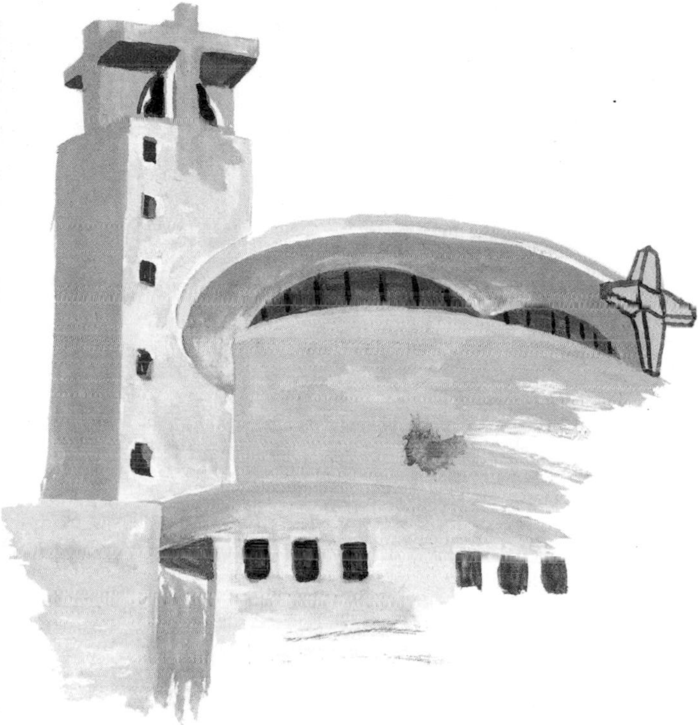
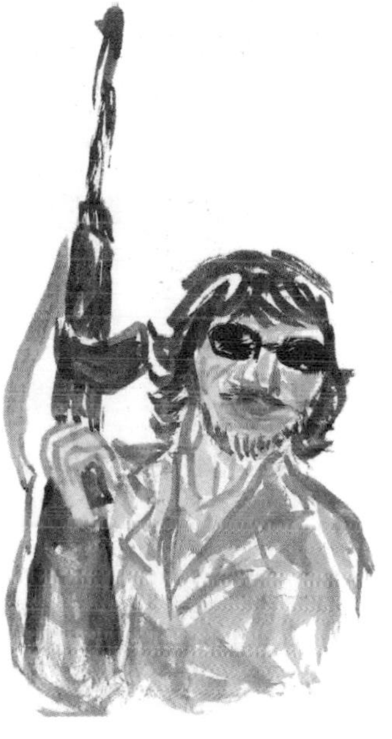

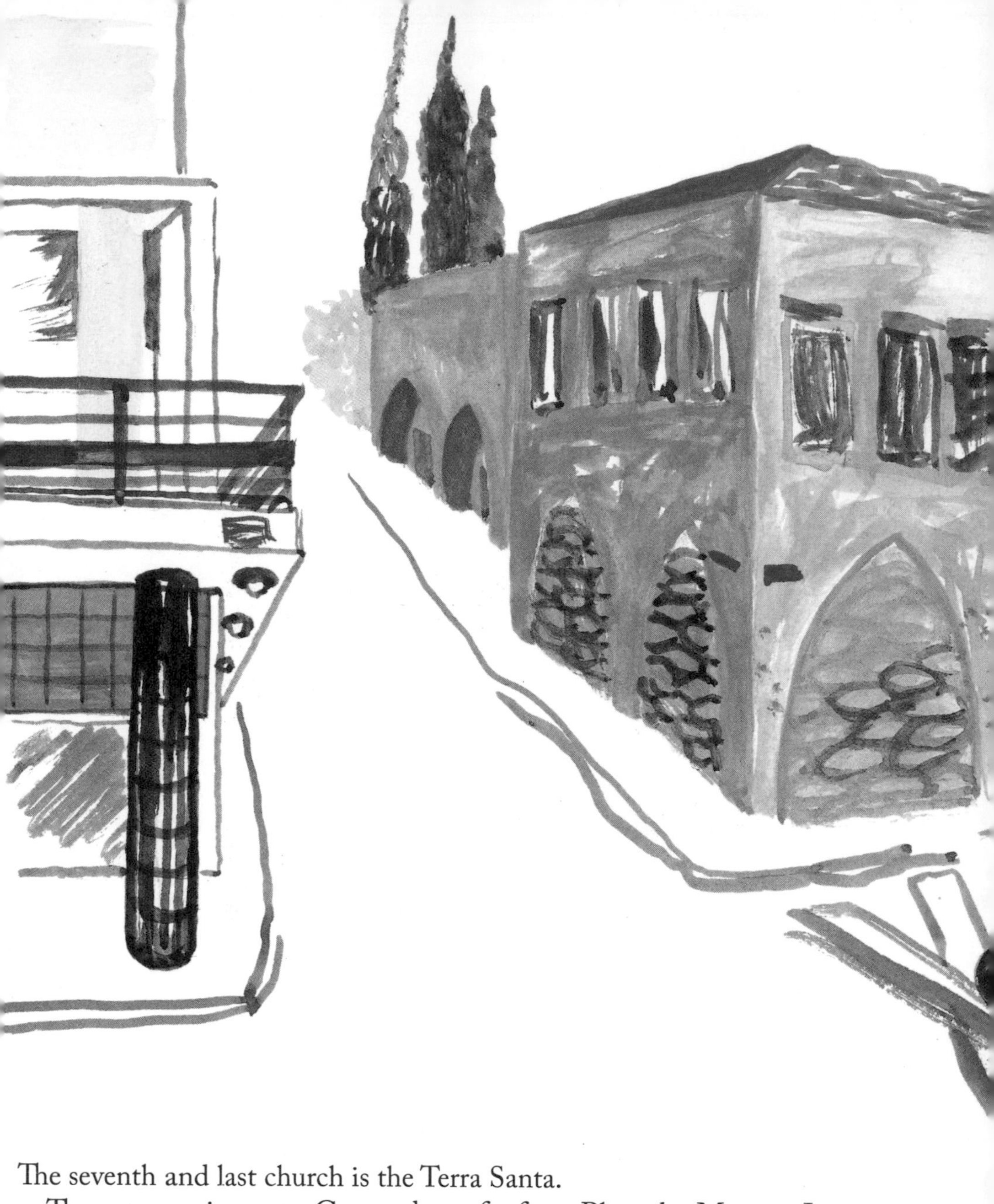

The seventh and last church is the Terra Santa.

The entrance is on rue Gouraud, not far from Place des Martyrs. It is a target for snipers. The few parishioners who still go to the church must use the perpendicular street, rue du Liban, and enter through the sacristy. 'It's safer', remarks Teta, who would be hard pressed to explain that the Good Lord could take someone who has just visited six churches.

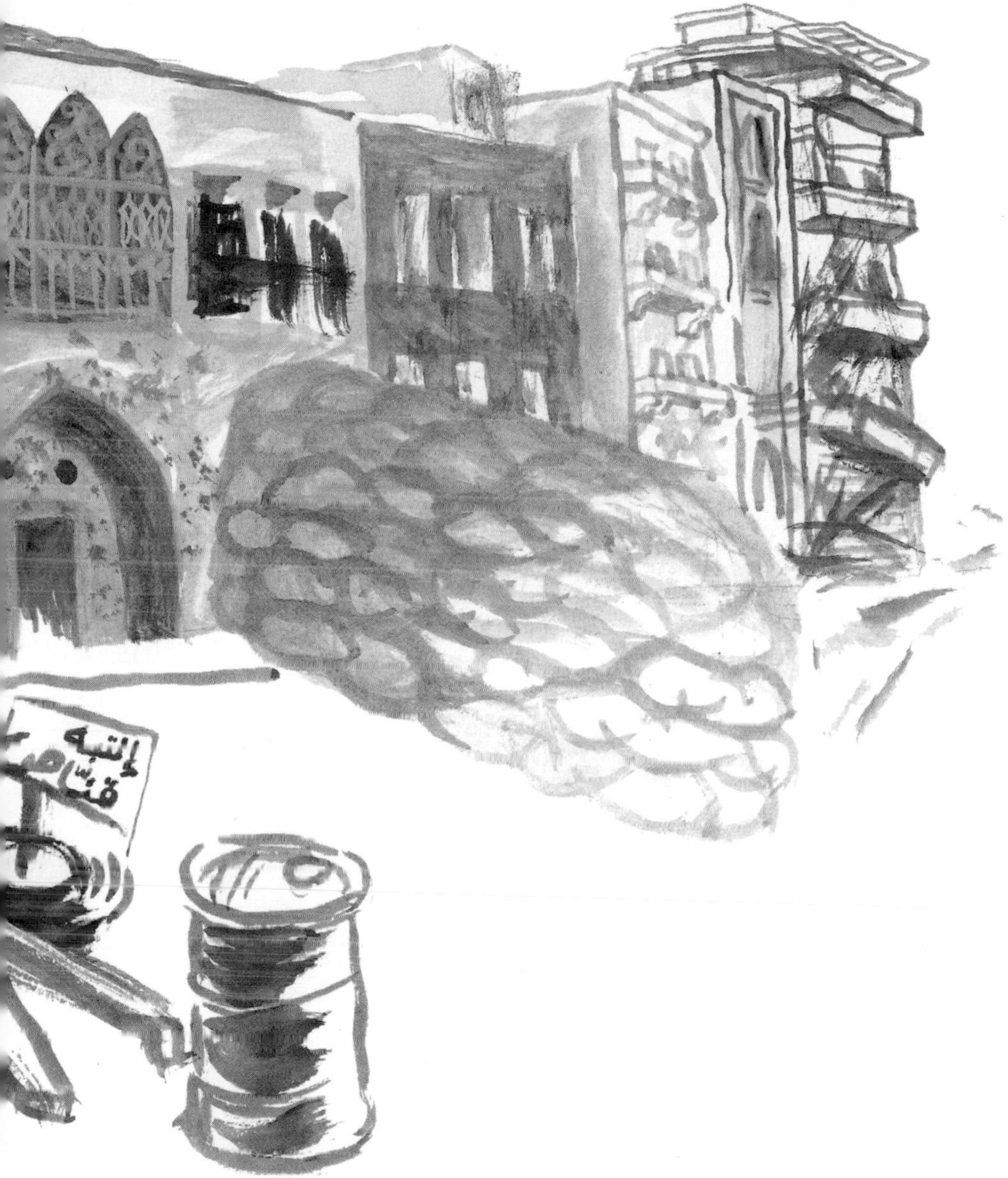
إنتبه

The old curtains

Then we move back into our apartment, which has been repaired.

New wallpaper, new curtains, it's all attractive and fresh.

But I hate the new curtains and I hate the new wallpaper.

I would die for the ones from 'before', the ones from back then . . .

At any rate they won't last. In the years to come our apartment will be hit several times while we are taking refuge in Kattine. But it will be smashed twice while we are inside.

The country has sunk into homicidal madness and the umpteenth Syro-Lebanese summit won't make any difference. Neither does the ballet of American envoys disturb the smooth progress of war.

We also learn that other serious events are occurring in the Middle East.

The circumstances in Iran during this legendary year of 1979 leave us, and the rest of the world, breathless. Unfamiliar faces appear, completing a sinister picture.

New monsters have arrived. The least frightening are definitely not on the Israeli side. During the 1980s they will not disappoint us and will achieve total self-fulfillment.

The war continues in spite of everyone, or rather, thanks to everyone's efforts.

The 1980s will be gloomy, bleak, appalling.

الإمام الخميني
قائد الثورة الإسلامية

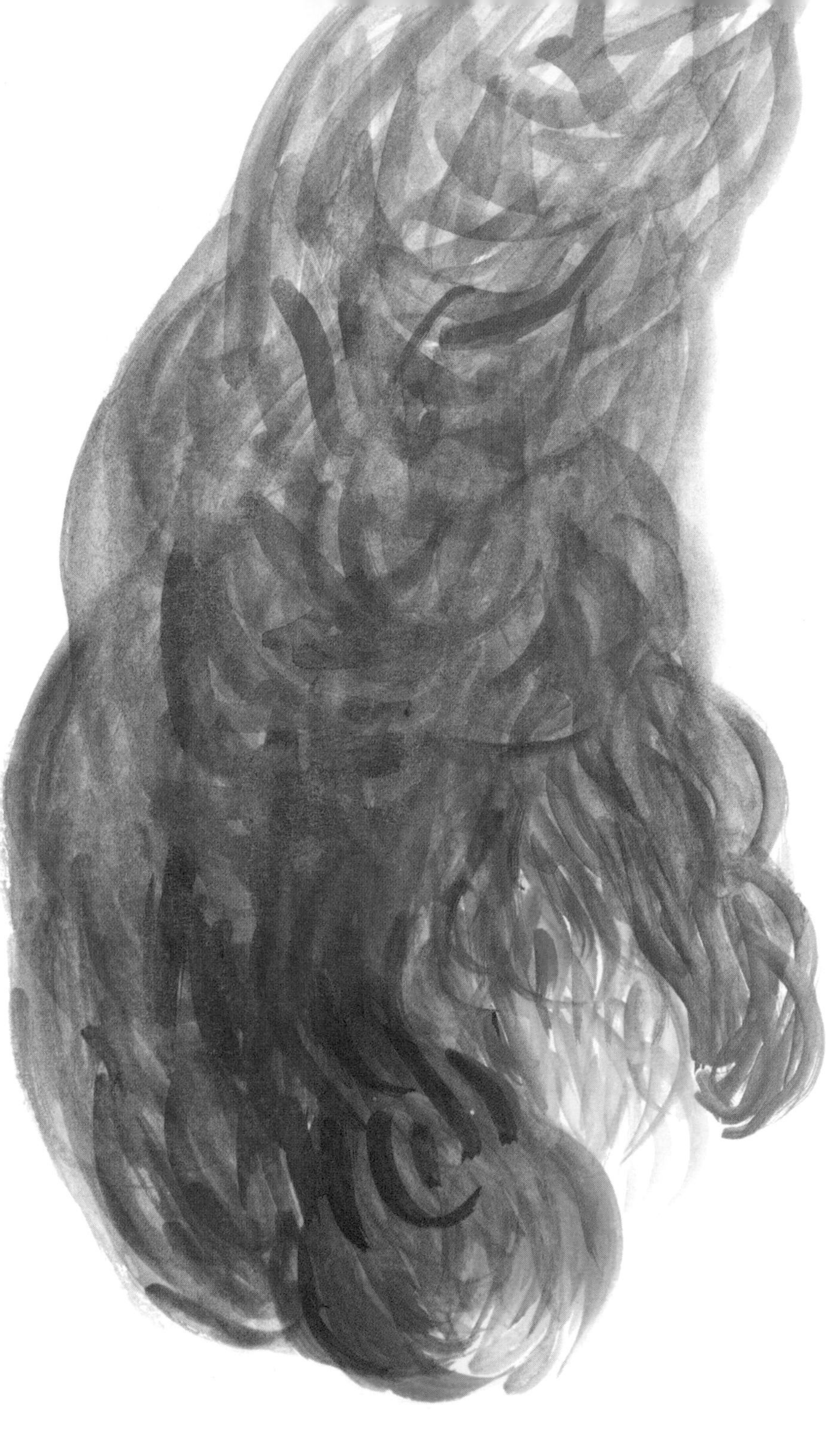

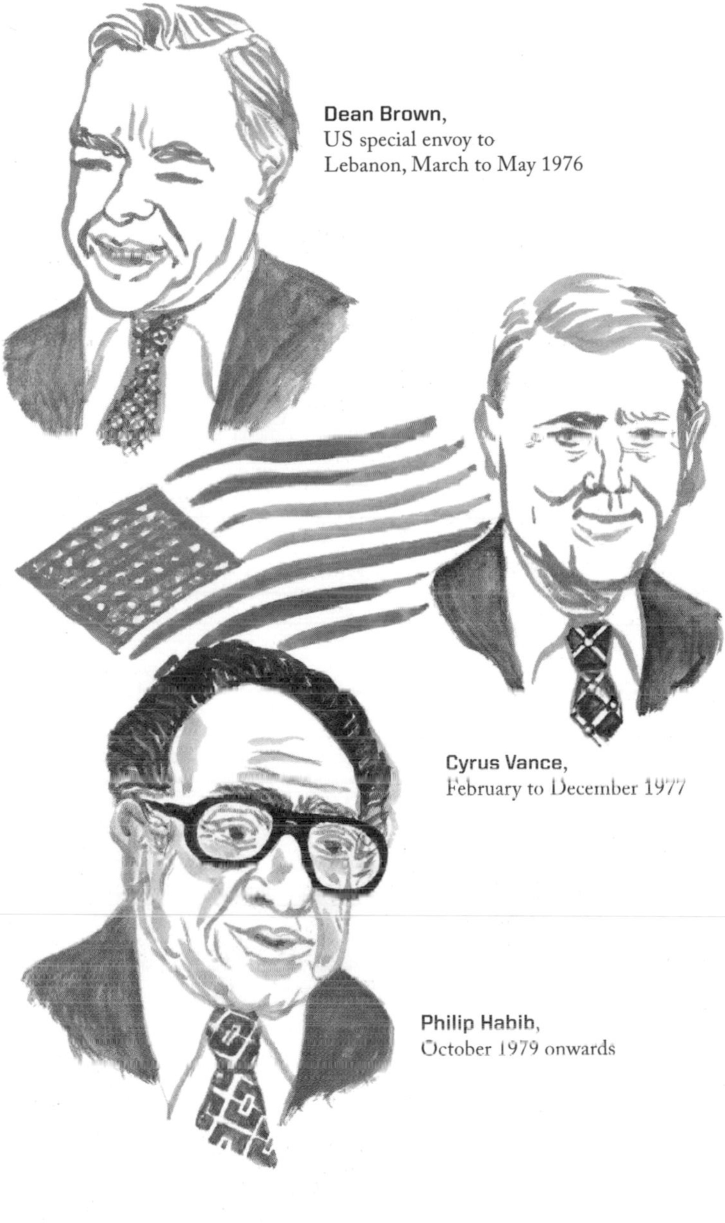

Dean Brown,
US special envoy to
Lebanon, March to May 1976

Cyrus Vance,
February to December 1977

Philip Habib,
October 1979 onwards

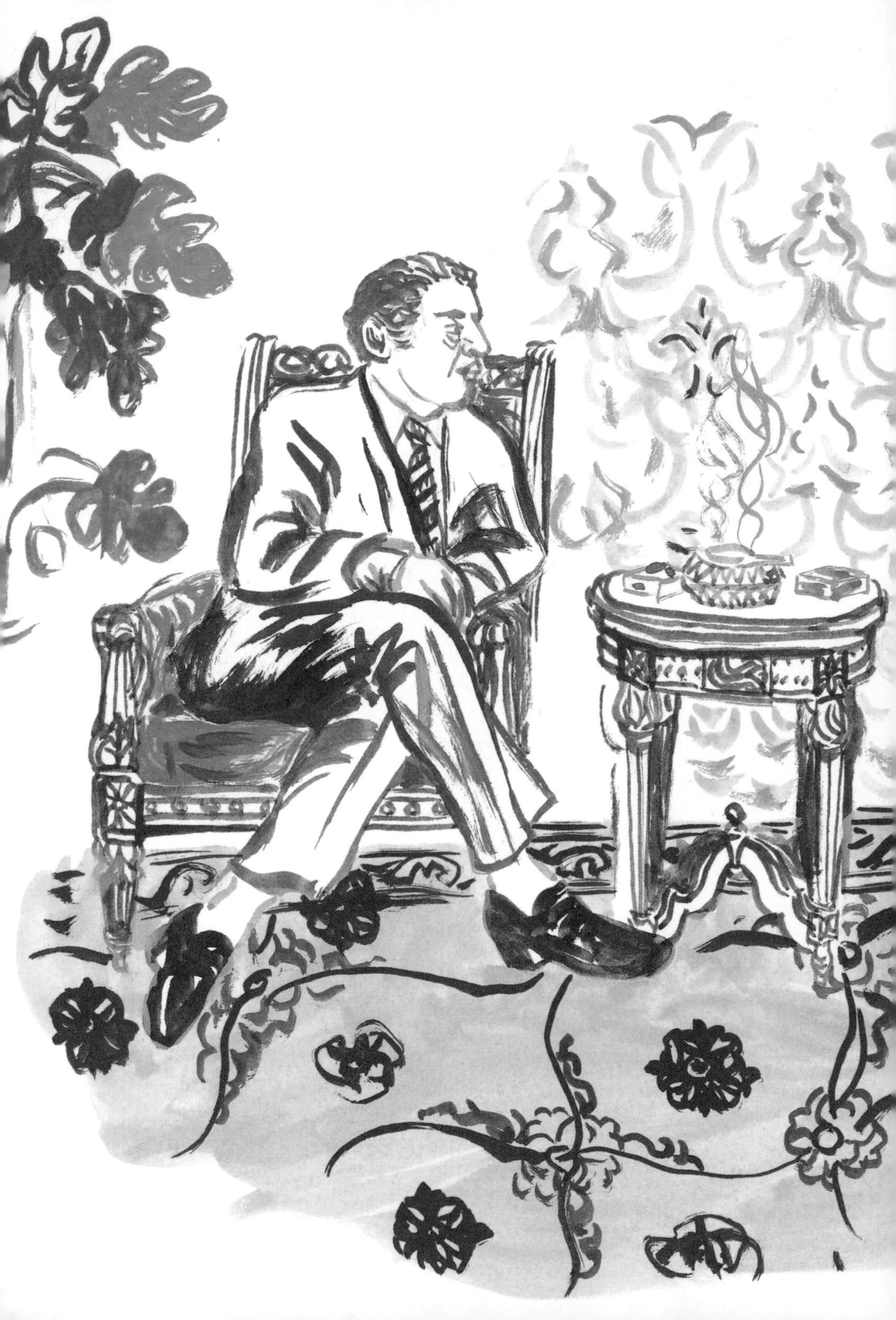

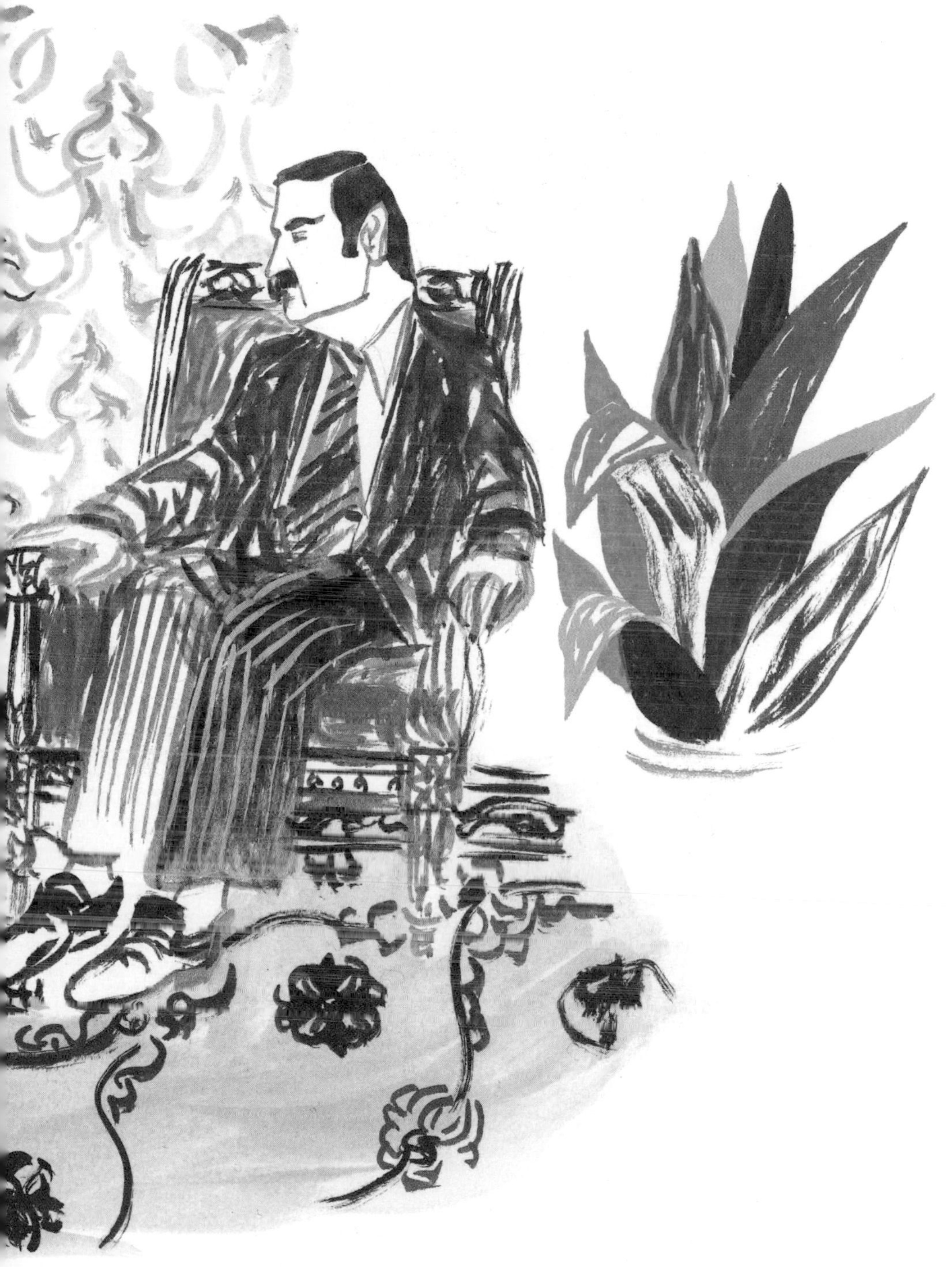

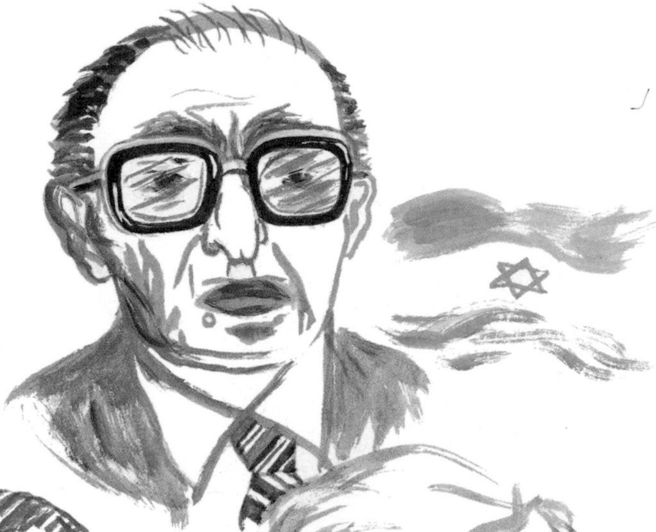

Menachem Begin,
Israeli Prime Minister

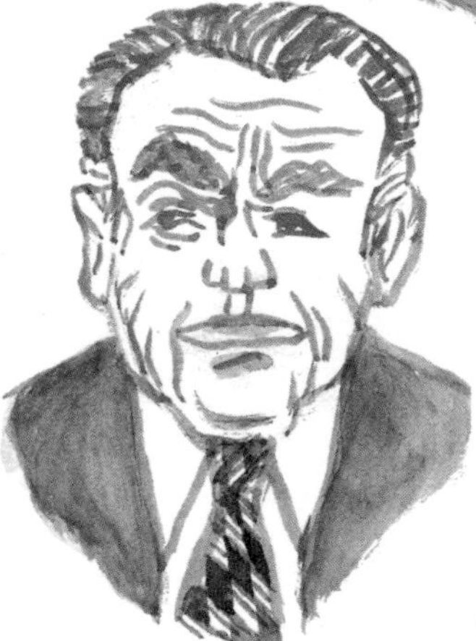

Yitzhak Shamir,
Israeli Minister of Foreign Affairs

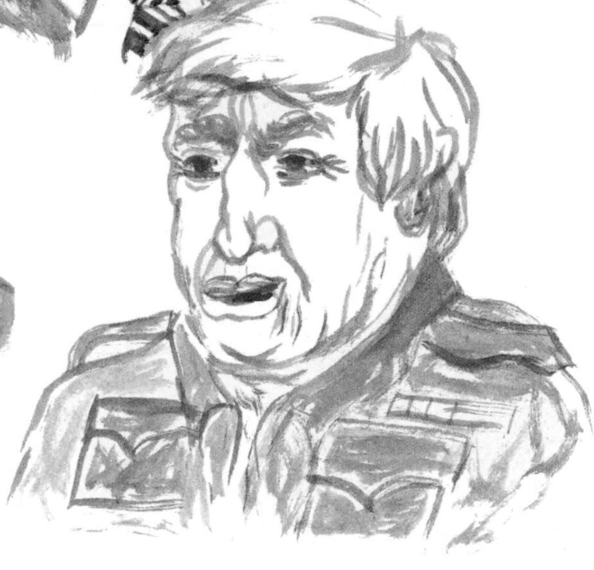

Ariel Sharon,
Israeli Minister of Defence

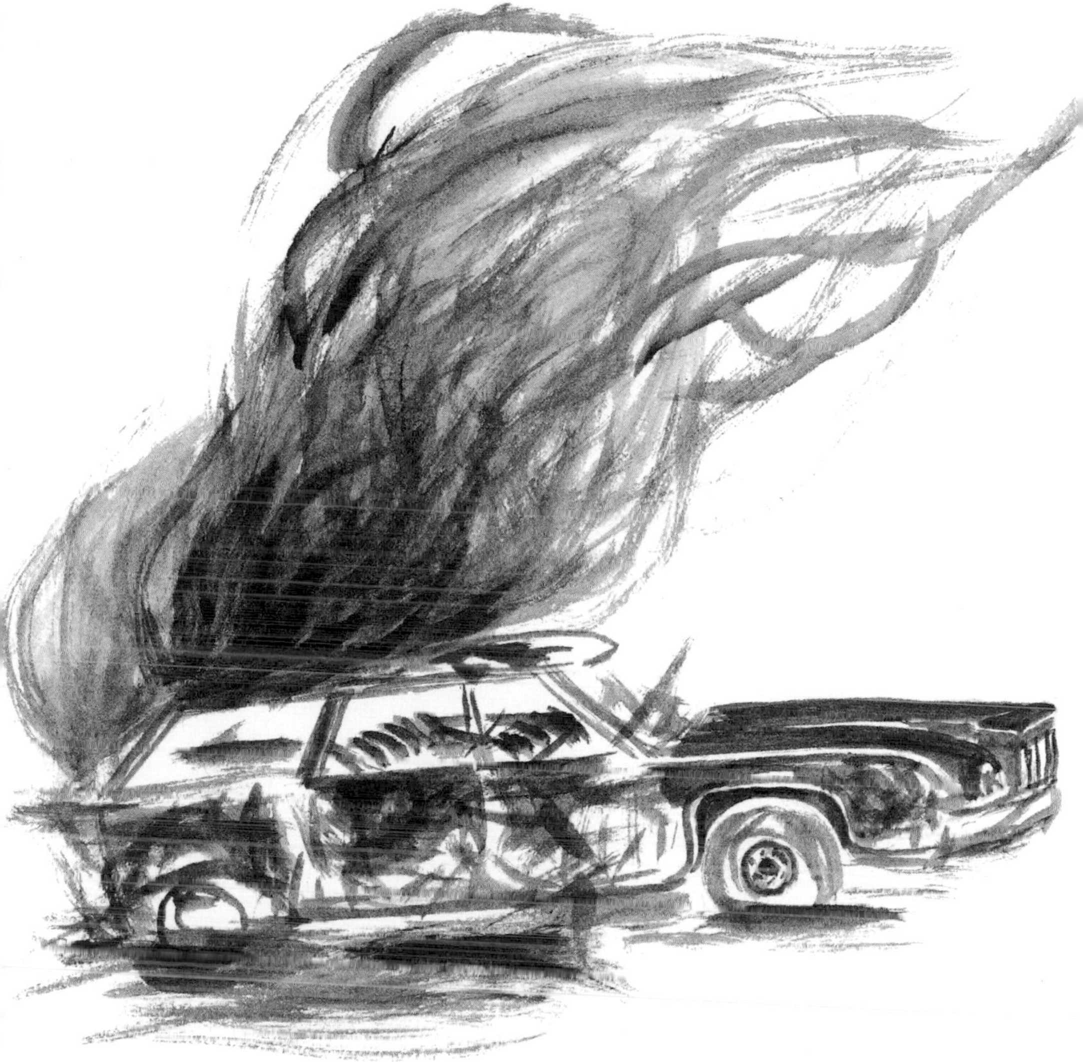

Besides everything else we have tested (snipers, bombings, kidnappings, massacres . . .), there's a new trend that spreads rapidly: the car bomb.

The young and handsome Ali Hassan Salameh, responsible for PLO intelligence and whom Arafat considered a son, will be one of the first victims. The next decade will be the golden age of the car bomb.

Since 1975, summer or winter, whenever there is unrest in Beirut we take advantage of a ceasefire and flee to Kattine, which is in one of the rare regions that is still sheltered from the war.

There are sometimes up to fifty people in the house, several of us per room, mattresses lined up on the floor to welcome parents and friends. Not everyone is as lucky as we are, having a family house in a protected area. Teta is the only one who has a room to herself that she shares with the Virgin Mary, Mitri and Michel, transported in their silver frames.

No more school, but board games, card games, fire in the hearth, snail or frog-hunting, egg-gathering, juice-box popping, making necklaces from pine needles, spinning acorn tops, blowing soap bubbles, new books, bike rides, visits to the farm. It's a holiday atmosphere that smells of tragedy.

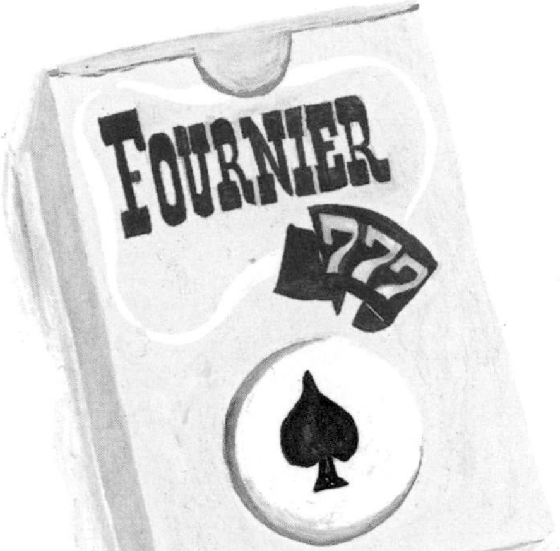
FOURNIER

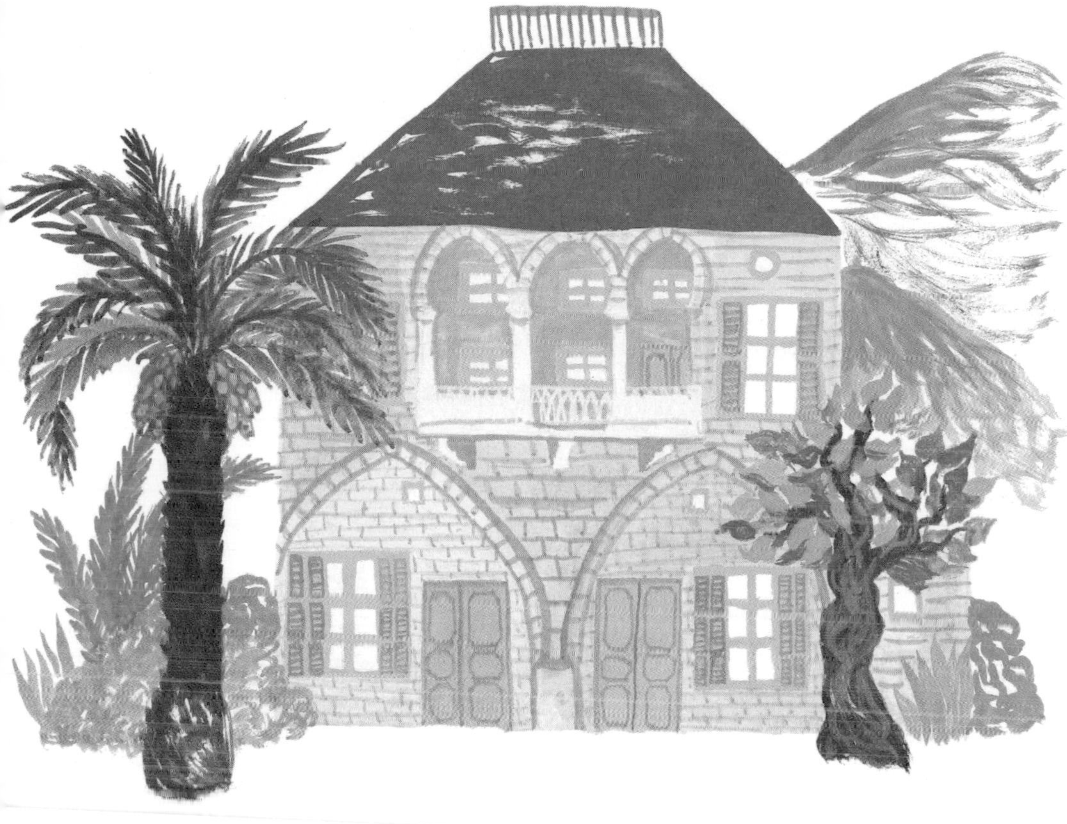

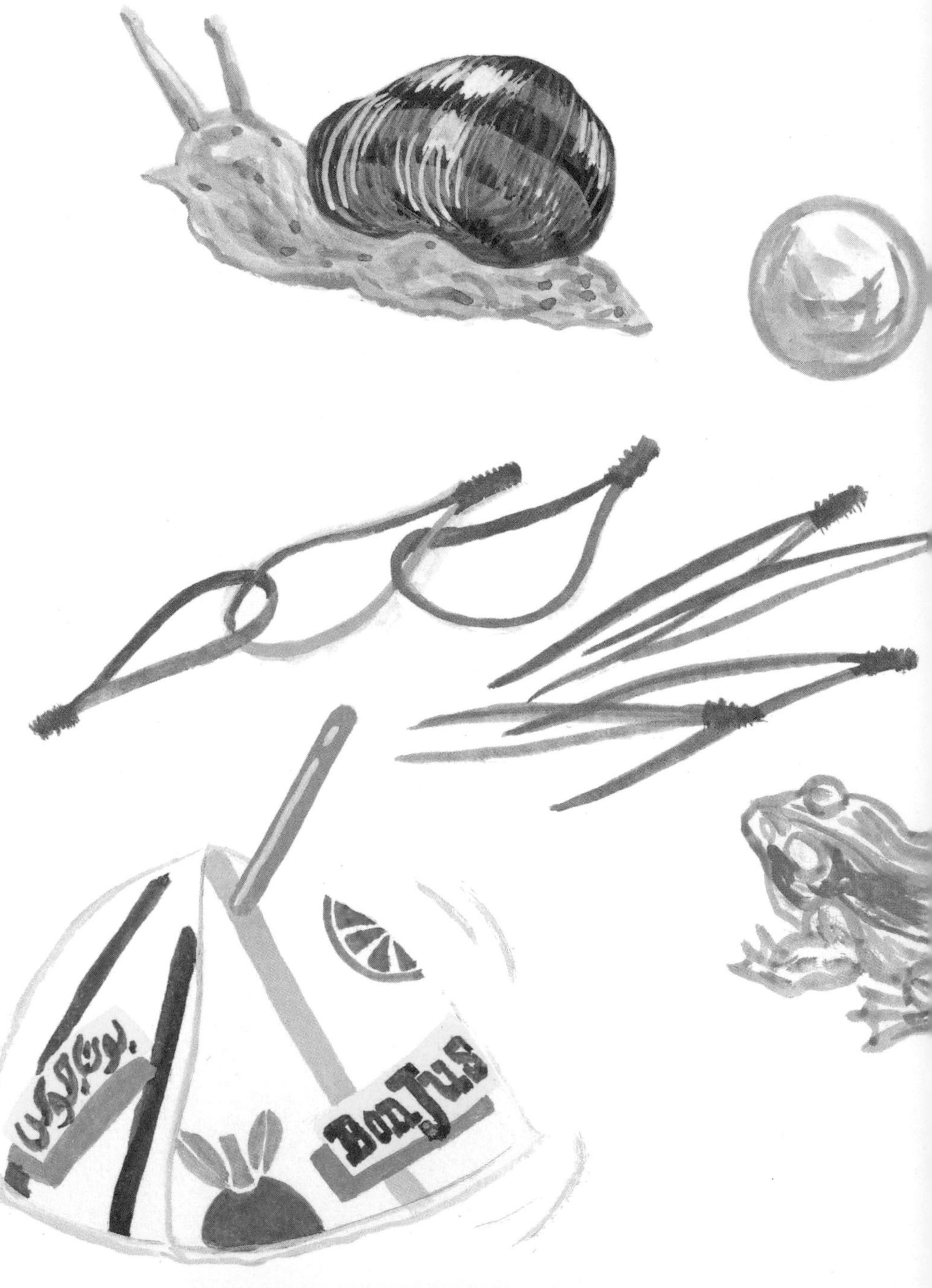
Bon Jus

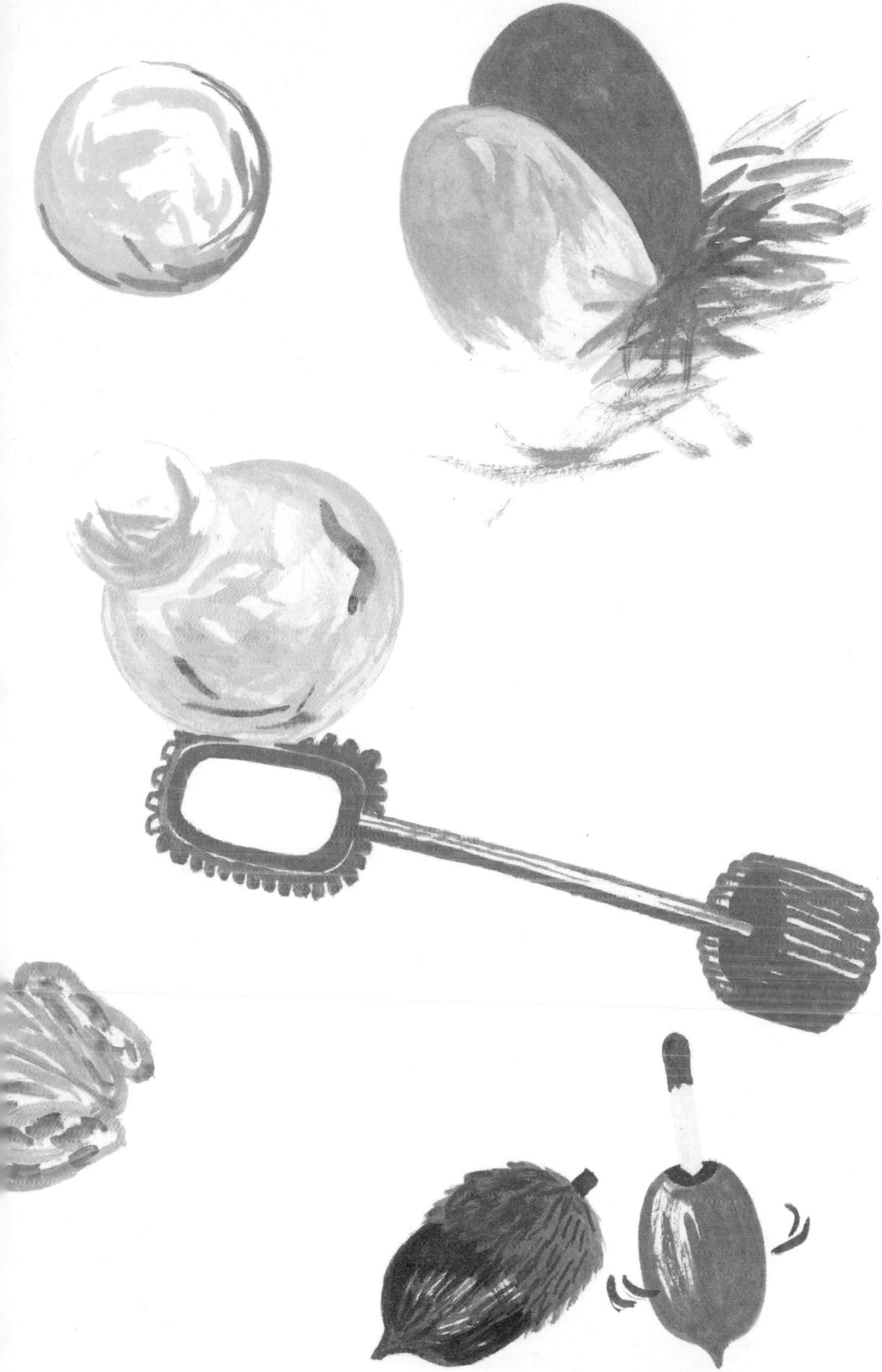

For those taking a stroll after dinner,
a wide bend in the road above the village offers
breathtaking views of Beirut in flames.

   It's the end of the 1970s, the war has been going on
for five years now, and we have no idea that the worst
is yet to come, for both the Lebanese and the Palestinians.

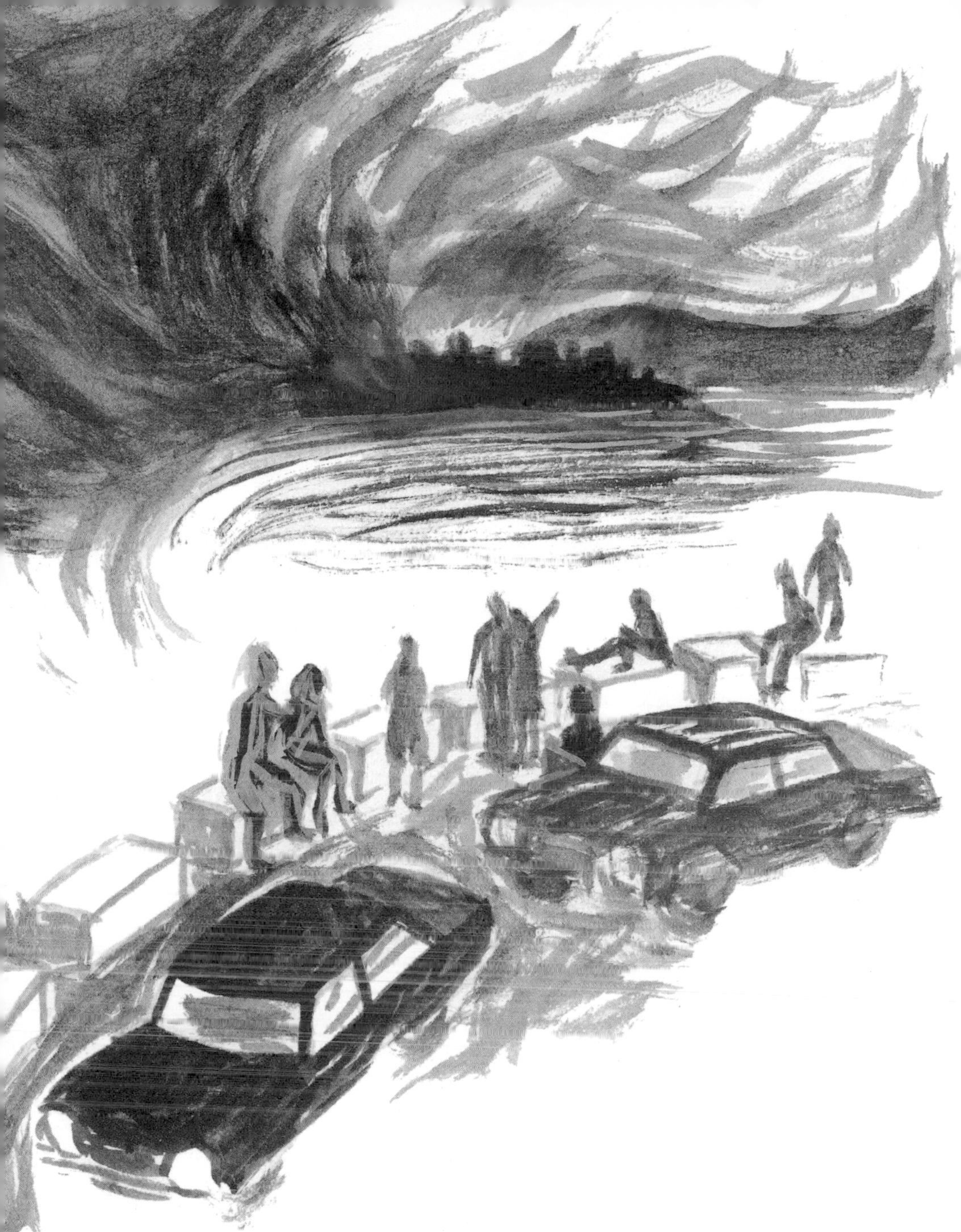

In a short while we won't be safe anywhere, not even in our tranquil little village of Kattine, which has long been spared. We will spend the summer of 1990 there, hemmed in between four walls of sandbags erected in the middle of the spacious living room on the ground floor. On 11 August, eleven large-calibre shells fall on the terraces, in the garden, on the roof and on the rooms facing the south. We find them the next day when we emerge to take stock of the damage. Walid and I have long since abandoned our collection.

It's my twenty-second birthday.

1918 Fall of the Ottoman Empire (Lebanon had been a part of it since 1516)

1920-1943 Lebanon is under French mandate and Palestine is under British mandate following the Sykes-Picot Agreement and a ruling by the League of Nations (LON)

1920 In Lebanon the first high commissioner, General Gouraud, proclaims the state of Greater Lebanon. In Palestine the Balfour Declaration (1917) promises the Zionist movement the establishment of a Jewish nation in the region

1943 Independence of Lebanon. French troops leave in 1946. The 'national pact', an unwritten agreement, institutes a multi-faith state dividing political power between Maronites, Sunnites, Shiites, Greek Orthodox, Druze and Greek Catholics

1948 End of British mandate in Palestine. Founding of State of Israel by David Ben Gurion. Egypt, Syria, Jordan, Lebanon and Iraq enter the war

1949 End of first Arab-Israeli war with Israel's victory and extension of borders. 750,000 Palestinians go into exile. The West Bank is under Jordanian control and Gaza under Egyptian control

1958 Creation of United Arab Republic, a union between Nasser's Egypt and Syria. Insurgency in Beirut between partisans and opponents to Lebanon joining the UAR

1959 Yasser Arafat founds Fatah (Palestinian National Liberation Movement)

1964 Founding of the PLO

1967 The Six-Day War. Israel is victorious, taking the Sinai, Gaza, the West Bank and the Golan Heights

1968 Israeli planes destroy fourteen civilian aircraft at Beirut Airport in December

1969 Tension mounts in Lebanon with Palestinian guerrillas. Signature of Cairo agreement legalising the presence and activities of Palestinians in Lebanon

1970 'Black September' in Jordan. King Hussein has thousands of Palestinians massacred. Yasser Arafat and his *fedayeen* move to Lebanon

1973 Violent clashes between Lebanese army and Palestinian organisations. Palestinian camps are shelled for the first time

1975

The right-wing Christians, among which the main leaders Pierre Gemayel, of the Kataeb party, and Camille Chamoun, of the PNL, feel threatened by the instability the Palestinian resistance is creating in the country

13 April Clash in Ain el-Remmaneh between Kataeb and Palestinians after a church service. THE CIVIL WAR ERUPTS

18 September First battles in downtown Beirut. The souks are torched. Snipers terrorise Beirut, kidnappings and civilian executions take place on the basis of religion

8 October Generalised skirmishes in Beirut. Shelling of Ashrafieh.

25 October Kantari is sacked by the left-wing parties. New front in *grands hotels* neighbourhood

6 December 'Black Saturday'. Hundreds of Muslim civilians are killed in Christian neighbourhoods following the axe murder of four Kataeb members

8 December Violent offensive in the *grands hotels* neighbourhood. The Saint-Georges falls into the hands of the Mourabitoun

1976

January Green line appears dividing Beirut into two

18 January Karantina massacre

21 January Damour massacre

16 March Prison doors are opened and inmates released

22 March The Holiday Inn is in the hands of the Palestinian-leftists

4 April Jumblatt denounces illegal entry to Lebanon of Syrian soldiers to help Saiqa party

8 April Robbery of banks in Beirut. Looting and burning of port

28 April Elias Sarkis announces he is running for president against Raymond Eddé

8 May Sarkis elected with rockets raining down around him

16 May Indiscriminate shelling of Beirut. Edouard Saab, editor-in-chief of *L'Orient-Le Jour*, is killed by a sniper

7 June Beirut airport closes. No water or electricity

16 June US Ambassador Francis Meloy, his economic advisor and his chauffeur are kidnapped and assassinated in Beirut

25 June 10,000 rockets fall on Beirut in four days and 3,000 the day after. No water or electricity

12 August Fall of Tal al-Zaatar Palestinian camp after a fifty-three-day siege

23 September Swearing-in ceremony of Sarkis in the Park Hotel in Chtaura

25 October Cairo Summit

15 November 250 Syrian tanks and 8,000 soldiers enter Beirut. 250 Syrian tanks and 3,000 soldiers enter Tripoli and Saida

1977

16 March Kamal Jumblatt is assassinated in the Chouf, one hundred metres from a Syrian checkpoint

19 November Anwar Sadat's historic visit to Israel

1978

7 February Clashes between Lebanese and Syrian soldiers. Syrians shell Christian neighbourhoods

14 March More than 25,000 Israelis, supported by planes, armoured cars and artillery, occupy a tenth of Lebanese territory in less than twenty-four hours.

13 June Ehden Massacre. Tony Frangieh, his wife, his daughter and his men are assassinated by a Phalangist commando

1 July Beginning of the Hundred-Day War. Syrian artillery shells Christian neighbourhoods for three months. Bullets hail on Ashrafieh. 130 rockets fall on l'Hôtel-Dieu. Huge fire at the port

11 September 'Disappearance' of Imam Musa Sadr in Libya

17 September Camp David accords signed by Egypt and Israel

28 September 'Black Thursday' in Ashrafieh. East Beirut burns. Thousands of rockets rain down on Christian neighbourhoods, primarily from the Rizk tower where the Syrian army is posted. Shortages of food and medicine

1 October Shelling of Ashrafieh. Buildings collapse. The population remains in shelters for several days.

7 October Ceasefire.

1979

16 January Hijacking of MEA Boeing by Shia militia. More plane hijacking will take place this year

22 January Ali Hassan Salameh, responsible for PLO intelligence, is killed by a car bomb in Beirut

8 May Battles between Armenian militia (Tachnag) and the Kataeb in Nabaa and Bourj Hammoud.

12 May Clashes with mortars between the Kataeb and the PNL

27 June Syrians and Israelis battle it out in the sky over Damour. Four Syrian MIGs are downed

22 July Israeli planes bomb Damour, Naamé and Sarafand

15 August Violent clashes between Lebanese Forces and Syrians. Rocket attacks on Gemmayzeh, Accawi and Ashrafieh

20 August Israeli planes bomb southern Lebanon

10 September Violent clashes between the Kataeb and the Tachnag

24 September Syro-Israeli duel in the sky, four Syrian planes shot down

2 November Battles in Chiyah between Amal militia and Syrians

BEIRUT 1975

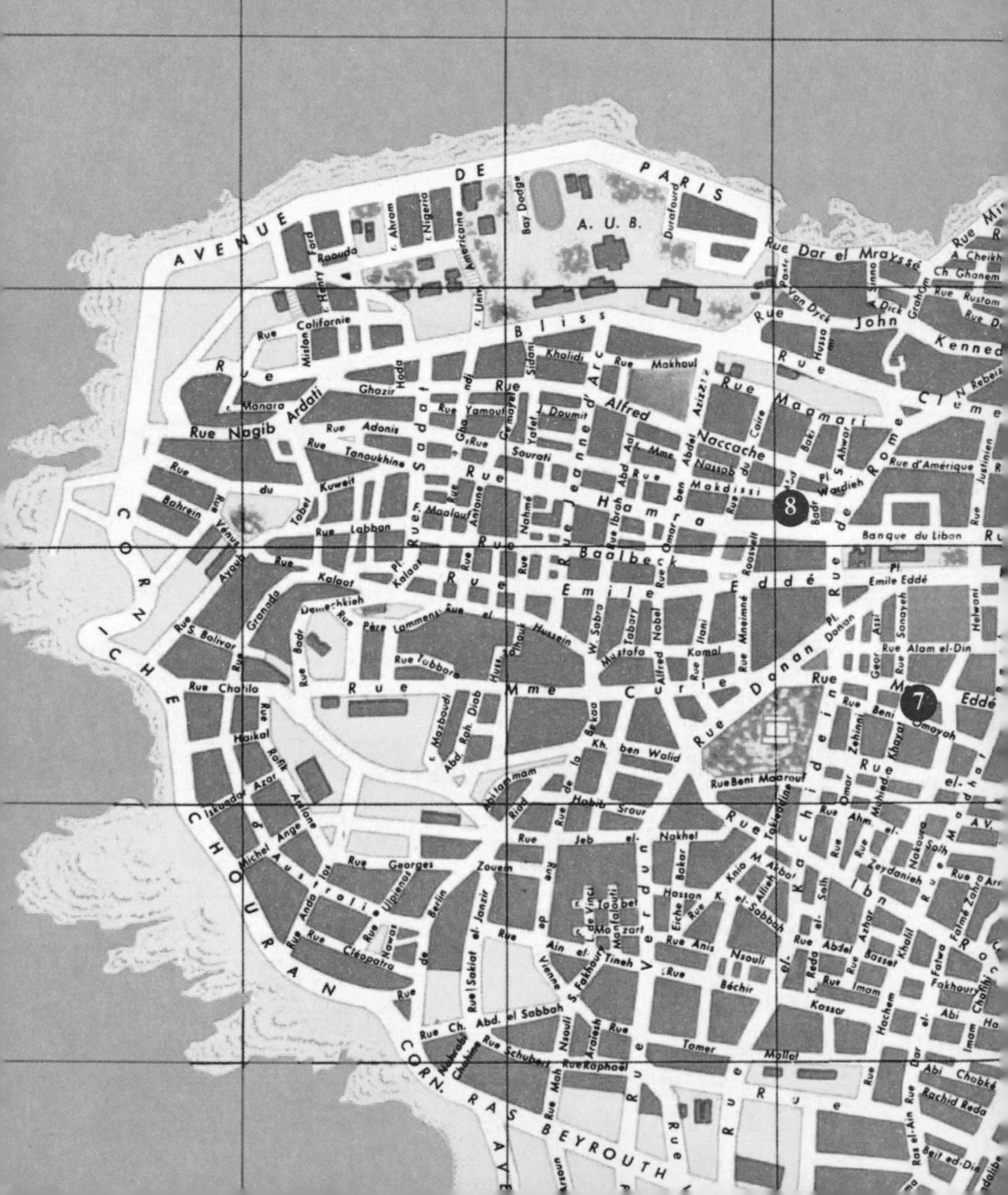

AVENUE DE PARIS
A. U. B.
Bay Dodge
Durafourd
r. Ahram
r. Nigeria
r. Americaine
r. Univ.
r. Henry Ford
Raouda
Rue Dar el Mraysse
Rue Van Dyck
Rue John Kennedy
Rue Bliss
Rue Californie
Rue Mislan
Rue Monara
Rue Nagib Ardati
Ghazir
Hoda
Sidani
Khalidi
Rue Makhoul
Rue Maamari
Rue Alfred Naccache
Azizie
Rue Yamout
J. Doumit
Rue Adonis
Rue Tanoukhine
Rue Sourati
Rue Jeanne d'Arc
Rue Abdel Nassab
Rue Makdissi
Rue Hamra
Rue du Caire
Rue Kuweit
Rue du Bahrein
Rue Vénus
Tabet
F. Maalouf
Antoine
Nahmé
Rue Labban
Rue Baalbeck
Roosvelt
Banque du Liban
Rue de Rome
Rue d'Amérique
Justinien
Pl. Emile Eddé
Rue Emile Eddé
Rue Kalaat
Pl. Kalaat
Rue Ayoub
Rue Granada
Demechkieh
Rue Père Lammens
Rue el Hussein
Rue S. Bolivar
Rue Badr
Rue Jabbara
W. Sabra
Tabary
Nobel
Mustafa
Kamal
Rue Ilani
Mneimné
Rue Donan
Pl. Donan
Sanayeh
Rue Alam el-Din
Helwani
Rue Chatila
Rue Mme Curie
Rue Mme Eddé
Beni Omayah
Zehinni
Khayat
Rue Bekaa
Kh. ben Walid
Rue Beni Maarouf
Rue Rachid Karamé
Rue Takieddine
Rue Mazboudi
Abd. Rah. Diab
Abi Hamam
Riad
Rue de la Habib
Srour
Rue Jeb el-Nakhel
Rue Verdun
Haikal
Rafik
Iskandar Azar
Aplane
Michel Ange
Rue d'Australie
Rue Georges Zouein
Rue Ulpianos
Rue Anda los
Rue Cléopatra
Nawas
de Berlin
Rue Sakiat el Janzir
Rue Ain el Tineh
Rue Anis Nsouli
Rue Béchir Kassar
Rue Abdel Basset
Azhar
Khalil
Rue Zeydanieh
Rue Nakoura
Rue Ahm. el-Solh
Rue Imam
Fatwa
Fatmé Zahra
Rue Ch. Abd. el Sabbah
Rue Schubert
Rue Raphael
Tomer
Mallel
Rue Mah Nsouli
Araiesh
Hachem
Rachid Reda
Abi Chabké
Ras el-Ain
Beit ed-Din
CORNICHE CHOURAN
CORN. RAS BEYROUTH
AVENUE

1 Notre Dame de Nazareth school
2 My parents' apartment
3 Jiddo Antoun and Teta Eva's apartment
4 Teta Simone's house
5 Jiddo's fabric shop
6 My father's office
7 Aunt Marcelle's apartment
8 Cavalier Hotel
9 Holiday Inn
10 Phoenicia
11 St Georges
12 Alcazar
13 British Bank of the Middle East
14 Pâtisserie Suisse
15 Librairie Antoine
16 La Rose du Liban
17 Rivoli
18 Roxy
19 Radio City
20 Empire
21 La Santa church
22 Chocolatier Attié
23 Élie's chocolates

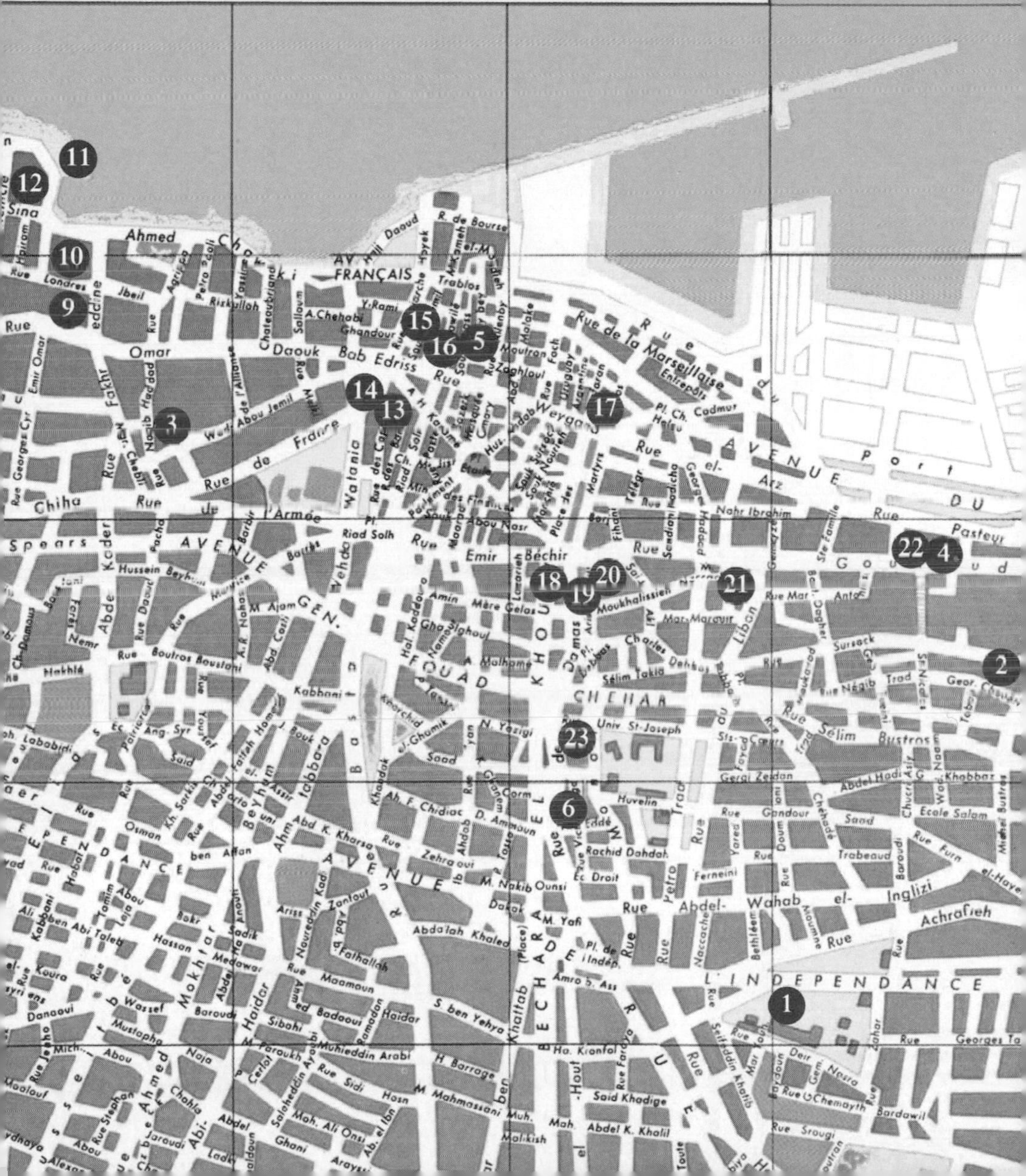

Rue de la Marseillaise
AV. FRANÇAIS
Bab Edriss
Rue de France
Rue de l'Armée
Riad Solh
Rue Emir Bechir
AVENUE GEN. FOUAD CHEHAB
AVENUE DU Port
Rue Gouraud
Rue Pasteur
Rue Selim Bustros
Rue Abdel-Wahab el-Inglizi
Achrafieh
L'INDEPENDANCE
Univ. St-Joseph
Rue Weygand
Rue Foch
Rue Allenby
Rue Damas
Rue Georges Cyr
Rue Omar Daouk
Rue Spears
Place des Martyrs
Rue Emir Omar
Rue Chateaubriand
Rue Mar Maroun
Rue Charles Debbas
Rue Sursock
Rue Hussein Beyhum

Thank you

To Camille, Leyla, Walid, Youmna and Nayla Ziadé.
To Jacques Binsztok, Micheline Boulos, Walid Boutros, Frédérique Cadoret, Julien Carreyn, Mouna Copti, Maher Daouk, Emile Khoury, Fouad el-Khoury, Michel el-Khoury, Alain Le Saux, Luc Martin, Najat Mhaoune, Hugues Micol, Georges-Emmanuel Morali, Paul Otchakovsky, Jawad Pakradouni, Christophe Prébois, Olivia Snaije, Zeina Tabet, Néda Takieddine, Patrick Tanguy, Emmanuelle Zanni, Joseph Ziadé.

And thanks for their books, a rare and precious source of research:
Joseph Chami and Gérard Castoriades, *Jours de Misère 75–76*
Joseph Chami, *Jours de Colère 77–82*
L'Orient-le-Jour, *La Guerre à la une*
Gabriele Basilico, *Beyrouth 1991* (2003)
Ghassan Tuéni, *El Bourj, place de la liberté et porte du Levant*
Samir Kassir, *Histoire de Beyrouth*
Maria Chakhtoura, *La Guerre des graffiti*
Francis Jalain and Gerard Boulad, *Lumières du Liban*
René Chamussy, *Chroniques d'un guerre*
Jonathan Randal, *La Guerre de Mille Ans*

And to Gabriele Basilico, Raymond Depardon, Fouad el-Khoury, René Burri, Joseph Koudelka and Robert Frank, who photographed downtown Beirut just after the war ended in 1991.

Translator's acknowledgements:
Thanks to Lamia Ziadé, Jon Randal, Colonel Jean-Louis Dufour and Major Jean-Marie van Hove.